A

B O O K

The Philip E. Lilienthal imprint
honors special books
in commemoration of a man whose work
at University of California Press from 1954 to 1979
was marked by dedication to young authors
and to high standards in the field of Asian Studies.
Friends, family, authors, and foundations have together
endowed the Lilienthal Fund, which enables UC Press
to publish under this imprint selected books
in a way that reflects the taste and judgment
of a great and beloved editor.

The publisher and the University of California Press Foundation gratefully acknowledge the generous support of the Philip E. Lilienthal Imprint in Asian Studies, established by a major gift from Sally Lilienthal.

Japan, the Sustainable Society

Japan, the Sustainable Society

*The Artisanal Ethos, Ordinary Virtues,
and Everyday Life in the Age of Limits*

—

John Lie

UNIVERSITY OF CALIFORNIA PRESS

University of California Press
Oakland, California

© 2022 by John Lie

Cataloging-in-Publication Data is on file at the Library of Congress.

Names: Lie, John, author.
Title: Japan, the sustainable society : the artisanal ethos, ordinary virtues,
    and everyday life in the age of limits / John Lie.
Description: Oakland : University of California Press, [2021] | Includes
    bibliographical references and index.
Identifiers: LCCN 2021035825 (print) | LCCN 2021035826 (ebook) | ISBN
    9780520383517 (hardcover) | ISBN 9780520383524 (paperback) | ISBN
    9780520383531 (ebook)
Subjects: LCSH: Sustainable development—Japan. | Japan—Economic
    conditions—History. | BISAC: HISTORY / Asia / Japan | BUSINESS &
    ECONOMICS / Economic History
Classification: LCC HC465.E5 L43 2021 (print) | LCC HC465.E5 (ebook) |
    DDC 338.952—dc23
LC record available at https://lccn.loc.gov/2021035825
LC ebook record available at https://lccn.loc.gov/2021035826

Manufactured in the United States of America

30   29   28   27   26   25   24   23   22
10   9   8   7   6   5   4   3   2   1

For Perry and Judy

CONTENTS

What ever happened to Japan?

In the year 2020, many topics other than Japan—the rise of China and the radicalization of Islam; the financial globalization and counterglobalization movements; the intensification of inequality and the resurgence of authoritarianism; transnational epidemics and natural disasters—are rightly deemed to be of pressing and paramount significance. In this context and at this point, one could be forgiven for not even mentioning, much less thinking of, Japan.

A far cry from the 1980s! Given that decade's shrill debates and vibrant, vituperative discussions about Japan's impending status as the world's premier economy, one likewise could have been forgiven for believing that the century ahead was destined to belong to Japan. Today, though, as far as I can tell, no one in or outside Japan subscribes to the conventional wisdom of a generation ago. *Fugit inreparabile tempus*; or, as we say, *tempus fugit*, and along with time fly assumptions and expectations of the looming Japanese Century.

The 1980s aside, however, my contrarian view is that Japan stands to be even more significant in the 2020s than it was four decades ago. The rise of Japan in the post–World War II decades was a variation on the rapid, compressed industrialization currently taking place in China—and a reprise of the Eurocentric past, if allowances are made for idiosyncratic variations across national experiences. But what about Japan as a *sustainable* society? That question alone places Japan at the front lines of the challenges now confronting the advanced industrial societies.

Economic growth entails well-known problems, including the exacerbation of inequality and poverty, not to mention the destruction of the natural environment. Needless to say, many people see it as the master solution to humanity's manifold problems. For some, belief in economic growth practically amounts to a religion; in contemporary Japan, there are politicians, bureaucrats, and executives who worship at its shrine. Yet it is probably impossible, and almost surely inadvisable, to take the road backward to the Golden Age of rapid economic expansion. Nor should we dismiss the catastrophic potential of contemporary science and technology—most obviously, artificial intelligence and biotechnology—especially because we have already witnessed environmental destruction and other deleterious consequences of earlier scientific and technological achievements. Instead of turning once more to the putative panacea of economic growth, shouldn't we be asking how we can live in a world without it?

From another angle, triumphs in the area of public health—Covid-19 notwithstanding—have meant that people in affluent countries are living longer, all the while having fewer children, and the counter-Malthusian specter of population decline haunts many politicians and pundits. But population stasis, even decline, may be desirable. The idea of the sustainable society may seem perverse to scholars and policymakers brought up on idolatry of growth, yet it's an idea well worth pondering at a time when we can no longer expect economic growth to save us—a time when economic growth may actually spell our doom. This is precisely the time for us to reevaluate our faith in growth and to ponder alternative modes of labor and leisure.

When we peel back the scab over postgrowth Japan, we expose the wound left by the excesses of the Bubble decade, and we lay bare the continued yearning for that bygone era of rapid economic growth. But we also find ways of living and working that are viable, if still occluded by the colossal complex of big government and giant corporations. In Japan, beneath and beyond the rhetoric of growth, many people are already leading sustainable lives and creating a sustainable society. Thus, contemporary Japan offers a glimpse or two of what a viable immediate future might look like, a future in which people acknowledge the limits of the environment and the economy, champion meaningful ways of working, and valorize everyday life and ordinary virtues.

Social scientists may find themselves flummoxed by the two empirical foci of this book—sushi and bathing. But it is in just such apparently trivial pursuits and practices that we find, in embryonic form, meaningful and sustainable ways of working and living. My intention here is not to present life in contemporary Japan as a ready-made model for the future of other affluent countries, and certainly not for the future of the rest of the world, but to offer Japan's sustainable society as one example of how to navigate the perilous present.

One caveat to the reader: when I discuss figures like Marie Kondo and Haruki Murakami, who are well known to anglophone readers, I place the first name first, both in the main text and in discursive portions of the notes, against the Japanese convention of placing the surname first. In the notes, however, for a work published in Japanese, I follow the Japanese publisher's convention of placing the author's surname first (though the same author's first name comes first in the citation of an English translation of his or her work, unless the translation's publisher follows the Japanese convention, as in the work of Kōda Rohan, for example, whose English-language publisher splits the difference, so to speak, by giving his name as Koda Rohan).

This book was completed in the summer of 2019, after a year of research leave made possible by a fellowship from the Japan Foundation. Takita Ayumi in particular was helpful at the Foundation. Hiroshi Ishida sponsored my stay at the University of Tokyo, as did Hama Hideo and Inaba Akihide for my affiliation with Keio University. I should also like to salute the staff at the Tokyo Metropolitan Library (Main Branch), Keio University libraries, and University of Tokyo libraries, who maintained salutary and salubrious reading environments. I also received financial and infrastructural support from the Center for Japanese Studies, the Center for Korean Studies, and the Department of Sociology at the University of California, Berkeley. I wish to express gratitude to my Berkeley colleagues, especially Jinsoo An, Kumi Sawako Hadler, Laura Nelson, and Dan O'Neill.

At the University of California Press, Reed Malcom proved once again to be an efficient and effective editor. Thanks also to Steven Baker, Cindy Fulton, Kate Hoffman, LeKeisha Hughes, and others at or with the Press. Alexander Trotter did the index. Two anonymous reviewers made useful comments and criticisms. I cannot thank enough the work of Xavier Callahan, developmental editor and line editor *nulli secundus*. She saved me from errors large and small, and she vastly improved the prose and the organization of this book.

For encouragement and support in the writing of this book, I am grateful to Michael Donnelly, Kyunghee Ha, Hasegawa Yuki, Hashimoto Setsuko, Imoto Yuki, Xuan Jin, Michael Kowen, Kexin Li, Charlotte Lie, Youngmi Lim, Sigrid Luhr (who drew the graphs), Majima Ayumi, Nakamura Yuki, Nakayama Keiko, Nishioka Yoko, Joohyun Park, Jay Ou, Sonia Ryang, Shirahase Sawako, Takenoshita Hirohisa, Charis Thompson, Watanabe Hideki, Jeff Weng, and Jun Yoo.

Finally, I wish to dedicate this book to Perry and Judy Mehrling, my dear friends for nearly four decades. Their bedrock stability and unmatched hospitality have provided one of the few constants in my itinerant life.

From Japan as "Number One" to
the Lost Decades

In 1979, the sociologist Ezra F. Vogel published *Japan as Number One: Lessons for America*.[1] It had modest sales and a tepid response in the United States. As Vogel recalled seven years later, "The general reaction [was that the book was] 'fascinating and amusing.' The implication clearly was that the professor had spent a little too much time in the Orient . . . for he vastly overestimated . . . the extraordinary successes of Japan."[2] A month after the initial publication, when the Japanese translation appeared, *Japan as Number One* became one of the best-selling nonfiction books in Japanese publishing history. What was "fascinating and amusing" to Americans evidently had tickled Japanese amour propre. After all, US bombs had smashed Japanese cities to smithereens a mere thirty-four years earlier, but now an American scholar—a Harvard professor, no less—was declaiming Japanese greatness. If there could be some external validation of Japan's having arrived, the publication of *Japan as Number One* was it. To be sure, many Japanese readers, or nonreaders, blithely ignored the subtitle, for the course of bestsellerdom is rarely littered with subtleties. Fame was thrust upon the book, which captured the zeitgeist proleptically as Japan embarked on its decade of economic exuberance.

Indeed, the notion of Japan as "number one" became something of a leitmotif during the Japanese Bubble of the 1980s. By then, Japan's rapid postwar growth had decelerated, but the newfound Japanese practices of financial and property speculation were creating an era of massive, instantaneous returns, especially after the 1985 Plaza Accord, which led to the strengthening of the yen. Land prices and the stock market seemed to know no upper bounds as fortunes crested on the backs of timely real estate deals or reckless financial gambles. At one point, the value of the Imperial Palace, an indisputably large parcel of prime real estate, was said to exceed the value of Manhattan as a whole, and the value of Tokyo was said to exceed that of the entire United States.[3] Easy money was goading Japanese companies and speculators into acquiring one iconic bauble after another, from a van Gogh sunflower painting to Rockefeller Center. The new normal was defined by conspicuous consumption, which could mean popping expensive champagne or sporting designer bags and rococo jewelry. And life on this order of lavishness ushered in not just a climate of fecklessness but also a time of extravagant taste and execrable morals.[4] Pundits in turn proclaimed the gospel of Japanese greatness; all things Japanese were extolled, from Japan's unique language to its superior culture. In particular, the Japanese way of doing business, encompassing industrial policy as well as corporate management, heralded a new model for *Homo economicus*, who was to become *Homo japonicus*, whether by emulating Toyota's inventory technique or perusing *Gorin no sho* (*The Book of Five Rings*), by Miyamoto Musashi, a sixteenth-century samurai. One ubiquitous commentator, Takemura Ken'ichi, predicted in 1989 that the 1990s would be "golden" for Japan and that Japan would become a global hegemon by 1995, exercising leadership not only in the economic realm but also at sea and in space.[5] Blessed it was, indeed, to be alive and Japanese in the 1980s! In that decade, the proverbial Martian visitor might have wondered who indeed had won World War II.[6] It wasn't simply that Americans were reading how-to books about doing business the Japanese way; they had also begun wolfing down sushi, previously a repugnant symbol of Japanese barbarity.[7] It was as if Philip K. Dick had written, not as fiction but as reportage, his 1962 fantasy novel *The Man in the High Castle*, with its conceit that the victors in World War II were Germany and Japan.[8]

But not everyone was similarly smitten with Japan. In the early 1990s, a critically derided but reader-friendly novelist of the era was writing a thinly veiled fiction-cum-jeremiad about the Japanese economic ascendance and menace.[9] At the same time, a flamboyant Manhattan property developer was sounding an apoplectic alarm about Japan's winning the economic war by means of unfair trade deals. He claimed that the Japanese were "openly screwing" the United States, and he labeled the Japanese practices "a disgrace." "The Japanese cajole us," he said, "they bow to us, they tell us how great we are and then they pick our pockets. We're losing hundreds of billions of dollars a year while they laugh at our stupidity."[10] Thus was the Yellow Peril of yore, decisively defeated only a generation before, now threatening the self-proclaimed greatest country in the world. The *reductio ad absurdum* of this Japanese threat, *The Coming War with Japan,* was published in short order.[11]

What goes up must come down, of course, and what happens to go up rapidly must come down the same way. Since the late 1980s, there had been rumors and rumblings of an overextended asset-price bubble in Japan, and land prices in Tokyo began to plummet in 1989. The following year, the Nikkei Stock Index took a nosedive and lost more than a third of its value. The speculative bubble had burst by 1992. Cultural manifestations of irrational exuberance continued to flicker for at least five years after this collapse in property values, but economic growth slowed, stopped, and even declined for a time. By 2002, an eminent magazine could report that Japan had "suffered the deepest slump in any developed economy since the Great Depression."[12] If the presenting symptom was a struggling political economy, auscultation of the Japanese body politic yielded diagnoses that included not just faulty macroeconomic policy but even a malady presumed to be deeply ensconced in the Japanese psyche.[13] And as economists deployed all the negative terminology at their disposal—"deflation" and "depression," "stagnation" and "slump"—the world's onetime economic showcase was recharacterized as a basket case. Boosters of the Japanese boom now spoke gloomily of Japan's lost decade, which over time became Japan's lost two decades.

Where had the prophets of the Japanese Century gone? No one was talking now about Japan as "number one" except perhaps as an exercise in nostalgia, and "turning Japanese" had become the nightmare scenario for other economic powers.[14] In a retrospective discussion about the Japanese literature of the Heisei period (1989–2019), a comment by the novelist Takahashi Genjirō stands out: "I cannot but think that Heisei was a period of decline."[15] Decline and fall: for post-Bubble Japan it was all downhill, and all down-and-out. As the influential philosopher Azuma Hiroki put it in 2017, "Over the past quarter-century, Japan has become absolutely destitute."[16] Most damning, however, is that a new catchphrase—"the rise of China"—became the twenty-first century's version of Japan as "number one"; few beyond the Japanese archipelago seemed to care about, or even to have noticed, the fate of the once-mighty economic engine.

THE POSTWAR REGIME

What accounts for Japan's post–World War II economic recovery and growth, frequently described as miraculous? To my knowledge, no one has attributed Japan's postwar economic success to divine intervention (Emperor Hirohito himself declared his human status on New Year's Day of 1946); nor is an explanation to be found in the misty Japanese past or in the inscrutable recesses of Japanese culture, tempting though such explorations might be. A more useful approach is to begin by elaborating the dominant narrative, which holds that Japan's economic recovery and growth in the postwar period were engineered by the postwar regime.

This narrative is not altogether wrong. But it is misleading, dependent as it is on a common reckoning of contemporary Japanese periodization, in which the events and phenomena under discussion stretch roughly from Japan's surrender in 1945 to Hirohito's death in 1989.[17] The dominant narrative is misleading because it exaggerates and mischaracterizes not only the triumphs of the Bubble era in particular, and of Japan's post–World War II economic recovery and growth in general, but also the dysfunctions of the post-Bubble period.

The term "postwar regime" encapsulates the congeries of institutions and the repertoire of actions that embodied rapid recovery and growth—the Liberal Democratic Party; the infrastructural, developmental state; large corporations; and, as a junior partner, a compliant but diligent labor force. All of them in turn were dedicated to growth as a habit of thought and behavior. The postwar regime of export- and growth-oriented political economy did not become entrenched until the early 1960s, after the collapse of the Nobusuke Kishi premiership, as a consequence of mass mobilization against the US-Japan Security Treaty. But its rudiments had been clear since the 1950s. Working under US hegemony, and in the context of the expanding global economy, Japan embarked on export-oriented industrialization and, in so doing, became "Japan Inc." At first, Japan manufactured and purveyed inexpensive and technologically unsophisticated goods ("Made in Japan" was once shorthand in the West for a cheap, shoddy product), but by the 1980s, with the fabrication of innovative, sophisticated gadgets and widgets, goods of Japanese manufacture had come to stand for class and high quality. At the same time, postwar Japan was experiencing massive population movements that included colonial-settler repatriation and rural exodus, the institutionalization of the patriarchal nuclear family, the integration of the national popular culture, and the crystallization of a Japanese national identity. The postwar regime was the Japan of rapid economic growth (that is, a tautology), and it was precisely in the post–Korean War decade that the idea of growth became firmly entrenched in the Japanese mind-set.[18]

The postwar regime did not rise like the phoenix from the ashes of destruction. In the years immediately after the end of World War II, there were many calls for revolutionary transformation, calls that were silenced by the US occupation forces.[19] It would also be misleading to flatten out the full dimensions of the conservative and reactionary politicians of the 1950s: some, such as the Class A war criminal Kishi, yearned to restore features of prewar Japan; others, such as Ishibashi Tanzan and Ikeda Hayato, stressed attaining and disseminating prosperity. By the mid-1950s, however, there were two points on which they agreed, at least in public. Postwar conservatives were at once pro-business and pro–United States in their acceptance of defeat, and therefore in their acceptance of Japanese subservience to the United States. Skeptics notwithstanding, Japan had entered headlong into a war against the United States. Now, in spite of some holdouts, Japan was not so much embracing defeat as embracing the United States, the end of the war, and liberation from the war's attendant tragedies and miseries. Symptomatically, 15 August 1945 is commemorated as the date of the end of the war (*shūsen*), not the date of the defeat (*haisen*). There were those who retained their spiritual allegiance to the prewar regime, with its stress on military power and territorial expansion, but even they eschewed open celebration of martial glory and imperial ambition. As in the case of Kishi, the fate of holdouts from the prewar period was political purge or even imprisonment. For the war-weary masses, the war was rendered as a series of private experiences, whether that meant grieving the dead, nurturing the disabled, or recalling, sotto voce, the war's hardships. Amnesia reigned with respect to wartime enthusiasms, whether these had involved the war's purported cause (liberation of the colonized Asian nations) or the course of the war itself (with its frequent celebrations of Japanese military might), but one lesson stuck— the undesirability and inadvisability of war.[20] Best to focus on the present and the future and forget the past; recovery was the primary desideratum. A mere two weeks after the end of the war, the charismatic army general Ishiwara Kanji would urge Japan to be "the advanced nation for peace."[21] Not only was the idea of the peaceful nation popular with the people, who had suffered during the war, but it also contributed to the nation's emerging economic orientation.[22]

The emperor was no longer the central gravitational force in Japanese politics. Instead, the erstwhile enemy became the new master, one who did not do unto the Japanese public what the Japanese military and colonial bureaucracy had done to Japan's hapless Asian neighbors. Emblematic of the Japanese readiness to welcome the occupying forces is the fact that the first guide to conversational English appeared on 30 August 1945 and went on to sell four million copies.[23] The new constitution was thrust upon the Japanese—whatever one may think of the postwar constitution, it was of and by the US occupation forces (drafted hastily by amateurs, to boot) and for the defeated—but it was nevertheless accepted. And this was not just a matter of military might; the former enemy not only was rich but also had such technological miracles as penicillin and DDT (in addition to atomic weapons). There is considerable truth, then, to the claim that Japan was the permanent loser to the United States and would remain a US protectorate.[24] Despite persistent nationalist criticisms of the Peace Constitution—Article 9 explicitly eschews a standing military force—it has remained robust precisely because it was a good fit with the pro-American, pro-business thrust of the postwar regime. Pro-American attitudes became hegemonic; expressions of anti-Americanism were almost as grave a taboo as overt denigration of the emperor.[25] Being pro-American meant adopting and adapting to the American way, which included unquestionable commitment to capitalist democracy and unwavering support for the US bloc in the Cold War.

Apart from its cardinal principles—a pro-business orientation and pro-American pacifism—the Liberal Democratic Party, which had been cobbled together in 1955 from a menagerie of conservative politicians, represented from the outset a contingent union of convenience. The postwar regime is often called the "1955 system" in Japan, not only because the dominant conservative party coalesced in that year but also because the basic elements of pro-growth political

economy were evident by then. As Voltaire might have put it, the Liberal Democratic Party was not liberal, was not democratic, and was not even a true party. But
it was a perennial majority party, in no small part because of rapid economic
growth and because of the party's hold on rural voters.

The Liberal Democratic Party was closely aligned with the state bureaucracy.
Bureaucratic continuity and expansion brook almost no obstacles, not even revolution or defeat. The enthusiastic, progressive vision of the US occupation forces
sought to remake Japan into the Switzerland of Asia and thus dismantled Japan's
massive military apparatus, though the onset of the Cold War upended even this
restraint on bureaucratic continuity. There was a new rule—no more recitation of
the Imperial Rescript on Education and, in its place, a fresh enthusiasm for peace
and democracy—but the state apparatus at once expanded and intensified its reach
and its penetration into the population. Micromanagement of public infrastructure and other matters—including decrees regarding exactly where post offices
would be built and maintained and which subjects would be taught in the final
term of third grade—was merely the most visible face of the postwar state.[26]

The glorification of bureaucratic prowess was especially evident in economic
affairs. The Ministry of Finance, the most prestigious and powerful of all the ministries, had long maintained a soft mercantilist position—sustaining a low yen, providing credit, and maintaining growth. In the 1970s and 1980s, especially outside Japan,
the Ministry of International Trade and Industry (MITI) came to be perceived as a
repository of omniscient bureaucrats proposing one triumphal industrial policy after
another. Indeed, Japan originated a genre unprecedented in world literature—the
celebration of bureaucrats.[27] For most people, the most consequential of the state's
manifestations was that of the infrastructural state. The bureaucracies, flush with
generous budgetary allocations that were in turn assured by the seemingly permanent Liberal Democratic Party majority, would restore areas ravaged by war and—
once rebuilding and recovery were complete—build roads and railroads, bridges and
tunnels, ports and airports here, there, and everywhere. In addition to its construction projects, the state had its fingers in manifold aspects of everyday life, such as the
workings of the Japan Post, whose savings branch, at least where total deposits were
concerned, became the world's single largest bank. Liberal Democratic Party politicians and state bureaucrats alike were pro-business, but an innocent observer might
have questioned their commitment to capitalism, at least in its laissez-faire form.
"State capitalism," "bureaucratic capitalism," "infrastructural capitalism"—no one
applied these or other descriptors to the nexus between the perennial ruling party
and the powerful state bureaucracy, but any of these terms would have been more
accurate than labels reflecting a view of the capitalist state as a kind of libertarian
night watchman.

Large corporations took center stage in the theater of economic recovery and
growth. The US occupation forces, beyond eliminating the Japanese military, ini-

tially attempted to deracinate the economic and social foundation of militarism by dismantling *zaibatsu* (oligopolies) and enacting land reform. By the time there was evidence of economic recovery, the slimmed-down oligopolies had already insinuated themselves into the Japanese economy as major players (and the remilitarization of Japan had become an explicit US desideratum). Given the impoverishment of Japan, the *zaibatsu* decided to follow the money, just as they should have, and therefore to export their products to the erstwhile enemy. Operating under the US-led global economy, with relatively free trade, Japanese corporations regained footholds in light industries, such as textiles, and soon scaled the hierarchy of higher-value-added, technologically sophisticated products, moving from black-and-white to color televisions, from transistor radios to cassette players, and from motorbikes to automobiles.[28] Not all these enterprises had prewar origins, for there was an entrepreneurial moment in Japanese economic life in the 1950s, but several companies—notably Toyota, Nissan, Sony, and Panasonic—became the standard-bearers of the new Japanese economy. The prewar *zaibatsu* transmogrified into *keiretsu*, or conglomerates. It was fortunate that Japan in the immediate postwar decades had virtually no competition inside the US sphere of influence; the economies of Latin America and of the other Asian countries were lodged in the primary sector, and those countries had neither the experience nor the inclination to engage in massive industrialization.

A persistent advantage for the postwar Japanese export drive was the country's relatively low cost and seemingly infinite supply of labor. In the decades just after the war, repatriated soldiers and returning colonial settlers as well as young rural workers flocked to the cities in droves. Japanese primary-sector employment declined precipitously in the postwar decades as the rural exodus and rapid urbanization transformed the archipelago. Also critical was the fact that the new workers were literate, motivated, and disciplined, most immediately because of their wartime mobilization. By the 1970s, rapid economic growth had made low-paid labor a thing of the past. Many corporations, goaded by labor unions, established new modi vivendi so that the norm became lifetime employment security, a seniority-based wage system, and enterprise-based unions—the vaunted "three treasures" of the Japanese system of labor relations. This norm applied primarily to the larger companies, but the reality of rapid growth eased tension between workers and managers, and between subcontractors and corporations; in other words, the postwar regime also gave rise to relatively harmonious relations between business and labor.

Critics bemoaned the relatively low wages and the exploitation of many Japanese workers. At the time, a number of Japanese social scientists, inspired by Marxism, would have agreed with the critics. But the new urban workers seemed to rejoice in their escape both from the ravages of war and from the impoverished countryside. And because the Japanese economy was operating at full steam, there was very low unemployment, and wages increased steadily. An economy growing at an annual rate of 10 percent will double every seven years. Although wage increases did not approach the level of accelerated aggregate growth, there was enough prosperity trickling down to satisfy all but the most ideological. Moreover, technological advances—the three divine appliances of the 1950s (a black-and-white TV set, a washing machine, and a refrigerator) and the three C's of the 1960s (a color TV set; a cooler, or air conditioner; and a car)—simultaneously purveyed convenience and unleashed desire.[29] "We won't want until we win" had been a piece of Japan's wartime propaganda, and now it was as if access to that slogan's promised usufruct had finally arrived. Meanwhile, as new buildings popped up featuring all the modern conveniences, urbanites donned Western clothing to complete the modernization of city life. Structural mobility, both for farmers in the countryside and for workers in the cities, provided a sense of movement and improvement. By the mid-1960s, it would have taken total immersion in Marxist literature to reverse the upbeat national mood of "onward and upward." It is not surprising that in this era of rapid economic growth, the emperor-worshipping right-wing nationalists who had dominated the war years became nearly silent and invisible, but it is curious that the left continued so long to rule the Japanese intellectual world. In any event, the postwar regime spelled success for the majority who enjoyed plenitude, and who in turn supported the Liberal Democratic Party and the corporations that were the visible engines of growth.

Thus the postwar regime—the robust rule of a pro-business, pro-American party; a powerful state bureaucracy dedicated to economic growth; export-oriented large corporations; and educated and motivated workers—brought prosperity and stability to Japan, no longer a pariah. The 1964 Tokyo Olympics and the 1970 Osaka Exposition were welcomed as validations of Japan's acceptance by the world at large. Growth had slowed by the 1970s, and there were bumps like the 1973 oil crisis, but in the sustained economic growth engineered and executed by the postwar regime, Japan not only recovered but also prospered.

THE LOST DECADES, OR THE "JAPANESE DISEASE"

Let's return now to the received narrative of Japan during and after the bursting of the Bubble. The decline of the postwar regime was coterminous with the death of Hirohito, in 1989, and the beginning of the Heisei period.

In contrast to the previous decades, the post-Bubble decades saw an economic slowdown. In 2000, the novelist Murakami Ryū published *Ushinawareta 10nen wo tou* (Questioning the lost decade), based on a TV program that in turn was based on Murakami's blogs. By that time, the phrase "the lost ten years" had entered the everyday Japanese lexicon.[30] Newspaper reports and television documentaries told countless stories of personal loss: the investment that had soured (such as the apartment one could no longer afford but could not sell except at a large loss), the downward spiral from popping Dom Perignon to sipping *shōchū* (an inexpensive Japanese distilled drink), and so on and so forth. The national mood felt like the day after a wild party, with groggy memories of good times offset by remorse and a migraine. And the hangover did not dissipate quickly. A Keynesian economist might have prescribed government investment to revive the slumping economy, just as the proverbial hair of the dog might be suggested for the morning after. But the sluggishness persisted, and the lost ten years became the lost fifteen years, and then the lost twenty years.

There is a rough-and-ready consensus on the proximate causes of the mania, the panic, and the ensuing crash. The 1985 Plaza Accord is seen as a critical proximate cause: not only did the accord show Japan to be a player in the international political economy, but the stronger yen also contributed to expansionary monetary policy in Japan. Property prices skyrocketed from a launching pad of excess credit, low interest rates, and lax regulatory oversight. And with easy credit chasing fast returns, real estate and the stock market both overheated. When a downturn came, a series of banks, stretched far beyond any prudent standard for lending practices, found themselves facing a credit crunch and then bankruptcy. In terms of historical time, it all happened quickly—from 1985 to 1989 or perhaps 1992. The bad debt that ricocheted throughout Japan ended the reign of easy money and financial speculation; the whales who had gorged on loose credit were soon beached and rotting, and the bursting Bubble spewed its undigested contents all over the weary Japanese populace. The most exuberant manifestation of the Bubble—the bling disco Juliana's—opened as late as 1991 and shut down only in 1994, as if to demonstrate both the materialist thesis that culture follows the economy and the adage regarding the willingness of the spirit and the weakness of the flesh.

Analysts who share an understanding of how the Bubble ended still tend to diverge when it comes to explaining the persistence of the economic slowdown.[31] Some cast blame on the Japanese government's macroeconomic and monetary policy; for these analysts, politicians and bureaucrats had exercised economic and financial oversight to clamp down on the economy instead of either investing aggressively to regain momentum or reopening the spigot of easier credit. Conversely, other analysts suggest that fiscal policy had remained loose while monetary policy was bearing the brunt of macroeconomic problems. Still others point to long-range transformations both in the business environment and in business strategy; for instance, there had been steady decline in corporate investment as well as in Japan's vaunted commitment to long-term growth, and the creeping conservatism of Japanese managers had failed to anticipate the oncoming digital revolution and the disruptions of information technology. Yet others highlight Japanese wage increases and the intensification of international competition, especially from neighboring Asian countries. As for myself, I would include additional external factors. For one thing, the 1990s were a time of global economic downturn, with one crisis after another, involving the UK pound in 1992, the Mexican peso in 1994, and most Asian currencies in 1997; the Japanese downturn was more the rule than the exception. For another, the bursting of the Bubble coincided with the end of the Cold War and the onset of US-led globalization, and globalization itself was defined by newfound enthusiasm for liberal economic policy, the ascendance of finance, and the revolution in information technology. In the environment of globalization, the United States gained momentum while Japan faltered. But few, if any, advanced industrial countries were able to sustain rapid growth immediately before and after the turn of the millennium. Indeed, after the 2008 financial crisis, the Japanese malaise merely anticipated the generic problem of all the world's rich economies.

These factors, and others adduced to explain the lost decades, are not necessarily incompatible. Indeed, it is likely that any long-term phenomenon afflicting a large country has multiple overlapping and even changing causes. Yet what interests me here is the shared consensus, in Japan and outside Japan, that the once-mighty Japanese economy had stalled. Foreign analysts who had spent the 1980s looking for positive lessons from Japan's success now sought negative lessons from Japan's failure. Only the rare observer has had anything positive to say about the Japanese economy of the post-Bubble decades.

A generalized articulation of the "lost decades" idea is the notion of the "Japanese disease." According to this line of thinking, the trouble is not just with the economy but also with the senescent, sclerotic Japanese body politic as a whole. Two factors encourage such dystopian thinking: first, the indubitable reality that the Japanese population is rapidly aging and may even decline in the near future; and, second, an anti-Malthusian discourse that for more than two decades has been sounding the alarm about the eventual disappearance of the Japanese people altogether.

With respect to the second factor, on 20 March 1995, when the bursting of the Bubble had come to seem incontrovertible, an act of domestic terrorism shattered the comforting assumption that Japan was a safe, secure country. As Haruki Murakami and many others have pointed out, the Japanese archipelago was convulsed when followers of the Aum Shinrikyō cult killed thirteen commuters with a sarin gas attack on the Tokyo subway.[32] Earlier that year, on 17 January, another sort of convulsion, the Kobe (Great Hanshin) earthquake, had already shaken the fraying confidence of the Japanese populace. Then, on 3 March 2011, when most people had forgotten about the two 1995 events, came the Tōhoku earthquake (usually called 3/11, after the date when it struck), which also entailed what is referred to as the Fukushima disaster, since a subsequent tsunami led to meltdowns, hydrogen explosions, and radioactive contamination at the Fukushima Daiichi Nuclear Power Plant. The Japanese people are certainly not unaware of the ubiquity of earthquakes in the tectonically unstable Japanese archipelago, but learning about earthquakes from textbooks and earthquake drills is one thing; witnessing the indelible spectacle of destruction and death is quite another. A massive natural disaster would dampen the spirits of any country, of course; for Japan, however, already a downbeat nation by 1995, these two earthquakes, sixteen years apart, were doubly distressing and depressing. In their wake, there has been widespread awareness of just how precarious everyday life can be in the Japanese archipelago. The Fukushima disaster in particular occasioned major reflection on the present and future of Japan; for example, the novelist and translator Ikezawa Natsuki found it necessary to engage in "a fundamental rethinking of the Japanese character," and Takemura Ken'ichi, the aforementioned prophet of Japan's "golden" future, described Japan as a *saigai taikoku* (natural-disaster superpower).[33] One can be well aware of the pathetic fallacy inherent in the latter characterization and still be tempted to wonder what is wrong with Japan.

Not surprisingly—indeed, inevitably—the "Japanese disease" discourse has a corollary—the discourse of the cure or prescription. Perhaps the loudest call for a cure is the demand to restore Japan's past glory (that is, the rapid economic growth that took place between the 1950s and the 1980s). In 2012, the second Shinzō Abe premiership announced "Abenomics," whose quiver held the three arrows of monetary easing, fiscal stimulus, and structural reforms. Designed to encourage both export growth (via a lower yen) and private investment, Abenomics also sought—by constructing roads, railroads, and bridges to everywhere and nowhere—to revive the infrastructural state that had bulldozed and built postwar Japan. In other words, Abenomics was a throwback to the postwar regime, presumably without the excesses of the Bubble years.

The Japanese narrative of decline contains an indisputable grain of truth. Indeed, the very idea of decline is as old as the foundational poetry and myths of the West; and, in the case of postwar Japan, we move from utter devastation at the end of World War II to the Golden Age of rapid economic recovery and growth to, suddenly, the Age of Disease, an epoch of perpetual economic stagnation and perhaps also of societal decline. Any effort to deny this grain of truth would be pointless. To begin with, it would be difficult (though not impossible) to deceive so many people for such a long time: first, from an ethnographic standpoint, seasoned observers would note that there was massive behavioral divergence from the high tide of the Bubble economy and people were no longer ready to bet everything on the stock market or real estate; and, second, the conventional wisdom would continue to paint Japan as a ship that, if not quite sinking, could nevertheless be described as adrift, aimless and languorous. Moreover, if Japan's domestic pundits (many of whom were cheerleaders of the Bubble years) were to prove untrustworthy, then Nobel Prize–winning economists like Paul Krugman and Joseph Stiglitz would step forward and declare that the Japanese malaise was a consequence of the Japanese economy's having been "crippled by caution."[34]

Krugman, Stiglitz, and other progressive economists were unlikely boosters of the conservative Abe administration; in fact, there is something of a consensus among Western observers that the heroes of the postwar miracle are the very culprits responsible for the post-Bubble doldrums. A common view is that Japan, in order to revive or resuscitate its economy, must first abandon the regime that brought about the nation's unprecedented prosperity and then emulate the once-derided laissez-faire orientation of the US economy. This line of reasoning holds that capitalism with Japanese characteristics, if it is to be properly capitalist, must cease to be Japanese. The mathematical edifice of contemporary economics, undeniably ethnocentric, serves as the rationale for the advice that Japan be more like the United States, and it restores the dominant pattern, briefly broken during the heady 1980s, of US advice to Japan. There is no question that the general trend in Japanese political economy since the 1990s has been to embrace more open, and more American, policies in everything from labor relations to corporate governance.[35] Paradoxically, the state bureaucracy has been at the forefront in proposing neoliberal policies. The core of state-led economic development, which had putatively conceived and executed Japan's rapid growth, has now corroded. Japan's dawn, in August 1945, inaugurated a brilliant arc that reached its apogee in the late 1980s (perhaps, like Icarus, Japan had come too close to the sun) and then seemed to fall, slowly and surely, into dusk.

Some like to think that chronological markers are immaterial, but few people can really resist the symbolic significance of a new year or a new reign. Be that as it may, the year when the Bubble began to burst, 1989, also marked the passing of Emperor Hirohito and of the lengthy Shōwa period (that is, the post–World War II portion of Hirohito's reign). In addition, 1989 was the year that saw the beginning of a process that culminated in 1992 with the collapse of the Soviet Union, and the ultimate disappearance of the Communist world; and by 1992, no serious observer could doubt that the Bubble had finally burst. In other words, between 1989 and 1992, the hubris of capitalist enthusiasts was squelched, and the dream of socialism—the sustaining faith of the major opposition parties in Japan—was destroyed. In retrospect, then, the triumphant rise of American-style capitalism is not surprising. The end of ideology, the end of history: Henry Luce and Francis Fukuyama seemed to have been proved correct; the twentieth century was the American Century.

RETHINKING JAPAN'S GOLDEN AGE: A MIRACLE?

The story of Japan's rise and fall offers a pleasing narrative arc—wartime devastation, economic recovery, rapid growth, the Bubble, and decline. But this story casts a tendentious light on post–World War II Japan, a light that distorts and occludes as much as it illuminates.

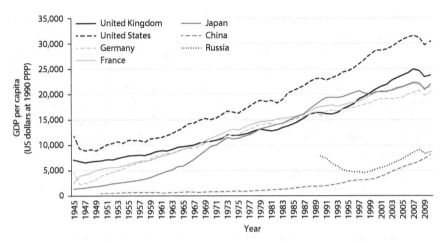

FIGURE 1. Comparative Per Capita GDP Growth. PPP stands for "purchasing power parity."
Data from Jutta Bolt and Jan Luiten van Zanden, *clio infra*, January 2013, https://clio-infra.eu/
Indicators/GDPperCapita.html.

My disenchanted perspective dethrones Japan and Japanese achievements as unique. It also decenters the mythistory of postwar Japan, a legend born of the inescapable correlation between the period of rapid economic growth and Japan's postwar regime. In reality, Japan's rapid postwar economic growth was not a miracle. The German *Wirtschaftswunder* and the Italian *miracolo economico* were no less awe-inspiring, nor did any Western country fail to achieve sustained economic growth between the end of World War II and the oil shock of 1973 (see fig. 1). Japan's economy certainly did grow after the war, but so did that of almost every other country, at least in the industrial world.

When Joseph Schumpeter described capitalism as a process of creative destruction, he wasn't thinking of Japan after World War II.[36] Nevertheless, the misbegotten war's massive destruction did facilitate a compressed process of postwar creation in Japan, with ample opportunities for construction and reconstruction. Yet, by the early twentieth century, Japan had already become a formidable industrial powerhouse, unlike every other non-Western country at that time. Moreover, Japan's prewar industrial know-how and work ethos survived the wartime pulverization of Japanese cities and industries. (As discussed at greater length in chapter 3, an ethos—a complex of normative thinking and habitual action that discloses a particular value orientation—is constituted by a habit of thought and a repertoire of practice.) In addition, the discipline and solidarity forged during Japan's war effort were channeled into postwar economic pursuits. Far from being a miracle, then, rapid postwar economic growth in Japan was a by-product of recovery or reconstruction.

In the immediate postwar period, Japan's recovery was in line with that of Germany and Italy in particular, and in general with that of other industrial countries, which were recovering not just from the destruction of World War II but also from the deleterious consequences of the Great Depression (and, by extension, from the destruction of World War I as well, though the latter generalization does not apply to Japan).[37] In the quarter century after the end of World War II, economic growth was the norm in the industrialized world; indeed, every industrialized society, whether capitalist or socialist, experienced growth that crystallized by 1950 and sputtered only after the 1973 oil shock.

Without denigrating Japanese achievements or denying Japanese diligence, it is possible to say that, with minor exceptions, the period from the end of World War II to the 1973 oil shock was the Golden Age of capitalism. In terms of gross domestic product (GDP), the world economy continued to grow even in the 1970s and 1980s, and Japan was a protagonist in the story of postwar economic recovery and growth. In the 1990s, as growth stalled in all the industrial countries, Japan's experience followed the same trajectory. Thus Japan's postwar regime oversaw both the spectacular upside and the unspectacular downside of the Japanese economy.

External Factors in Japan's Postwar Growth

Whether from benevolence or self-interest, the United States promoted reconstruction after the war. The Marshall Plan in Europe, and its unnamed equivalent in northeastern Asia, provided stopgaps to alleviate hunger, encouraged economic recovery, and supported democratic institutions. And it is just as significant that the United States desisted from imposing draconian measures on the defeated Axis powers, in part because US postwar policymakers were mindful of the presumed connection between the harsh measures meted out to Germany after World War I and the subsequent rise of the Nazis. Consequently, pro-American sentiment reigned for decades in Japan.

During the tenure of General Douglas MacArthur, progressive reforms swept away some of the foundations of Japanese prewar militarism and imperialism. The unchallenged US occupation forces vitiated economic concentration by dissolving the *zaibatsu*, and they enacted large-scale land reform. The United States also legislated a revolutionary overhaul of Japanese political economy, something that a socialist revolutionary could only have dreamed about in 1944, but that a conquering power could impose on a virtual colony in 1946.[38] MacArthur's revolutionary reforms removed impediments to competition and innovation and enabled the ascent of entrepreneurial firms, such as Sony and Honda, that in turn would drive the postwar Japanese economy. What is more significant, land reform loosened the large landlords' stranglehold on the countryside. Henceforth, relatively equitable land distribution eliminated abject poverty in rural areas and facilitated the rapid rural exodus that provided the requisite labor force for accelerated industrialization.[39]

The US-led capitalist world economy maintained an open-trade regime after World War II. No one in the United States complained about trade imbalances or Japan's artificially low currency rate until the 1970s.[40] In the regnant global division of labor, Japan found itself occupying the sweet spot: on one hand, Japan possessed great technological sophistication and skilled labor; on the other, it could offer a large, comparatively inexpensive labor force. Or, in more concrete terms, while the United States was focused on technologically more sophisticated and higher-value-added production (such as manufacturing color television sets instead of black-and-white TVs), Japan remained one of the few countries ready and willing to take over the production of technologically less sophisticated, lower-valued-added goods. Japan more than made up in human capital whatever it lacked in natural resources. And there were lucky breaks; for example, in the early 1950s, demand generated by the Korean War brought a spike in light industrial production and exports (the so-called Jimmu Boom). There were some dark clouds before the 1973 oil crisis, but there was nothing to deter the forward march of export-oriented Japanese corporations.

The State and Corporations

During the first decade of rapid recovery after World War II, every industrializing society was on the same upward trajectory as Japan. After that initial decade, it was the developmental orientation of the state, and of capital, that contributed to Japan's continuing growth. By the 1960s, the mantra of the political-economic establishment was "Grow and export, export and grow." The state—both the ruling, pro-business politicians and the economic bureaucrats—maintained a laser-like focus on the economy, and in particular on the enhancement of Japan's competitiveness in exports. There is also no reason to downplay the impressive effort to improve efficiency and generate innovations.[41] The state was no longer sidetracked by imperialist and militarist ventures, or by excessively self-aggrandizing, corrupt circles of politicians, bureaucrats, capitalists, and landlords. And the state was now disciplined by a vibrant democratic and labor opposition. As a result, the state promoted economic growth.

Nevertheless, it would be wrong to give too much credit to farsighted politicians or bureaucrats. For example, some of the politicians were more interested in reviving the prewar system than in promoting economic growth.[42] And elite politicians and bureaucrats, focused as they were on defense or recovery, merely rode the wave that had caught them up. Meanwhile, as already mentioned, corporations—facing both liberal-leaning economic policy and newfound competition from the dissolution of the *zaibatsu*—followed the money and, in so doing, pursued exports.

Labor

Low labor costs, in addition to the low yen (pegged at 360 to 1 US dollar), meant that Japanese goods were competitive until the 1970s. Around 1960, the mean Japanese manufacturing wage was about one-seventh that of the United States, and those labor cost advantages fueled Japanese exports until the 1980s when Japanese workers reached rough parity with their counterparts in the West. But even though labor was beginning to reorganize, its strength was limited, less by anticommunist propaganda, or even by the postwar regime's pro-business orientation, than by the presence of a large reserve pool of labor in the countryside. Furthermore, many workers were not wrong to see themselves as *shokunin* (skilled artisans). The egalitarian ethos cultivated during the war also served to weaken class conflict.[43]

Japan's Size

No matter what postwar life was really like in Japan, we would do well to remember that Japan is a large country—larger, at least in terms of population, than its major European counterparts, and small only in comparison to China or to the United States (which was the primary source of all international comparisons in the postwar period). To be sure, Japan's per capita GDP exceeded that of its European counterparts, but not by a significant margin; that is, the Japanese miracle was in part a nominal illusion of Japan's large size. Only some years after the Bubble decade would Japanese businesspeople and pundits recognize the enormous size of Japan's domestic market.

Furthermore, what distinguished the phenomenon of postwar Japan from the experience of West Germany was Japan's massive structural transformation: as a result of postwar Japan's rapid exodus from the countryside, what had been, in 1945, a predominantly rural, agrarian country became a thoroughly urban, industrial society only a generation later. What captures the turbulence of postwar Japan is not so much GDP as the transformation of everyday life—new norms involving Western clothes, urban life, and work that was not farmwork. As young people fled the stifling insularity of rural life, they flooded the modern cities and, in so doing, became modern themselves—living in nuclear families, working as salaried employees, and acquiring industrial consumer goods. In a song from 1984, Yoshi Ikuzō rapped about a village without "television, radio, telephone, gas, or electricity," describing the precise reality of those who had left rural areas in the postwar decades. The first half of the Meiji regime's goal—creation of a rich country—had been achieved in the 1960s and 1970s; by the 1980s, even skeptics could assent to the previously unthinkable proposition that Japan was an affluent country. If to be different is to stand out, to be immodest, then by the 1980s almost all of Japan was putting on a conspicuous show of middle-class status, since almost everyone by then had a color television set, a radio, and a telephone, not to mention natural gas and electricity.

REASSESSING JAPAN'S GOLDEN AGE

It would not merely be a mistake to heap uncritical praise on Japan's Golden Age or on the postwar regime. It would actually be misleading. To put this issue simply, Japan's postwar economic growth was fraught with problems. Let's now consider seven kinds of evidence—involving the environment, workers, the family, the bureaucracy, and other domains—to show how Japan's postwar regime and the rapid economic growth it wrought were anything but brilliant.

Environmental Destruction

An indisputable feature of Japan's rapid postwar economic growth was reckless disregard for the natural environment. Mountains and trees were razed; effluents flooded rivers and lakes. Industrial pollution did not begin during the postwar period; indeed, the beginnings of industrial pollution were coeval with the post-Meiji industrial revolution in Japan, if not with an earlier time. But the ravaging of the environment intensified after the war. Pollution was to Japan in the 1960s what it became to China in the 2010s. By the 1960s, the dysfunctional consequences of industrial pollution were obvious in the air (most notoriously in the photoelectric smog), in the water (with murky rivers and sludgy ponds), on the land (which was drenched with pesticides, including DDT), and in the bodies that necessarily absorbed all these pollutants. W. Eugene Smith's photographs of people poisoned by mercury in Minamata are only the most indelible images to emerge from the dark side of Japan's Golden Age. That the Minamata tragedy inspired a landmark work of postwar Japanese literature, Ishimure Michiko's *Kugai jōdo* (The sea of suffering, the land of purity), is scant consolation.[44] And what came to be called "Minamata disease" was only one of four major pollution-related illnesses that wreaked havoc in Japan during the 1960s; no wonder the vast majority of Japanese people worried endlessly about the environment.[45] Paradoxically, or predictably, Japan not only became a leader in the academic study of pollution but also was the site of a sizable antipollution social movement; both impulses made partial amends for the wanton destruction of the nation's habitat and its people.[46] Nevertheless, given the postwar regime's ingrained reflex to pursue conventional growth and to follow the West, Japan has never realized its potential to become a global leader in renewable energy or pollution reduction.

Exploitation

With the eradication of nature came the exploitation of people, not so much in the Marxist sense (as in the systematic cutting of wages) as in the sense of colonizing workers' time and lives. Long working hours, however they may have been compensated with overtime pay, came to shape working in and for Japanese organizations. The term *karōshi* (death from overwork) entered the Japanese lexicon from

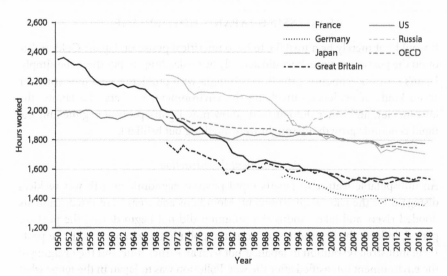

FIGURE 2. Comparative Working Hours. Note from OECD data website: "Average Annual Hours Worked is defined as the total number of hours actually worked per year divided by the average number of people in employment per year." The OECD data set does not appear to include China. Data from "Employment: Hours Worked," *OECD iLibrary*, accessed 16 June 2019, doi: 10.1787/47be1c78-en.

the time of the first identified case, in 1969.[47] Even after Japan became one of the wealthiest countries in the world, Japanese workers were still among those putting in the longest hours (see fig. 2). And the phenomenon of *pawahara* (power harassment), including such particular manifestations as discrimination on the basis of gender, nationality, or ethnicity, pervaded the corporate hierarchy as superiors used symbolic violence and sometimes outright physical abuse to punish their subordinates. Well into the twenty-first century, so-called black corporations condoned the abuse of workers. In addition, long commutes and substandard housing contributed to the impression that ordinary Japanese workers' well-being took a backseat to the quest for corporate profits and growth. If successive French presidents were insensitive in disparaging, respectively, a Japanese prime minister as resembling a transistor radio salesman and his fellow citizens as living like caged rabbits, the French officials' observations nevertheless illuminated some ugly truths about urban Japanese life.[48] Worse, women as well as ethnic and national minorities suffered unemployment as well as discrimination in promotions, and their situation recalled the famous quip by the British economist Joan Robinson: "The misery of being exploited by capitalists is nothing compared to the misery of not being exploited all."[49] The postwar Japanese government finally began to tame gender- and ethnonational-based discrimination when it consented to honor international agreements and standards; in 1985, for example, the government made a formal commitment to gender-based employment equality.[50]

The Family

Apart from job-related stress, not to mention death from overwork, there was impoverishment of Japanese family life in the postwar period. Clearly, work-life balance was all but nonexistent. But another noteworthy (if in fact little noted) feature of postwar Japanese life was asymmetry in gender relations. At home, the figure of the housewife became normative, just as subordination of female employees became the norm at work.[51] These twin gender-based forms of subordination, while providing psychic compensation for male workers' long hours, also kept the wheels of the postwar regime turning. In these ways, heteronormativity and misogyny reigned in postwar Japan. Japanese men in factories and offices, if underpaid or overworked, found the life of production palatable, and that of reproduction easy: at work, they lorded it over their female colleagues; at home, no "second shifts" of housework or childcare were expected of them. Indeed, Japanese wives and mothers were collectively the Atlas supporting the self-satisfied, androcentric world of rapid economic growth. And, as shown in chapter 6, Japanese men's collective shirking of family-related work caused damage to their relationships with their wives and children.

Bureaucratic Overreach

Scholars and pundits in the postwar years had high praise for farseeing government bureaucrats, especially at the elite ministries concerned with finance and commerce. Yet bureaucratic autonomy brought about concentration of decision-making power and instituted a rigid scheme of rules and regulations. Brilliant though bureaucrats may be when it comes to passing difficult examinations, there is something bizarre about having a bureaucrat determine the exact placement of a post office on an island more than a thousand kilometers away. One need not read Friedrich Hayek in order to sense the gulf between information and wisdom, nor does bureaucracy, however efficient and effective, have all the answers. And, unsurprisingly, centralized, top-down decision making reigned in Japanese bureaucracies that were devoted to the notion of a centralized, top-down hierarchy. Thus, in the name of serving the people and democracy, state bureaucrats promoted their own corporate interests, often at the expense of democratic means and ends.[52] Especially during the period of rapid economic growth—and in no small part because of expectations carried over from the immediate past when the imperial regime had exercised almost absolute authority—top Japanese bureaucrats, within the parameters set by US hegemony and the Liberal Democratic Party, made and sustained the rules that governed the postwar regime. Their dictates during a

period of rapid growth, whether these involved promoting export-oriented industrialization or building airports in every prefecture, seemed marvels of infinite
wisdom. In leaner times, however, their decisions simply looked wrong, and
wrongheaded; in rural Japan, for instance, a traveler who wanders off the beaten
path will find pristine roads and magnificent bridges that lead to nowhere in particular.[53] In any case, zealous bureaucratic oversight did little to relieve the eradication of nature or the exploitation of humans. Moreover, the elite bureaucrats, notwithstanding their ostensibly effective, farsighted policies, could do little to prevent
the bursting of the Bubble or to reignite rapid economic growth afterward. Instead,
they became enmeshed in one corruption scandal after another.

The Iron Triangle

The long reign of the Liberal Democratic Party institutionalized an iron triangle
among powerful Japanese politicians, elite bureaucrats, and large corporations.
Although the iron triangle was interrupted and partially destroyed by the US
occupation, the triangle can actually be dated to the late nineteenth century and
the Meiji regime. Consider only the generational reproduction and tight network
of leading conservative politicians: Shinzō Abe is the grandson of one prime minister, Nobusuke Kishi, and the nephew of another, Eisaku Satō; Tarō Asō is also the
grandson of a prime minister, Shigeru Yoshida, and is married to the daughter of
yet another prime minister, Zenkō Suzuki. The proliferation of *zoku* (tribal) or
second- and third-generation parliamentarians has turned politicians into an
occupational caste.[54]

This seemingly endless reign of conservative politicians, in concert with elite
state bureaucrats, has created cozy corners of elite policymaking. Despite the institutionalization of electoral democracy in Japan, one-party rule and the relatively
autonomous state bureaucracy have shielded the policymaking elites from full
democratic scrutiny. Large- and small-scale corruption have corroded the polity
in matters that include sexual harassment and ethnic discrimination, contributions from corporations and *yakuza* (gangsters) to conservative politicians and
institutions, and the nondemocratic nature of Japanese democracy. Excessive protectionism and excessive spending have also contributed to Japan's massive public
debt, consistently the highest among rich industrial countries in the twenty-first
century (see fig. 3).

A particular problem is that conservative politicians have protected public
companies, or special corporations, which function as state-socialist organizations; at once corrupt and inefficient, they are part and parcel of the postwar developmental state and remain fiefdoms within the iron triangle.[55] No organization
exemplifies such questionable protection better than the Tokyo Electric Power
Company. Shielded from serious oversight, the company operates with a rule-
bound rigidity that nevertheless failed to protect the Fukushima nuclear power

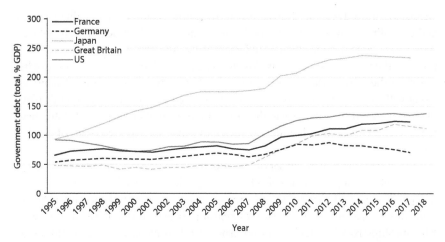

FIGURE 3. Public (Government) Debt. Note from OECD data website: "General government debt-to-GDP ratio is the amount of a country's total gross government debt as a percentage of its GDP. It is an indicator of an economy's health and a key factor for the sustainability of government finance. "Debt" is commonly defined as a specific subset of liabilities identified according to the types of financial instruments included or excluded. Debt is thus obtained as the sum of the following liability categories (as applicable): currency and deposits; securities other than shares, except financial derivatives; loans; insurance technical reserves; and other accounts payable. Changes in government debt over time reflect the impact of government deficits. . . . All OECD countries compile their data according to the 2008 System of National Accounts (SNA)." The OECD data set does not appear to include China or the Soviet Union. Data from "General Government Debt, *OECD iLibrary,* accessed 16 June 2019, doi: 10.1787/a0528cc2-en.

plants after the Tōhoku earthquake and tsunami of 2011, and the resulting wreckage could neither have been prevented nor successfully be cleaned up. The habitual ease with which large corporations are able to sidestep governmental regulation has produced a series of financial irregularities, not to mention manufacturing misadventures that include some of the greatest corporate scandals of the twenty-first century—the discovery of Takata Corporation's faulty airbags, for example, or of Kobe Steel's dishonesty about its products.[56] The bond between large corporations and state bureaucracies—a bond sealed by *amakudari* (the practice of inviting top bureaucrats, upon their retirement, to serve in the corporations that they presumably spent their careers regulating)—has ensured that corruption remains pervasive and entrenched.[57]

Clientelism

Japan remained a virtual protectorate of the United States even after regaining sovereignty, in 1952. Ostensibly nationalist prime ministers, whether Yasuhiro

Nakasone in the 1980s or Shinzō Abe in the 2010s, retained Japan's alliance with and geopolitical subservience to the United States as the bedrock of their politics. As a senior government official told me during Abe's tenure, "The key to Abe's power is the perception that he is close to the US president. That's the source of his power in the Liberal Democratic Party, and that's why all the business leaders go along with him." For everyone who ever wondered about Abe's repeated displays of obeisance and subservience to the forty-fifth president of the United States, here is the answer—the foundational character of Japan as a protectorate of the US empire.

Notwithstanding such subservience, Japan's sovereignty is unquestionable for most people. Yet a pentimento of subjugation can be perceived under the patina of independence. Emblematic of this phenomenon are rare literary depictions of Americans in Japan, as in the novel *Kurutta kajitsu* (Crazed fruit), published in 1956 by Ishihara Shintarō, who later became governor of Tokyo and is renowned for his ultra-nationalist statements. The novel and its film adaptation are often remembered as portraying a classic love triangle—the struggle between two brothers for the same woman—but readers and viewers forget that the *objet d'amour* is married to an elderly American man who floats along unperturbed by the tragic rift between the brothers, and by the damage to his wife.[58] And in Kojima Nobuo's 1965 novel *Hōyō kazoku* (Embracing family), an apparently happy nuclear household—a heteronormative couple with a son, a daughter, and (eventually, for good measure) a dog—implodes as a result of the wife's adultery with an American GI. The family's new, Western-style house is both physically flawed and interpersonally fraught; the wife experiences masculinization as a side effect of chemotherapy and later dies, whereas the GI thrives as a businessman in Japan.[59] It would be reductive to read these two literary works as allegories of US dominance in Japan, but the more interesting point is the near silence on the part of the Japanese about de facto US military sovereignty in Japan. As in the story of the two brothers in *Kurutta kajitsu,* domestic disputes provide a veneer of democratic vitality but also occlude US hegemony. Not surprisingly, the most articulate expressions of anti-Americanism have come from Japanese intellectuals with firsthand experience of life in the United States.[60] For them, the United States is far from being a land of liberty and affluence; these observers have borne witness to (and sometimes personally experienced) ethno-racial discrimination, stark inequality, and a barbaric anti-intellectualism.[61] By and large, though, the fact of Japan's subservience to the United States is a tetragrammaton of sorts for the postwar regime, an overarching reality that remains largely unspoken.

Hubris

The idea of Japan as "number one," a mere rumor in the late 1970s, had become something like dogma in bureaucratic and executive circles by the late 1980s, precisely when the Bubble was poised to burst. Part of the explanation is that the

Japanese people had begun to believe all the encomiums in the press, especially those from friends abroad, but failed to notice that the fundamental formula of the Japanese miracle could be replicated elsewhere, especially in neighboring Asian countries, including Taiwan and South Korea at first and, later on, China and Vietnam. Particularly pernicious was belief in the notion of Japanese uniqueness, a notion based on a number of implausible predicates. Some of these were innocuous enough, such as self-validating affirmations of the uniqueness of the Japanese language. But other, more sinister articulations of this notion involved, for example, the cultural and ethnic homogeneity and superiority of Japan, considered a major reason why the country was performing so well, by contrast with the multicultural, multiethnic (and therefore inferior) United States. By the 2010s, in a near reprise of the prewar period, there was a thriving industry founded on *Nihon wa sugoi* (the idea of Japanese greatness) as expressed in numerous television programs, print publications, and the ascendant social media.[62] In truth, however, cultural involution had created an echo chamber: whereas Japan had prospered precisely because it had been willing to learn from abroad, the Japanese now began to look inward, smug in the conviction of their superiority.

Japanese hubris was most evident in corporate boardrooms. The initial phase of postwar economic recovery had been powered by the assembly and manufacture of goods according to the requirements of received technology, and so state bureaucrats and corporate executives were implicitly and perpetually locked into catch-up mode. It is true that by the 1970s reliance on low-paid labor was a thing of the past; Japanese corporations had begun by then to invest heavily in research and development. But just when Japanese corporations were superseding US and other companies as industry leaders (think of Sony or Honda in the 1980s), they fell prey to the seductions of pursuing profit through finance, and they lowered their commitment to seeking and making disruptive technology. I interviewed Sony executives in 1985, and when I asked them about the prospects of a newly founded South Korean company called Samsung Electronics, those normally taciturn men could barely suppress a chuckle, and there were even a few guffaws. Sony was confident in its mastery of analog technology, and the company was reveling in the success of the Sony Walkman, the iPhone of the 1980s. But Sony failed to catch the oncoming wave of the digital revolution and soon fell behind its upstart South Korean competitor.

Twentieth-century Japan, then, was marked in particular by two moments of hubris—the military hubris that ended with atomic bomb blasts over Hiroshima and Nagasaki, and the economic hubris that concluded with the bursting of the Bubble. In both instances, the hubris lasted only four years, at least in its manic phase (1941 to 1945 for the war, and 1985 to 1989 for the Bubble), but it would have been difficult to miss the frenzy, short-lived though it was. In any event, all talk and aspirations of, on one hand, Japanese military might and, on the other,

Japanese economic superiority were quashed for at least a generation. As for the Bubble, by the third decade of the twenty-first century it has become something that only the older people talk about; people would have to be well into their forties to have experienced it firsthand.

THE POSTWAR REGIME IN CRISIS

Exploitation of nature and humanity; rigid bureaucrats and myopic politicians; overconfidence and failure to anticipate change and competition—these problems are far from unique to postwar Japan. Yet not only have they been, in and of themselves, a blight on Japan's postwar regime, but they also point to the regime's deep flaws.

The postwar regime was in full crisis by the late 1980s, but it had been riddled with problems from the outset. Most regimes, in the sense in which I am using the term, don't last very long. The Thousand-Year Reich, for example, survived barely a dozen years. Japanese militarism, encompassing the Fifteen Years' War (1931–45), was at its most stridently martial and authoritarian for only four years (the period of the Pacific War, 1941–45). Again where Japan is concerned, what is most emblematic of this phenomenon is that the forty-year reign of the Liberal Democratic Party came to an end in 1993 (if only for one year). The party then resumed its reign until 2009 and came to power once again in 2012, though its myth of invincibility has evaporated; today the legitimacy of the Liberal Democratic Party rests squarely on its purported managerial skills.[63]

Like the Liberal Democratic Party, elite bureaucrats have also lost their luster. Symptomatic of their decline are repeated revelations of high-level corruption involving money and sex (the usual suspects). From a more systematic perspective, the constant shuffling and reshuffling of ministerial names and functions suggests that politicians and bureaucrats recognize the problems afflicting the once-mighty state apparatus; these name changes and functional shifts do not inspire confidence in the permanence and solidity of the state bureaucracy.[64]

Moreover, among the power elite of the post-Bubble period, not only in the financial and business establishments but also in the state bureaucracies, there has been a strain of neoliberalism that espouses less state intervention and more free-market economics. (Neoliberalism in its pure articulation, of course, would radically curtail the scope and functions of the state.) The two longest-serving prime ministers of the post-Bubble decades, Jun'ichirō Koizumi and Shinzō Abe, differed considerably in matters of personality and policy but nevertheless shared a commitment to structural reform, meaning a more neoliberally oriented economic policy. The continuing dominance of the United States in the global economy underscores the appeal of US-style political economy, as opposed to the postwar regime or to European-style social democracy.[65] But the state bureaucracies are recalcitrant, and where they have instituted liberalizing reforms (such as the partial privatization of public universities), those initiatives have been watered down or have otherwise not fared well.[66] Elite politicians and bureaucrats may enjoin their younger counterparts to study abroad or show some entrepreneurial spirit, but it is precisely the policies and practices of these elites that constitute a challenge, if not an outright barrier, to foreign ventures and domestic innovations.

Large corporations navigated the high tide of rapid economic growth with great dexterity. Able young people aspired to a smooth ride—a lifetime of prestigious, meaningful employment. Corporations like Sony and Panasonic, Toyota and Nissan were avatars of Japanese economic might. Yet the story of how Samsung overtook Sony is but one among many woeful tales in which a once-formidable Japanese corporation begins to stumble or even tumble. The psychological shock of the Bubble cannot be separated from many Japanese citizens' disbelief that a reputable financial firm like Yamaichi Shōken could become insolvent; clearly, however, large Japanese corporations were neither immortal nor invincible. The twenty-first century has not been kind to the giant Japanese corporations that engineered and steered the nation's rapid postwar economic growth. As already noted, heretofore unthinkable news of corporate scandal proliferated. By the late 2010s, "Made in Japan" was no longer an indisputable guarantee of quality. Japanese corporations today seem at best to be treading water, if not poised to be carried off by the receding tide.

Another feature of the postwar regime in its decline was the waning of Japan's system of labor relations, encompassing the "three treasures" (recall that these are lifetime employment, a seniority-based wage system, and enterprise-based unions). The idea that an employee might remain with a single firm for an entire career has been shaken as most companies have come to rely on temporary and short-term help. And even though seniority remains a powerful norm, it was predicated on the expectation of lifetime employment. Labor unions, too, are greatly diminished. Long workdays and managerial authoritarianism remain, but college graduates—many of whom have spent the last two years of their four-year university curriculum in *shūkatsu* (job hunting)—are caught up in the mad rush for stable employment. By 2020, it would have been difficult to hear anyone singing the praises of the Japanese employment system.[67]

Yet another casualty of the post-Bubble decades has been belief in Japan as an egalitarian nation, where all 100 million–plus citizens were said to be middle-class. The earlier perception of equality was a product of the postwar period. It was due not so much to the quantitative uptick in per capita GDP as to processes of structural transformation (by which one could change, for example, from a farmer to an urban worker) and to processes of technological change, especially as these allowed acquisition of labor-saving appliances and access to previously undreamed-of luxuries, such as foreign travel. By the 1990s, however, both processes had decelerated considerably. A color TV, for instance, was still a wonder, but the marginal benefit of a larger screen or assorted mystifying bells and whistles was vanishingly small or nonexistent. And flying on a jumbo jet to take in a *tour d'horizon* of European sights was an eye-opening experience, but not many who had enjoyed it felt the urge to have it again. The dominant perception during the 1990s was no longer that everyone was middle-class. It was that Japan had become a society of *kakusa* (qualitative difference or, more simply, inequality). Thus Japan's celebration of growth accompanied by equality became a lament over economic decline and inequality.

Consider Japan's ranking on the following measures (Japan, far from being "number one," was middling at best):

2018 Global Entrepreneurship Index: 28

2017 Gallup poll measuring workers' engagement in 139 countries: 133

2018 Global Gender Gap: 110

2018 Corruption Perceptions Index: 19

2019 World Press Freedom Index: 67

2017 Government Expenditure on Education as Percentage of GDP: 134

2018 Environmental Performance Index: 20

2018 Good Country Index: 24

2018 World Happiness Index: 54[68]

Such indexes and rankings are fraught with problems, of course, and Japan actually does well on measures of education, health, and other domains. But one unavoidable conclusion is that Japan is not performing well on quite a few measures of desirable outcomes.

Very few people in Japan now expect Japan to be "number one" in anything. The occasional triumphs—Yuzuru Hanyu winning at figure skating, Naomi Osaka winning at tennis, Japanese scientists winning Nobel Prizes—do nothing to restore the brilliance of Japan's bygone day in the sun. Epistructural transformations notwithstanding, the iron triangle still holds considerable sway, and almost all the problems of contemporary Japan, as discussed in earlier portions of this chapter, can be traced to the iron triangle's dysfunctions. In short, the postwar regime is no longer working well, and Japan's current problems point to the ways in which it never really did.

THE SO-CALLED LOST DECADES

Despite the problems already recounted, contemporary Japan is anything but a basket case. The "Japanese disease" discourse of the lost decades is a tendentious description of post-Bubble Japanese society. As the journalist David Pilling puts it, "Though I arrived at the end of Japan's first 'lost decade' and in what was supposed to be a deep recession at the start of its second, there was scant evidence of deprivation, certainly much less than I was used to seeing in my native Britain."[69] Pilling's impression is not at all unique; Japan appears to be functioning rather well, from its trains that run on time to the solicitude of its restaurant servers, and from the remarkable security of even its large cities to its low incidence of extreme inequality.

The vision of the lost decades relies disproportionately on the imagery of senescence and death. Population decline, for example, is of dire concern to the policy elites. Yet population in and of itself, whether it grows slightly or declines somewhat, is not a serious issue. First, Japan, like every other major industrial country, is not experiencing much natural population growth, as opposed to the kind brought about by immigration. And, second, given not only the long-standing impression that Japan is overcrowded, especially in its large metropolises, but also the general burden that human beings place on the environment, bureaucrats and policymakers perhaps ought to welcome demographic stability or even decline. But the fear still exists—at times it borders on hysteria—that population decline denotes Japanese degeneration or even the disappearance of the Japanese people altogether. A statistical miscalculation is what accounts for the belief that the Japanese people will disappear if the population continues to decline. If longer life expectancy is creating a greater proportion of elderly people, this fact might even be celebrated. After all, who wants to die young? Nevertheless, in what has been a gerontocratic society, pervasive ageism is evident in the troubling image of the doddering, decrepit retiree, an image that doubles as the personification of twenty-first-century Japan—a geriatric society without vitality. Policymakers and pundits also articulate issues that are more concrete. For example, the Japanese pension system necessarily relies on younger workers to support the current crop of pensioners, and an imbalance in favor of the inactive may be overburdening the active population. In addition, corporate executives worry not just about maintaining an adequate supply of workers but also about how sheer pressure for higher wages, if nothing else, may be weakening Japanese competitiveness.

Where the issue of population decline is concerned, the politicians, bureaucrats, and executives ensconced in the postwar regime remain committed, often unconsciously, to masculinist, patriarchal institutions and policies. As a result, government officials and corporations enact simple, unambitious, limited measures to facilitate pronatalist outcomes. But many women can no longer enjoy a middle-class lifestyle as full-time homemakers, and so they continue to work long after they marry and have children. Moreover, women's comparatively low wages, along with family-unfriendly working conditions and the severe lack of urban day care facilities, discourage women from having more than one or two children. As for

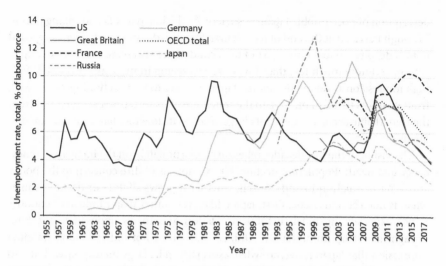

FIGURE 4. Comparative Unemployment. Note from OECD data website: "[The u]nemployment rate is the number of unemployed people as a percentage of the labour force, where the latter consists of the unemployed plus those in paid or self-employment. Unemployed people are those who report that they are without work, that they are available for work and that they have taken active steps to find work in the last four weeks. When unemployment is high, some people become discouraged and stop looking for work; they are then excluded from the labour force. This implies that the unemployment rate may fall, or stop rising, even though there has been no underlying improvement in the labour market." The OECD data set does not appear to include China. Source: "Unemployment rate (indicator)," *OECD iLibrary*, accessed 16 June 2019, doi: 10.1787/997c8750-en.

competition, it would not be unreasonable to propose that long working hours be shortened or to curb the so-called black corporations that promote death by overwork; the Japanese might consider competing with the Nordic countries, rather than with South Korea or China, by creating a society of well-paying jobs, with social support.

The Japanese economy is far from moribund. Even if we consider a crude basic indicator like GDP, Japan's growth, if modest, has been steady. No doubt Japan's current growth is minuscule compared to the growth that occurred during the nation's Golden Age, and the present cannot match the exuberance of the Bubble decade. But a more relevant comparison would be between the Japan of today and today's other rich industrial societies. Japanese growth is far from negligible in comparison to that of the mature economies (fig. 1); in fact, some industrial countries, such as the United Kingdom, are suffering the longest period of real-income decline in their recorded histories. That has not been the case for Japan. It is true that inflation in Japan has been very low, but economists have usually regarded low inflation in a positive light. Japan's unemployment figures are also low, even if there is an under-

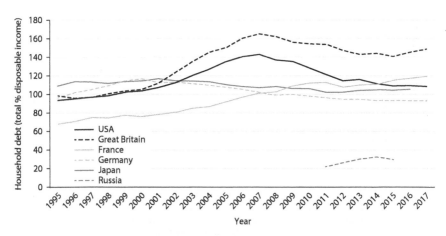

FIGURE 5. Private (Consumer) Debt. Note from OECD data website: "Household debt is defined as all liabilities that require payment or payments of interest or principal by [the] household to the creditor at a date or dates in the future. Consequently, all debt instruments are liabilities, but some liabilities such as shares, equity and financial derivatives, are not considered as debt. Debt is thus obtained as the sum of the following liability categories, whenever available/applicable in the financial balance sheet of the households and non-profit institutions serving [the] households sector: currency and deposits; securities other than shares, except financial derivatives; loans; insurance technical reserves; and other accounts payable. For households, liabilities predominantly consist of loans, in particular mortgage loans for the purchase of houses. This indicator is measured as a percentage of NDI [net disposable income]. All OECD countries compile their data according to the 2008 System of National Accounts (SNA)." The OECD data set does not appear to include China. Data from "Household Debt," *OECD iLibrary*, accessed 16 June 2019, doi: 10.1787/f03b6469-en.

count of discouraged job seekers (fig. 4). In addition, credit card debt and student loan debt—the bane of many Americans—are much lower in Japan (fig. 5). Moreover, in spite of Japan's massive public debt, Japanese public and private debt combined are no greater than the combined public and private debt of the United States. And if we consider income inequality or rates of poverty, we see that Japan's figures, if hardly inspiring, are no worse and often better than those of most other affluent countries (fig. 6). In the United States and the United Kingdom, life expectancy is down and infant mortality is up, but the corresponding figures for Japan attest to the robustness of the Japanese public health system as well as to the absence of an opiate crisis and other epidemics (fig. 7). As any systematic review of aggregate economic data or national vital statistics reveals, Japan is doing well, especially in comparison to other rich countries in the wake of the 2007–8 financial crisis.

The Japanese infrastructure also remains robust—not just roads and bridges but public transportation too. Commuters and riders may grumble about this or that shortcoming, but Japan's railways and private subway companies perform

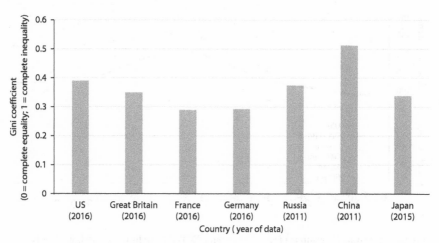

FIGURE 6. Inequality and Poverty Rate. Note from OECD data website: "Income is defined as household disposable income in a particular year. It consists of earnings, self-employment and capital income and public cash transfers; income taxes and social security contributions paid by households are deducted. The income of the household is attributed to each of its members, with an adjustment to reflect differences in needs for households of different sizes. Income inequality among individuals is measured here by five indicators. The Gini coefficient is based on the comparison of cumulative proportions of the population against cumulative proportions of income they receive, and it ranges between 0 in the case of perfect equality and 1 in the case of perfect inequality. S80/S20 is the ratio of the average income of the 20% richest to the 20% poorest; P90/P10 is the ratio of the upper bound value of the ninth decile (i.e., the 10% of people with highest income) to that of the first decile; P90/P50, [the ratio] of the upper bound value of the ninth decile to the median income; and P50/P10, of median income to the upper bound value of the first decile." Data from Income Inequality, *OECD iLibrary*, accessed 16 June 2019, doi: 10.1787/459aa7f1-en.

remarkably well. For example, Shinkansen, the famous bullet train, processes a constant stream of departures and arrivals but has remained accident-free for half a century. The tangled web of the Tokyo subway system is a precision instrument, unlike the rodent-infested subway system in New York City or the olfactory nightmare that is the Bay Area Rapid Transit system in and around San Francisco. And Japan's public and private delivery services are nothing short of extraordinary for their alacrity and careful handling of parcels.

The many large Japanese corporations which found that rapid economic growth was synonymous with struggle have still managed to survive and even thrive; in other words, not all of Japan's large corporations disappeared or declined after the Bubble burst. The conventional view often conflates Japanese political economy with such large corporations and their export-oriented industrialization. What the conventional view leaves out, however, is a vibrant sector of the Japanese economy, a sphere of economic and social life made up mostly of smaller firms, that is dis-

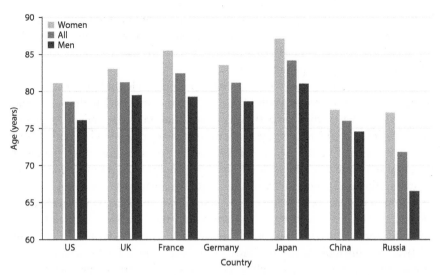

FIGURE 7. Life Expectancy. Note from OECD data website: "Life expectancy at birth is defined as how long, on average, a newborn can expect to live, if current death rates do not change. However, the actual age-specific death rate of any particular birth cohort cannot be known in advance. If rates are falling, actual life spans will be higher than life expectancy calculated using current death rates. Life expectancy at birth is one of the most frequently used health status indicators. Gains in life expectancy at birth can be attributed to a number of factors, including rising living standards, improved lifestyle and better education, as well as greater access to quality health services. This indicator is presented as a total and per gender and is measured in years." Data from "Life Expectancy at Birth," *OECD iLibrary,* accessed 16 June 2019, doi: 10.1787/27e0fc9d-en.

tinct from and largely occluded by the postwar regime. In so doing, the conventional view also exaggerates the pessimistic perspective on contemporary Japan. The smaller firms usually manufacture specialized precision parts or machines; similar to companies found in the small- and medium-size sector of German enterprise that is usually called *Mittelstand,* these Japanese counterparts have continued to do well in the twenty-first century. On an even smaller scale are the family-based businesses or microenterprises that deliver the rudiments of Cool Japan. Encompassing a range of entrepreneurs and enterprises from anime studios to sushi restaurants, and pervaded by a remarkable artisanal ethos, the smaller firms create many of the groundbreaking products that Japan is becoming known for all over the world.

In short, then, contemporary Japan is not a sick society suffering through its final phase of disease and decline. A quick look around the world should make this clear. For example, Russia, the once-mighty superpower, is and definitely has been in decline, no matter how that phenomenon is measured. And, although the

United States may look superior because of its paramount position in finance and its profitable information technology, few in Japan would countenance its appalling inequality and crumbling infrastructure. Present-day Japan loses its luster only when compared to the Japan of the 1960s.

Japan's period of rapid economic growth lives on as a legendary time, but not many Japanese people today would choose to turn the clock back to the immediate postwar era. That champagne cork has popped, and only considerable force and ingenuity could get it back into the bottle of what in any case would be nothing but flat, sticky dregs. To resist the dysfunctions of the postwar decades is a matter of common sense today. Contemporary Japanese people would reject Chinese-level pollution (that is, Japanese pollution as it existed in the 1960s). They would also be unwilling to endure a so-called 3K job—*kitai, kitsui,* and *kiken* (in English, a 3D job—dirty, difficult, and dangerous). Nor would they readily accept extremely low-paid employment, not least of all because the lost decades have been a time of relatively low unemployment. In almost all analyses of post-Bubble Japanese economic malaise, moreover, bungling politicians and corrupt bureaucrats and myopic executives are considered to be at or near the heart of what caused the economic downturn. As mentioned earlier, the heroes of the postwar regime have morphed into the villains of the lost decades.

Hubris, gone now, has been replaced by a sense of unease, even despair. After all, the global economic outlook is not propitious. There are keen competitors, especially in neighboring Asian countries, and no rich country in any part of the world has managed to achieve accelerated growth since the time of Japan's Golden Age. Almost no one now looks to Japan for corporate innovations, as many once did in the 1980s. Few Japanese people now believe that double-digit GDP growth can come back. In any case, the last thing Japan needs is a return to the postwar regime with all its flaws. But if Japan is nostalgic for its Golden Age, much as the Netherlands or Spain might yearn for their own, not many of the countless Japanese people I've talked with would choose to live in the Golden Age or in the Bubble years rather than in the present, in the putative lost decades. As we have seen, no one younger than forty even remembers the Bubble, and a person would need to be well over fifty to have had firsthand experience of Japan's rapid economic growth. For almost everyone under forty, Japan has always been a relatively affluent and comfortable country. Just who, then, is nostalgic for the Golden Age or the Bubble decade?

THE PASSING OF TWO GENERATIONS

The "lost decades" idea and the "Japanese disease" discourse reveal a disjunction between the postwar regime and twenty-first-century Japan. Although it would be simplistic to reduce this disjunction to a cleavage on the order of "the state" versus "society," there are indeed two major competing visions of Japan—the vision of those who are committed to the postwar regime, and the vision of those who are not. Those who are steeped in the memory and ideology of the postwar regime find that the present deviates from their notion of how Japan ought to be; an unshakable belief in growth preoccupies the architects and engineers of Japan's rapid postwar economic growth. Yet the postwar regime has not completely colonized economic, social, and cultural life in Japan: a distinct and vibrant sector of Japanese life continues to produce superlative goods and to sustain the good life.

Why is the "lost decades" idea so resonant in contemporary Japan? For one thing, now that the notion of China's rise has superseded the buzz about Japan as "number one," the unavoidable reality is that Japan is no longer even "number two." And the rise not just of China but also of South Korea and other Asian economies only accentuates the sense of Japan as arguably stagnant. Moreover, beyond historical and geographical comparisons—which are reasonable from a psychological standpoint, but not from that of economics or the social sciences—the "lost decades" idea persists as a cultural phenomenon, the mood or zeitgeist that dominates Japan. This mood arises from the visible decline of the postwar regime, which, as already noted, was considered the essential correlate and probable cause of Japan's rapid economic growth after World War II. Nostalgia for the time when Japan seemed poised to overtake the United States, or for the earlier time when Japan's GDP was doubling every seven years, is one factor, especially among older Japanese people. Exemplary in this regard is the 2005 hit film *Always san-chōme no yūhi* (*Always: Sunset on Third Street*), directed by Takashi Yamazaki.[70] Set in the late 1950s, the film depicts a time when neighbors were caring and supportive and everything seemed to be improving; people could watch the proverbial grass grow. It was, again, all onward and upward in the period of rapid economic growth, by contrast with contemporary urban Japan, where civil indifference and economic stasis are the norm. This *saudade* for Japan's Golden Age, like Yamazaki's sepia-toned film, appeals mainly to two generations in decline—the wartime (*senchū*) and Japanese baby boom (*dankai*) generations—and the basic phenomenology of the "lost decades" trope reflects their decline.[71]

The wartime generation, especially its men, narrowly escaped death, having been exposed to the mortal combat and destruction that their parents' generation had brought about. As the protagonist in Yoshiyuki Junnosuke's short story "Honoo no naka" (Into the fire) reflects, "I was forced to think only about death during the war, but now I have been thrown into a time when I must think about living."[72] Similarly, one of my interview subjects, a senior executive at a major Japanese company, reflected on his own life: "I was not living my life, but I was allowed to live. I think of all the friends who perished in that meaningless war. I've been living on borrowed time."[73] For Japan's wartime generation, the emptiness of defeat also meant emancipation from certain destruction. These young people, growing up with no apparent future, later rejected the wartime lies of their parents and teachers and came to pride themselves on having created Japan's recovery and prosperity. They brought about massive transformations in Japan, but they are greatly outnumbered by the baby boomers, especially the *dankai* generation, who were born in the three years after the end of the war. This younger generation, of course, does not remember the wartime horrors; nevertheless, it would be difficult to find a Japanese person born in the first decade after the end of the war who did not experience or observe the war's resulting destruction and poverty at first hand during childhood. They and the *senchū* generation embraced the new, the democratic, and the modern, all the while resisting the traditionalism of the older generation, which had contributed to the national disaster.

And Japan's economic growth was tangible for both of these younger generations. Growth meant not just lifetime employment security, a seniority-based wage system, and enterprise-based unions, not just a color TV, an air conditioner, and a car, but also the upward trajectory of wages and disposable income. For both the *senchū* and *dankai* generations, the postwar period spanned the glory of youth, a vibrant middle age, and the hope and brilliance of a future that became lived experience, all of it compressed into just a few years. Emblematic of this mind-set is a critical study by Miura Masashi, *Seishun no shūen* (The end of youth); Miura, born in 1946, locates the end of youth in Japan in the late 1960s and early 1970s, precisely the time when his own youth came to an end.[74] Much the same can be said about Sekikawa Natsuo, born three years later, and about his book *Shōwa ga akarukatta koro* (When the Shōwa period was bright); for Sekikawa, the Shōwa period was bright during his childhood.[75] One finds in both authors an overlapping of biography with history that makes for a potent idealization of the past.

There is something deeply disturbing about the persistence of the postwar period into the third decade of the twenty-first century. After all, there are not many Japanese people left in the 2020s who were even conscious during World War II. Moreover, the Japanese have been discussing the end of the postwar period since at least the early 1950s. In the meantime, Japan's rapid growth has waned and the Cold War has ended. But the postwar regime endures—in the geopolitical dominance of the United States, in the iron triangle, in the Liberal Democratic Party, in the state bureaucracy, and in Japan's large corporations. For those who lived through the nation's glory days, and for those who hold to the ideology of growth, it is a matter of Japan's very survival that its Golden Age be revived. The *senchū* and *dankai* generations carry with them the glorious memory of Japan's postwar period; to them, the post-Bubble decades seem stagnant, reeking of decline, decay, and death. It is as if these two generations and the nation itself have grown old together and are now wearily facing the inevitable. Thus has the deep

sleep of received and settled opinion, articulated by and for two passing generations, encased the discourse of Japanese decline.

OLD AND YOUNG

Let's return now to the problem of demographic decline and the prospect of an
aging society. Is demography destiny? A common expression of crackpot realism
is expatiation on one population crisis or another. But time and time again in the
two centuries since Thomas Robert Malthus's dire forecast, demographic determinism (and pessimism) has been refuted.

All the same, it is difficult not to notice the widespread panic in Japan over
fantastic claims of impending calamity, whether it is imagined as the disappearance of the Japanese nation because of the plunging fertility rate or as the collapse
of the old-age pension system because of a decline in the active population that
must support it. Today it is strange to recall that until the 1980s it was common
sense in Japan to regard the nation as overpopulated and overcrowded. Some four
decades later it still seems that way to many people. And, as we have seen, the
Japanese economy is not in decline. There are also ways, such as automation and
immigration, to compensate for unmet labor needs.

As for Japan's rapid aging, it emerged as a serious issue in the post-Bubble decades. As mentioned earlier, longer life expectancy and the steep decline in Japan's
fertility rate have meant that Japan's population is now made up of a larger proportion of elderly people. In the course of the 1990s, the relatively new term *kōreisha*
(people of advanced age) came to supersede such older terms as *rōjin* (old people).
Around 2010, Japan had what was probably the world's highest proportion of elderly citizens (defined as those sixty-five years and older) and highest mean age,
though South Korea and Taiwan may have overtaken Japan on that score by the
mid-2010s.[76] In the Japan of the 1970s and 1980s, foreign social scientists were able
to detect the distinct Japanese national trait of honoring the elders, but few Japanese people or outsiders would have noticed it by the 1990s, apart from a national
holiday to honor the elderly, or the priority seating ("silver seats") reserved for
elderly people on mass transit (as such seating is also reserved for pregnant women
and people with disabilities), in keeping with a policy introduced in 1973.[77] Just a
year earlier, Ariyoshi Sawako's novel *Kōkotsu no hito* (The twilight years) had
offered a melodramatic, sensationalistic depiction of dementia and its devastating
impact on elderly people and their caregivers.[78] By the 1990s, the individual problems and private tragedies of aging had been transformed into a general social
concern. The proliferation of poverty and homelessness among elderly people also
became a serious social issue, though the number of poor elderly citizens, as a proportion of all elderly Japanese people, now appears to be shrinking.[79] And the rapid

aging of society affects all of the world's affluent countries; aging in neighboring South Korea is even more acute than in Japan.

But the problem is not so much the graying of society in and of itself as the fact that traditional support for elderly people, including the help provided by nuclear and extended family members, friends, and neighbors, is indisputably in decline. In 2010, a sensational program on NHK (Japan's BBC) about *muen shakai* (the "no relationship" society) reported that every year, thirty-two thousand elderly people died alone, with no one at their side and no one to claim them. Formal mechanisms of care, such as employer- or government-sponsored old-age pensions, remain inadequate. Needless to say, this trend is only exacerbated by prolonged life expectancy. We should also be mindful that traditional families and communities in Japan were not always gerontocratic; recall the practice of abandoning the elderly on a mountain to die, as depicted in Fukazawa Shichirō's novel *Narayamabushi kō* (The ballad of Narayama).[80]

More to the point, since the late 1960s—the time of the student movement against the war in Vietnam and of the protests against the construction of Narita Airport—the *dankai* generation has been projecting a self-centered perspective. The year 1946 was the beginning of the *dankai* generation; and, given Japan's mandatory retirement laws, the dawn of the new millennium marked the start of that generation's sunset years, at least in terms of their centrality as movers and shakers. It is a garden-variety epistemic error to confound one's own decline and demise with that of the world. With so many of the *dankai* cohort in the same situation, this generational delusion risks becoming a national confusion.

Pessimism about the proximate future of Japan's aging society also gives rise to an exceedingly negative perspective on younger generations. Journalistic and scholarly writings on the topic often sound like older people's complaints about their young counterparts—their children, in short. For example, members of the *dankai* generation are utterly incapable of understanding the lives of the *furītā* or *nīto* (under- and unemployed young people) whose parents they happen to be.[81] These young people, often in their thirties, appear content to live at home with their parents and are called *parasaito singuru* (parasite singles).[82] Dependent on their parents, they move from one employment gig to another, refuse to marry and settle down, and seem passionate only about one favorite pastime or another. Prod almost any middle-aged *sararīman* (salaryman, or white-collar worker), and out comes a torrent of verbal abuse directed at the young: they are addicted to their cell phones and don't care about the larger society, they are spoiled and dependent (*amae*) on their parents, they are useless (*dame*), and so on. As one retiree in his late sixties told me, "I just don't understand. My sons grew up with every-thing—everything I didn't have growing up. What do they want to do? I don't know." And a housewife whose children, both in their thirties, still live with her and her husband said, "I don't understand my children. They don't even seem Japanese to me."

The educational psychologist Hayamizu Toshihiko—born in 1947, and therefore a member of the *dankai* generation—argues that the sentimental life of the Japanese has been transformed by the emergence of young people who have lost the desire to work, who disrespect others, and who display an excess of self-esteem; the solution, he says, is discipline.[83] When I mentioned Hayamizu's argument to Japanese teenagers and people in their twenties, the uniform reaction was, not surprisingly, disbelief (*ge*, a phatic expression, was probably the most common response). What is more spectacular, a discussion of *nīto* that was published around the turn of the millennium describes them as "devouring" the wealth of their parents and their country, as allied with society's destruction, and as being, "in a sense," a "bomb."[84] *Ojisan* and *obasan* (middle-aged men and women, respectively) and young people live in mutually uncomprehending worlds.

The proliferation of, at first, *furītā* and, later, *nīto* became noticeable in the post-Bubble decades, initially because of the economic downturn, but their presence has been sustained over time by the transformation of the Japanese labor market. Even when Japan experienced something close to full employment, in the mid-2010s, no steep decline occurred in the population of irregular workers, precisely because a large and vibrant job sector in Japan sought nontraditional employees, who came without the burden of guaranteed lifetime employment. But no matter how closely members of the *dankai* generation scrutinized the daily newspaper, they found it hard to grasp the fact that employment in the 2010s was not what it had been in the overheated labor market of the 1960s and 1970s. And just as puzzling to them was the fact that younger Japanese people, born to relative comfort, are not hungry or ambitious, and that they do not expect and often do not want the salaryman's life.[85] To put this idea differently, these are ordinary young women and men, products of their upbringing, who are facing and reacting to the changing Japanese labor market. No longer can they blithely count on the school-to-work transition that their parents took for granted. Moreover, the salaryman's life strikes many young Japanese people as a life of quiet desperation. As a man in his early thirties said to me, "I'm not getting up early and getting on a crowded train to do some meaningless job. For what? So I can buy a house farther away? And not be able to enjoy my little garden?" And several other men in their thirties told roughly the same story: "Why leave a nice house where my mother cooks and cleans? What's the advantage of working and living like that? I'd have a tiny apartment. I'd have to do all the housework. And I wouldn't have any free time."

The corrosion and contraction of the putative miracle of Japanese employment, a system that even at its height was limited to perhaps a third of the labor force, has produced a new reality of flexible employment, a reality that necessarily includes unemployment for young people. Yet what is remarkable about contemporary Japan is the relatively low rate of unemployment, with comparatively stable rates of inequality and social mobility.[86] It is bizarre, then, to encounter what almost amounts to a moral panic in Japan, and to hear a US social scientist bemoaning the fate of *furīta* and *nīto,* when conditions in the United States and other advanced industrial countries are themselves far from enviable.[87] It is also baffling that hardly any social scientists have seriously addressed the persistence of artisanal employment or the vitality of small- and medium-size firms in contemporary Japan.

2

Growth Reconsidered

The idea of modernity, along with associated notions of growth, progress, and improvement, remains at the heart of the Western, and the Western-influenced, way of life. Against the pernicious and perfidious past—which saw the reign of stasis instead of growth, of cycles rather than progress, of continuity over disruption, and of tradition in lieu of innovation—we can regard the advent of modernity only as an unalloyed good. Who, after all, could possibly be *against* modernity, except perhaps a few tree-hugging environmental activists or antediluvian reactionaries?

But has Japan since the Meiji Restoration (1868–1912), Japan in its mad rush to catch up with the West, been a singular story of success? Doubtless no Dr. Pangloss today would celebrate the dark decades of Japan's descent into militarism and authoritarianism, and it would take a Herculean effort merely to justify the deaths (perhaps 2.7 million Japanese dead), not to mention the many millions more victims of Japanese aggression.[1] In fact, modernization and Westernization engendered one war after another, whereas the Edo period, or the Tokugawa shogunate (1603–1867), had overseen nearly three centuries of uninterrupted peace.[2] It hardly takes much historical information or imagination to see that Japan's emulation of the West produced not just industrialization and nation building but also capitalist exploitation, imperialist adventures, and runaway militarization. All the same, one might protest, isn't Japanese life in the second decade of the twenty-first century surely superior, in general, to Japanese life in the 1850s? But my counterfactual query has to do with the putative blessings of post–Meiji Restoration modernization; that is, I question whether the Meiji regime and its sinister avatar, the prewar regime, were as positive as some Japanese people are still inclined to believe.

Be that as it may, I am more curious about the wisdom of Western emulation and the presumption of Japanese backwardness. It may be that Western technology was incompatible with Japanese culture and society; the ideal of *wakon yōsai* (Japanese spirit, Western techniques) may have been an oxymoron. But were all things Western—diet, clothing, housing, mores—truly superior? Scientific advances have cast doubt on the superiority of a protein-heavy, high-calorie diet and on the suitability of sitting in a chair for long periods.[3] In any case, a pescatarian or vegetarian diet seems advisable in our age of obesity epidemics and animal liberation.[4] It seems incredible today that in the early-nineteenth-century Edo period there were more than 7,600 eateries in Japan, with distinct and delectable cuisines.[5] And was it really so shameful that Japanese men had sex with other men, or assumed nontraditional gender roles, or bathed with women and children? Indeed, gender relations seemed more egalitarian before the Western onslaught.[6] Many peasants and townspeople led reasonably sanitary, disciplined, orderly lives.[7] Were Tokugawa-era artistic achievements inferior to their European counterparts? That is, was Augustan literature or Restoration art (Alexander Pope, Jacques-Louis David, Eugène Delacroix) better than the literature and art of Bakin, Hokusai, and Hiroshige? Is Christianity the only true religion, and were the Japanese of the Tokugawa era benighted heathens? Were the market system and the protoindustrialization of late Tokugawa Japan inefficient and unproductive? The assertion that Western visitors found the pre–Meiji Restoration Japanese well off and happy is now supported by economic historians.[8] To put it simply, then, did Tokugawa-era Japan really need to be saved from its backwardness?

GROWTH AND ITS DISCONTENTS

A counterfactual comparative history would be, needless to say, a disreputable academic pursuit, nor can we go backward, in any case, even if doing so would solve any disputes. Surely it would be irrelevant to compare 1819 Edo-period Japan with Tokyo in our own day; better to compare particular moments of the Edo period with contemporaneous moments in Paris or London or New York. Anyway, nostalgia is all too often an exercise in insipid fantasy, a hankering for a past that never was. The important point is that the vast majority of the Japanese came to believe that the West was superior to Japan and that the Tokugawa past had to be superseded if not expunged. What is not clear, however, is why the path of Western emulation or the pursuit of growth came to be seen as always so wonderful.

It may be problematic enough that a seditious scholar is looking for the bright side of what is traditional and sustainable in Japan, and not excluding the much-derided Edo period. That this scholar should then seek to generalize his findings would be all the more perverse. But that is precisely what I propose to undertake here—a grand tour of reasons to be skeptical about economic growth.

My argument is not against change. In a universe of constant change, there is precious little we can do but accept and deal with it. Nor am I against promoting affluence, minimizing poverty, and celebrating artistic or scientific efflorescence and innovation. Rather, my argument has to do with the primacy of economic growth and its valorization as the master solution to our problems.

But doesn't it seem strange to question growth? Who would not want more, or at least more of the things we value? Who, for example, would not find pleasure in seeing children or plants grow? Growth has been at the heart of modern political economy and social sciences. All that *can* be grown *must* be grown, in a linear, upward trajectory of progress and improvement, and so it's only common sense that growth should have been explosive and continuous since the Industrial Revolution. The primacy of economic growth—or economic development, or progress, or whatever this phenomenon may be called—is an article of faith in the modern world; perhaps it even constitutes the modern world's one true monotheistic faith.

The most powerful and prestigious of the modern social sciences is economics, and its founding figure is Adam Smith. In the memorable year 1776, *An Inquiry into the Nature and Causes of the Wealth of Nations* appeared and, as the conventional narrative goes, classical political economy was born.[9] Smith was writing before what we call the Industrial Revolution got under way, but he championed, in elegant prose, "the obvious and simple system of natural liberty," which, by ensuring the pursuit of individual freedom, would bring about sustained and productive growth.[10] The subject of economics was, in almost every account of its genesis and development, all about economic *growth*.[11] Moreover, even though the marginal revolution of the 1870s (the basis of neoclassical economic theory) shifted the analytical focus away from macroeconomic growth and onto utility maximization and economic efficiency, few economists would question either the centrality or the desirability of economic growth. On this point, Karl Marx remains very much a classical economist; whatever he may have thought about the future of industrial capitalism, he marveled at its revolutionary potential and certainly preferred it to feudalism, or to whatever else preceded the modern industrial revolution, and Marxists have followed the master's example.[12] It is not surprising, then, that the intellectual struggle between capitalism and communism during the Cold War was over which system could better achieve economic growth and, to a lesser extent, enact egalitarian distribution. At least on the question of growth, it was clear by the late twentieth century which side had triumphed.

Contemporary economics is a vast and sprawling academic discipline with manifold influences and consequences for formulating economic policy and shaping social thought. Its intellectual imperialist tendency has reached far and wide. To take but a small example, the law-and-economics movement has sought to bring the theories and tools of neoclassical economic theory to bear on legal cases and decisions. It is true that there are critics of applying economics to law or marriage, and there are those who criticize economics itself, from its fetish for simplistic models to its insouciant disregard for noneconomic factors and forces.[13] But the principal point I have in mind is that even though economics claims to be a science and therefore strives to be value-neutral, there is constant slippage between the study of growth or economizing, on the one hand, and advocacy of development and utility maximization, on the other. Take, for instance, the words of a textbook from 2009: "Perhaps the most compelling reason [to study economic growth] is that economic growth is what mainly determines the material well-being of billions of people."[14] The notion that growth is the major determinant of billions of people's material well-being is far from certain, but it would seem even more perverse to question why we would not be concerned about the material welfare of our fellow human beings. Another text, this one from 2005, assumes that "practically nobody opposes economic growth per se" and goes on to assert that "economic growth bears social and political consequences that are morally beneficial as well."[15] In short, contemporary economists, not to mention almost all contemporary social scientists and policymakers, cannot resist the primacy and desirability of economic growth.[16]

Later I inquire into the nature of material well-being. For now, let me outline my reservations about the very idea of economic growth. The fundamental reason for us to question the primacy of economic growth is our finitude. Indeed, our blinkered vision has exaggerated not only the triumphs of growth, development, and progress in our recent history but also the future sustainability of these achievements. To put this idea another way, there are potent limits to growth, whether we mean growth's conceptual, environmental, technological, historical, and sociocultural limits or its more oblique, but perhaps even more important, moral-psychological limits.

Conceptual Limitations

We talk incessantly about economic growth, and in so doing, we assume that we know what we're talking about. But when it comes to defining or critiquing the concept of economic growth, many commentators rely on the phenomenology of perception—and in this, they are not unlike US Supreme Court justice Potter Stewart, who had trouble defining pornography but knew it when he saw it.[17] After all, to someone who visited Tokyo in 1949 and returned there in 1989—or, for that matter, visited Beijing in 1989 and again in 2019—economic growth seems as clear as night and day; it is everywhere and in everything from gleaming skyscrapers and traffic congestion to well-appointed apartments and luxurious shops.

But there's more. Gross domestic product (GDP), a metric that almost everyone uses to gauge a nation's economic growth, may appear to reveal over a relatively brief period—say, seven years—a nearly twofold increase in the nation's economic growth for that seven-year period, as calculated on the basis of an annual increase of 10 percent in GDP for each of those seven years.[18] Thus the concreteness of a number, however stratospheric that number may be, renders the concept of economic growth tangible, objective, and cogent. And who can resist the power that seems to inhere in something as simple and clear as a concrete number? Who can keep from using this number? It's difficult to argue with a number that has the imprimatur of a national government and its experts, a number that in turn is based on a metric used in nearly every country in the world.[19]

But what, exactly, is being measured? Here, the key is *commodification* or *commercialization*, since much useful work does not count as a contribution to GDP. For example, if a woman grows and consumes her own vegetables, she isn't contributing to GDP (or to economic growth), but if she grows them for sale, she does make a contribution. Or consider housework and care work, often unpaid and performed disproportionately by women in contemporary Japan. If Japanese women were to drop or reduce their performance of the critical tasks of household reproduction in favor of paid work, would that necessarily be a positive development?[20] As another example, commuting by automobile adds to GDP if commuting is understood in terms of the manufacture and use of cars, the construction of roads, the creation and maintenance of traffic surveillance systems, and myriad related expenditures, but it is unclear why the *act* of commuting—which entails spending unproductive time in traffic, suffering higher cortisol levels, burning fossil fuels, and inevitably contributing to air pollution—should be considered a net benefit to the economy or to society.[21] And do intermediary products such as home insurance or defensive outlays for private security cameras make a substantive contribution to human welfare? Such products may contribute to individual feelings of safety, of course, but is a surveillance society desirable? Then again, we may choose to live in a safe neighborhood where extensive systems for home security are not even needed, but what conforms to our individual preferences and well-being may not be good for GDP and economic growth.

Needless to say, many economists and policymakers are aware of the manifold limitations of employing GDP as a measure of a nation's economic growth. Hence, there are numerous alternative indices, including the Human Development Index, the Better Life Index, gross national happiness, and net national product.[22] Yet it would be extremely difficult to find an economist or a politician—or anyone else, for that matter—who is skeptical about the intrinsic value of economic growth itself.[23]

The fundamental problem with GDP or any other measure is not its flaws of measurement or aggregation. Science is all about corrigibility and progress. Rather, all the talk of GDP masks a more elementary question about the nature and desirability of economic growth in particular and about the economy in general. Having created the fetish of GDP, we not only look to it as a gauge of our economic (and therefore social) health but also strive to protect and nurture our manufactured fetish. The measurement and growth of GDP, which were once universally recognized as means, have somehow become unquestioned ends in themselves. The paradox is that these ends are almost never justified except as means to various other desirable ends, including economic growth. According to the conventional wisdom, economic growth is coveted because it supposedly decreases, perhaps even eradicates, poverty and inequality, as by eliminating insecurity with respect to food and housing. Yet we know that this is often not what happens, certainly not in our post–Cold War period of globalization. The contemporary United States, for example, suffers from widening gaps in equality and well-being, and Japan is no different.[24] Moreover, apart from the problems of inequality and poverty, repeated survey results are robust in confirming the Easterlin Paradox (that is, the fact that people's subjective sense of well-being does not increase beyond a certain level of economic growth).[25] As a case in point, per capita GDP in Japan increased fivefold between 1958 and 1987, but there was no uptick in Japanese people's mean subjective sense of happiness.[26] In a comic strip by Shiriagari Kotobuki that depicts this state of affairs, an experienced artisan spends three days meticulously preparing ramen and sells it for a mere 750 yen per bowl (the equivalent of about seven US dollars at the time of this writing).[27] His customers spend precious time waiting in line to taste this delicacy, and one of them says, "We must really like things with low productivity."[28] Indeed, if higher productivity and greater GDP are so important, wouldn't it be better to eat mass-marketed, industrially produced fare from fast food joints? In any case, it is easy enough to acknowledge the gap between theory and reality; more difficult is to jettison a theory that has assumed the form of an ostensibly irrefutable concept manifesting as a concrete figure.

But economic growth, assumed as the master solution to all manner of economic, political, sociological, and psychological problems, has not been dethroned by all the brouhaha over GDP as an inadequate measure, or by the accumulating evidence that economic growth not only doesn't eradicate but may actually exacerbate poverty and inequality. One would have to be mad to deny, *tout court*, the desirability of growth, but it seems equally perverse simply to embrace economic growth wherever and whenever we happen to measure it.

Environmental Limitations

Global climate change, with global warming at its center, is an indisputable fact, and it has ushered in a new geological epoch called the Anthropocene.[29] Whatever the impact of cyclical changes in temperature may be, it would be impossible to refute the impact of industrialization on the global constitution. Environmental pollution has worsened the condition of air, water, and land in general; the oceans and the Earth itself are clogged with human-generated waste. Human beings have come to lord it over our environment and, in so doing, to bring about the rapid

extinction of species, accelerate the disappearance of the wilderness, cause defor-
estation and desertification, acidify the oceans, and draw perilously close to
destroying our ability to live on this planet. Where our continuing ecological crisis
is concerned, positive reports are few and far between. And, contrary to a common anthropocentric misunderstanding—which, paradoxically, has us worrying
about the Earth and enjoins us to be kind to it—we should be worried about *ourselves*, about our place on this planet. The Earth will survive us, but we may not
survive at all, at least not in any way in which we would like to live. Environmental
scientists bring their own emphases and nuances to the discussion, but few of
them would disagree that we are on the road to catastrophe.

The looming ecological crisis has generated a critical discourse against the
almost uniformly positive assessment of economic growth.[30] In the early 1960s,
Rachel Carson's *Silent Spring*, drawing on a robust lineage of conservation writings, gave rise in the United States to a movement to save human health and the
natural environment.[31] In Japan, as mentioned in chapter 1, Ishimure Michiko's
incandescent *Kugai jōdo* (The sea of suffering, the land of purity) appeared in three
volumes originally published between 1969 and 1974, but the history of Japanese
environmental protectionism dates at least from the late nineteenth century, with
Tanaka Shōzō's conservationist activism around the Ashio copper mine and the
mine's deleterious environmental impact.[32] Indeed, the history of environmental-
ism overlaps with the history of industrialization. And yet economic growth
remains sacrosanct among academic economists and social scientists. Even Daniel
J. Fiorino, a writer extremely critical of mainstream economists and their blithe
confidence in the virtues of growth, describes growth's "benefits" as "obvious" in
that growth "delivers a better quality of life, improves education and health care,
allows for social safety nets and retirement systems, funds government service,
enhances political stability, finances new medical technologies and treatments,
and expands the prospects for flourishing in modern societies."[33] With an enemy
like Fiorino, economic growth doesn't need any more friends.

A major cause of human inaction on the climate crisis is the fact that the comfortable classes around the world are shielded from the most devastating consequences of pollution and other environmental ills. In the case of modern Japan,
this robust generalization also holds true for the victims of Ashio, Minamata, and
the 2011 disaster at the nuclear power plant in Fukushima. For the comfortable
classes in a world of sovereign nations, environmental destruction constitutes
externalities that must be endured by others who are downstream or who will
come after us. The brunt of environmental degradation will be borne by polar
bears seeking to cross expanses of solid ice on melting glaciers, and by impoverished lowland residents whose land is sinking from overuse of aquifers while
sea levels rise and torrential rains and hurricanes bear down. When we map intra-
national and international distributions of risk onto national and global inequality

in power and wealth, we find a good, close fit.[34] The frontline victims of environmental destruction are voiceless and invisible, by and large, but even the comfortable and the privileged are capable of observing the victims' plight, and of becoming enlightened about the perils ahead. What will later generations make of our wanton ways? More economic growth can only exacerbate an already dire situation—which is to say, in short, that there are environmental limits to economic growth.

Very few systematic observers deny the potential problem. Rather, many believe, confidently and conveniently, that the tipping point of ecological catastrophe is still decades away. More optimistic, and probably more numerous, are those who believe that human ingenuity and technology will rescue us. But the weight of those who have passionately researched the issues tilts the odds decisively toward a relatively imminent catastrophe, and it may be that the really interesting question is why we have ignored all the warning signs. Conventional wisdom, or public opinion, is a singularly powerful force in the human world. We are familiar with beliefs that have cast a spell over hundreds and thousands and even millions or billions of ordinary people, whether these beliefs manifest as short-lived cults or as religions lasting many centuries. But what should we call the belief in economic growth, a belief that has had so many of the best-informed people in its thrall for the past century or two? Whatever we call this belief, it remains the bedrock of the modern, Western-influenced world.

Technological Limitations

Technology may seem to offer a potential master solution. Whereas nineteenth-century political economy saw the heyday of the prophets of stagnation (population, rather than pollution, was then the limiting variable), today's techno-optimists and techno-utopians claim that advances in science and engineering have facilitated massive productivity growth and better living conditions around the world. Indeed, faith in technology, buttressed by science as a form of salvation, is widespread in the modern world.[35] And who would wish to turn the clock back a century, to what was prime time in Europe for war, famine, pestilence, and death?[36] We may hope that scientific achievement and technological innovation will ameliorate and possibly solve our current environmental crisis. For example, we may believe that improved recycling will blunt the impact of expanding waste—though it remains unclear that recycling, as currently practiced in the Global North, even comes close to alleviating, much less solving, the problem.[37] Moreover, the periodic celebration of revolutionary breakthroughs, such as plastic-consuming bacteria, ignores the fact that many environmental disasters have arisen from overconfident scientific panaceas like plastic—not to mention DDT, Thalidomide, and nuclear energy, which has left us with millions of tons of radioactive waste. The scientific mastery of nature is forever incomplete, and nature's revenge, whether in the form of remnant pollutants or resistant microbes, remains a resilient countervailing force.[38]

As giddy as the techno-utopians of Silicon Valley and elsewhere may be about the imminent arrival of the Singularity or about never-ending progress, the realities of the twenty-first century belie the wild exuberance of the post–World War II decades. Atomic weapons, space rockets, and laser beams fed the imaginations of young and old alike, encouraging speculation about the imminent arrival of intergalactic travel, teleportation, intelligent high-functioning robots, and immortality. Likewise, science fiction and manga depicted colonies on Mars by the twenty-first century, along with the communication problems that would be generated by travel at almost the speed of light. But almost none of the expected breakthroughs have come to pass, from the Jetsons' flying car to Tetsuwan Atomu (Astro Boy). And yet who can confidently deny that life-altering disruptions aren't just around the corner? All the same, they seem unlikely, less because of the apparent slow-down in scientific revolutions and technological innovations than because of systematic underinvestment in basic research, along with a focus on profit-generating advances for the comfortable classes.[39]

There is another sense in which the contemporary world may be facing technological limits. The somber reality is that all our innovations in computing, information technology, and the internet have only slowly enhanced aggregate productivity, and therefore growth.[40] Nineteenth-century inventions or reinventions, from electrification and urban sewerage to railways and chemical fertilization of crops, may seem primitive from the vantage point of the twenty-first century, but they altered the industrializing world, and they enhanced productivity in ways that the digital or genomic revolution, however sophisticated, has not done and probably will not do.[41] To state the matter polemically, postwar technological inventions (think of the washing machine or the refrigerator) altered domestic lifestyles and possibilities for work, but later inventions like smartphones and genetic therapy are mere improvements, with notable side effects. Contemporary innovators and inventors may earn billions, but that says nothing to contradict the simple economics of productivity stasis in today's Global North.

There is, then, a possibility that economic growth, as an economic reality, has ceased because of this stasis in productivity growth. I have not considered the economic constraints on growth, a theme especially popular among Marxists, who argue about whether overproduction or underconsumption will bring about a crisis and then an end to the capitalist world-system. But there is more than a glimmer of evidence that not just productivity growth but also the rate of profit may be slowing and rapidly approaching zero.[42] At least in the Global North, there are some indicators that retain the spirit of the economist Simon Kuznets's desire to measure positive goods (as opposed to commercial products and activities that inflict ills), and these indicators reveal a stationary state since the late 1960s and early 1970s.[43]

Technological advances are also disruptive. Although disruption is seen as a positive attribute in vast stretches of the contemporary world, it has manifold negative consequences and connotations. The flip side of technological progress is the proliferation of risk. Nuclear power, for example, was heralded as a massive advance, and it promised a source of safe, low-cost energy with almost no environmental impact. As we know, however, when we account for the expense of storing nuclear waste and dealing with accidents, we see that the total actual costs of nuclear power have been extremely high.[44]

Thus an advanced technological society is a high-risk society. And because the risk is distributed and experienced unevenly, technological progress is often disruptive in a second sense: it exacerbates inequality in terms of the costs borne by the less privileged and the benefits reaped by the fortunate. For example, our innovations in information technology have not increased productivity; instead, they have contributed to greater inequality, both intranationally and internationally.[45]

Technological progress also alters, even destroys, everyday life. Tokyo's elevated expressways are beautiful and majestic in their own right, but one section of them overhangs and occludes Nihonbashi, the famed terminus of the Tokugawa-era artery Tōkaidō. What we gain in convenience, we lose in glorious architecture and in the world of pedestrians and slower-moving vehicles; we accept aesthetic blight and white noise as the cost of a faster commute, and what we have instead of leisurely strolls are traffic congestion and automobile exhaust. Our newly convenient world is different but not necessarily better. With public health officials worried about the negative consequences of a sedentary society, not to mention the dangers of obesity, how can we insist that a car-based civilization is necessarily superior?

The prophets of growth and the preachers of technology have discarded God in favor of the Enlightenment. But precisely as they proclaim the virtues of secularization, they profess one myth after another and counsel a religion of growth and technology. And yet technological disruption is not always and already positive in any uniform sense. It often makes for unfortunate trade-offs as well as unpleasant, unintended consequences. As such, and as in the case of economic growth, only a fundamentalist faith in progress makes it possible to see technological disruption in a uniformly positive light.

Historical Limitations

The modern Western notion of history remains stubbornly linear and progressive—onward and upward, as the saying goes. Needless to say, some historians question the reigning prism of growth and progress, and at other times and in other places there was a distinct reckoning of time's passage, with time viewed as cyclical or stagnating or even as part of the eternal now. Nevertheless, to espouse the dominant mythistory of the present is to believe, more or less uncritically, that things have been gradually improving over the past few millennia, or at least the past few centuries.[46] Economists in particular are happy to deluge the skeptics with tables and figures, such as those depicting GDP growth, to underscore their theoretical commitment to the sacrosanct idea of growth. Much the same can be said of scientific and techno-logical utopians.

But was the past so terrible? Those attached to the received narrative would adduce a barrage of numbers, such as those that represent lower GDP and lower life expectancy, to prove the obvious and irrefutable reality of backwardness. It is indeed indisputable that improvements in sanitation and nutrition have length-ened modal life expectancy in the rich countries of the world. Yet it is far from clear that the story is as simple and clear-cut as the progressive narrative would suggest. In so-called primitive societies, hunter-gatherers enjoyed a much more leisurely life, with limited working hours and certainly no stress related to com-muting; as Marshall Sahlins has memorably put it, theirs was the original affluent society.[47] Affluence, after all, is not just a matter of abundance. Consumption enhances GDP but not necessarily the quality of life. Students of preindustrial life have suggested time and time again that the Neolithic Revolution—that is, the introduction and dissemination of settled agrarian life—may not have been the unquestioned advance that many believe it was. After we transitioned to settled agriculture, with its concomitant centralized polity, constant warfare, and exploi-tation and inequality, it took a long time for us to regain the quality of life that our primitive forebears had enjoyed.[48]

Beyond the unsolvable calculus of sacrifice—conquest and imperialism, war and enslavement, expropriation and exploitation—lies an even more disturbing conjecture about the fictive character of growth and progress. We usually take it for granted that Meiji Japan was more prosperous than Tokugawa Japan, and that the 1930s in Japan were better than the 1830s, because GDP gives distorted figures for intercountry and cross-historical comparisons; as noted earlier, noncommer-cialized products and activities are not included or counted. Yet this conclusion is not as incontrovertible as it may seem. Tokugawa Japan enjoyed nearly three cen-turies of peace, and it developed a relatively eco-friendly and reasonably prosper-ous society. Its food, though impoverished by the standards of the carnivorous Western diet, was healthy and tasty, and its food culture included the development of such distinctive dishes as sushi and tempura.[49] In addition, ordinary housing and everyday clothing, however they may have diverged from the prevailing West-ern norms, had an aesthetic and functional quality that suited them to the climate of Japan, with its unbearable heat and humidity in the summer, not to the rela-tively cool Europe of the recent past.[50]

But more crucial than these empirical considerations and comparisons is the underlying ideology of progress. The fundamental flaw of the progressive narrative resides in its ever-receding endpoint. When is enough enough? John Maynard

Keynes wrote in 1930, "For the first time since his creation man will be faced with his real, his permanent problem—how to use his freedom from pressing economic cares, how to occupy the leisure, which science and compound interest will have won for him, to live wisely and agreeably and well."[51] He thought this point would be reached a century from 1930, but it seems unlikely that the year 2030 will mark the end of human progress, or at any rate the end of human desire for material plenty. Plenitude, after all, is just around the corner, a bit beyond the horizon; it represents a permutation of one of Zeno's paradoxes, the dichotomy paradox. Many people in the rich countries may indeed perceive the end of the rainbow, the point when enough becomes enough, but they can never reach it. The quest is inflected by the notion of *more*, and we act like spoiled children, personifying desire unbound. We remain unaware of the limits, as well as of the burdens placed on parents and on the world, that have enabled the fulfillment of desire. Progressive history, like desire, is all about more and more, the ever-receding endpoint that is always beyond our grasp.

Sociocultural Limitations

In the economic history of the past millennium, preindustrial growth was minimal. Unusual upward spikes were usually predicated on plunder, whether it occurred through superexploitation of the masses or through the conquest of people elsewhere. The post-Columbian exchange encompassed multiple distinct spheres of life—flora and fauna, diseases and beliefs—but a major axis was acutely asymmetrical, representing the theft of natural resources and the enslavement of native peoples. Even at the high tide of the Industrial Revolution, the pervasive character of economic exploitation was incontrovertible in the classic Marxist sense of seizing time, money, and vitality from the masses of people escaping rural desuetude or urban poverty. In contrast, as we canvass the world today, we find no new landmasses to conquer, nor is there even much left of the proverbial reserve army of would-be proletarians. Residents of the Global North are reluctant to engage in dirty, difficult, dangerous tasks or to suffer high levels of pollutants or contaminants. The movement of human populations does bring trickles of people from desperate straits to the environs of richer neighbors; but, given automation and mechanization, the erstwhile exploiters are no longer so keen to exploit labor power. In any case, it's hard to imagine that the current system of production and investment will discover new modes of massive economic expansion by way of human expropriation and exploitation.

Rapid economic growth almost always generates a countervailing force. Individual and social tolerance for rapid, massive transformation—the destruction or renovation of a neighborhood, the closing or opening of factories or offices, the end of a particular way of life—is often low and limited. As George Eliot put it, "There is no general doctrine which is not capable of eating out our morality if unchecked by the deep-seated habit of direct fellow-feeling with individual fellow men."[52] The doctrines of capital and profit did indeed tear into the viscera of pre- or noncapitalist men, women, and children, and these doctrines were often deaf to the cries and whispers of those human beings. People, unlike capital or commodities, tend to resist rough handling, and at times, they seek, individually or collectively, to thwart heteronomous forces. Although this theoretical rendering may seem simplistic—a dialectic, as it were, of commodification and countercommodification—there is no question that growth tends to generate instability and exacerbate inequality. If economic growth were actually such a panacea, why did the working classes of England so bitterly resist the capitalists in the nineteenth century, a time of rapid growth, and why did the workers and students of Japan struggle against corporations and the government in the 1960s, precisely when rapid growth was at its high point? If classical industrialization, whether capitalist or state socialist, really does thrive on creative (or, at times, uncreative) destruction, skeptical citizens of the Global North have developed immunity and resistance to disruptive capital and technology. From the standpoint of growth maximization, it would be far more efficient to eliminate old-age pensions and other social welfare benefits and to invest instead in innovative machinery, but such a measure, its ethical aspects notwithstanding, would meet with great social resistance. In short, there is a social or political limit to unencumbered growth.

The individualist calculus of felicity comes face to face with the recalcitrant reality of other people. As long as others have their own wills and wants, there is no good reason to suppose that others will act to ensure one's own utility maximization. Brute reality itself suggests the infeasibility of such an approach, apart from the fact that rationalist deliberation cannot reverse what is admittedly the primacy of individual utility or egoistic hedonism over collective utility or the universal good.[53] Norms and laws may impinge on one's nonnormative or extralegal desires, whether pederasty or polygamy, murder or mayhem. Envy of greener grass is difficult to extinguish, and the antisocial impulse of extreme individual desire needs regulation, no matter how conducive to growth such desire may be. In an unregulated state, our desires would make us susceptible to, in the words of Thomas Hobbes, "continual fear and danger of violent death"; we would be pawns in an untrusting social intercourse leading inexorably to a life that would be "solitary, poor, nasty, brutish, and short."[54] We cannot survive without interpersonal trust, or without the norms and regulations that buttress it.

Another aspect of the social limits to growth has to do with the restricted availability of many goods.[55] How many houses can be built on a mountaintop with a striking vista or on a beachfront where soothing waves roll in? Nowadays there are even traffic jams at the top of the world as professional mountaineers and wealthy hobbyists scramble to summit Mount Everest. And in contemporary Tokyo there is a mad rush to erect *tawaman* (tower mansions, or skyscrapers), which promise their tenants fabulous views. But the contiguous jungle of other buildings will block the views of tenants on the lower floors; not only that, but even tenants on the higher floors will find their formerly fabulous vistas blocked by new high-rises. In any case, there cannot be more than a few penthouse apartments, and this is one reason why the demand for skyscrapers may continue to accelerate.

Positional, or oligarchic, goods are inherently limited; scarcity cannot be overcome. In addition, even when particular goods are much more widely distributed, access to more such goods or to better versions of them, does not necessarily imply satisfaction, because one's well-being may depend on what *others* have. In the nineteenth century, for example, a university degree was rare and prized, but university degrees in the twenty-first century are increasingly common and therefore less prized and prestigious except for those earned at marquee colleges and universities.[56] If everything and everyone could be something and someone, then everything and everyone would be nothing and no one. In other words, scarcity—or, more accurately, envy—cannot be overcome by mass production and mass consumption.

Furthermore, as discussed earlier in connection with the historical limitations to growth, scarcity is not a quasi-natural constant. The idea of generalized scarcity emerged in the modern West at times when, and in places where, the experience of specific, fluctuating wants and desires was transmuted into what came to be seen as a fundamental human condition.[57] The industrial and commercial revolution and its attendant science introduced economizing as a perennial problem of human beings, who were understood to be trapped in potentially infinite wants and desires, and we learned a particular way of thinking—an economic habit of thought. Particular wants and specific scarcities are simply a part of life; in modernity, however, infinite desire and universal economizing have become recognized *conditions*. Our wants, desires, and needs (as institutionalist economists repeatedly instruct us) can be invoked and fanned by social emulation or seductive advertisements. And even though the arrival of affluence is announced from time to time, these proclamations have done little to cool the fervor for consumption. Again, the social condition of scarcity cannot be overcome by more production or consumption.

There are also cultural limits to growth. As Edmund Burke exemplified in his criticism of the French Revolution, conservatives emerged as a political force against the romance of total revolution, which would have severed the ligaments of received society and culture. Similarly, whereas the revolutionary Karl Marx almost rapturously sang the praises of the new industrial capitalism, Thomas Carlyle railed against capitalist industrialization for its destruction of the social and cultural fabric of traditional England. Economic growth, then, whether capitalist or socialist, brings about the destruction of a received way of life. And even though such destruction may be creative and progressive, it is also true that the past two centuries of economic growth and Western expansion have eliminated distinct ways of life all over the world. The ensuing cultural loss, the unlinking of present from past, can be justified only if the alleged benefits of growth can be said to have produced something superior to what such growth has superseded. As we have seen, though, the claim that everything about the past was worse than the present is highly dubious. Call this view cultural conservationism, but there is no reason for us to assume that we the living are epistemically superior to our ancestors. The story of progress is also necessarily a story of loss.

Moral-Psychological Limitations

Morality boasts a long, vast bibliography. Nevertheless, it seems spurious to speak of what is moral in the context of economics. My use of the term "moral" is not particularly about ethical injunctions against overconsumption and its harmful consequences. Consumption as a form of addiction—so-called affluenza—may be counterproductive in that it can lead to unmanageable debt, to overwork taken on to repay the debt and feed the addiction, and to even more consumption. In short, except for the happy few, material pursuits don't bring happiness or contentment.[58] Soulless materialism, it is said, destroys our humanity, and I don't disagree with that diagnosis. Here, though, in speaking of the moral-psychological limits to growth, I am more concerned with cognitive or subjective constraints.

The idea of growth brooks no limits or fixed goals. There is always room for one more in the actual or virtual shopping cart, but satisfaction is fleeting and happiness is momentary; I get tired of or bored with what I have, and I want something else.[59] There will always be another, newer, shinier trinket: "Affluence breeds impatience, and impatience undermines well-being."[60] Hegel described this cycle as spurious (or bad) infinity; in what should be a finite series, we can't help seeking to add one more item. The essentially restless nature of desire means that desire has no apparent means of permanent satisfaction. Until we die, we cannot satisfy our desire without generating still more desire.

Beyond desire, spuriously infinite or not, lies the reality that choice can be fallible and that consumption, over time, may be unsustainable.[61] The psychological distress occasioned by excess spending and crippling debt is not the only harmful effect of overconsumption. The term "addiction" denotes a range of short-term benefits and long-term costs. Few doubt the salutary effects of a glass of good wine, for example, but fewer still wish for alcohol dependency or poisoning. We can never know what the future will bring: how long we can seize the day, live life to the full, burn the candle at both ends, all with impunity. Over time, the short-term benefits of our overconsumption look like mere immaturity, but who can really hope to remain a teenager forever? Even if the spirit remains willing, the flesh becomes not just weak but downright old.

Then there is the corrosive effect of commercialization. Commercial life has been progressively extending its ambit. Different societies and periods exhibit variable levels of tolerance for monetization, but the general trend is toward commercial expansion and intensification. As one example, gift giving in the contemporary United States approximates a cash transaction when it takes the form (as it often does) of the ubiquitous gift card. To be sure, whatever is within the domain of the cash nexus is subject to normative constraints—no one today, at least not in respectable company, openly proclaims the legitimacy of the slave trade or slave auctions. What I stress here is not so much the Kantian critique (that people should be treated as ends, not means) as the reality that basing human interaction or acquisition on market considerations or monetary exchange demeans the very transactions or products in question when people consider those transactions or products to be noncommercial in character. This is the commercialization effect.[62] Vespasian may have believed that *pecunia non olet,* but almost no one (perhaps we should wait for the superman of the future) seems capable of following through on that conviction. There are still many arenas in which monetary exchange corrodes the nature of a transaction. For instance, many people who hanker after romantic love and sexual satisfaction also find the buying and selling of love and sex less alluring and often illegitimate, since the real thing is supposed to be based on mutual attraction, not on factors involved in a market exchange. You can dress the cash nexus up in fur or emoji, but it doesn't come close to, much less replace, a nonmonetary romantic relationship, however illusory (and expensive) that relationship turns out to be. Countercommercial impulses and relations—the giving of gifts, voluntarism, and other nonmonetary modes of exchange—thrive in the most commercial of societies, and these impulses and relations can neither be expunged nor be reduced to material transactions. In other words, when people hold on to noncommercial bases of relationship as being right, genuine, appropriate, or worthy, the taint of money cannot be expunged from such exchanges; its stench lingers long after the commodity has been consumed.

The value of noncommercial interactions, products, and achievements remains robust even in a thoroughly commercialized society—or perhaps *precisely* in an extremely commodified economy. To quote a classic TV ad: "There are some things money can't buy. For everything else, there's MasterCard"; pricelessness is the ultimate desideratum.[63] It is possible to buy sexual interactions and academic degrees, but most people remain convinced not only that these things should not be bought but also that they cannot be bought; that is, the effort of obtaining them is what generates their value. There is, then, the *effort paradox*; that is, we want to minimize effort, but we also value the outcomes of effort. To put this idea more concretely, it is possible to be flown to the summit of Mount Everest, and not too long in the future it may be possible to have a foreign language downloaded into one's brain (with pathways to the associated organs of speech), but most would regard these outcomes as illegitimate. Likewise, advances in robotics and artificial intelligence may one day produce a violinist superior to Jascha Heifetz or David Oistrakh, or a mathematician more original than Leonhard Euler or Kurt Gödel, but popular morality (at least as of the early twenty-first century) would find these achievements problematic at best and more likely reprehensible. Mastery of a musical instrument or completion of a marathon is valuable and meaningful precisely because one has expended blood, sweat, and tears. And even though this conviction may represent nothing but our last stand against AI—a romantic, humanist bathos—we find it difficult if not impossible to treasure competence and achievements that are purchased or bestowed. We retain a lingering suspicion of beauty created through plastic surgery, though we forgive people who improve their looks through the skillful application of cosmetics. That is to say, the artisanal ethos survives in our valuing of outcomes that cannot be bought, outcomes that, however imperfect, are brought about through effort. (I have much more to say about the artisanal ethos in chapter 6.) And even though it's true that achievement can be thrust upon someone, people often reframe it within a narrative of striving. This moral-psychological outlook may be anthropocentric, but we cannot even entertain the notion of what it would be to live in a society of complete commercialization, or in a society that had eliminated human effort and achievement altogether. One day, we may overcome our revulsion to the thought that we would be happier and more satisfied as a wired-up brain in a jar. For the time being, however, our revulsion represents a moral intuition that remains almost universal.

Similarly, most people remain allergic to the sort of person who (to paraphrase Oscar Wilde's quip) knows the price of everything and the value of nothing. The pursuit of money and wealth gives off a foul odor, and (pace Vespasian) it's not always possible or practical to hold one's nose. Even in a society where billionaires are celebrated and ordinary people shop till they drop, the unvarnished paean to capitalism, commercialism, and consumerism is rare. We cannot keep from suspecting that the acquisition and retention of wealth have a corrosive impact. Literature and popular culture and folk wisdom, from Ebenezer Scrooge to King Midas to the Wolf of Wall Street, attest to the vanity of mammonism. We are almost instinctively repelled by people who physically or figuratively brandish wads of cash in their quest to purchase favors and things.

A powerful moral limit to growth is our knowledge that more money and more things are not a master solution. They cannot solve our existential problems—far from it. Meaning and significance, like social relations and interactions that bring pleasure, satisfaction, and contentment, lie ineluctably beyond the sphere of the pecuniary and the material.

The essentially social character of our existence, like the simultaneous limit of economic or commercial thinking and transactions, is shown in our reluctance to flaunt our money or our wealth. We need to convert it into currencies that mask its origin. Just as might strives to turn into right, and power to turn into legitimacy, money seeks at every turn to convert itself into nonmonetary virtues—elegance or intelligence, credentials or titles, beauty or refinement. To pursue selfish gains and fulfill personal desires may feel liberating, but one of the paradoxes of egotism is that the individual finds at once more fulfillment and more freedom in social intercourse.[64] And social relations are corroded if they are based solely on instrumental interactions, such as monetary transactions.

We come now to human finitude. Almost everyone of a certain age experiences time, whatever it is, as an acutely scarce good. We cannot be in two places at once, and we all die; and so we must allocate our time, and we must experience its scarcity even if we happen to be as rich as Croesus. The death's-head or memento mori inevitably suggests that we want to live longer for a reason, and that we should interrogate that reason. But no one, at least to my knowledge, has ever proposed that earning more money or experiencing more economic growth is the foundational reason for wanting to live longer. As mentioned earlier, rich people almost always convert capital into cultural capital, such as singular works of art or rare wines. Similarly, most rich societies find nonmonetary justifications for expending accumulated wealth. Perhaps the character who comes closest to justifying accumulation for accumulation's sake is Noah Cross, the megamillionaire played by John Huston in Roman Polanski's 1974 film *Chinatown*. Asked by Jake Gittes, a private eye played by Jack Nicholson, why he wants even more money ("What could you buy that you can't already afford?"), Cross grunts, "The future, Mr. Gittes! The future!" The viewer cannot avoid judging the millionaire's desire as pathetic and immoral, cannot avoid perceiving the fundamental futility of playing down the present for the sake of impossible desires.

And yet, as we have seen, economic growth remains the master solution to almost every economic, political, social, or psychological problem. More growth is said to alleviate, if not entirely eliminate, an array of difficulties. And, as if we were forever in a state of infancy, we seem to believe that the most rational response to our needs and wants, our shortcomings and quagmires, is to cry, "More!" But we cannot abandon the notion of economic growth, though we are aware of the many problems associated with it. Even calls for sustainable development are articulated in terms of "socially inclusive and environmentally sustainable economic growth."[65] In short, the goal remains growth. But what precisely is the question to which economic growth is the answer? This question is not often discussed in explicit terms, but it usually has to do with the issue of how we should live, individually and collectively. Thus the terminus of millennia of human thinking is the presentation of a solution that has been refuted from time immemorial. We have always already known that economic growth—along with its permutations, such as more money and more possessions—cannot be an entirely satisfactory solution to our problems. Nevertheless, that knowledge doesn't stop politicians, economists, and many influential others from insisting on the primacy on growth.

THE IDEA OF THE SUSTAINABLE SOCIETY
AND ITS MODUS VIVENDI

What is a world without economic growth? The idea of growth has been hegemonic in the modern era, but it has also met with numerous criticisms and countervailing thoughts. Indeed, if we reach further back into history or look at other, non-Western traditions of thought, we see that the notion of an upward trajectory is actually deviant. Much more common are schemas positing that we are in a state of decline, from Hesiod's Age of Gold to the Age of Bronze and baser states, or that we exist in endless cycles, whether these occur in the course of an individual life (birth, growth, decline, and death) or as part of diurnal and seasonal changes. Once upon a time, the vision of unending progress promulgated by Condorcet and others was considered lunatic; now it is dominant. Now we think we are evolving and improving, and to question the imperative of economic growth is to all but deny the reality of personal development, to say that we should remain infants all our lives.

But because growth is not a constant reality, modern thinkers have also posited a variety of other possibilities, including stasis and stagnation.[66] The most important articulation has been that of the stationary state. David Ricardo, for example, argued that the rate of profit would decline and reach the stationary state of zero. His prediction has not come to pass, even though murmurs of a declining and disappearing rate of profit have been widely discussed in the twenty-first century. But Ricardo, along with almost every other analyst of stasis, regarded this development as undesirable, if unavoidable.

The major exception to this trend was the nineteenth-century polymath John Stuart Mill. Much maligned by Marx (and Marxists) for his dogged commitment to radical utilitarianism—pursuit of the greatest happiness for the greatest number, and the defense of individual liberty—Mill welcomed the prospect of a near future in which material growth would cease. Because the "struggle for war" preceded the "struggle for riches" in human (or at least Western) history, Mill argued that both may have been necessary stages but neither was any longer desirable: "I confess I am not charmed with the ideal of life held out by those who think that the normal state of human beings is that of struggling to get on; that the trampling, crushing, elbowing, and treading on each other's heels, which form the existing type of social life, are the most desirable lot of human kind, or anything but the disagreeable symptoms of one of the phases of industrial progress."[67] For Mill, the end of economic growth did not spell the absence of progress altogether: "It is scarcely necessary to remark that a stationary condition of capital and population implies no stationary state of human improvement. There would be as much scope as ever for all kinds of mental culture, and moral and social progress; as much room for improving the Art of Living, and much more likelihood of its being improved, when minds ceased to be engrossed by the art of getting on."[68] Mill did not delineate in any detail the concrete contours of the coming stationary state. These points hark back to his commitment, however moderated by the principle of liberty and the fear of tyranny, to the greatest happiness for the greatest number: "But the best state for human nature is that in which, while no one is poor, no one desires to be richer, nor has any reason to fear being thrust back by the efforts of others to push themselves forward."[69] Having rejected the simple version of utilitarianism, Mill came to appreciate the rich and complex character of the individual: "Human nature is not a machine but a tree, which requires to grow and develop itself in all sides, according to the tendency of the inward forces which make it a living thing."[70] In other words, a calculus of happiness must be supplemented by the pursuit of meaning and significance and the quest for fulfillment and efflorescence.

It would be easy, of course, to mock Mill's argument; the clarity of hindsight reveals that the 1840s hardly represented the peak of human productivity or economic enrichment. As also happened in connection with Keynes's vision of material abundance, sketched out nearly a century after Mill, there has been more growth, and it may continue until precisely the moment when the Earth becomes uninhabitable by human beings. Mill was almost surely thinking of absolute poverty—hunger and homelessness—but relative poverty is a permanent feature of social life. Unless we were to legislate conditions of absolute equality, some would always feel deprived in comparison to others. And even if all material needs could be met with a strictly even distribution of all goods and services, there would still be spheres in which some would feel inferior to and envious of others. Which is to say, we would need to create a totalitarian state, one in which more able, more beautiful, more intelligent, or stronger people would be "thrust back" by those who resented their advantages and excellence.[71]

Where any totalizing solution is concerned, the failures and flaws of past state-socialist societies should give pause. These societies' claims to superiority were based on their competition with capitalist economies on the latter's favored ground—the achievement of economic growth. The state-socialist societies' project of advancing human welfare, in the form of widely distributed medical care or public schooling, was later superseded by the much more powerful idea of growth and by faith in technology; that is, advances in human welfare became the end that justified the means.[72] Centralized economic planning, especially as it was undertaken without reliable statistics or the benefits of modern computing, lurched from one exercise in guesswork and disaster to another. Even more troubling was the fact that contemporary socialist states everywhere sought to engineer the human soul into one or another variant of *Homo Sovieticus,* thus producing societies of grim and grudging obedience; spirits purportedly liberated by socialist policies were tamed, then tortured, and the upshot was a spate of human-rights disasters.[73] Communist propaganda and centralized control from above, as if imposed by a government made up of authoritarian parents, rendered people cynical, competitive, selfish, and even materialist. The belief that the ends justify the means is self-subverting, since the means always supersede the ends. As the old Soviet joke had it, capitalism is a system of exploitation of men by men; in communism, it's the other way around.[74]

Nevertheless, the implausibility of an instant utopia—the romance of total revolution—does not prove the impossibility of any and every scheme for human improvement. After all, many countries after World War II employed democratic, nonforcible means of disseminating the benefits of public health, mass schooling, and social welfare, even though such efforts may have been facilitated by rapid economic recovery and growth. And human history is not exclusively a tale of suffering and oppression, despite all the rogues and tyrants. Even the much-maligned social sciences offer insights into which policies or arrangements are to be avoided, and libraries are overflowing with schemes for individual and collective empowerment and flourishing. The manifold and manifest failures of state socialism should neither suppress people's longing for a better world nor extirpate all manner of utopian thinking, or of hope for possible futures. The fact is that laissez-faire capitalism, or unfettered globalization, is not without its own utopian impulse and its own ideological backbone, both of which have brought about innovation, certainly, but also devastation. In Japan and elsewhere, inequality (however imperfectly we understand and measure it) and its evil accompaniments—relative and absolute poverty, including hunger and homelessness—are on the rise. In the circumstances, it would be churlish at the very least to expatiate on principles and theories. It does not take deep philosophical thought or even a big heart to worry about the not so invisible wretchedness all around us.

If economic growth is not the master solution to and cure-all for our social problems, and if growth may not even be all that desirable, then what other options do we have? We can simply offer information and imagination, insights and possibilities, about our own lives and about others' ways of living. Wallace Stevens once described the function of the poet as "not lead[ing] people out of the confusion in which they find themselves" or "comfort[ing] them" but rather making "his imagination theirs" so that "he fulfills himself only as he sees his imagination become the light in the mind of others. His role, in short, is to help people to live their lives."[75] And John Stuart Mill, as we have seen, articulated a vision for widespread satisfaction as the outcome of a stationary state. In keeping with Stevens and Mill, but in a different context, the workable slices of contemporary Japanese life—the viability and desirability of the artisanal ethos, and the valorization of ordinary life—offer another source of light. It is not that ordinary people of the Edo period had ceased to search for escapes and alternatives, even utopias; such a renunciation is not the reason why we turn to those people now. Rather, it is precisely in their concrete legacy—interrupted, mediated, and transformed though it may be—that we can find and instantiate the potential for a sustainable society.

The Regime as a Concept

The date of 11 March 2011 is a fateful one in modern Japanese history. Remembered as 3/11, it was the day the Tōhoku earthquake and tsunami shattered buildings and swept them away, along with many people. Even more devastating was the meltdown at the Fukushima Daiichi Nuclear Power Plant, a disaster that threatened Japan's very survival.

I happened to be in the air on that day. My plane touched down at Tokyo's Haneda Airport a few minutes before the earthquake struck. I was actually on my way to the Tōhoku region itself, to Sendai, and was thinking about my connecting flight as workers on the tarmac moved the jet bridge into place and linked the plane to the terminal.

Just as I was about to get up from my seat, the plane jolted and rumbled. At first I thought the jet bridge had malfunctioned, but as a violent shaking began, and continued for well over a minute, it became obvious that the cause of the disturbance was something much larger and deeper. Then came a hurried, clipped announcement over the plane's PA system about an earthquake, and we were instructed to remain seated. I fidgeted, thinking myopically that I would miss my connecting flight.

Once we were allowed to leave, I rushed off the plane. Inside the terminal, I learned that all remaining flights for the day had been canceled, so I went to the train station, only to be told that all the train lines, too, were shut down indefinitely. Nor were any buses running. There remained only two ways into central Tokyo—walking or taking a taxi.

I was not surprised by the long queue at the taxi stand. But I was surprised by the apparently matter-of-fact way in which everyone was waiting. It could not have escaped anyone's notice that the wait would be a long one. I didn't know whether to be impressed by my fellow travelers' placid fortitude or to bemoan their complete passivity. The trouble was that there were very few taxis in the first place; after an hour, the queue had barely moved. Then I noticed that when the rare taxi did show up, it often took only a single passenger.

After a while, annoyed, I found the official in charge of the queue and asked him why he wasn't easing the burden on everyone by arranging for passengers headed in roughly the same direction to ride together.

He answered me in the tone perfected by bureaucrats everywhere, a tone both insouciant and officious—that is, insufferable. "It's the prerogative of the customer," he said. "If the customer wishes to share a taxi, that's fine, but I cannot force the customer to take others."

"But this is an emergency," I protested. "Look at this line! It will take hours if every taxi picks up only one person."

The official bristled ever so slightly at my impudence. "Yes," he replied, "but that's the rule. It's in the manual. It's the customer's right. There's nothing I can do."

I reached my hotel twelve hours later, having utterly failed to muster any enthusiasm for the collectivist solution toward which events had impelled me.

It's something of a cliché to say that individual people, not to mention collectives, show their true colors in times of crisis. More often than not, however, individuals and collectives think and act just the way they've been thinking and acting all along. It is in this sense that I am using the term "regime"—in the sense of a regimen, an ossified habit of thought, a routinized repertoire of action and behavior. All of us, myself included, are creatures of habit, like the official in charge of the taxi queue. It is this fact that I hope the concept of the regime will elucidate.

THE REGIME

The concept of the regime is an extension of the pragmatist notion of the institution. As pragmatist philosophers have proposed, the institution is, at bottom, a habit of thought.[1] Pragmatism or institutionalism may sustain economic traditionalism, or it may help in embarking on capitalist industrialization. It may sustain the process of the received mode of production, or it may help in revolutionizing the mode of production altogether. In any event, it highlights the way of thinking that underlies economic activity. For example, if the dominant habit of thought serves to encourage economic growth, then it will come as no surprise that efforts to form or shape policies and organizations will consequently be directed toward the goal of economic growth, no matter how much that goal may actually be compromised by cognitive misrecognitions or unanticipated outcomes.

I use the term "regime" to encompass the behavioral realm—ways of being and acting—instead of focusing only on the cognitive. Together, a habit of thought and a repertoire of practice constitute an *ethos,* or a complex of normative thinking and reflective action that in turn discloses a particular value orientation. In the case of the Meiji regime, for example, the dominant habit of thought stressed the achievement of greatness in politics and commerce. As a consequence, those who subscribed to the Meiji regime were people who worked and lived in ways that were compatible with greatness in politics and promoted that kind of achievement, including preparation for war and the goal of industrial growth. Naturally, then, the dominant Meiji character traits included valorization of hierarchy and loyalty, or the habit of thought and the repertoire of action that stressed the dialectic of domination and obedience.

To use the regime as a concept is to wield a blunt instrument. For one thing, in concrete terms, the regime itself exhibits multiple and distinct variations. For another, in more abstract terms, the concept of the regime is a guide not to textured abstraction in and of itself but to granular generalizations. Consider the Edo regime, and the habit of thought at the turn of the eighteenth century, as exemplified by the resplendent plays of Chikamatsu Monzaemon. His *kizewa*—stories of ordinary people often doing such extraordinary things as committing double suicide—bear a family resemblance to the habit of thought at the turn of the nineteenth century, but they remain only distantly related to that time; after all, there's a huge leap, and a hundred years, from the moral seriousness of Chikamatsu to Juppentei Ikku's *Tōkaidōchū Hizakurige* and the comic shenanigans of that work's gay lovers on their road trip. Nevertheless, at the precise moment when Juppentei's ludic, sometimes ludicrous tales were the talk of the town, the Tokugawa government, to the chagrin of ordinary urbanites, was seeking to suppress popular entertainment (and not for the first time) so as to uphold popular morality.[2] Thus the Tokugawa government was closer in spirit to the Meiji government than to the ethos of the Edo regime proper.

What I am proposing here is *not* an essentialist and deterministic explanatory framework. Rather, I offer a first approximation to making sense of a complex, confusing, and, above all, changing reality, so consider this chapter not so much a guide as a guide to a rough draft. In any case, the concept of the regime is neither total nor totalizing. It would be tempting to equate the regime with the zeitgeist, in Hegelian fashion, but I make no claims about an essentialist habit of thought or an essentialist repertoire of action that would apply equally to everyone in a particular place and at a particular time. In modern Japan, for example, remnants of the Edo regime have remained a powerful subterranean force despite the dominance of the Meiji regime and the postwar regime. Contemporary Japan is a complex and contradictory society in which different impulses are at work. If the Abe administration sought to revive the Meiji regime, this does not imply that all of Japan had been striving to return to that well-trod path. To take another example, the Edo regime did not become a visible presence until the Genroku period (1688–1704), and it should not be surprising that after decades of unremitting, bloody warfare, the habit and the practice of militarism were slow to fade away.[3] Likewise, everyday violence in post-war Japan persisted for several decades after the end of the Pacific War, but in contemporary Japan one almost never sees a raised fist in public or hears a raised voice, and that decorum is due precisely to the hegemony of the postwar regime.

As a concept, the regime is close to that of culture, but culture tends to be depicted in ahistorical ways (as something that is slow to change) as well as in ways that are totalizing (as something that applies to everyone in the same domain). For example, consider Clifford Geertz's influential, though heavily criticized, idea of culture as a web of significance that seems to structure individual thinking and behavior.[4] By contrast, using the regime as a concept allows us to acknowledge that both cognition and action can change quickly; witness the rapid (though by no means instantaneous) shift from the prewar regime to the postwar regime, before and after 15 August 1945.

If one temptation is to equate the regime with the zeitgeist, another is to elucidate distinct regimes and illuminate the past five hundred years of Japanese history. But that academic exercise is not my intention here. Instead of offering macrohistorical interpretations, I hope to make sense of the Japanese present and aid thinking about Japan's future. And, make no mistake: the struggle over the future of Japan is precisely a struggle over which regime will predominate.

TWO DOMAINS, TWO STRATEGIC PATHS, FOUR POSSIBILITIES

Should Japan revive its postwar regime of rapid economic growth? Should Japan recapture the glory and dynamism of the post–Meiji Restoration decades? Should Japan return to its pre–World War II militarism, as some may desire? Or is Japan perfectly fine with what seems to be its current stasis? One way to think about these distinct possible scenarios is to consider Japan's political, geopolitical, and military role as well as the Japanese economy. Should Japan become a major political and geopolitical power, one that has a strong, assertive military and that occupies a powerful place in the world? Or should Japan rest content with being a neutral, peaceful polity and having a small, modest role? Should Japan pursue growth and a powerful, growth-oriented economy? Or should it seek sustainability and a modest or even no-growth economy? These questions represent two domains (Japan's geopolitical-military role and economy), two strategic paths (advance or retreat), and the four possibilities shown in table 1.

Strategic Advance

A strategy of advance, deployed in both the geopolitical-military and the economic domain, might enhance Japan's geopolitical role as well as the Japanese

TABLE 1 Effects of Strategic Advance or Retreat on Japan's Geopolitical-Military Role and Economy

Strategy	Geopolitical-Military Role	Economy
Advance	Strong military; greater power in the world	Growth-oriented economy
Retreat	Peaceful polity; modest power in the world	Sustainable or no-growth economy

economy, thus capturing the post–Meiji Restoration slogan *fukoku kyōhei* (enrich the country, strengthen the military). This slogan, initially articulated by Dazai Shundai in 1729, became a defining description of Meiji government policy.[5] The Meiji leaders, bringing together the diverse strands of thought that had percolated during the later Tokugawa period, toppled the Tokugawa shogunate and restored the Kyoto-based Imperial Household. What is more significant, they embarked on industrialization and militarization. In so doing, they enacted a revolutionary overhaul of Japan, casting aside nearly three centuries of Tokugawa rule, which had established and sustained peace and prosperity in the Japanese archipelago.

The Meiji regime pursued strong military power and an equally strong industrial economy. No one, broadly speaking, would dispute that the Meiji regime promoted Western-style industrialization over and above (and, in fact, often in contradiction with) Edo-era proto-industrialization, which had been based on handicraft manufacture.[6] Instead of extending the industries of the time, the Meiji leaders sought to replace them with Western organizations and technology. Although the environment had already been somewhat degraded by later Edo-era proto-industrialization, the environmental impact of post-Meiji industrialization was definitive. From light industries like textiles to heavy industry, including chemical production, Meiji political economy sought to catch up with the Western economic powers. At the same time, the Meiji leaders created a powerful military that would become the force sustaining Japanese territorial expansion, whereas Tokugawa rule had sought to minimize the influence of foreign powers and had certainly eschewed external conquest. Indeed, the modern Japanese military fought one war after another until it reached its devastating end in the Pacific War.

Japanese modernity was born of efforts to model Japan on Western, or modern, powers. It is indisputable that some of the Japanese opposed the very idea of such modeling. Others sought to infuse Japan with indigenous ideas and practices, and the general recalcitrance of everyday life ensured that Japan did not emerge as a mere replica of the West. We should of course recall this reservation and resistance, as well as the inevitable hybridity of any Western import once it landed in Japan, but we also should not forget the looming threat and lure of the West. After all, the first minister of education, Mori Arinori, proposed English as the official language of Japan, and Takahashi Yoshio suggested that miscegenation with Westerners would improve the Japanese people.[7] Thus it is commonly observed that Japanese modernity was a translated modernity, and that Japanese intellectual life, especially in the universities, sought to adopt and adapt to Western knowledge.[8] Even in the twenty-first century, when few outside Japan would consider Japan anything but a major country with an impressive culture, the default Japanese tendency is to learn from the West, whether in matters of political and economic policy or in the cultural and intellectual realms. Even the Japanese language itself, compared to the global language of English, has come to seem inferior and irrational.[9]

As any historian would caution, my summary of the Meiji regime's influence is simplistic, and it misses all sorts of nuances and subtleties (concerning, for example, the ways in which tradition was refashioned, or how eclectic and syncretic the outcomes were). Nevertheless, it would be difficult to deny the radical, even revolutionary design and outcome of the Meiji regime. The Meiji leaders, striving to be outstanding pupils of the superior West, rejected the traditional and revered the new, or the West. As a result, the Meiji regime's success came to be measured in terms of how Western Japan had become. And so, for example, post-Meiji Japanese men wore Western clothes, and they displayed facial hair in rank imitation of Western men.[10]

In addition, success was often measured in terms of Western approbation. One instance of this tendency is an observation by Douglas Sladen from 1904: "Japan is no longer the hermit of the East, but the most Western of the nations of the West."[11] It should not be surprising that this statement by a Western visitor was taken as a compliment; in principle, the post-Meiji leaders agreed that the more Western Japan became, the better Japan would be. To cite another small example, German sociologists found myriad problems in the Japan of the 1930s, and they had the answer, too: "It may well be that the only possible solution for this nation is to transform itself into a new Japan that will have nothing in common with the old except a name."[12] In other words, if Japan was to succeed, it needed to shed its Japaneseness. According to this line of thinking, and in retrospect, the Meiji Restoration appears liberal because it introduced a Western-style constitutional monarchy and presented a Japan in the image of the West, which constitutes the very definition of being liberal. Once the self-imposed Western metrics had come to dominate, there was only lack, or emptiness, in anything about Japan that remained Japanese. What did Japan have that the West didn't? The Meiji liberal Nakae Chōmin's devastating claim—"There is no philosophy in Japan"—is symptomatic of the apparent defeatism of Japanese thinkers in confrontation with the mighty West: "People without philosophy are without a will to deep thought on any project and cannot achieve anything but superficiality."[13] Nakae is right to the extent that Descartes, Kant, and their ilk are not Japanese, and that the products of traditional Japanese cogitation do not belong to the same genre as modern Western philosophy. If only imports count, there's no point in domestic production. There is hollowness at the heart of post–Meiji Restoration Japan.

It would be facile to say that cultural importation is a long-standing tradition in Japan. Yet the inescapable reality is that world history is nothing but a series of borrowings and adaptations. The myth of ancient Greek autochthony elides the profound impact of Eastern philosophy; the European Renaissance would have been impossible without the critical role of Arabic and Islamic intellectuals.[14] It would also be a massive misrecognition to neglect the distinctiveness of Japanese culture; already by the early eleventh century, Sei Shōnagon had written *Makuranosōshi* (*The Pillow Book*), and Murasaki Shikibu had written *Genji monogatari* (*The Tale of Genji*).[15] Both works are major literary achievements, and each is quite distinct from anything the Japanese had learned from the advanced civilizations of the West, or the East for that matter.

The Japanese sense of inferiority engendered a peculiar attitude and discourse of difference. What the Japanese produced may not have been philosophy or literature by Western standards, but that fact alone made the Japanese inscrutable to people from advanced Western civilizations. Sour grapes, perhaps; in times of Japanese ascent, however, they yielded the heady wine not just of Japanese uniqueness but of Japanese superiority. Therefore, a subterranean strain of thinking about Japanese greatness emerged. At present, hardly a day passes in Japan without a television special on the greatness and uniqueness of things and customs Japanese.[16] Hubris on the way up, sour grapes on the way down—the Japanese inferiority complex vis-à-vis the West is overcome in part by the assurance of Japanese impenetrability.

At the same time, Japan's excellent students looked down on their compatriots who were less educated in matters Western, as well as on their predecessors. The Meiji regime, in imposing an imported institution, sought to vanquish a society in which, at least to nineteenth-century Western eyes, significant liberties existed for ordinary people.[17] In the name of squelching the traditional and the feudal, the Meiji regime imposed draconian rules on the population, ranging from higher taxes and military conscription to control over or destruction of folk religions and received peasant life. And in these areas, not surprisingly, Meiji rule encountered fierce resistance.[18] In one of those rare literary prophesies that turn out to come true, a character in Sōseki Natsume's *Sanshirō* (1909) responds as follows to a question about Meiji Japan's future: "It will perish."[19] And perish it did as a viable regime, though by August 1945 the regime had already taken on a different form.

At times during the 2010s, the Shinzō Abe administration, true to the vision of Abe's grandfather Nobusuke Kishi, seemed intent on restoring elements of the glories of post–Meiji Restoration industrialism and militarism. For example, in his New Year's address of 2016, the prime minister declared, "Japan will once again be a country that will shine at the center of the world."[20] Abe put considerable energy into revising Article 9 of the Constitution of Japan (the clause that concerns disavowal of a standing military force) in order to legalize a large and legitimate military force; the Japanese Self-Defense Force has the eighth largest military budget in the world.[21] Without question, the Abe administration sought a more assertive role for Japan in world affairs. It is not surprising, then, that the administration was keen to celebrate the sesquicentennial of the Meiji Restoration and to underscore the essential continuity from the beginning of modernization (and Westernization) to the present.[22] Perhaps the Meiji regime will be revived, but its span as the embodiment of a dominant habit of thought stretched from the Meiji Restoration only to 1931 or so, when it was superseded by the prewar regime.

The prewar regime deviated from the Meiji regime in that it valued militarism and imperialism over the economy. That is, the prewar regime—roughly coeval with the Fifteen Years' War, beginning with Japan's serious military incursion into the Chinese mainland in 1931 and ending in 1945—privileged military and geopolitical power over what had been, during the Meiji regime, a more equal emphasis on the economy. A symptomatic slogan of the prewar regime was *hoshigarimasen katsumadewa* (we will not want until we win).[23] Luxury (that is, nonmilitary) spending was the enemy. In other words, the Japanese were to forgo nonessential consumer goods and limit nonmilitary production until Japan had prevailed over the United States and the other Allied powers. The prewar regime was also a time of strictest orthodoxy in matters of public opinion: the triumph of Grundyism.[24] Everyone agrees that there was increasing military influence over Japanese political economy in the early Shōwa period. Violence and even death were celebrated, and they permeated everyday life. In any case, it was precisely the predictable disaster of the prewar period that prompted Japan, with more than a nudge from the victorious United States, to reject militarism and war and usher in the postwar regime.

Needless to say, the prewar regime approximated its pure form only briefly—perhaps for four years between 1941 and 1945, or the duration of the Pacific War—and primacy of the military had not meant neglect of the economy. After all, war cannot be waged without industrial production. It is also true, as discussed in chapter 1, that wartime mobilization contributed to the postwar formation of Japan's industrial production, including the enhanced efficiency and greater discipline of the Japanese labor force. As also noted in that chapter with respect to the wartime generation, the experience of war profoundly shaped business leaders in the postwar period and most likely enhanced their commitment to economic growth.[25] The prewar regime's primary goal was military and political power, whereas the postwar regime favored the economy over the military.

Strategic Retreat

A strategy of retreat, again deployed in both the geopolitical-military and the economic domain, might diminish Japan's geopolitical-military role and lower the country's economic standing. This strategic path deviates from the Meiji and prewar regimes in that it forswears political and military greatness. The postwar regime has been insistently pacifist.[26] Indeed, during the 2010s the commitment to peace, or at least an aversion to war, was widespread in Japan, despite a certain pop-cultural enthusiasm for the wartime heroics of kamikaze pilots in particular and for violence and war in general; in this, Japan had come close to realizing Douglas MacArthur's project of turning itself into the Switzerland of Asia. The postwar regime—the brainchild of Ishibashi Tanzan and other Liberal Democratic Party grandees, though it was brought more fully into being during the 1960s by two successive prime ministers, Hayato Ikeda and Eisaku Satō—had a single-minded focus on economic growth. The fact that the postwar administrations pro-moted Japanese exports around the world led to the perception that the Japanese were economic animals. It is safe to say (though there are revisionists and resisters) that Japan in the postwar period has sought economic growth but not geopolitical and military power.

The devastating defeat in 1945 seemed to upend all values. Shiga Naoya, god of the novel, proposed French as the new national language of Japan. Not surprisingly, young writers were finding almost nothing worthy in Japanese literature, which was all "particularity" with "nothing universal or cosmic"; there was "nothing further from universality or more impoverished than Japanese literature," and the extant Japanese writers had not "mastered even a single foreign language," nor did they know anything of the Bible or Aristotle, of Kant or Marx.[27] If Tanizaki Jun'ichirō or Nagai Kafū could not redeem Japanese literature, perhaps literature itself was irre-deemable. Yet according to this line of thinking, everything Japanese was backward and particular and therefore incapable of containing or conveying general or uni-versal significance.[28] It was as if Japan had nothing to show to other civilizations, nothing to teach them.

Be that as it may, after 1945 the powerful Eurocentric current in modern Japa-nese life and thought was revived, this time with an American accent. Every aspect of Japan seemed pathetic and drab by comparison with the mighty, shiny West. Since miscegenation was not widely practiced after the Meiji Restoration—the sole government-sponsored effort had been to encourage marriage between ethnic Japanese people and ethnic Koreans—what remained was a pervasive sense of physical inferiority.[29] It would be simple to observe that, objectively speaking, the Japanese were, on average, shorter than their Western counterparts, but the prob-lem was less physical than psychological and aesthetic. What is most obvious is that Japan, in defeat, has long remained a virtual client of the United States and, in matters of geopolitics, a minor presence on the world stage.

The postwar regime, partly in reaction to the nationalist prewar regime, approx-imated the Meiji regime in its enthusiasm for things Western. Facial hair was out, since it was closely associated with wartime military leaders, but Western clothes became even more widely worn. To take another example, Daisetz Teitaro Suzuki echoed many other people when he observed that haiku "may be said to reflect the Japanese character," but after the end of the war, in 1946, the influential literary scholar Kuwabara Takeo wrote that haiku was "appropriate for the elderly or the ill" who wished to "fritter time away."[30] There were nationalist reactions against these trends, of course, but the profound impact of the West, and in particular the impact of the United States, is visible today in the language, the food, and the everyday life of postwar Japan.

In 2020, the postwar regime continued to embody the dominant mind-set among Liberal Democratic Party politicians, elite state bureaucrats, and leaders of large corporations. The dominant idea has been (in contrast to the momentary hubris of the Bubble decade) to redirect the postwar political economy in a more neoliberal direction. Degrees of commitment and emphases have varied, of course, but few in the iron triangle have been inclined to deviate from geopolitical reliance on the United States or from unswerving faith in economic growth as the master solution to social, political, and economic problems. Most people in contemporary Japan, like majorities probably everywhere else, have remained overwhelmingly in favor of the idea of economic growth.[31] For example, a notable habit of thought and practice has to do with the development of infrastructure—build it, and when it gets old, rebuild it. In 2018, this ethos led to the destruction, but not the reconstruction, of the Tsukiji Fish Market, which one master sushi chef has described as "not just Tokyo's best known brand" but as "the people's market."[32] Indeed, the Tsukiji Market had often been the most highly prized tourist destination in a country eager to court tourists, but its obsolescence (it was first built in 1935) was making it an eyesore for construction-oriented politicians and bureaucrats.

The Bubble years can be seen as a souped-up version of the postwar regime. In those years, the culture of getting and spending—no longer restrained by the Edo or prewar legacy of thrift, or by general disapprobation of moneymaking itself—expressed one possible and extreme outcome of the postwar regime. As Horie Takafumi, a celebrated entrepreneur turned white-collar criminal and pop-culture pundit, observed in 2004, "There is nothing in the world you can't buy with money, and everything is equal before money."[33] Deep within the Japanese body politic, a free-market radical slouches between the shades of Ayn Rand and Milton Friedman to be born. At the same time, however, there has been an undercurrent of criticism toward the single-minded pursuit of growth. Already by 1970, a favorite catchphrase—mōretsu kara byūtifuru e (from the extreme to the beautiful)—was proposing that Japan cease its obsessive focus on growth and pay attention instead to improving the quality of life.[34] In contemporary Japanese life, too, there is a steady countercultural trend reminiscent of the hippie ethos that swept the Western world in the late 1960s and early 1970s. In any case, as chapter 4 shows, by 1980 Japanese people were placing more value on matters of the heart than on things; the trend has intensified since then and has ushered in a postmaterialist ethos.[35]

Yet it would be misleading to suggest that the postmaterialist ethos has superseded the power and dynamism of the postwar regime. The process of creative destruction can still be seen, most clearly in the continuing development of Tokyo's built environment. For example, the first skyscraper in the Kasumigaseki district was not built until 1968, but Tokyo, once a low-slung city, has now become a dispersed Manhattan, and this process has only accelerated since the turn of the new century. In 1989 there were only 26 buildings over thirty stories high, but by 2016 there were more than 320.[36] Moreover, the creation of these forbidding, impersonal towers was accompanied by a bureaucratic campaign of renaming that has done away with colorful old Tokyo street addresses and replaced them with sterile numbers.

And, finally, no discussion of a possible strategy of retreat regarding Japan's geopolitical-military role and the Japanese economy would be complete without a consideration of the Edo regime, that is, the reign of the Tokugawa shogunate, as most Japanese scholars mean when they mention the Edo period. *Edo* is a toponym, the name of the city that is Tokyo today but was largely a swamp when it became the capital of Japan in the early seventeenth century. *Edo* is also a political label synonymous with Tokugawa rule. And the term "Edo" has yet another connotation—that of a way of life exemplified by the ordinary denizens of Edo, and it is in this sense that I use the term.

During nearly three centuries of peace—after a period of constant warfare that followed the collapse of the Ashikaga shogunate, or the Muromachi period (1338–1573)—Japan in general, and Edo in particular, enjoyed growing prosperity and a cultural efflorescence. Indeed, what most people find distinctive about Japanese culture—foods like sushi and tempura, for example, and arts like kabuki and *ukiyo-e* prints—was born in and thrived during the Edo period, especially in Edo itself, after the Genroku period.[37] Entertainment, including popular literature, flourished.

But the Edo regime did not pursue political or economic greatness. The Tokugawa shogunate was committed to stasis and order. Content to sustain the status hierarchy, the shogunate did not promote commercial or industrial activities. The shogunate was far from closed to foreign contact. Nevertheless, Tokugawa Ieyasu and his progeny desisted from serious incursions into foreign territory, unlike the previous ruler and in contrast to the succeeding Meiji regime. Thus the Edo regime developed a form of sustainable society that, without seeking political expansion or economic growth, still achieved economic improvement and a cultural flowering, at least for much of the Edo period. Why is it, then, that so few Japanese people today seem to appreciate the Edo period as a remarkable era of peace, affluence, and creativity?

THE EDO REGIME: BACKWATER OR RENAISSANCE?

Just as the Tokugawa shogunate curtailed its forays into other countries, it also sought to limit the influx of foreign ideas and influence. For this reason, the Edo regime is often misleadingly described as having been a *sakoku* (locked country), a region hermetically closed off from the rest of the world. Modern Japan, or the Meiji regime, has eclipsed and elided the Edo regime, and the contemporary Japanese dismissal of the Edo regime's achievements says something profound about the legacy of the Meiji regime. Government-approved textbooks of Japanese history still depict Tokugawa-era foreign policy as having been all about *sakoku*, about the seemingly xenophobic practice of closing a country off from foreign contact, and not about 250 years of uninterrupted peace—a rare achievement in world history.[38] But some slow progress has been made on historiographic revisions.[39] In any event, it is common enough for a regime to bury its predecessors while claiming to sing their praises. But the post-Meiji leaders didn't even bother to go through the motions of eulogizing the Tokugawa period; instead, they impugned it in unrelentingly negative terms, labeling it backward and feudal. And the postwar regime followed right along. After all, the dominant analysis of what had gone wrong with prewar Japan held that Japan had not become adequately modern—that Japan was immature and behind the West.[40] The Tokugawa period, then, if it was nothing else, was non-Western and therefore a drag on Japan's inevitable modernity.

In retrospect, the transition from the twilight of Tokugawa rule to the dawn of Meiji governance has come to be understood not as a mere caesura but as a profound chasm between old and new. As exemplified by the title of Shimazaki Tōson's 1935 epic, *Yoakemae* (Before the dawn), the pre–Meiji Restoration period was the time before the dawn, and thus the post–Meiji Restoration corresponds to sunrise, in the very country of the rising sun.[41] Modern Japan, Manichaean in the extreme, has embraced the new and the West, rejecting the old and the Japanese (and the East in general). Good riddance, then, to the sordid past; if the Meiji political-economic establishment and the Marxist revolutionaries agreed on little else, they agreed on that. The forward march of history, and Japan's pursuit of the loftiest of lofty heights, constituted a chronicle of murder and mayhem, a chronicle decorated with triumphant images of imperial expansion that adorned the maps that every student perused. But that seemed immaterial; anyway, all the murder and mayhem were blamed on the prewar regime and its domination by fanatical military leaders. By this calculus, then, the Meiji regime looks like a necessary step on the way to the present, whereas the Edo regime appears to be beside the point and looks like an excrescence of rank backwardness that had to be removed for the sake of the future.

Moreover, Edo life remained terra incognita long after the historiography of the post–Meiji Restoration had obscured it. Not only did the Meiji regime take the Tokugawa era severely to task, but the Meiji series of language reforms also ensured that vanishingly few Japanese readers would ever be able to access the vast trove of Edo literary treasures.[42] As the fortunes of Heian, or modern, literature rose, those of the Edo masterpieces fell. Some literary figures—Nagai Kafū and Tanizaki Jun'ichirō, Ishikawa Jun and Tanabe Seiko, among others—did draw sustenance from the legacy of Edo culture, but the vast majority remained ensconced in their love of the new and the West. It is not surprising, then, that so few sought to make sense of the Edo cultural efflorescence or to write about it with appreciation. A striking exception to this rule is Kuki Shūzō's explication of the aesthetics of *iki*.[43] Like Nagai and Tanizaki, Kuki undertook a long sojourn in the West, one that alerted him to the esprit (perhaps the closest equivalent of *iki*) of ordinary Edo people. Kuki highlights the salience of eros, of will (or resistance), and of resignation or indifference in the everyday life and worldview of Edoites: desire unleashes the fashioning and presentation of the self; the will to live life to the fullest discloses an antinomian and antiauthoritarian bent; and persistent awareness of memento mori prompts acknowledgment of life's recalcitrance and transience. In more concrete terms, Edo culture is a ludic culture, a culture of getting and spending. A true Edoite, it was said, never saves money; in the words of a contemporary adage, "Seriousness is a human being's downfall."[44] The Edo regime—and here it is important to distinguish the regime itself from the Tokugawa shogunate, which cared little about ordinary townspeople or farmers—was dedicated to artisanal work, to work for its own sake, to worldly enjoyment and an ethic of ordinary virtues. Edo life valorized artisanal work that was undergirded by a strong social ethic—primacy of human relations and mutual help, protection of the weak, and an egalitarian ethos (overlaid though it may have been with the reality of status distinctions).

In contrast, the Meiji regime was all about eradicating eros, or the individual will, and implanting obedience to the higher authority of the emperor, for the greater good of the nation. The Meiji regime was punctual, staid, organized, and boring. In the language of Edo culture, which was all about being chic and dashing, spirited, and worldly, the Meiji regime was *yabo*, or the antonym of *iki*. For example, modern Japanese people favored Western paintings over *ukiyo-e* prints, placed the striving for upward mobility above individual expressiveness, and valued a future orientation and transcendence above passion and immanence. The vaunted Meiji virtues, far from *iki*, were diligence and studying, as embodied by being *majime* (serious), the precise attitude that the Edo ethos had ridiculed.[45] If the dashing and romantic Sukeroku, a popular kabuki hero, exemplified *iki*, the Meiji man of seriousness and ambition was represented by the character Ninomiya Kinjirō, who read and studied even as he walked and worked. Thus it is not surprising that, as mentioned earlier, the Meiji regime sought to eclipse and elide the esprit of ordinary Edo culture, since the Meiji regime was all about bureaucratic formality. The Meiji and Edo modes of governance and livelihood were diametrically opposed. In other words, the Meiji government (and the military) wanted ordinary Japanese people to sacrifice themselves for the glory of the country (and the emperor) and to pursue a compressed process of industrialization, even at the expense of their own well-being. As a result, many ordinary Japanese people, city dwellers as well as farmers, experienced the Meiji government and its disciplinary rule as something akin to colonization.[46] It was not just that the Meiji regime created a new Japanese body politic, dedicated to industrial might and military strength; the regime also forged the modern Japanese people, whether that meant enlarging their bodies through Western-style consumption of meat, intervening in and disciplining their sex lives through an imposed heteronormativity, or putting them in thrall to modern (that is, Western) knowledge. Premodern Edoites—and, for decades, their descendants—had been pescatarians and vegetarians; their non-carnivorous diet had also made possible the extensive recycling of human waste (though Western and Meiji observers judged this ecologically correct practice to be backward).[47] The premodern Edoites were also remarkably tolerant of different sexualities and lifestyles, and they enjoyed comic works of popular culture. But the Meiji regime was sensitive to the gaze of Westerners, who were often Christians and censorious of popular Japanese morality, as expressed in mixed-sex bathing, for example, or in same-sex intercourse. Thus the Meiji regime, by imposing what it took to be the Western way of life, also painted the recent past of the Edo period as a dark age of rigid feudal hierarchy, xenophobic isolationism, and superstition-ridden stasis. Nevertheless, it is also true that many vital features of contemporary Japanese life survive from the Edo period. Despite the Meiji regime's calumny, the Edo regime remains a vibrant, if weakened, presence.

By the early eighteenth century, the Tokugawa rulers had brought about remarkable affluence by preserving peace and resisting political as well as economic misadventures. The development of interregional commerce was particularly important in stimulating artisanal production. Proto-industrialization emerged; that is, the growth of an artisanal ethos and the virtues associated with mastering a craft (such as long training, diligence, and a commitment to high quality). The expanding economic base in turn facilitated a thriving popular culture, created largely by and for the townspeople. Edo now became a locus of artistic and cultural innovation and challenged Kyoto's long-standing dominance in the arts. Especially during the Kasei period (1804–30), Edo produced a concentration of artistic achievement rare in world history, with Hokusai and Hiroshige in the visual arts, Bakin and Nanboku in popular literature, and many other remarkable figures.[48] And just as remarkable was these figures' longevity: Nanboku died at seventy-five, Bakin at eighty-two, and Hokusai at ninety. But all three remained active to the end, thanks to the security and prosperity that made meaningful pursuits possible. Symptomatically, however, the only major overview of Kasei culture in print is in the genre of manga.[49]

As for the enduring vibrancy of Edo culture, in Japan today its quintessential achievements have become highly visible trappings of rich people's lives. Dining at an expensive sushi restaurant, attending a kabuki performance, collecting ukiyo-e prints—these three activities are the province of the comfortable classes, and yet the ruling samurai classes scorned all three. But how could contemporary perceptions of the Edo period's cultural flowering be idiosyncratic or mistaken, if outsiders see the pinnacle of traditional Japanese culture in the very products of ordinary Edo townspeople?

There are certain parallels and resemblances between the Edo regime and the postwar regime. To begin with, both followed a period of intense warfare and sacrifice, and both achieved a peace and prosperity that then trickled down to the masses, ushering in a level of material and cultural enrichment after a paroxysm of violence. Moreover, the samurai and the post–World War II soldiers gave up, respectively, the sword and the rifle for office work. Imagine the samurai's sword replaced by a briefcase, and his kimono by a Western-style suit, and the samurai, like his postwar counterpart, becomes a salaryman. In addition, according to the received stereotype, Edokko—that is, the ordinary townspeople of Edo—worked hard, but they played harder. Their orientation was to the present, and they were willing to shift jobs and forgo savings. In this they resemble today's *furītā* and *nīto*, the postaffluent young Japanese people introduced in chapter 1, who do not seek permanent employment, especially not as office workers.[50]

It is also worth noting that the continuity of the Edo ethos of work and life is precisely what allowed the Meiji regime—and, for that matter, the prewar and postwar regimes—to function so well, if only by making sure the trains ran on time. At present, though, the survival of the Edo regime is tenuous. The reigning political powers, not to mention bureaucrats and corporate executives, hope to rejuvenate the postwar regime, if not go all the way back to the Meiji regime itself (or, worse, to the prewar regime). That said, my intention here is not to celebrate Edo culture or to revive it in contemporary Japan. After all, celebration of Edo culture can simply be a fig leaf for xenophobic nationalism, a vehicle for touting Japanese superiority.[51] And we can't turn back the clock, nor is the past a place to which we would choose to return. But neither is the present completely utopian, for Japanese society is fraught with seemingly intractable issues—not only what the policy elites worry about, such as slow economic growth and a rapidly aging society, but also problems that include political corruption, corporate senescence, gender inequality, and regional underdevelopment. What I seek to do instead, by delineating the continuation and further development of the Edo regime, is to showcase some ways of living that remain not just workable but spirited and vital, too.

WHITHER JAPAN?

Some proposals for Japan's future embrace elements of the Edo regime. For example, one manifestation of the Edo regime's continuing influence is faith in Japanese traditions, together with resistance to globalization. This remains a minority perspective, but occasionally it strikes a nerve with the reading public, as in 2005, when Fujiwara Masahiko sold nearly three million copies of *Kokka no hinkaku* (*The Dignity of the Nation*), which advocates *bushidō* (the way of the samurai) and reaffirms Japanese traditions and greatness.[52] Fujiwara laments Japanese abasement, including Japan's subservience to the United States as well as the Japanese stress on English-language education, and he lambastes such Western influences as faith in logic and rationality, advocacy of liberty and equality, and indulgence in selfishness and greed. The Japanese, he says, should value beauty and feelings instead of seeking to be logical or to acquire material wealth. Fujiwara wants the Japanese people to recover Japan's aesthetic and ethical traditions, including reverence for nature and respect for the weak. In short, he wants Japan to be an "abnormal" country, a country that will abandon the pursuit of materialism, embrace Japanese aesthetic and moral traditions, and thereby save the world.[53] This, then, is one articulation of what I am calling the Edo regime, though this one includes a twist of the ruling Tokugawa regime along with that regime's samurai ethos and values.

The playwright Hirata Oriza proposes an alternative to Fujiwara's vision. Hirata takes for granted three types of sadness, which he says the Japanese must accept: sadness that Japan is no longer an industrial society, that there will be no more growth, and that Japan is not the only advanced country in Asia.[54] Once upon a time, he says, Japan scaled the heights of economic and political power, but now the moment has come for Japan to climb back down, slowly and skillfully. As an illustration of how Japan might navigate the future, he proposes the example of Shōdōshima, the island that served as the location for the 1954 film *Nijūshi no hitomi* (*Twenty-Four Eyes*), directed by Keisuke Kinoshita. In the decades after that prosperous era, Hirata says, Shōdōshima has not stagnated; instead, the island has done well because of its vigorous agricultural production, its beautiful natural environment, its rich culture (the island has a tradition of rural kabuki more than three hundred years old), and sound local governmental policies, which include the provision of convenient transportation.[55] Hirata's example of Shōdōshima can be taken as also representing the Edo regime, though with an emphasis on ordinary people's ethos and virtues, as opposed to the ethos and virtues of the samurai.

A regime, once it has attained dominance, finds it easy to legitimate a course of action because the regime is necessarily hegemonic and difficult to resist. But no regime triumphs completely; at any point in time, there are competing regimes and ethos. The prewar regime, for example, especially toward the end of World War II, seemed totalitarian and appeared to brook no resistance or alternatives, yet there were critics and doubters, despite the squelching of open, vocal dissent. And every regime has a long tail, in part because individuals and organizations bear its legacy and carry on after its hegemony has passed. For instance, the Meiji regime partly undergirds the remarkable success of Japan's contemporary transportation infrastructure (as noted earlier, the trains are reliable), and even though artisans made and continue to make this achievement possible, the modern system could not have been conceived and realized without the mammoth bureaucratic apparatus of the Meiji regime and, later, the postwar regime. But another, more disturbing way to talk about a regime and its afterlife is to say that what seemed dead and buried may yet return, perhaps innocuously at first, through reading or hearsay, then by way of politics or social movements or by means of group or organizational emulation. And what is all the more terrifying is that there is no fixed telos toward which we are moving.

This is also to say that, despite the hegemonic character of any regime, it is always possible for people to change their minds, to work and live differently. Thus, as discussed at the beginning of this chapter, a bureaucrat of the postwar regime may feel compelled to do things by the book even in an emergency, and he may persist in his mind-set of *yabo*, but perhaps even he will come to learn the spirit of *iki*; the future's not ours to see. At any rate, when it comes to Japan's future, whether one gravitates toward the vision of a Fujiwara or that of a Hirata, what is now most consequential about the Edo regime is its long afterlife, whose permutations may offer the most viable mode of working and living in an age of limits.

4

Ordinary Virtues

In the mid- to late 2010s, a curious trend swept through the rich countries of the world. Against the capitalist virtues of accumulation and consumption, Marie Kondo proclaimed the emancipatory gospel of decluttering, that is, the practice of dispossession and the principle of minimalism.[1] The so-called KonMari method (its name combines the author's surname and given name, Kondō Marie, as they are styled in Japanese) poses a simple question to the person overwhelmed by a particular possession: Does it "spark joy"?[2] If yes, keep it; if no, toss it. As the Kon-Mari method launched a thousand tweets and retweets, and "the life-changing magic of tidying up" converted one pack rat after another, Marie Kondo became a household name in the rich world, and yet another self-help volume was added to many a groaning bookshelf.

The theory and the practice of simple living are as old as civilization. In the modern era, the Americans can point to Henry David Thoreau, and the British to William Morris ("Have nothing in your house that you do not know to be useful, or believe to be beautiful"), or to any number of contemporary self-help books.[3] But Kondo's advice goes beyond Morris's criteria of useful and beautiful. It is a radical prescription for personal liberation based on a simple, minimalist rule—instead of being enthralled to your belongings, live with the things you love. Kondo claims a perfect record for the success of her counsel; apparently no one she has coached ever committed the recidivist act of reaccumulation.

Probate records from eighteenth-century England, perhaps the first consumer society, reveal a Spartan inventory that would make Marie Kondo proud—a typically modest household contained fewer items than some homeless people in the United States call their own in the early twenty-first century.[4] But if tidying up has been deemed essential for as long there have been human settlements, it took mass production and mass consumption to make cluttering a mass phenomenon. In 2001, the performance artist Michael Landy grabbed headlines by systematically destroying all his belongings—more than seven thousand items, including his father's sheepskin coat and his Saab 900 automobile. With the help of a dozen assistants, the project, *Break Down,* took two weeks.[5] If the artist Barbara Kruger's *I Shop Therefore I Am* can be said to apply to Michael Landy, then Landy lost not only his stuff but also his sense of self.[6] But Landy, far from bereft or distressed, had this to say about his process of depossession: "It was the happiest two weeks of my life."[7]

Decluttering is not a virtue peculiar to Japan, but merely one possible response to the world of plenty. We want things, and they overwhelm us. At least in affluent countries, except among people who are extremely indigent, the problem has become less about adequate calories and enough goods than about an excess of things to eat and buy. In other words, an epidemic of overeating and cluttering will produce a bonanza for publishers of books about dieting and decluttering. Each culture or civilization retains received virtues, such as the virtue of thrift (not wantonly wasting resources) and that of diligence (not frittering one's time away meaninglessly), but contemporary Japanese society has sustained its received virtues better than most. To be sure, the importance of these ordinary virtues was exaggerated during the wartime mobilization, when they were enforced, but it is also possible to draw connections between these virtues and the latter Edo-period virtues born of mercantile thrift and *shokunin katagi* (the Edo-era artisanal ethos).[8] Such ordinary virtues were also given renewed emphasis after the excesses of the Bubble period's exuberance, rational or irrational as it may have been.

Consumption is certainly alive and well in contemporary Japan. Indeed, it was a defining feature of the postwar period of rapid economic growth, when love of things and shopping seemed to be the mainspring of life. Corporate workers and their wives waited for bonuses or saved for big-ticket items: washing machines, refrigerators, and black-and-white TVs in the 1950s; a car, an air conditioner, and a color TV in the 1960s. The very definition of respectable livelihood came to depend on material possessions, and people began to calibrate their satisfaction in terms of things. The apotheosis of this postwar trend came in the 1980s, when conspicuous consumption seemed to rule Japan. By the 1990s, however, even though consumption remained sovereign, there was also a profound undertow of aspiring to minimize consumption and lead a minimalist life. Even as the Liberal Democratic Party—and, in particular, the Abe administration—worked with corporations and their endless advertising campaigns to promote spending, a significant segment of Japanese society was pursuing and continues to pursue another way of living. Whatever the motivation—an individual response to the environmental crisis, a reaction to the go-go years of the Bubble, a lack of disposable income—slices of contemporary Japanese society evince a minimalist way of life.

FROM THE PURITY OF POVERTY TO
THE VIRTUES OF MINIMALISM

In 1992, precisely when the asset-price speculation bubble burst beyond all recovery, Nakano Kōji's *Seihin no shisō* (The philosophy of pure poverty) came along to encapsulate the zeitgeist of the immediate post-Bubble years and, in the process, become a best seller.[9] Had the book appeared earlier, it probably would have been remaindered or pulped, having piqued interest only among business-minded readers who had misheard the title's homonym (*seihin*) as touting the philosophy of manufactured goods. Like some other best sellers that ride a wave of popular enthusiasm, the book begins with an unlikely litany of premodern Japanese poets and essayists—Saigyō (1118–90), Kenkō (1283–1352), Bashō (1644–94), and Ryōkan (1785–1831), among others—who have in common the rejection of a life of ambition (whether for prestige or wealth) in favor of a simple rustic life. Their Zen-like aesthetic, often called *wabi-sabi*, is all about the benefits of impoverishment and impermanence. *Seihin no shisō* is Nakano's encapsulation of the adage that urges a pure and impoverished but nevertheless beautiful life. By restraining or redirecting the desire for fame or property, he says, one can paradoxically achieve inner freedom and emancipate oneself from anxiety. He suggests that the genealogy of *seihin* (pure poverty) constitutes a major strand of Japanese life, one that has been threatened by materialist influences: "Japanese people used to look down on people who talked about money in front of others, and to disparage people who thought about nothing but profit."[10] The Westernization that accompanied the Meiji Restoration, he goes on to say, planted the seeds of worldly, material success, that is, the capitalist spirit of accumulation and consumption. Or, to paraphrase Nakano in the lexicon of chapter 3, the Meiji regime overwhelmed the Edo regime.

My précis of Nakano's book may give the impression that he was a conservative crank and right-wing nationalist. On the contrary, he was associated with left-wing peace activists. He wrote novels—perhaps the most successful was *Harasu no ita hibi* (Days with Harasu), a thinly veiled fiction about his life with his pet dog—and he translated primarily twentieth-century German-language writers, such as Franz Kafka, Max Frisch, and Günther Grass, all the while serving as a professor at Kokugakuin University. Immersed as he was in German and Western literature, his influences and models of the philosophy of pure poverty range from Buddhism to the ideal of the English gentleman.[11] Yet he came to appreciate the values attendant on a modest life liberated from the endless quest for fame and fortune—values articulated, in writing and in life, by a series of Japanese writers. Bashō is the best known of them, but Kenkō and Ryōkan also exemplify a life of forgoing fame, fortune, and promotion and instead living simply and reflectively. The nineteenth-century poet Tachibana Akemi's *Dokurakugin* (Solitary pleasures) is representative of such values; indeed, all the poems in the collection begin with "pleasure is" (*tanoshimi wa*), though they depict the small pleasures of a life spent in poverty, such as the rare occasions on which Tachibana and his family eat fish and everyone is happy.[12] Another exemplar is the female teacher in the 1954 film *Nijūshi no hitomi* (*Twenty-Four Eyes*), who leads the idealized life of purity, poverty, and beauty.[13] Beyond these artistic achievements, Nakano admires the poor people with whom he grew up in the prewar period, the people who lived in a small, nearly empty "house made of wood and paper," the people who were scorned by Westerners but who worked hard and took pride in their work, who loved nature and hated waste, the people who enjoyed life—the artisans introduced in chapters 5 and 6.[14] It would be easy to conclude that Nakano was reacting to the excesses of the Bubble years, when the quest for money and conspicuous consumption seemed to be the rule, and he suggests that the values of those years stemmed from foreign influences.[15]

Whatever the impact of Nakano's book—best sellers rarely change lives, but surely there were some converts to his proposed way of living—there is no question that its publication was coeval with a cultural turn in Japanese life. In the Bubble years, some had gambled away their life savings; others had pursued a comfortable life of speculating and rent seeking; still others had just wanted a little more. Financial speculation ended abysmally for many people, and because its reach was wide and deep, it inevitably affected the entire archipelago. The rapidity and thoroughness of the financial crunch pushed debts into bankruptcies and, in the process, turned dreams into nightmares. The massive post-Bubble hangover led some to double down (and the initial relief from that hair of the dog may have hastened their overdependence); others took the cure and became financial teetotalers, a course that appeared to dominate in post-Bubble Japan.

The original slogan of the Meiji Restoration—*sonnō jōi* (revere the emperor, expel the barbarians)—had fairly soon been replaced by *fukoku kyōhei* (enrich the country, strengthen the military). Without exaggeration, then, one could summarize the seventy-five years after the Meiji Restoration as reflecting the twin (if sometimes conflicting) goals of pursuing economic growth and pursuing military power. But the post-Bubble turn toward austerity contradicted the dominant narrative of modern Japan. If the enforced austerity of the Fifteen Years' War—especially during its last phase, the Pacific War (1941–45)—decisively turned Japan away from the military and toward identifying itself as a peaceful nation, the postwar period saw Japan embrace growth as something of a substitute. Thus it is not surprising that many Japanese people converted their newfound wealth and leisure into shopping sprees and luxury travel. Over the course of a single generation, Japan had achieved recovery and become affluent. The most visible and visceral indicators of these changes were the consumer goods that reached almost the entire population.

An uglier manifestation of Japan's newfound austerity has been the contemporary Japanese attitude of derision and condescension toward the Chinese vice of *bakugai* (explosive shopping). And yet the things that Japanese people accuse today's Chinese tourists of doing are the very things that their own parents and elders were doing from the 1960s to the 1980s. The title story of Tsutsui Yasutaka's 1973 collection, *Nōkyō tsuki e iku* (The farmers' co-op goes to the moon), pokes fun, none too gently, at farmers and the co-op under whose auspices they not only travel around the world but also embark on a lunar journey, only to engender a global crisis when they find aliens on the moon.[16] Meanwhile, back here on Earth, some Japanese hotels and inns have been refusing to admit Chinese tourists, suspecting that they will walk off with everything in their rooms. But as the writer Ikenami Shōtarō (if no one else) recalls, Japanese tourists themselves stripped many a hotel room in the 1970s.[17] And, now that ordinary Japanese people have moved on to a life of modest (if not quite pure) poverty, the repressed misdemeanors of their parents and elders have returned as malfeasance on the part of foreigners.

In the three decades since the publication of Nakano's screed, there has been a steady stream of books, television programs, and life coaching dedicated to modest or simple living, or at least to avoiding the excesses of consumption, possession, and unfettered desire. Again, the most widely known and most celebrated of this movement's avatars is Marie Kondo, but she is only one among a loosely organized group of writers and bloggers who espouse *minimarizumu* (minimalism) as a way of life. Thus we have a race not just to the bottom but to actual nothingness, and in the lead is Sasaki Fumio, whose 2015 book has a title that clearly conveys his message: *Bokutachini, mō mono wa hitsuyō nai* (We don't need things anymore).[18] To free oneself from possessions, and from the desire for things, means to live *tebura* (hands-free), that is, to live without things, or at least with only a few essential things.[19] And these essential things should not be stamped with fashionable brands, in keeping with the earlier efforts of a company, Muji Ryōhin, that produced no-brand, high-quality goods for everyday living. The next step would be to wander about like Bashō.[20] Thus the spirit of pure poverty manifests as both freedom to move (mobility) and freedom to do as one likes (in the manner of a bohemian).[21] Once things (in the form of possessions) have been dispensed with, the project of minimalism extends to eliminating things one doesn't want to do and people one doesn't want to deal with.[22] The title of a popular 1990 anime says it all: *Kumo no yō ni, kaze no yō ni* (Like the Clouds, Like the Wind).[23]

Many of the minimalist movement's best-known bloggers are young men who came of age after the Bubble burst. It is not at all difficult to detect their propensity to skirt responsibility, as many young men (and women) are inclined to do, but it would be difficult to deny their cultural propensity for minimalism. A common observation about minimalism stresses the peculiar quality of urban Japanese life, especially the tiny dimensions of most apartments and houses. It stands to reason that minimalism would be an inevitable consequence of living in a small space. There is more than a grain of truth in this hackneyed conclusion, but what is striking is the tendency toward, or at least a discernible fashion of, living in even the smallest lodgings. For example, one author, Katō Kyōko, presents eight houses that range in size from 30 to 59 square meters (roughly 323 to 635 square feet) and that can accommodate two to five people; she accompanies her text with beautiful photos as well as question-and-answer sections offering guidance on choosing and living in a tiny house.[24] And the people who live in these microlodgings seem far from oppressed by their narrow living spaces. Instead, they appear to feel that their tiny houses give them the opportunity to live *sukkiri* (freely and refreshingly). Given that our wants and desires expand to fit the space available, we are doomed to be burdened with too many things, with too cluttered a house (even when the house is of gigantic proportions), with too many items to take care of. For the sake of all our belongings, we may choose to live far away from our workplace, in a community where we can afford a larger residence, and thus we saddle ourselves with a long commute that leaves us with less time for what we really want to do, such as enjoying urban amenities or spending time with family members and friends. One man, who lives with his wife in a house of only 35 square meters (377 square feet), told Katō, "There are no limits to human desire, which expands infinitely. No matter how big our house is, we think it would be better if it were a bit bigger. As long as there is any space to put things, we think we want this or we need that."[25]

Minimalist living may strike its detractors as an ascetic, hermit-like way of life. But in contemporary writings on minimalism, and in conversations with people following this lifestyle, I have seen and heard almost nothing about religion or spirituality. In fact, many of the people who live minimally also resist the label or philosophy of minimalism, believing that it's too abstract or that it smacks of intellectualism. If Nakano's practitioners of pure poverty tended to be inspired by Buddhism, they were premodern figures who could not avoid being influenced by Buddhist rituals and practices, arts, and values. But the sacred has largely departed everyday urban Japanese life. The general thrust of the minimalist movement is to live well, without being in thrall to one's belongings or living according to others' dictates. As one young minimalist told me, "It just doesn't make sense to ride on a train called 'Life' that's all set up in advance—all the destinations and all the stops in between. I want to live *my* life, not someone else's idea for my life." To the extent that there is a grander theory behind the postmaterialist orientation, it has to do either with ecological thinking (the desire to be kind to the Earth) or with the idea that we are living in a time and in a world beyond the excesses of conspicuous consumption.[26] If this doesn't quite add up to the Buddhist insight that the source of all suffering is desire, it does acknowledge that unrestrained desire can wreak havoc.

The type of minimalism just described is only one expression of the theme of simplicity in everyday life. Another involves food. For example, Doi Yoshiharu, a well-known chef, has proposed that a meal should consist of one soup and one (vegetable) dish to go with the Japanese staple of rice, and he sets this proposal forth as a "philosophy," an "aesthetic," and a "way of life" for the Japanese people.[27] In this way he suggests that a meal, from preparation through cleanup, is not a means to an end but rather an essential component of everyday life, a way of appreciating the rhythms of the hours and the seasons, the bounty of nature, and the intrinsic tastes and nutrients of each food. In short, he says, a meal is a way of enjoying life and should be regarded as a source of everyday luxury and as a means of participating in the essential rhythms of living. Doi is proposing not only a particular diet—a healthy, nonfattening way of nourishment—but also a common-sense way of living in harmony with nature and with other people.[28] In a similar spirit, Koizumi Kazuko suggests that the Japanese people should revert to the practices of the postwar period in order to minimize "environmental destruction and the deterioration of living skills."[29] She recommends minimizing use of and dependence on not just electricity and water but also the many disposable goods that, convenient though they may be, unduly burden the natural environment while diminishing the human skills needed for the everyday work of living.

It would be all too easy to trace a straight line from Japanese tradition to contemporary minimalism.[30] As Nakano shows, eminent poets often eschewed worldly success—though a cynic might note that, having failed at worldly success, they fled the corrupt world in a fit of sour grapes and only then embraced a life of simplicity and reflection. The inescapable reality, however, is that at all points in Japanese civilization the majority has seemed to be in thrall to the game of fame and fortune. The hedonists popping champagne, the conspicuous consumers toting Birkin bags—were they also reflecting on life's impermanence and the aesthetic of imperfection? Perhaps. But the postwar period undeniably valorized material pursuits, with a singularity of focus that may remind some of the prewar obsession with war and empire. Whatever antecedents the present-day minimalists of Japan may invoke—and they are just as ready to name Thoreau or Tolstoy, Laozi or Gandhi, as Ikkyū or Ryōkan—the unavoidable backdrop of the current minimalist scene is the modern Japanese pursuit of power and wealth. As we have seen, however, material well-being is necessary but insufficient, and to pursue it relentlessly proves unfulfilling, in part because there are no satisfactory endpoints.

ORDINARY VERSUS EXTRAORDINARY VIRTUES

As noted in chapter 3, an ethos is made up of a habit of thought and a repertoire of practice; that is, an ethos is a complex of normative thinking and reflective action that together disclose a particular value orientation. As applied to expectations regarding individual action and behavior, an ethos is grounded not in abstract principles but in conventional wisdom, a sense of rectitude, and settled norms. There are countless norms in everyday life, such as responding to a friendly greeting or not cutting in line. Most people regard norms as simple rules of conduct and give little thought to their significance or ethical ramifications.[31]

Nevertheless, as just implied, every norm incorporates one value orientation or another. For example, there are poor people in Japan who make serious and sustained efforts to belong to respectable society, such as by observing the norm of washing regularly and thereby both exercising their stake in society and sustaining their self-respect.[32] An elderly homeless man who regularly visits the public library makes special efforts to observe the norm of looking respectable so as to maintain a normal appearance and avoid disturbing others; in other words, he has not given up on belonging to the larger society, and its institutions have not excluded him. As another example, consider the everyday Japanese practice of giving one's seat on the subway to an elderly or infirm passenger. This norm is grounded in the traditional value of revering an elderly person or assisting a person who has a disability. To be sure, this norm is not observed as often as might be expected, and is in something of a freefall in metropolitan Tokyo subways, for instance.

Once norms have weakened, they must be sustained by what I am calling "ordinary virtues," or norms of a specific kind. Ordinary virtues include explicit normative components and ethical injunctions, which is to say that even though these norms are not always observed, the expectation is that they should be. Unlike other norms, then—which are often observed unconsciously, or at least are not explicitly articulated—ordinary virtues entail conscious acts of upholding or enhancing the world of norms, or what Hegel called the *Sittlichkeit,* an ethical order grounded in custom and reproduced by action.[33]

Norms and ordinary virtues stand in contrast to extraordinary, or heroic, virtues, which are often based on abstract moral principles. Extraordinary virtues demand considerable sacrifice for the sake of a transcendental rationale, which is usually articulated abstractly, as in the Kantian categorical imperative. Or take Simone Weil's call for total sacrifice, a virtue whose achievement would catapult one into the ranks of the secular saints.[34] As another example, if Japan's political and military leaders were to seek Japanese military greatness, they might call for heroic self-sacrifice, as was asked of the kamikaze pilots, or if leaders were to seek a society of radical sustainability, the call might be for an ascetic degree of self-abnegation.

But ordinary virtues are just that. They do not demand heroic sacrifices or self-abnegation, nor do they appeal to a higher plane of principles. They reside squarely in the realm of common sense or convention. Indeed, the realm of everyday life is usually not where heroic acts or abstract ideas are to be found, because it is difficult to mobilize people for heroic action or to make them embrace abstract principles and intellectual arguments. Rather, ordinary life relies for its sustenance on norms and ordinary virtues. Someone who wants to lose weight, for example, is well advised to practice the ordinary virtues of eating moderately and exercising instead of adopting the extraordinary measure of an extreme fast. Likewise, if the goal is a sustainable society, people may be able to draw on an earlier ethos, or even earlier norms, for the purpose of practicing, say, the ordinary virtue of conserving resources. In this context, sensible conservation is often more effective than the born-again conservationist's obsession with turning off lights, a remedy as unsustainable as it is annoying to almost everyone else. Ordinary virtues, then, have nothing to do with extreme actions or revolutionary overhauls, though they are ultimately about the limits of what can be consumed, individually or collectively, and about the essentially social character of our existence (as noted in chapter 2, a paradox of egotism is that we are tempted by selfishness but actually obtain more fulfillment and greater freedom through social intercourse).

Where unlimited economic growth is concerned, the flip side is a mode of life that makes sustainability itself sustainable—makes it, that is, both possible and reproducible. Apart from the overall legacy of the Edo regime, and the virtues proper to the Edo period, some cultural correlates of ordinary virtues from that era exist in post-Bubble Japan. It was the bursting of the Bubble that allowed those earlier virtues to resurface after the unsustainability of the postwar regime had been made clear.

AMBITION AND ITS DIMINUTION

To speak of modern Japan at all is to speak of ambition—the heart and soul of the Meiji regime. After the Meiji Restoration, the modal idea imparted to almost everyone (though intended largely for men) was that of *risshin shusse* (autonomy and mobility). This neologism combines the Confucian vocabulary of *risshin* with the secularized rendition of the Buddhist *shusse* to capture the end of the static status order and the beginning of a new world of possibility. *Risshin shusse*, in short, is the individual articulation of *fukoku kyōhei*. The notion of ambition—amplified by the teaching and examples of the Scottish author Samuel Smiles, whose *Self-Help* sold more than a million copies in its Japanese translation and inspired countless copycat works, and by Yukichi Fukuzawa's representative work *Gakumon no susume* (*An Encouragement of Learning*)—was pumped into the atmosphere during the first decade after the Meiji Restoration and was thereafter diffused into the air that every Japanese person breathed.[35] A stock character in modern Japanese fiction is the ambitious lad who comes from the countryside to study in Tokyo, filled with hope and seeking to become a leader of one institution or another. In other words, the modern Japanese man was to make something of himself. The oft-repeated injunction by William S. Clark to the graduates of the Sapporo Agricultural College in 1877 ("Boys, be ambitious!") became one of the major memes of Japanese modernity.[36] And the surest path to success was to study hard, do well on tests, graduate from a top school, and land a job with the government or a large corporation—to be, that is, a nonviolent soldier in Japan's struggle to catch up with the West.[37] This is the classic mold—classic because it would be possible to identify the forebears of this figure in the distant past—of the salaryman.

The emancipation of ambition unleashed dreams of fame and fortune in post–Meiji Restoration Japan. Collectively, the Japanese ambition was to catch up with the West. The dominant conceptualization of *bunmei kaika* (civilization and enlightenment) sought to separate the spiritual and cultural realm from the economic and technological sphere; this was the idea of *wakon yōsai* (Japanese spirit, Western techniques). In reality, however, emulation of the West encapsulated almost every domain.[38] The Meiji emperor set the scene and the tone: while in Kyoto, he wore Heian-style clothes, whitened his face, shaved his eyebrows, and blackened his teeth; in Tokyo, after the Meiji Restoration, he wore a Western-style military uniform and a Western-type mustache.[39] In the national gallery of Meiji leaders, who were so eager to emulate the West and project virility, it is rare to find a cleanly shaven face; they might just as well have been Prussian leaders. Whatever evoked traditional (or Tokugawa-era) practices carried a whiff of shame by comparison with the shimmer of the modern. Indeed, modern Japanese life did not lack for instances of auto-Orientalism (a form of self-hatred) and Occidentalism (adulation and idealizing of the West). For example, as noted in chapter 3, the government encouraged meat eating in order to make Japanese people taller and bigger, like Westerners; discouraged such traditional practices as male homosexuality and mixed-gender bathing; and instituted hegemonic heterosexuality as well as sex-segregated bathrooms.[40] In the Japanese body politic, Occidentalism was manifest in the drive to conquer and rule over the Orient; its maximalist articulation was the Greater East Asia Co-prosperity Sphere, which envisioned Japan at the head of a vast empire stretching across eastern Asia and the Pacific. Even the realm of pure literature came to be all about emulating Western masters and masterpieces.[41] Boys were enjoined to sacrifice their private desires, such as their desires for sex and love, and to pursue individual and public advancement.[42] In keeping with what was then the dominant idea of Social Darwinism, both Japan as a country and the Japanese people as individuals had to struggle for survival in the new world of competition. And just as a boy was expected to preoccupy himself with power and wealth while he achieved manhood, the goal for a girl growing into womanhood was to become a *ryōsai kenbo* (a good wife, and a wise mother).[43] Thus the struggle for an ambitious and modern Japan, far from breaking tradition's stranglehold on Japanese women, ensconced women in the satisfactions of the private sphere—if a boy, following the exhortations of William S. Clark, was to be ambitious, a girl's desires had to be projected onto her husbands and sons. The mother-wife was the mirror of perfection achieved via the cloud of unknowing.

The abject and total defeat of Japan in World War II spelled the end of Japan's martial glory and of imperial adventure as a viable future for the vanquished country. The sadness of surrender was then transmuted into the imperative of recovery. The substance of ambition was expunged, but the form remained, hence the continuity between the Meiji regime and the postwar regime. The postwar period of rapid economic growth instilled a materialist expression of the erstwhile collective goal—catching up with the West, this time economically. By the 1980s, some were taking the cheerleading press seriously, and they dreamed of superseding the United States in the economic realm. But the bursting of the Bubble destroyed that longing. No one in Japan in the 2020s, as far as I can tell, still believes that Japan can become a major military power and geopolitical presence (World War II put an end to that) or even a premier economic engine (the memory of the burst Bubble has lingered). It is not that contemporary Japanese people are not proud of their country's achievements, or that they are not eager to hear praise from outsiders, especially white Westerners. But few believe that Japan is or can be "number one" in any major sphere of human achievement. In other words, the overweening ambition that defined Japanese modernity has withered away in the post-Bubble decades. At least in matters of national ambition, humility is everywhere.

To anyone born in Japan after 1980, the heroics and excesses of the 1980s seem the stuff of fairy tales The propensity to invest heavily, for example, or the expression of entrepreneurial ambition is sometimes taken as a generational marker of Japanese elders who cannot quite renounce the go-go 1980s. Equally difficult to fathom for post-Bubble Japanese young people is the grit and ambition of those who engineered, or merely took part in, the Golden Age of economic growth. The postwar period, as discussed in previous chapters, is in large part a story of economic recovery. The prewar oligopolies (*zaibatsu*) became postwar conglomerates (*keiretsu*), and the large conglomerates became kinder and gentler. Yet we should not overlook the entrepreneurial moment in the immediate postwar decades. Many young people, having faced imminent death during the war, turned their lives toward enriching themselves and reconstructing the country. Ambition was resuscitated and reconfigured from the ashes of defeat. The arrival of a new, democratic era also seemed to open up venues of mobility for rural youth, poor people, and even derided minorities. Indeed, economic recovery and growth could not help trickling down, however unevenly, to the populace at large, with enrichment and ambition nurturing each other.

The postwar generation was steeped in a culture of growth that valorized overwork and ambition. Many Japanese people born in the postwar period and caught up in the notion of *shusse* (advancement) studied in crowded classrooms and sought career advancement—admission to a college or employment by a corporation—

by taking competitive entrance examinations. They embraced material pursuits while rejecting their parents, who not only had failed in their collective project of war and imperialism but were also traditional, and authoritarian to boot. The signal virtue of this younger generation was relentless effort, as emblematized in the notion of *konjō* (guts or grit). Thus it is no surprise that the best-selling manga of the 1960s, at least for boys, told stories about impoverished protagonists who struggled to conquer the world of baseball or boxing (girls had their own heroines, in stories about volleyball or ballet). This postwar genre, now remembered as *supokon* (sports) manga or *konjō* manga, featured protagonists who gushed blood, sweat, and tears as they struggled to improve their skills; they tested their mettle against rivals and strove for Japanese or world championship in their chosen sports. It's hard to resist casting these *konjō* narratives as allegories of postwar Japanese growth. As the contemporary cliché had it, Japan was a small country with meager resources and small bodies (at least in comparison to American bodies), and so Japan had to rely on the diligence and determination of the Japanese people. The cliché itself was a permutation of the wartime Yamato (Japanese) spirit, which was supposed to lead Japan to victory over the much-better-resourced and better-endowed United States. The secret of the protagonist's success in being *majime* (serious) and *kinben* (diligent) was the liberal use of elbow grease. Who cared if the protagonist suffered, more or less continuously? The point of the story was not even the goal or the glory. It was all about the struggle and the striving. The aesthetics of ambition valued the process as much as, if not more than, the end result. Ambition was, in short, a way of life in postwar Japan.

As chapters 1 and 2 reveal, the general direction after the war was onward and upward. The Japanese people had emerged from burned-out houses and fields, shortages of food and other goods, and a general sense of poverty, and they now believed themselves integral to the nation's recovery and growth. And, because everyone belonged to a large birth cohort, no one could escape competition. A sizable portion of the postwar Japanese population harbored dreams, sometimes small but very often large: to become a baseball star, an Olympic athlete, president of a company, a Nobel laureate; to summit Mount Everest; to be wined and dined, and to wine and dine, in Paris. In every sphere of human activity, one could not avoid bumping into some Japanese individual who was seeking out the highest and the best, the rarest and the most expensive. For many, the purpose of life became inextricable from worldly success on a grand and global scale. Japanese ambition knew no bounds.

But the culture of the *dankai* generation (the postwar Japanese baby boomers) looks exotic at best to that generation's children, who came of age during the Bubble decade of the 1980s or later. Usually, though, their parents' culture looks risible or *dasai* (uncool); the blood, sweat, and tears of *konjō* manga have become fodder for satire. Thus *supokon* manga are mercilessly parodied, even as many of the younger generation admit a begrudging respect for some of the genre's protagonists. As one young woman put it, the masochism of *supokon* manga is *itai* (painful, not so much physically as psychically). For example, in one of the iconic *supokon* manga, *Kyojin no hoshi* (Star of the giants), the protagonist, Hoshi Hyūma, born not just poor but also short, has a lifelong rival, Hanagata Mitsuru, who is tall, good-looking, from a wealthy family, and, for good measure, marries Hoshi's sister. Hoshi himself is the product of his father's Spartan training, not to mention the older man's foiled ambition, which has metamorphosed into unremitting and all but sadistic efforts to beat baseball skills into his son.[44] And Hoshi, of course, is all about grit and determination—the theme song from the anime version reprises and rehashes a wartime song in the lyrics "I will try to the end when I have decided to try. / This is the spirit of man."[45] As for the seemingly effortless genius of Hanagata, Hoshi's brother-in-law and rival, it too is the product of relentless exertion. Just as a swan appears to move gracefully over the surface of a pond, but is in fact pedaling furiously under the waterline, everyone (or so the point seems to be) must remain hardworking.

Yet the Japanese sports heroes who emerged in the 2010s radiated sweetness and light, not pain and suffering, though no one doubts that they trained vigorously and systematically. In this, like almost all other Japanese heroes of the post-postwar decades, they were more in the mold of Hanagata than of Hoshi. The superstar figure skater Yuzuru Hanyu is as representative of the type as any. He is completely without the darkness and desperation of a *supokon* manga protagonist, and it is no accident that he adopted Winnie the Pooh as his mascot. As he said after winning the gold medal at the 2018 Olympics, "My really true feeling is that I don't really want to be hated."[46] And it's not just Olympic-level ice skating that has changed. Baseball and boxing, with their fusty ways, have been eclipsed by the more up-to-date sports of soccer and tennis. As for traditional sumo wrestling, the less said, the better—Mongolians now dominate what was once a sacrosanct national sport. Clearly, an era has passed.

War and poverty, too, seem as remote as samurai tales to members of the post-Bubble generation. To them, Japan was always already well off; Japanese affluence has brought them not only comfort but also a general level of satisfaction. Their *dankai* parents had almost no sense of a safety net, but their children can usually rely on them for food and shelter (hence the unflattering moniker *parasite singles*, first encountered in chapter 1).

The notion of advancement is alien to them as well, given the current and widely acknowledged difficulty of gaining admission to a top university or corporation. And in contemporary Japan generally, it is hard to find the type of blind ambition suggestive of the corporal punishment seen in *supokon* manga. There is no more hunger or desperation. There are no outsize goals. There is no longer any need for superhuman grit. As a corporate executive in his sixties told me, "We're not hungry for success—not like Jō." The executive was referring to another hero of 1960s-era *supokon* manga, a boxer who rises from the lower depths and whose ambition is to train and fight until he burns himself all the way down to pure white ash.[47] By the 1990s, the ambition that had fueled Japan's postwar recovery (and the modern Japanese quest to catch up with the West) was already well on its way to being extinguished. What remains today are nostalgia (for the old) and parody (for the young)—the desire to be white has indeed burned down to pure white ash.

Thus the entire culture of effort and ambition has come to be viewed with suspicion and is often labeled *usankusai* (stinky) or, more simply, *uzai* (annoying). Even the idea of visiting exotic locales or of consuming luxury goods seems to the younger generation like the behavior of nouveaux riches, such as Chinese tourists. Foreign travel and fine dining are not dismissed out of hand, but the sense is that one might as well enjoy domestic attractions and that one might do better to scout out spectacular local restaurants serving meals for the equivalent of less than ten US dollars, even if the meal requires a long, long wait.

The generational chasm, then, is decisive, and it comes with a screen of mutual incomprehension. Elders who complain about or criticize their younger counterparts are met with ready responses. If the new generation is accused of lacking the desire for *shusse,* or of being deficient in the spirit of *konjō,* the older generation is asked to explain the point of all the diligence and sacrifice. In the postwar decades, *gaman taikai* (neighborhood-based contests of suffering and persistence) were not uncommon. Their point was to find out, for example, who could hold their breath the longest. But the term *gaman taikai* has become obsolete, and the activity it once denoted can only strike an incredulous twenty-something as absurd.

What, after all, is the point of winning? Entrance into an elite university or corporation, an accomplishment that often seems out of reach, means a life of obligation, rectitude, and sacrifice. The very idea of a lifetime employment guarantee represents, in a sense, a trap. It is not that being a member of the precariat offers an ideal life course. But in a society where class divisions are inscribed in educational attainment, which in turn is based largely on class origins, the vast majority of Japanese people recognize that they are excluded from what has always been a privileged stratum of work. Inequality, often called *kakusa* (status difference), is omnipresent even for privileged young people, and it blocks them with the solidity of a concrete wall.

And so the diminution of ambition has brought forth a culture of contentment. This culture, having forsworn the overweening longings of earlier times, is skeptical of past and future glories, the grand narratives of a Japanese utopia. It represents a form of cultural conservatism in that it doesn't ask for massive changes or improvements. But it does not necessarily reject all change—continuous tinkering is expected, just as artisans may seek to improve on their predecessors' achievements. It is as if the general Japanese attitude toward life has come to reflect a memorable if quite understated exchange between the elderly couple in Yasujirō Ozu's 1953 film *Tokyo monogatari* (*Tokyo Story*). At the end of what appears to have been a disastrous trip, the husband (played by Ryū Chishū) tells his wife that there are no limits to desire and that he and his wife have actually been lucky. His wife (played by Higashiyama Chieko) agrees, saying that the two of them have been not just lucky but happy, too. It is possible to interpret this mind-set as reflecting a Zen metaphysics of sorts, a stoic acceptance of fate. But it can also be seen as symbolizing the wartime generation's denial of its complicity in the misbegotten war. In Kenji Mizoguchi's movie *Ugetsu monogatari* (*Ugetsu*), released the same year, the peasant characters seek to satisfy a variety of worldly desires—to profiteer from war, to seduce an aristocratic woman, to be a samurai—but it all ends badly for them (and this is one of the morals of the book by Ueda Akinari on which the movie is based). *Tokyo monogatari* and *Ugetsu monogatari* were both released a scant eight years after the end of the war, and it wouldn't be much of an interpretive stretch to discern in each of them an allegory of imperial Japanese overreach. In the case of *Tokyo monogatari*, we can transpose distinct generational experiences onto the canvas of a larger and, at that time, very recent history. The elderly couple's generation promoted and fought the war; their children, represented in the film by their youngest son, paid the price. After the war, there were those who busied themselves with the reconstruction of Japan. Others were children, oblivious to the past and the future. In this context, the elderly couple truly is lucky to have survived and even thrived. The Bubble period was not as destructive as the Fifteen Years' War, but in post-Bubble Japanese life there is an undercurrent of feeling that the Japanese people, like the couple in *Tokyo monogatari*, should appreciate what they have. And the Japanese people, like the peasants in Mizoguchi's film, have come to understand the dangers and delusions of ambition and are experiencing renewed gratitude for what they do possess.

For Japanese youth who came of age after the 1990s, it is not so much the getting and spending of the Bubble years that they find difficult to understand. It is the outsize, unreasonable expectations that their elders (usually their parents) have for themselves and their scions. As one recent college graduate told me, "What's the point of studying abroad? Sure, it would have been nice to say I'd gone to Harvard. But it's freezing there, and the food is terrible." Living in Japan is considered much more agreeable than struggling to live in the United States, once the greatest country in the world. A Japanese university may not be the best in the world, but it is pleasant, convenient, and satisfactory. This is the mind-set that is sometimes called *nurumayu no sekai* (the world of the lukewarm bath). And Japan is like a lukewarm bath—pleasing enough, if unsatisfying in some respects, but wonderful to plunge back into after stepping out into the cold cruel world. The people of twenty-first-century Japan are not the swashbuckling heroes of post-Meiji Restoration Japan, or the people who chased dreams of *fukoku kyōhei* and *risshin shusse,* or the striving Stakhanovites of postwar Japan who sought to resuscitate and revitalize their nation as a peaceful, wealthy country. Japan itself in the twenty-first century is simply Japan, a comfortable country. What, again, would be the point of strife and struggle?

With Japanese ambition crumbling, the idea of Japan as an egalitarian society was also undergoing demystification. If the Meiji Restoration had formally ended most aspects of status-based Tokugawa life, Japan's wartime mobilization instilled egalitarianism, however imperfectly.[48] In retrospect, the militarization of prewar Japan has been vilified as nationalist, imperialist, and fascist, especially with respect to Japan's powerful army. But ideological support for the prewar militarization stemmed in no small part from the military's concern with agrarian poverty and inequality. The attempted coup in 1936 by young military officers—the so-called Incident of 2/26—is emblematic of the nationalist and quasi-socialist sentiment that prevailed among some of those youthful officers.[49] By the end of World War II, many Japanese people had already been trained to work collectively, to suppress their individuality, and to spout egalitarian platitudes. The habits born of wartime mobilization, along with the virtues of solidarity, now contributed to the nation's apparently single-minded focus on recovery and growth, diligence and industriousness. The reality of growth, added to those habits and to the ideology of egalitarianism, gave Japan all the rudiments of belief in itself as a classless society. Indeed, in the 1980s, the high tide of Japanese economic growth, equality was one of the most frequently mentioned characteristics of Japanese society.[50] In the Japan of the 1980s almost no one, apart from the odd sociologist or leftist, would have described Japan as an unequal society. By the first decade of the twenty-first century, however, almost everyone was talking about Japan as a society of *kakusa,* a society of disparity.[51] By then, the *furītā* and *nīto* who had begun to appear in the mid-1980s seemed to be everywhere, and around 2004 they became a topic of wide discussion. These ubiquitous under- and unemployed young people marked a sea change from the *dankai* generation, all of whose members appeared to have ended up in long-term employment.

Once the recalcitrant truth of inequality and the tremendous barriers to mobility had been recognized, they could be found everywhere in Japan. This is not to say, however, that the dream of mobility—as represented by the supreme achievement of gaining admission to Tōdai (the University of Tokyo), the most prestigious university in Japan—has withered away completely. The popular manga *Doragon sakura* (Dragon cherry blossom), which appeared in the middle of the first decade of the twenty-first century, kept the dream alive for less privileged students—those from less affluent households, neighborhoods, and regions of the country.[52] But the more powerful trend is to wonder what all the fuss is about. Consider only the proliferation of stories about University of Tokyo graduates who, after all their grinding away, have become full-time mah-jongg players or professional players of video games.[53] Books criticizing Tōdai, which seems at times to be the wellspring of everything that is wrong with contemporary Japan, could fill many shelves. Such totalizing criticism is possible only because of the preponderant role that Tōdai and other elite universities have played in the making of modern Japan. To gain a sense of Tōdai's implausible significance, consider the fact that a renowned journalist wrote a two-volume work positing the emperor system and Tōdai as the twin apex of modern Japanese history.[54] In any event, the edifice erected after the Meiji Restoration has begun to crack, and the fissures are all too evident, not only in Japanese society's structural inequality but also in the futility of the educational rat race. Parental injunctions to study and do homework ring hollow to those who have abandoned the rigged competition for entry into Tōdai. Effort itself is now considered boring, if not *dasai*, overdetermined as its results are by the myriad mechanisms of reproducing inequality.

In short, then, Japan has seen a massive contraction of ambition, and this change shows up even in contemporary language, where *yabō* or *yashin*, used to express "ambition," gives the word a pejorative ring, in contrast with the way ambition was previously valorized and glorified. Now, instead of a society focused on glory and world conquest, we see a world of *chiisana shiawase* (modest happiness), a valorization of ordinary, everyday life.

CULTURAL INVOLUTION

The pursuit of modest happiness—the contraction of ambition—denotes a turn away not only from the extraterritorial expansion of the prewar period but also from the postwar period's relentless hankering after growth and the crude materialistic manifestation of growth during the Bubble era. Instead of expansion aimed at conquering other nations or capturing other markets, there is a reflexive shift away from international adventures. The common sense of the postwar era held Japan to be a small country with a limited market, but the post-Bubble conventional wisdom imagines Japan as a large, culturally homogeneous market rare in the world. Cultural involution has been a dominant motif of the post-Bubble decades. In polemical terms, cultural involution is tantamount to a return to Tokugawa-style soft isolationism.

The phenomenon of Japanese cultural involution implies a sense of arrival. Modernization in Japan was all about catching up with the West, and the postwar articulation of this idea took the form of economic recovery and growth. But there is a dawning recognition that Japan has already caught up or is no longer seeking to do so. Again, no one today is saying that Japan is "number one," and few expect Japan to reign as a premier power in the economic or political realm. Rather, the sense of arrival stems from the idea of Japan as a comfortable, pleasant place, a country sufficiently affluent, one with a long and proud cultural tradition.

Cultural involution is not necessarily reactionary, in the sense either of ejecting all things foreign or returning to the traditional past. The ubiquity of right-wing internet trolls and bloggers notwithstanding, there is no effort to excise all foreign influences from Japanese life. If only because of the contemporary convention of using katakana, a script that denotes foreign provenance, people are well aware that beer and wine originally came from abroad and that baseball and soccer are not indigenous Japanese sports.[55] In addition, no one is actively pushing to turn the clock back to the Tokugawa or Heian period. It is true that a fad for time travel in manga and movies—permutations of *Doctor Who*—has protagonists ending up in one period or another from the Japanese past. All the same, though the past may be interesting, it is no place for contemporary Japanese people. After all, where would one find convenience stores selling sushi? Progressive historiography, whether conservative or Marxist, is united in the conviction that the present is better than the past. If contemporary Japanese people are reluctant to emigrate abroad, they are also disinclined to return to the past, which, they realize, is also a foreign country.

So much for what cultural involution is not, and what it does not represent. What cultural involution does represent is the Japanese people's appreciation of contemporary Japanese society, and their sense that Japan neither needs to nor should keep trying to catch up with the West. The United States and its citizens have long been admired and even loved in Japan for their advancement, wealth, and power and above all for being *kakkoii* (cool), but there is no longer unquestioned adulation. Among young Japanese people, for example, a surprisingly common first impression of the United States has to do with the proliferation of gun violence and the ubiquity of obese people. One young man told me, as his other listeners nodded in approval, "Americans are fat, which is puzzling because the food in the United States is not very good. It's dangerous there, and people don't go out at night, because there's nothing to do." Popular books and television shows that compare living in Japan with living in other countries of the Global North find ordinary Japanese life more convenient and more pleasant.[56] But is it really so surprising that a Japanese national would find it difficult to navigate a foreign language and culture, or more convenient to stay in Japan, however interesting and invigorating a foreign country might be? Admittedly, many women and minorities in Japan find the country less than completely palatable, given the prevailing misogyny and ethno-racial discrimination, but the larger point has to do with the relative comforts of home.

Whatever the validity of such cross-cultural comparisons, contemporary Japanese society is geared to the consumer's convenience. It may be challenging to work long hours in a hierarchical corporation, but Japanese stores, restaurants, and other such establishments provide high standards of service—and, indeed, what makes working for these establishments so challenging is precisely the imperative of service. As a popular postwar saying had it, "The customer is a god."

That may not be quite true, but the customer is at the very least a VIP.[57] Sometimes the sovereignty of the consumer can look like authoritarianism, as when an aggrieved customer, normally polite in the Japanese style, morphs into a demanding, self-righteous tyrant.[58] But attentiveness and politeness are cardinal virtues in the contemporary Japanese service ethos, and they undergird the idea that Japanese culture is one of *omotenashi* (hospitality). Despite the self-serving, ideological character of celebrations of Japanese service, this idea is not wholly untrue. The transactions involved in service are profoundly asymmetrical, of course, and many people find it much less agreeable to serve than to be served. Nevertheless, the idea that service should be excellent is a widely accepted norm.

Convenience for consumers is a key feature of Japanese cultural involution, but it did not appear out of the blue. Casual shopping has long been easy in Japan, thanks to the many convenience stores open every day around the clock, not to mention the omnipresence of vending machines. Even before the advent and rise of Amazon, Japanese consumers enjoyed the luxury of having merchandise delivered from specialty retailers and department stores. And the Japanese system of package delivery is unparalleled. Mechanisms in place in Japan make the shopping experience easy as long as one's credit holds out (though a surprising number of people still pay in cash).

Thus Japan's cultural involution is sustained by the culture of convenience. But the most striking contrast between the contemporary era and the Bubble decade involves the generic preference for things Japanese. Some believe that this turn toward domestic tourism and products stems from confidence or belief in the superiority of Japanese goods and services. Others cite the difficulty of traveling abroad and managing in a foreign language. We should not forget that luxury goods are still largely the province of foreign, or Western, suppliers—a number of great retail pâtissiers and chocolatiers based in France and Belgium, such as Pierre Hermé and Pierre Marcolini, have opened more branches in Tokyo than in their home countries. Nevertheless, the day is gone when ordinary people regarded *hakuraihin* (foreign goods) as unquestionably superior to domestic products, and this change is of a piece with the Japanese reassessment of things Japanese as satisfactory, if not necessarily superior.

But cultural involution has its dark side, too, and in Japan that dark side is widely believed to be the so-called Galapagos syndrome. (The term denotes the isolated development of products, especially technology, that fail to gain global traction.) Like the eponymous island with its unique flora and fauna, post-Bubble Japan has become a land of one-of-a-kind products and services. Whether it's the ultraportable laptop, or the supersophisticated toilet seat that opens by motion sensor or plays music and doubles as a bidet, a striking number of Japanese products are either unavailable abroad or difficult to find outside Japan. Similarly, many Japanese cultural products, including manga and movies, are not exported. For example, the postwar period witnessed the production of incandescent works by Kurosawa, Mizoguchi, and Ozu, among others. It was the Golden Age of Japanese cinema, but how many cineastes can now recall more than a few contemporary Japanese directors? And over the past two decades, when I asked publishers why they weren't trying to translate and export manga, and asked music producers why they weren't making Japanese acts and their records available abroad, the typical answer was that it would be *mendōkusai* (too much work). It would indeed be a nuisance to deal with foreigners in what might be one's broken English—the specter looms of expensive attorneys, if not litigation. And maybe the particular manga or musical act would not do well abroad in any case. But this frequent fall-back on sour grapes is antithetical to the prevailing attitude of the postwar period, when Japanese businesspeople sought to export anything and everything.

Another negative manifestation of cultural involution has been social isolation at the individual level. *Hikikomori* (physical and psychological unwillingness to leave one's room) is a form of agoraphobia that afflicted a number of young Japanese people in the mid-1990s and was widely discussed at the time.[59] The protagonist of *Shinseiki Evangelion* (*Neon Genesis Evangelion*), an anime that was explosively popular precisely when *hikikomori* was a major issue, withdraws completely at the moment of crisis into a metaphorical womb, thus failing to complete his mission and fulfill his presumed destiny to save the world. The phenomenon of *hikikomori* eventually receded, but then along came *sekai-kei*, the tendency to equate one's human (usually romantic) relationship and its problems with a world crisis or even the end of the world itself, all with complete disregard for larger social or historical considerations.[60] Ironically, then, modest happiness comes to concern the entire universe. (It is true, however, that the tendency toward *sekai-kei* is common enough all over the world, at least among youth of romantic bent.)

The internet, of course, by offering anonymity under cover of pseudonyms, fosters balkanized political discussion, thus exaggerating individual differences and perspectives while facilitating a type of extremist speech not often used in face-to-face encounters. In this way, it also engenders a subpolitics of hatred directed against one element or another that is judged not to be "one of us." And so the internet reveals still another facet of Japanese cultural involution's dark side, an inner recess where cultural involution sometimes takes a turn toward nationalism, ethnocentrism, and chauvinism as internet trolls strike out at their enemies—ethnic minorities in Japan, foreigners (especially neighboring Koreans and Chinese), leftists, feminists, and others who deviate from the trolls' prescribed straight-and-narrow path. They can also count on plenty of foreigners, usually white Americans, to lend them a respectable veneer by praising the Japanese and denigrating other Asians.[61] One of the most aggressive social movements in Japan during the 2010s was Zaitokukai.[62] Its adherents don't stop at spewing racist hatred on the internet. They stage public demonstrations where they openly call for the massacre of Zainichi (ethnic Koreans in Japan) and wave the Nazi Hakenkreuz flag.[63] It is paradoxical that Zaitokukai's wrath is focused on this historically oppressed minority, since many present-day Japanese people, not to mention such key aspects of Japanese culture as rice cultivation, trace their origins to the Korean peninsula.[64] The racist Zaitokukai movement is flanked by chauvinist and xeno-phobic fellow travelers who disseminate *netouyo* or *netto uyoku* discourses (that is, discourses of the internet-based right). Some analysts see this phenomenon as unique to Japan, but it is surely worldwide; in the Global North it is commonly identified as populism. Given the global upsurge in xenophobia and racism, the potential exists for the Zaitokukai movement, with its particular focus on Zainichi, to find new adherents and contribute to Japan's drift toward isolationism. A similar discourse and strand of thought is now undertaking a reappraisal of both Japan's prewar past and the kamikaze pilots.[65] This will not mean a return to prewar Japan. It would take years, probably decades, for Japan to rebuild the necessary military power, to say nothing of the massive cultural change that would be required. But it is not completely out of the question for the people of Japan to unite in hatred and struggle against enemy outsiders.

Nevertheless, we should not regard all xenophobic and racist outbursts as her-alding a turn toward isolationism. Such outbursts represent, in part, an expression of counterglobalization sentiment aimed at sustaining a particular way of life. It is true that the Abe administration pursued a pro-business policy of expanding the supply of foreign workers, but that policy was far from a program for admitting anyone and everyone. Rather, it was an effort to secure a supply of relatively inex-pensive labor. The postwar regime, then, has sought to align itself with the forces of global capitalism, and the regime's desire for exports and growth remains powerful. Among many Japanese people, however, especially the young, there is no longer much of a cultural basis for Japan's vaunted ambition and global orientation.

SOCIALIZED INDIVIDUALISM

In commentaries on Japan, it is almost an article of faith that Japan is different from other countries and that, among its many differences, its holistic and collec-tivist nature stands out; that is, Japan is said to valorize group orientation at the expense of the individual. In keeping with the old proverb that tells of how the nail that sticks out gets hammered down, it is believed that in Japan it is unwise to enact social deviance or express an individual opinion. In addition, the power of conformity and group orientation is said to discourage the exercise of personal autonomy and expressive individualism in Japanese life. Thus Japan is seen as a country where Enlightenment ideals, including the ideal of the autonomous indi-vidual, remain insufficiently rooted and underdeveloped, whether because of tra-ditional Japanese influences or because of the lack of Westernization. And there is some truth in the conventional wisdom regarding the absence of Western-style individualism in Japan. Surveys repeatedly show that the most valued principle of living in contemporary Japan is *tanin ni meiwaku wo kakenai* (not bothering others). Japanese ideals do not involve such abstract principles as truth or beauty, God or the sovereign individual, but tend instead to be amorphous, ostensibly neither abstract nor principled. Or, to take the high road of intellectual history, Japanese reflections on the nature of the self have repeatedly found that the modern, or Western, idea of the individual or the ego either does not exist in Japan or cannot be assimilated into Japanese life. In fact, the typical narrative of modern Japanese literature or philosophy tends to focus on the formation of *kindaiteki jiga* (the modern ego) as the basic problematic. Almost all the flaws in modern Japanese life—including militarism and imperialism, the autocratic emperor system, and antidemocratic forces and sentiment—have been traced to failed attempts to transplant the Western notion of the modern ego into the arid Japanese soil.[66]

This modernist, ethnocentric narrative is tendentious, however.[67] On the one hand, it is far from clear that the modern ego has flourished even in the modern West. In the United States, the brilliant findings of post–World War II social psychology, beyond recalling unfortunate historical events (and the modern twentieth century is replete with instances of unreflective xenophobia, even genocide), have shown precisely the absence of cognitive autonomy in supposedly individualist Americans of intelligence and conscience. In research such as Solomon E. Asch's experiments on conformity and Stanley Milgram's study of obedience to authority, the majority of subjects failed miserably to act on their individual judgment or conscience.[68] On the other hand, it is not as if modern Japanese history were devoid of people acting on the basis of individual conscience, even in the face of the majority's disapproval, a majority that includes family members, friends, teachers, and colleagues. Apart from concrete cases of everyday heroism, such individuals have also been lionized in novels and movies, manga and anime. Consider Hayao Miyazaki's classic anime *Sen to Chihiro no kamikakushi* (*Spirited Away*). In the opening scene, the ten-year-old protagonist is a dependent, spoiled child, but she learns over the course of the film to think and act on her own. She achieves her independence in part by avoiding negative models—her parents, who gobble suspect food and are turned into pigs, and the eerie Kaonashi (a faceless demon), which doesn't know what it wants to do and pursues its desires mindlessly—and in part by valuing the principles of mutuality and helping others. This anime is intended mainly for children, of course, but its powerful criticism of environmental destruction and capitalist greed goes hand in hand with the potential of the individual to fight for justice, however frightening and challenging the fight may be. I mention Miyazaki's anime partly because when I reflect on my own moral education, the four years I spent in a Japanese public school were formative. Some of the generalized postwar democratic lessons in moral education included the virtues of honesty, kindness, persistence, cooperation, following rules, not bothering others, and valuing human life.[69] Needless to say, moral education has been rendered suspect by its prewar, militarist articulation and by recent efforts to enhance conservative patriotism; but, formally or informally, one does learn moral lessons in school. I recall vividly some of the moral lessons I learned from teachers I didn't much like, such as treating others equally, speaking one's mind, and standing up for one's convictions even if they seem unpopular. This kind of ordinary virtue, involving individual conscience and courage, undoubtedly stems from the vogue for peace education as well as from Japan's regret over its prewar militarism. Be that as it may, lessons of individual conscience do permeate contemporary Japanese life.

We can see differences between the United States and Japan in another prevalent twenty-first-century genre of popular culture—stories about zombies. Past their common point of departure—a dystopian near future in which mindless, semideceased individuals roam about and act like rabid, anthropophagic dogs—US and Japanese zombie narratives display considerable cultural divergence. In the United States, *The Walking Dead*, a wildly popular cable television series based on a comic book, presupposes a Hobbesian state of nature in which desperate individuals gather into groups and usually succumb to one authoritarian leader or another, though the chief protagonist, Rick, maintains a glimmer of personal dignity and democratic respect for others.[70] Despotic communities engage in constant tribal warfare. Even after a social contract has been established, life remains cold and brutal for the show's characters. The contrast between *The Walking Dead* and the Japanese manga series *I AM A HERO* is striking, though the postapocalyptic zombie world is no less virulent and frightening in Japan. The protagonist, Hideo, has an idiosyncratic hobby—riflery—and it is precisely this hobby that allows him to survive. There are few guns and rifles in Japan, and so there is correspondingly less bloodshed than in the fictional post-apocalyptic United States. But the reason for this disparity is not merely technological; after all, guns don't kill people all by themselves. Rather, there is less bloodshed because Hideo, a manga writer and prototypical *otaku* (geek or nerd), maintains his pre-apocalyptic mode of interacting with others. He is utterly ordinary and normal in the sense that almost no one seems to notice him.[71] Whereas his counterparts in *The Walking Dead* have no qualms about pillaging abandoned retail outlets, Hideo continues to leave money on the counter when he helps himself to something from a convenience store. Needless to say, there is something odd about Hideo's continuing his pre-apocalyptic behavior and retaining his politeness, just as there is something rational about the way in which *The Walking Dead*'s Rick and his fellow characters have made a decisive break with the past. After the veneer of civilization has been stripped away, the Americans conform to nature, red in tooth and claw as they find it, whereas Hideo and the other Japanese characters continue to follow a great number of their pre-apocalyptic social rules. It appears, then, that Americans can imagine only a post-apocalyptic life of struggle, and that Japanese people cannot imagine a post-apocalyptic life that lacks a modicum of civilization, including manners. We should not make too much of comparative zombiology, of course, or of this divergence in imagining an extreme situation. More often than not, however, we die as we have lived.

The Japanese have their fair share of moral cowardice and unthinking conformity, and it would be pointless to deny this. But the ideal of the modern ego, precisely because it has been debated, questioned, and examined, does exist and exert its pull on contemporary Japanese society. People know about the modern ego, and about the presumptive Japanese failure to achieve it, and so it exists as a regulative ideal that, in surprising moments, shapes people's actions and decisions. But the modern ego is not just a matter of unbounded self-interest. It is also a matter of conscience and conviction. In this context, the idea of not bothering others is much less about stifling one's desires and conforming to the collectivity than about tempering the tendency to enforce one's will and impose one's desires on others. By 2020, for example, cell phones had become ubiquitous in Japan, but I found it striking that almost all the passengers on a train would put their phones away and use them only in one of the areas between the train's compartments. This behavior may look like nothing more than automatic conformity to a prevailing social norm, but when I asked Japanese people why they refrained from using their phones on the train, most replied that talking on the phone, though tempting, would disturb others. "It's a violation of common etiquette," one middle-aged man told me. "There are other people on the train, and I don't like it when someone next to me talks on the phone. It's an unspoken rule, and everybody follows it—or should." In other words, this is a norm that verges on being an ordinary virtue, a form of socialized individualism—recognizing the existence of others and exhibiting a minimal level of care for them as people like oneself. It is not just this particular norm but also the exercise of this ordinary virtue that makes the libraries and lounges of Tokyo so much quieter than those of almost any other metropolitan center in the world.[72] Alas, this particular manifestation of ordinary virtue appeared to be in steady decline in the early 2020s.

In no sense does contemporary Tokyo fit the classic definition of a community. One can identify in Tokyo neither a commonality of will nor any widespread social and cultural likeness and homogeneity. Rather, contemporary Tokyo is a sprawling, dense, impersonal entity where civil indifference reigns. How, then, does the city function? It functions in part through the mechanisms of large bureaucracies—for example, the trains and buses that run on time. But the city also works in part because of socialized individualism, that is, the social norms and ordinary virtues by which individuals subscribe to the values of humility and modesty and curb excessive egocentric behavior.[73] It is not that contemporary Japanese people dislike pursuing their individual interests and desires, or that their close relatives and neighbors impose strictures on their behavior. Rather, they have adopted what can be described as, for lack of a better phrase, a broadly sociological understanding of the place of individuals and their expressions.[74] Contemporary Japanese people understand the existence of others. They understand social relations and networks, and even abstract concepts like society and the globalized world—the ABCs of scientific sociology. As a result, any propensity for excessive and expressive individualism operates within that largely shared context of social forces. Socialized norms and ordinary virtues outline the broad contours of a space in which people, by force of necessity, live with others while maintaining a level of propriety and politeness usually possible only in smaller cities and towns.

All this politeness notwithstanding, there is no shortage of hate speech in contemporary Japan, as we have seen, but it is limited to cyberspace, where it flourishes behind the screen of anonymity. The domain of face-to-face interaction continues to be governed by civil inattention and ritualized politeness. At the same time, just as privacy is a cherished ideal in Japan (and this accounts for the fact that almost all blog posts and other online commentary are pseudonymous), so is the right of free speech. Indeed, I spoke with many left-leaning intellectuals who said that for the sake of this basic human right, hate speech should be protected rather than curbed. Thus, even though Japanese ideals tend not to be based on abstract principles, such principles do play a role in Japanese life and are often invoked to justify the taking of one stand or another.

And there is more to say about socialized individualism. The principle of not bothering others, though formulated negatively, is an explicit rejection of grand projects and narratives that would sacrifice individual desires and happiness to the greater good. As discussed earlier, modern Japanese history has not lacked for great visions—most tragically, visions of war and conquest. The Bubble years, though far less destructive than the project of imperialism and militarism, still loom as a stark reminder of limitless greed in particular and of grand narratives in general. The celebrated feats of a kamikaze pilot, or those of a parvenu financier, are another reminder that such achievements are not particularly conducive to, and may even prove fatal to, modest happiness. Demystified or disenchanted, the ethos of the sustainable society depends precisely on a socialized individualism shorn of illusions and delusions. It depends, that is, not on the practice of extraordinary virtues by heroic individuals but on the practice of ordinary virtues in everyday life.

TOILET CLEANING, OCCUPATIONAL EGALITARIANISM, AND THE ORDINARY VIRTUE OF CLEANLINESS

At elite universities in the contemporary United States, there are dormitory crews made up of students who clean their fellow students' restrooms. This state of affairs obviously contradicts the egalitarian ethos touted at the self-described best universities in the world. According to one student who works on such a cleaning crew, "A restroom, urine and feces, is the worst of the worst. . . . To have to get on your hands and knees and scrub their toilets, it says a lot about the divides here between who has to work and who doesn't."[75] The author of the study that is the source of this student's comment endorses her observation: "When poor students scrubbed rich students' bathroom counters and toilets, their relationship mirrored worker-client relationships in the outside world and set up a hierarchy between them."[76] The point is well taken, though it leaves unaddressed the question of just who *should* be cleaning toilets—presumably those who do not have the opportunity to study at elite universities.

Consider, in contrast, the crew that services Shinkansen, the famed Japanese bullet trains that are not only fast and punctual but also remarkably clean. The job of restroom cleaning is done in seven minutes. Given that there are inevitably drunkards who vomit or even defecate in urinals—and trains do sway, so there are plenty of opportunities for eliminative streams to miss the target—one would expect the task of toilet cleaning to fall on the newest employees. It turns out, though, that skilled or experienced workers usually do the job.[77] I have talked with dozens of Shinkansen toilet cleaners, and their responses converge on the gist of what one man in his fifties told me: "Yes, it's dirty and smelly, and it's tough. I wouldn't do it if it weren't my job. But it's a very important job, and it's a challenge. It makes me feel good to see a *pika pika* [shiny] toilet." Like the student quoted earlier, these toilet cleaners must get on their hands and knees and scrub. It's easy to see that the student suffers from the ignominy of doing a job so far beneath her talents and prospects. But the Shinkansen toilet cleaners, even though they dislike the sights and smells, and even though they have fewer years of schooling and correspondingly modest prospects, come out of the same experience with a feeling of self-respect and even pride in a job well done.[78] A woman in her sixties who talked with me said, "Sometimes I take my gloves off to get rid of the tough dirt. But it's rewarding. It makes me feel good to think that all the trains I cleaned will have riders who won't be inconvenienced by the sight or smell of a dirty toilet."

An old-fashioned Marxist might see in this attitude an instance of false consciousness—cleaning jobs are not particularly well remunerated in Japan, and the Shinkansen toilet cleaners should be paid more. But they take pride in their work and find it meaningful. They partake of *shokunin katagi* (the artisanal ethos), and they share a worldview in which all occupations are worthy of respect and dignity, however unequal they may be in terms of pay or status. It's completely banal, of course, to say that something worth doing is worth doing well, but there is a quiet grandeur in this view of life. Without this belief, there is only the reality of a low-level, poorly paid job.

Niitsu Haruko is a master custodian who has been working at Tokyo's Haneda Airport for twenty-five years. She is fully aware that some regard her as invisible or as having low status, but she takes enormous pride in her work: "Once I'm at the airport, I work like it's my own home."[79] Her job, far from simple and unskilled, requires a combination of expertise and experience, effort and dedication. "How much effort you put into your work is something you yourself know best," she says, and this is why she invokes *ichigo ichie,* an idea from the Japanese tea ceremony that points to the singular character of every encounter or experience.[80] It may be something of a stretch to see a world in a clean urinal, or eternity in a traveler's single encounter with an airport toilet, but there is poetry and philosophy in this worker's pride and dignity. The ordinary virtue of endowing one's work with significance and of diligently bringing one's skill and experience to bear on one's work has helped make Haneda Airport the cleanest in the world and a source of pride and rewards for its cleaning crews.

Niitsu, who comes from a humble background, is not the only one who takes toilet cleaning seriously. Matsushita Kōnosuke—the late founder of the electronics giant Panasonic, who is regarded as the god of business management in Japan—used to insist on training all new employees to clean not only their office spaces but also the restrooms. The manifest logic of this practice was that a sanitary environment is beneficial to work and facilitates efficiency. Just as important, Matsushita said, the act of cleaning inculcates the value of persistence and provides practical lessons in business thinking as employees figure out how to use a cleaning cloth more effectively and which cleaning motions work best. Matsushita reportedly once cleaned a toilet himself when his employees failed to do so. His outlook reflects an underlying belief in Japanese life that cleaning a toilet is a way of polishing oneself.[81] A senior executive of a large automobile company offered another example when he told me, "Cleaning is really basic. It's important for sustaining the human spirit." Still another is the businessman in his fifties who said, "How can you trust someone who is not clean or who cannot clean? Cleaning is fundamental not just to business but to life." Or, as the founder of Honda Motors put it in 1953, "Superior products won't be born in a dirty or cluttered environment."[82] Marie Kondo didn't come out of nowhere.

The entwining of cleaning with business has made for a thriving industry in Japan. No one has systematically investigated the relationship between cleaning and business success, but the cleanliness outlook and its practices appear to have become widespread in the later Edo period.[83] Nineteenth-century Western observers in Japan often remarked that ordinary Japanese people were constantly cleaning themselves and their surroundings. And artisans were at the forefront, performing cleanliness rituals before, during, and after work, as they do today. In tradition-minded establishments, the received practice is not only to clean inside but also to sweep in front of the store or restaurant and to splash water outside to keep the dust at bay (most streets now are paved, but the practice continues).

Visitors to contemporary Japan continue to find the country clean. Passengers of All Nippon Airways, ranked the cleanest airline in the world, enter a spotless cabin. What is more striking, and by contrast with the dismal situation on US planes, the passengers benefit from the frequency with which the flight attendants clean the restrooms.[84] Moreover, the job of flight attendant is a prestigious one for women in Japan, where almost all flight attendants are indeed women; many are university graduates as well. And as a walk around Tokyo reveals, it is unusual to find trash on the streets of this sprawling metropolis of more than nine million people, but it is not unusual to find people cleaning—and not just professional cleaners, either, but ordinary people going about their daily lives. The norm until recently was to sweep in front of one's own house as well as around other houses in the immediate vicinity, and this practice set up a minicompetition of sorts among neighbors. Although the practice has nearly disappeared from central Tokyo, the city remains remarkably neat and clean.

Sushi chefs in Japan are also constantly cleaning while they work. Their obsession with cleaning extends to constant handwashing.[85] The successful operation of most sushi restaurants relies on the health of one person—the chef—and it is extremely rare to find a sushi establishment closed. The people who become sushi chefs in Japan are probably not the beneficiaries of an exceptional genetic endowment. I can only speculate that at least a significant part of their robust physical health is due to their obsession with cleanliness, apart from the fact that they work in a scrupulously clean environment, eat fresh food, and are in constant motion while they work.

Cleaning is an integral part of Japanese family life and is enforced at work, but Japan has also institutionalized classroom cleaning. A salutary feature of primary education in Japan is that all students participate in cleaning their classroom (though they usually do not clean toilets in primary school). In one survey, 97 percent of teachers agreed that students should learn about cleaning and other living skills.[86] These practical lessons in cleaning extend to an ethical lesson regarding the dignity of all lines of work.

The cleanliness culture has its tainted side, of course. At its extreme, a preoccupation with cleanliness becomes obsessive-compulsive disorder. It is also not without significance that the Meiji regime, especially the military, was highly focused on cleanliness, and that the cleaning rituals in primary schools sometimes entail excessive discipline and imposition of a teacher's will, to the exclusion of students' well-being.[87]

Cleanliness, needless to say, is not a virtue unique to Japan. A mother in the United States is just as likely as a mother in Japan to admonish her children to wash and be clean. But what distinguishes the two countries on the dimension of cleanliness is the attitude of each toward toilet cleaning in particular and occupational egalitarianism in general. Indeed, one waits in vain for a business leader in the United States to proclaim the virtues of toilet cleaning, much less scrub a toilet himself. Furthermore, in the self-proclaimed egalitarian United States, toilet cleaning is a grossly underpaid job, and schoolchildren are urged to study hard so they won't have to grow up to be janitors, though why a janitor's work is anything less than honorable is never explained.

Occupational egalitarianism in Japan has deep roots in *shokunin katagi*. Proud and independent artisans propagated the artisanal ethos, which stressed both self-confidence and responsibility.[88] The relatively privileged position of some Edo-period artisans undoubtedly contributed to their sense of pride in their work.[89] In spite of existing status hierarchies, each status group engaged in equally significant and noble pursuits. And Edo-era egalitarianism, compromised though it was by status hierarchies and other expressions of inequality, continues to exert influence over Japanese life. Every occupation today in Japan has its value and is therefore considered deserving of respect and dignity. The idea of occupational egalitarianism is also an important tenet of moral education. It is unclear how strong an impact the practice of cleaning or the theory of work's dignity had on ordinary Japanese people of the Edo period, but the associated lessons seem to have become part of ordinary Japanese life today.

If the world of artisans remains unequal and hierarchical today, it is because there are status distinctions between masters and apprentices as well as different levels of talent and skill, income and prestige. Nevertheless, artisans share a sense of equality born of their pursuing the same craft, and that sense encompasses basically all crafts and occupations. The imperative to respect all occupations was strongly emphasized during the war years in order to elicit support for the war. The same imperative was enforced by postwar democratic impulses, and it remains a powerful current in contemporary Japanese life, attenuated though this current is by income inequality and a globalization ethos that separates winners from losers.

But the notion of occupational egalitarianism also risks becoming an ideology that can serve to justify inequality. Isn't it better to hate one's degrading, meaningless job than to make it into an occasion of pride? It would be best if the value of occupational egalitarianism were tangibly honored in the form of equal, or at least more egalitarian, pay. But the cold reality is that there's a job to be done. Shouldn't it be done well, if it is to be done at all? And shouldn't people take pride and find significance in what they do instead of loathing their jobs and hating themselves for working at them?

Some Japanese people are openly contemptuous of the whole notion of occupational egalitarianism. Not uncommonly, people express disrespect of and disgust for jobs that are considered dirty, such as toilet cleaning. Nor is it uncommon in

Japan to find women cleaning men's public toilet facilities while the men themselves go about their own thing. Neither is it entirely uncommon to hear men, especially younger men (and some women), talk about the undesirability of custodial employment. This newer, more instrumental outlook is a departure from the older artisanal ethos. As such, it threatens the view that all work is worthy and deserving of respect. Instead, it measures work's value in terms of the income it generates or the prestige it commands. All the same, the value of occupational egalitarianism—the idea that all types of work are worthy of respect and dignity—remains alive in contemporary Japan.

5

The Book of Sushi

There is a sushi restaurant in central Tokyo that I have been patronizing for more than thirty years.[1] It is somewhat typical of the city's postwar Edo-style sushi purveyors. There are only nine seats. There are three different *omakase* (prix fixe) courses, ranging in price from the equivalent of roughly ten to thirty US dollars, including tax and tip. And the dishes are served in a matter of minutes, in keeping with sushi's origins as fast food or street food. The establishment serves primarily walk-in customers, as was usual during the postwar period, though many customers are *jōrensan* (regulars), and the restaurant does take dinner reservations. I have eaten there perhaps once or twice a year, but the chef recognizes me and presumes that I live somewhere near the restaurant. He is also aware of my spending habits, and he raises one eyebrow ever so slightly when I order a more expensive course than usual. We generally don't talk much, beyond greetings, though we do have the occasional extended discussion about the fickle weather or about which kinds of seafood are in season. He makes sushi, and I devour it.

In the mid-2010s, a printed notice appeared next to this restaurant's counter, and the apologetic chef also paraphrased it for me. The notice said that the establishment was raising its prices by 10 percent. There is nothing remarkable about inflation, seemingly as inevitable as death and taxes. The remarkable thing was that this was the restaurant's first price increase in thirty-eight years. The restaurant had opened in 1970, with several subsequent price increases and occasional turnover in apprentices and assistants, but for nearly fifty years the same chef had been composing one plate of sushi after another.[2] It was the chef's first day back after the New Year's break (most Japanese workers take off anywhere from three days to a week after New Year's Day), and his apology segued into his good wishes for the new year. As he set the first plate on the counter before me, he said he was glad to be back at work. During the break, he complained, there had been nothing to do; he had puttered around, been bored, and slept a great deal. When I said that his enforced leisure sounded heavenly, he chuckled. He couldn't live without making sushi, he said—sushi was his *ikigai* (raison d'être or reason for living).

It may be irrational not to raise one's prices to what the market will bear, just as it may be irrational to minimize one's leisure time by working long hours, day after day. But the sushi chef exemplifies the spirit of the *shokunin* (skilled artisan) and the *shokunin katagi* (artisanal ethos). In the words of an adage that is much bandied about, "If you want to make money, become a *shōbainin* (businessperson); if you want to make sushi, become an artisan." It's a contrived distinction, of course, since a businessperson lacking in skill and effort can realize little profit in a competitive economy, and no amount of spiritual zeal will allow an artisan to survive without remuneration. But the world of Tokyo's sushi chefs is powered and given meaning by a symbolic economy of pride and prestige. The work of a sushi chef exemplifies the artisanal ethos, a topic expanded on in chapter 6. For now, suffice it to say that where the artisanal ethos reigns, work is an end in itself and a source of personal satisfaction for the worker, or artisan. And when the artisan is a chef, the work also provides extraordinary levels of alimentary delight for the chef's customers.

THE EMERGENCE OF EDOMAE SUSHI

According to one authority, 90 percent of the world's estimated two hundred thousand sushi chefs do not regularly handle raw fish, which is what the word "sushi" means to most Japanese diners.[3] But there is actually a bewildering variety of sushi, both in Japan and in the world at large. Let's focus for now on Edomae (that is, Edo-style) sushi.

Edo, as noted in chapter 3, is the former name of Tokyo. Edo was the seat of the Tokugawa shogunate during what is known in Japan as the Edo period (1603–1868)—in Western academic parlance, the Tokugawa period. It was in the early decades of the nineteenth century, and in the littoral zone of Edo, that the modern form of Edomae sushi emerged—a piece of seafood (or occasionally cooked egg or vegetable) served over vinegar-infused rice.[4] In spite of its belated emergence, Edomae sushi soon took pride of place as an exemplary Edo food, along with tempura, *soba* (buckwheat noodles), and *unagi* (freshwater eel).[5] In a 1915 novel by Nagai Kafū, a character is asked to name the most representative way of eating in Tokyo, and he replies, "Eating sushi or tempura, standing up."[6] And as Nagase Ganosuke points out in a work published in 1930, "Not one out of a hundred dislikes sushi," which he considers a food appropriate to what he calls "the age of speed."[7] Sushi, he continues, "is for teetotalers and drunkards; children like it, old people like it, women ... and men," and up and down the status hierarchy.[8] In short, sushi has been recognized as a representative national dish for more than a century. Western foods may have attained more prestige and become more expensive in modern Japan, but they have never dethroned sushi as an object of culinary love and desire.[9]

Edomae sushi was born in the Kasei period (1804–30), a time of spectacular cultural flowering. Kitamura Nobuyo, a nineteenth-century chronicler of Edo life, observes, "The world of sushi changed completely when Matsuga Sushi appeared in Fukagawa [an area in Edo] around the beginning of the Bunka era [1804–18]."[10] The establishment's fame can be gleaned by *senryū* (haiku-like poems) that mention its delicious, beautiful, expensive sushi.[11] Other commentators point to Yohee Sushi, a restaurant founded in 1824 in Ryōgoku, as the pioneer of Edomae sushi. Although no one can be sure, Yohee Sushi appears to have focused on *nigirizushi*, the form common today.[12] This struggle over bragging rights is moot, given the absence of contemporary successors, though the restaurant Yoshino Sushi, in Nihonbashi, founded in 1880, claims a relationship to Yohee Sushi.[13] But there are older continuously operating sushi establishments, such as Bentenyama Miyako Sushi (founded in 1866) and Futaba Sushi (founded in 1877). Sushi, offered as street food sold in stalls as well as by peddlers, was a snack prepared by and for ordinary townspeople. It was widely available and, despite some expensive venues, reasonably priced. Kitagawa Morisada, a merchant hoping to make his mark by recording accounts of everyday life, wrote: "It is rare to be anywhere in Edo without a few sushi establishments."[14] One of the earliest restaurant guides, published in 1848, lists numerous venues, and some of them appear to have offered seating to diners.[15] Thanks to Kitagawa's detailed descriptions, we know that Edomae sushi from the beginning featured *kohada, tamago,* and *kanpyō* (more on those terms later), which still define Edomae sushi. A poor samurai writing in his diary around 1860 reports having eaten sushi fourteen times a year; he mentions wasabi and *gari* (pickled ginger), still the essential accompaniments to Edomae sushi, and he comments on sushi's affordability.[16] From the standpoint of the present-day world of Edo-style sushi, then, Edomae sushi appears to have been born fully formed, if not fully grown.

It is a truism in contemporary Japan that sushi is expensive. I spoke with many sushi chefs who talked about the existence of a sushi bubble and about the price-based polarization of sushi restaurants, but the reality is that sushi had already become a delicacy by the postwar period, if not earlier. For example, the signature story by Shiga Naoya, putative god of the novel, was published in 1920 and is based on a young apprentice's inability to afford a piece of sushi.[17] In the story, the apprentice's older colleagues talk about the food stalls where customers eat standing up (or perhaps sit on makeshift chairs, not at a counter or table), and it is their talk that elicits the apprentice's own desire to eat sushi. But the fact that this impoverished youngster cannot afford sushi does not mean that sushi was only for the wealthy at the time when Shiga's story was published. After all, the young man's colleagues (whose ranks the apprentice will probably join soon enough) have modest jobs. Sushi's plebeian origins made it a food more for the common people than for the ruling samurai class. Nagase, writing in 1930, observes that sushi is like a sandwich—a snack, not a meal—and that one should eat only three or four pieces at a time, as befits a bite between meals.[18]

After the Meiji Restoration, the rich and powerful began slowly to sample this lowly street food. Sushi is rarely mentioned in Murai Gensai's *Kuidōraku* (Gourmet), one of the earliest gourmet novels, published in 1904–5, though this long novel includes more than six hundred recipes for Western and Chinese dishes, as well as for types of Japanese food other than sushi.[19] Similarly, a history of Japanese cuisine published almost a hundred years after *Kuidōraku* has almost nothing to say about sushi, tempura, or, for that matter, most of the other popular dishes found in contemporary Japan, such as *karē* (curry), *tonkatsu* (fried pork cutlet), and ramen.[20] For traditionalists, Japanese food is Kyoto-based *kaiseki* cuisine; sushi is for the masses.

Perhaps the first modern specimen of a *zeitaku sushi* (luxury sushi) restaurant was Shintomi, which opened in Shinbashi in the late 1910s. Baroness Ōkura Kumiko, writing in the mid-1920s, observes that the takeout sushi from Shintomi is not very good, but when her husband invites the chef to make sushi at their estate, it is "fabulous."[21] Most *Edokko* (Edoites) consumed sushi from street vendors or itinerant peddlers, and most post–Meiji Restoration Tokyoites relied on the same venues. By the early twentieth century, the clientele had expanded to include the nobility and the wealthy, but sushi remained within the reach of the masses (if not that of lowly apprentices). Yasui Tekiji's 1935 guide to good eateries in Tokyo includes some sushi shops, but they were mostly establishments where the customers ate standing up.[22] In Okamoto Kanoko's resplendent 1939 story "Sushi," the protagonist, the daughter of a sushi restaurant proprietor, is embarrassed by her father's occupation.[23] The customers Okamoto describes—a dentist, the owner of a rifle shop, a vendor of rabbit meat—run the gamut from those who live in the affluent Yamanote area to those from Shitamachi (respectively, the higher and lower sectors of Tokyo, geographically and socially). Well into the postwar period, however, snobbish Western-oriented or wealthier gourmets continued to prefer Western food or Kyoto-based Japanese food over Edo-style cuisine.[24]

As late as the 1960s, sushi was still regarded as street food or as fare for snacking by some Tokyoites. Tanemura Suehiro recalls that he and his father ate sushi on the way to or from the *sentō* (public bathhouse) and that sushi was not for "white-collar workers."[25] During the prewar period, some sushi restaurants began to approximate the architecture and interior décor of contemporary sushi restaurants, but it was only in the 1960s that such conventions became widespread.[26] The ubiquitous counter, for example, though it had first appeared in the 1920s, did not become commonplace until the postwar period.[27] Miyao Shigeo, in a pioneering book on fine sushi dining in Tokyo that was published in 1960, claims that by the late 1950s the city had about seventy good sushi restaurants.[28] Even then, however, most Tokyoites continued to eat sushi on the run or had it delivered for a feast at home. Thus, although it is common to date the advent of dining out in Tokyo to 1970, that chronology is misleading because Edo had long been a town with plenty of street food and peddlers, teahouses and restaurants.

The yearnings of the apprentice in Shiga's story are one thing, but it would be quite another to find a contemporary Tokyoite who can't afford the inexpensive sushi sold in convenience stores—almost no one suffers from that level of food insecurity. Personal finances aside, however, it's not at all unusual for people to be hesitant about stepping into a sushi restaurant. Especially at the more expensive venues, everything seems opaque. How much does a meal cost? How does one order? How should one behave? On all these questions, to be sure, there has been a visible trend toward transparency, particularly since the phenomenal success of the restaurant Tsukiji Sushi Sei in the 1980s. In that decade, the restaurant, which dates to the early Meiji era, introduced price transparency and a dining experience that, if relatively inexpensive, was still luxurious, and the restaurant soon expanded to become a chain. Even more accessible and inexpensive are the *kaitenzushi* (conveyor-belt sushi) establishments, easily spotted throughout Tokyo if only because of their large signs. And almost every neighborhood in Tokyo has a sushi restaurant for locals who stop in for a small treat (or, not uncommonly, request home delivery). Again, sushi is an enduring favorite of the Japanese people.

CONFESSIONS OF A SUSHI EATER

An estimated thirty-six hundred sushi establishments now operate in contemporary Tokyo, though that number is misleading because it excludes restaurants that deliver and offer takeout as well as many that serve sushi only incidentally, not to mention the great number of sushi-purveying convenience stores, supermarkets, and department store food courts.[29] But, whatever their total count, Tokyo's sushi establishments offer a staggering diversity of prices, quality, and dining experiences. For example, some lunch spots serve sushi for less than the equivalent of eight US dollars; these places are known as *B-kyū gurume* (class B gourmet) restaurants. Other restaurants feature a course menu whose cost approaches the equivalent of five hundred US dollars. Then there are the demotic outlets, including the aforementioned *kaitenzushi*, which also exhibit considerable diversity. And for the frugal, prepackaged sushi is available from convenience stores and supermarkets, as mentioned earlier. Sushi sold in plastic containers may resemble the sushi offered by a Michelin three-star restaurant, but some of the world's most famous chefs and gourmets insist that the difference in quality between mediocre and outstanding sushi is greater than for any other comestible.

In this chapter, I focus on establishments that tend to be independently owned and that self-consciously strive to serve Edo-style sushi. I have restricted my focus in this way not only because such restaurants best exemplify the artisanal ethos but also because Edo-style sushi sets the standard for sushi making. For the same reason, I emphasize the experience available at relatively expensive venues. These are not always family owned, but they are almost always individually operated on a small scale.[30] Paradoxically, the duration of the meal and the style of service, including the number and types of sushi served, may be almost the same in the most expensive venues as in the most unprepossessing outlets. For example, Sukiyabashi Jirō—perhaps the most celebrated sushi restaurant in the world, with a chef in his nineties—may serve an entire course in a matter of thirty minutes, and with practically the same toppings as those found at the relatively humble establishment I describe at the beginning of the chapter (after all, most sushi chefs agree on what's in season). But what separates Sukiyabashi Jirō from the modest place in central Tokyo is not so much Sukiyabashi Jirō's ethos and orientation as the price of its raw ingredients and the cost of its rent.

The twentieth-century mecca for sushi was the Ginza district of Tokyo, where some six hundred shops vied for the world's most discerning sushi aficionados, who are usually quite affluent. It can be difficult, however, to tell the difference between those who have deep knowledge and appreciation of sushi and those who merely have deep pockets.

What, then, is a day in the life of a serious sushi eater? For starters, the day must be set weeks if not months in advance because making a reservation is now a real challenge. Even at relatively exclusive venues, the norm until the turn of the twenty-first century had been simply to show up whenever one was moved to eat sushi. It was still possible in those days to call ahead and find out whether the place was full. But by 2020 the need for a reservation had become universal, and the regimen of planning had come to be observed even in the neighborhood sushi shops. There is also a long-standing practice of precluding *ichigensan* (first-time customers) from dining at the more exclusive restaurants in Japan; this practice is intended to protect established and valued customers from nosy, uncouth outsiders or to forestall the newcomers' complaints about high prices. As a result, some highly regarded sushi venues—perhaps a dozen in all of Tokyo—take no new reservations and rely instead on repeat business from regulars, or from customers whom their *jōrensan* have introduced. This seemingly arbitrary practice brings complaints of xenophobia from foreigners, but a common claim is that a restaurant needs to know its customers in order to serve them properly. The royal road to regular service at the most exclusive places, after one has gained entrée, is to make the next reservation at the end of the meal (or upon arrival at the restaurant, to circumvent the amnesia that can accompany inebriation).

Another characteristic of the most exclusive restaurants is that they are very hard to find. There is a reason why such a restaurant is called a *kakurega* (hidden house). Until the era of GPS navigation, it took a heroic effort to track the place down. But the customer's thrill at joining what feels like a secret club also serves as a marketing ploy. For example, one restaurant supplies a private code along with the reservation, and the customer must register the code in order to enter the establishment, even though there is no actual need to do so. Internet-based reservations and reservations systems have not affected the sushi world to any real extent. Most proprietors accept reservations only by phone, on the rare occasions when they bother to pick up. A few now use the new technology, but with devastating results for would-be customers: once or twice a month, an opening may appear for the following month, or for the month after that, but the opening may vanish in the flash of a pixel. To watch digital icons representing open seats disappear before one's eyes is a frustrating experience, to be sure, and only solidifies the sense of scarcity, and of course the restaurant's desirability as well.

But to old-timers and others who are not in the sushi bubble, the very idea of making reservations months ahead is a travesty. How does one know one will even want to eat sushi seven weeks from now? The new world of nouveau riche sushi is especially alien to men older than sixty, who consider themselves the legitimate heirs to the bygone world of exclusive sushi restaurants. The occasional chef, in a rare expression of cynicism, may ridicule what is known as the *yoyaku konnanten* phenomenon, whereby coveted restaurant seats become minor trophies for self-styled gourmets; at one restaurant, the waiting list exceeds three years. Some suggest that unscrupulous owners try to inflate their restaurants' perceived value by pretending to be much busier than they really are. That may be true, but the sense of scarcity is now exacerbated at least as much by the sheer expansion in the number of potential customers. In Ginza, for example, the world of exclusive sushi dining was once largely the province of older men—executives, professionals, and others on expense accounts—who, often accompanied by their potential mistresses, would stop in for a quick meal before going to a nightclub. Nowadays, though, elite dining is available to the world at large, and the competition for seats has only intensified under the influx of younger, internet-based foodies, including foreign tourists. Most of the time when I asked a sushi chef about his aspirations, he told me that he did not want his restaurant to become a *yoyaku konnanten*, nor did he want to serve only the nouveau riche, which could be thought tantamount to selling out and thus losing the spirit of the true sushi artisan. In any case, there is a definite downside to booking reservations months or even years ahead. It can be difficult to deal with the occasional deluge of cancelations, and if even one customer fails to show up, that single absence may mean a waste of precious food as well as loss of income. And even if the food is not wasted, the next day's staff lunch is hardly the ideal showcase for the chef's careful selection and meticulous preparation.

The so-called sushi bubble finds its most concise articulation in the growing rift between expensive, exclusive sushi restaurants and cheaper, more accessible joints. Some venues are celebrated in print as well as on social media, and their chefs are lionized. But the dirty little secret of many a publicity blitz is that it was engineered by the media-savvy staff of the big business that owns the sushi establishment, where the chef is an employee rather than the chef-owner. With several notable exceptions, star chefs tend to be young and photogenic. These chefs are often playful as they make and present sushi to their delighted younger customers, who are usually in their thirties and forties, cheerfully ignorant of sushi basics, and apparently less interested in eating sushi than in taking pictures and uploading them to their social media accounts, thus hoping to cement an invidious distinction between themselves and their less privileged friends or acquaintances. These customers also tend to have allergies and specific dislikes. When I heard one young woman declare that she could not eat *hikarimono* (oily fish), shellfish, or red-fleshed fish, a middle-aged woman sitting next to me murmured, "What's left to eat?" Until recently, typical customers at exclusive restaurants either studied the ABCs of sushi beforehand or expressed embarrassment about their lack of expertise. In the world of the sushi bubble, by contrast, the dining experience has become very much a means rather than an end. And, fittingly, the beverage of choice among the young and wealthy is champagne.

Notwithstanding such breaches of protocol, there are stringent norms for those whose privilege it is to eat expensive sushi. For example, punctuality is expected. One chef expressed a widely shared sentiment when he told me, "We prepare everything to coincide with the customer's arrival so we can present all the ingredients at their peak." There are also tacit rules to be followed while eating sushi, such as not wearing strong perfume and not talking loudly. Even people who have never set foot in a regular sushi shop are aware of the rules. These norms are mandated in part by the prevailing seating arrangement, with seats tightly packed around a counter that is straight, L-shaped, or U-shaped, and the seating arrangement in turn is dictated by the expensive real estate that many top sushi venues occupy. As mentioned, though, newer and younger customers, among them foreign tourists, blithely ignore many of the established rules of conduct. When I asked individual chefs why the rules were not enforced, the usual response was that the chef could not expect foreigners to be aware of Japanese customs. A more salient explanation is the trap created by the internet and social media: the internet brings publicity and new business, but it can just as easily become a conduit for accusations of rudeness, even racism. A successful *oyakata* (chef, owner, or master) in his forties told me, "I never know when some customer is going to lose it and complain on social media."

An older chef who has been working in Ginza for more than three decades summed up the situation: "You can't win with customers these days."[31]

As for the customers themselves, they arrive in groups of anywhere from six to eleven, almost always within a few minutes of one another (surely their punctuality has something to do with Tokyo's highly efficient trains). The chef welcomes them, and for novices, in addition to the bow and the greeting, there is the question about allergies and dislikes, distasteful though most chefs find this discussion: "How do they know what they do or don't like, when they've never eaten it?" ("It" may refer to a specific part of a particular fish, at the height of its delectable glory and prepared in the way the chef thinks best.) The chef also tells the customers where to sit—and in the matter of seating, as in much else, there is a hierarchy. The most desirable seats are directly in front of where the chef makes sushi. The least desirable are at the far end of the counter. The very worst seat in the restaurant is the one closest to the restroom. The best seats are reserved for the regulars—and, not surprisingly, the longer a guest's acquaintance with the chef and the more frequent the guest's visits, the better his or her seat. There is a commercial imperative to welcome all guests with equal warmth, but most chefs express special delight in welcoming an old-timer, especially if the guest was an early customer, presumably in the days when the chef was young and struggling. Customers hardly ever resist the chef's seating instructions, though I did witness such resistance on one occasion, when a customer took the seat reserved for someone else. The chef fumed but swallowed his tongue and let the customer have his way. Later, though, he evidently regretted his decision—he returned to the topic several times after the offending guest had left.

The prevailing stereotype of the sushi chef, especially the chef who is celebrated, has long been that of a mulish curmudgeon (the older term is *ikkokumono*; the newer is *ganko oyaji*). The stereotypical sushi chef shares many traits with Edo natives and is said to be impatient, too, with a fondness for festivals and gambling. The chef is also reputed to be intimidating. For example, the writer Sano Yōko recalls the first time she ate at a sushi restaurant: "I was afraid the entire time I was eating, but I've never eaten such delicious sushi."[32] And Sano is far from alone in having felt such trepidation. In the postwar period, the reputable sushi shop became a forbidding place: rumor had it that sushi restaurants were for rich, powerful, or famous people, that the prices were stratospheric, and that the *oyakata* discriminated between legitimate and illegitimate customers. In addition, the *oyakata* was said to test and judge his guests.[33] In the mid-1980s, I occasionally dined at a place run by a legendary older chef. When I walked in the first time (no need for reservations back then), the master glared at me and asked gruffly if I was a student. "No," I said—not true, technically, because I was a graduate student at the time, but I interpreted him as having asked whether I was still an undergraduate. When he heard my answer, he nodded almost imperceptibly and seemed to approve of my presence. But I didn't understand the significance of the chef's question until another evening, when a young man walked in and admitted under questioning that he was indeed a student. The master thundered, "If your parents are supporting you, you shouldn't be eating such fancy food!" The young man replied that he was working part-time to support himself, but his explanation was in vain. The master raised his voice once again and instructed him not to come back until he was *ichininmae* (an adult, fully self-supporting).[34] By contrast with contemporary upscale establishments, everything on this restaurant's menu was à la carte. The chef almost always said that guests should eat whatever they wanted, in any order they chose, but the tacit assumption was that he was calibrating his guests' aptitude for sushi according to what they ordered.[35] There are urban legends about intransigent chefs who handpick their customers, then needle them and even go so far as to show them the door. In the 1980s, for instance, it was said that the *oyakata* at a mid-level sushi restaurant had taken a strong dislike to a particular customer and kicked him out after the customer finally ordered the same dish one too many times. Tales of abusive chefs, handed down in popular folklore or distilled from lived experience, still circulate among potential diners, with the result that some first-time customers fret over how to conduct themselves at a sushi counter.

But by the 2010s, as can be deduced from the earlier discussion of *yoyaku konnanten,* the stubborn, irascible sushi chef was a figure from the past. It is rare now to encounter an *oyakata* who does not project a friendly aura or behave with almost unfailing politeness; incidents that would have invited a sushi master's sharp rebuke a generation ago barely elicit a shrug from today's younger *oyakata*. One evening, at the establishment of a chef I knew well, I was seated near a pair of bankers who couldn't manage to sit up straight or stop talking about how they wished they were eating Kentucky Fried Chicken instead of sushi. The chef showed only the slightest hint of exasperation, though he did uncharacteristically allow himself to explode with irritation after the annoying guests had left. In any case, the balance of power has now shifted decisively toward the customer.[36] A few norms have changed, too. Some customers used to smoke in sushi restaurants, and others ordered *mizuwari* (whisky and water). But smoking and whisky had disappeared by the first decade of the new century, thanks to public health campaigns and generational changes in taste. The transition was not always smooth. When one establishment announced that there would be no more smoking, an irate middle-aged customer proclaimed the imminent arrival of fascism and vowed never to return to such a highfalutin joint.[37] And yet time passes. Today when I recount scenes that played out thirty years ago in a legendary sushi restaurant, some younger chefs and customers say, "Yes, my *oyakata* was like that." But others, who came of age in a more genteel environment, simply cannot believe me. "What? No reservations for a top sushi place? Whisky? And *smoking*? Are you talking about the Edo period?" For that matter, whisky, too, has come back in the form of the "high ball," a mixture of whisky and soda water. Sometimes what we take to be our accumulated wisdom looks to others like our decrepitude and fast-approaching demise.

Much of the contemporary common sense regarding fine sushi had solidified by the early years of the twenty-first century. But the mad spiral of reservations—a twenty-first-century phenomenon, to be sure—has a prehistory that can be traced to the gourmet boom of the 1980s, when food-oriented television programs and magazine articles brought home to many people the fact that there were other, better restaurants than the local sushi spots where they had happily been eating until then. Also in the early years of the new century, after the Bubble had burst, people were looking for new but affordable small luxuries. A new gourmet boom took off, and *yoyaku konnanten* emerged. Moreover, the first edition of *Le guide Michelin: Tokyo* appeared in 2007. Before the Michelin guide, there had been other books, even guides to sushi places. But most sushi lovers, if they knew the names of any top sushi places at all, were aware of only the storied few. As discussed earlier, however, any top sushi place in Tokyo necessarily has a small footprint. That fact, together with what had already become a global fascination with sushi, transformed sushi into an extremely scarce commodity.

The currently inevitable *omakase* menu has an older provenance. Some credit (or blame) Sushi Shō, which opened in Yotsuya in 1993, for introducing the contemporary practice of offering a prix fixe course that alternates sushi with nonsushi items.[38] But there was already something akin to the *omakase* menu in most sushi restaurants during the postwar period. The customer would rely on the master's sense of what was best on a particular day, and the *oyakata* would usually serve some raw fish and appetizers before making sushi. In any case, the *omakase* menu, love it or hate it, has made sushi accessible even to first-timers—no need to squirm under the gaze of the master. And the *oyakata* in turn can more easily determine how much of an expensive seafood to buy. The *omakase* menu, because it benefits both the customer and the chef, has understandably become dominant in sushi restaurants.

By contrast with the *yoyaku konnanten* trend, the older, established places and the local inexpensive restaurants rely less on reservations. They serve a striking proportion of repeat customers, often older men. Some also allow considerable latitude for *okonomi* (ordering à la carte), the prevailing norm until a generation ago. Even in the postwar period, however, distinct levels of prix fixe plates were already common. These plates, usually called *shōchikubai*, were (in descending order of price) the pine course, the bamboo course, and the plum course.[39] And the *omakase* menu was more common than not. Many longtime sushi eaters drink either beer or sake—wine is, well, foreign (beer, like baseball, assimilated quickly). There is also a great deal less use of cameras on the part of customers, and some chefs ban them outright. The atmosphere in these places tends to be less formal, at times approaching that of the ubiquitous *izakaya* (tavern or pub-like restaurant). The seating arrangement has not changed, but casual banter among the guests has declined—toward the end of the evening, however, alcohol sometimes loosens tongues—and so have spontaneous offers to share sake. Civil indifference reigns in the expensive establishments, though some guests seek to impress their companions by demonstrating a relationship with a famous chef. This is in striking contrast to the norms of a generation ago, when the constant presence of regulars and the camaraderie born of presumed similarity (because the restaurant was the province of middle-aged male office workers) routinely encouraged casual conversation (punctuated though it was by shrill debates on proper sushi etiquette) as well as the sharing of sake and other alcoholic drinks. That communal atmosphere has now become as alien as smoking.

But perhaps the single greatest change in the world of fine sushi has been the transformation of the clientele over the past generation. Three decades ago, as noted earlier, the typical sushi consumer was a middle-aged businessperson. Almost all sushi restaurants depended on cultivating regulars, and that was as true for a top-flight Ginza restaurant as for a lowly neighborhood shop. Unlike France, however, Japan offered precious few guides or critics to identify desirable establishments.[40] Therefore, would-be gourmets relied on word of mouth and were usually guided by older connoisseurs (*tsū*). Given the scarcity of reliable information about restaurants, sushi establishments in turn depended on their regulars but, in so doing, often neglected their new customers, especially if the newcomers did not look as if they would become regulars. For some restaurants, the practice of not welcoming newcomers was a hallmark of exclusivity. In addition, many an *oyakata* of a generation ago gave free rein to his prejudices. The same chef who sent the college student packing also had a tendency to lecture me (I was usually the youngest customer in the place) and impart life lessons for my benefit, such as lessons about the virtue of diligence. But that behavior would never fly today. Now most customers, especially at upscale restaurants, are couples on dates, men and women in their thirties and forties.[41]

Several reasons have accounted for this change in the clientele of fine sushi restaurants. The most obvious was the disavowal of the postwar practice of *settai*, whereby expensive restaurants or bars served as places for business to be conducted or government deals to be made. Public disapproval of this form of corruption became widespread, and fewer people were able to treat their guests to dinner at an expensive restaurant. Also in decline was the practice of *dōhan*, in which a nightclub hostess was taken out to dinner by her customer. In the postwar period, most Japanese executives had relied on expense accounts rather than personal income, and so they were able to spend lavishly at restaurants and nightclubs. But after the Bubble burst, the permissive attitude toward spending large amounts of money in this way evaporated, and so did the dominant presence of middle-aged men in expensive sushi restaurants. By the mid-2010s, however, the older practices were being revived, albeit in new forms.

At the same time, the barriers to entry have been lowered. Many new guidebooks appeared after the publication of *Le guide Michelin: Tokyo*. More important, there are now a number of sushi-oriented websites, of which Tabelog is the most influential. Demotic though these sites may be, they convey a good sense of what is popular and desirable among the younger, status-conscious set. And it's not just the customers who have become younger. At the most popular sushi restaurants, the chefs, too, are often in their thirties, and a few are even in their twenties. As these younger chefs serve their young customers in our digital age, one indisputable effect has been the rise of Instagramable sushi, created more for viewing than for chewing. Another effect, of course, is the waning of traditions, such as that of serving labor-intensive, cost-ineffective *kanpyō* (stewed calabash, a type of gourd). For some, then, as discussed earlier, dining on sushi is more about the pleasure of displaying one's social distinction than about enjoying delectable food. For these diners, eating sushi amounts to a form of alienation from the manifest and perhaps outdated function of savoring a tasty meal.

With so many foreigners now drawn to eating sushi, tales of their malfeasance abound. The stories that sushi chefs tell about foreigners tend to feature two themes—the chef's pride in cultivating knowledgeable, well-behaved customers (by contrast with the visitors from abroad, who refuse to eat raw fish, for example), and the foreign guests' expressions of lurking xenophobia. Many sushi chefs have spent time working in other countries, and so they are attuned to the desires of their foreign customers. (Even so, almost no chefs in Tokyo serve salmon or avocado, two North American–style sushi staples. Some chefs do serve *sakuramasu* [cherry trout], which is almost indistinguishable from salmon.) Some sushi venues won't allow non-Japanese-speaking customers to come by themselves, and two reasons are usually given for this policy: first, foreigners tend to cancel at the last minute; and, second, the *oyakata* cannot assume that foreigners have even the most basic knowledge of sushi etiquette (the norm of conversing quietly, for example, or of not mixing wasabi with soy sauce so as not to dilute the wasabi's pungency and flavor). But the problem is not just with foreigners—indeed, many of them are well informed. Another problematic group can be older customers, especially those who come from outside Tokyo. They may prefer non-Edomae sushi, such as *natto* (fermented soybean) roll, or they may stay for hours but order only a few inexpensive items. Moreover, some sushi chefs acknowledge that younger, affluent Japanese urbanites are no different from ignorant foreigners. At any rate, in the age of social media, almost all *oyakata* recognize that they are powerless to admonish a customer, much less toss one out. Whatever a chef's claims to being an artisan may be, he knows that his business cannot survive the alienation of customers that would result from a negative blog post or tweet. And, because the norm of politeness prevails, efforts to dissuade an unwanted customer can be quite subtle (for example, the customer can be offered a less desirable seat). Thirty years ago, chefs and diners alike talked about how an establishment that selected its customers could be evaluated on the basis of their knowledge and sophistication. Today it's the rare sushi restaurant that is successful enough to rely on its regulars and dispense with attracting new business. When it comes to diners, chefs have their likes and dislikes, but they are far from uniform in their thinking about what makes a good customer. As a younger chef told me, "Customers are customers. We have a duty to serve them as best we can."

And how do the customers decide where to dine? Younger people, as mentioned earlier, get their information from the internet, social media, guidebooks, and gourmet acquaintances. Older, more experienced sushi eaters take a much more varied approach. Some canvass far and wide, using the internet and guidebooks, but most of them frequent the places where they have long been regulars, usually because they were introduced by older gourmets. Others use visual or olfactory cues—the cleaner the place, the better it is assumed to be. It remains widely believed that a great sushi chef is the product of training by a master sushi chef; this is the argument from genealogy or descent. Another belief is that one can discern the ability of the *oyakata* by examining his face. Yet another article of faith is that the key to the chef's quality is his wife, who often works beside the master and is called *okami* (madam, or female general). A man in his seventies told me, in all seriousness, "In the past, the *oyakata* would marry his most beautiful daughter off to the most promising apprentice. Therefore, good chefs almost always have beautiful wives."

Once the customer has advanced through the strait gate, generally after having endured the steeplechase-like reservation process, the drinks arrive and the *oyakata* begins to serve the food. Most chefs begin by serving whoever has arrived first, even though the difference in customers' arrival times may be only a few seconds. But that order of priority may not last throughout the meal, and if one takes an extended phone or cigarette break, one can lose one's place when a particular dish is served. Appetizers—that is, dishes that are not Edo-style sushi—are usually flavored with salt or dipped in soy sauce or *nikiri*, which is soy sauce mixed with sake or *mirin* (sweet sake). At times a chef may recommend one of these condiments over the other. Self-conscious foodies tend to opt for salt and wasabi, though it's not always clear that this is the better option. Most Japanese diners are aware of the taboo against mixing wasabi with soy sauce. It should also be noted that in the past, the entire course was presented at once, *à la française,* on a serving block (and this practice continues at most neighborhood sushi establishments). In general, the diner used to start with the closest pieces and work her way out to those farther away. But this prescribed sequence, like most other aspects of the older sushi etiquette, has succumbed to the reign of laissez-faire.

Aficionados of a generation ago conducted heated, fruitless debates about every step of eating sushi. Should one dip each piece in *nikiri* while holding the top portion (*neta*, that is, the material, apart from rice, that is used in sushi) or the bottom portion (*shari*, the rice used in sushi)? Some argued that smearing fish into the sauce would alter the flavor of the *nikiri*, and others warned that the compacted rice would crumble if it got wet. Each expert seemed convinced of the correctness of his own protocol, and his conviction was sometimes shared by the chef. The prevailing practice now, fortunately, is for the chef to add any desirable condiments to each piece of sushi so that all the customer has to do is pick it up and eat it. But as simple as the customer's doing that may seem, the act of picking up and eating a piece of sushi is still liable to incite a highly vocal discussion. Is it all right to use chopsticks? In the past, some sushi venues did not provide them, and those restaurants' intention was clear. At others today, chopsticks are fine. About the only apparently remaining rules are that each piece should be swallowed *in toto*, not eaten in separate bites, and that each piece should be consumed as quickly as possible after being placed in front of the diner—within three seconds, according to Ono Jirō of Sukiyabashi Jirō fame.[42] But even here, alas, there is disagreement; another famous chef, one with many disciples, told me that a piece of sushi tastes better if the diner waits a little while before eating it. In any case, there are no longer any universal truths in the world of sushi. Most of the unspoken rules of a generation ago—eat the sushi promptly when it's placed in front of you, because it quickly degrades from its ideal state; don't wear perfume or cologne, because it interferes with the delicate taste of the sushi; don't talk about sushi trivia, including other sushi venues—have disappeared.[43] Nevertheless, it is still unusual for even a top sushi restaurant to impose rules, such as a ban on taking photos of the food. Indeed, by 2020, especially with the rise of the younger star chefs, the trend had shifted to making sushi places much more like Spanish tapas bars and heightening their appeal to younger, hipper customers who were less formal and more talkative. By the mid-2010s, some customers had even begun turning up in shorts, a choice of attire that once would have been unthinkable.

There also used to be quite a debate about the proper sequence of a sushi course, especially in the postwar period when many customers opted to dine à la carte. But that debate is now moot because almost all restaurants (I can think of only one exception among the famous sushi restaurants) serve an *omakase* menu. When the *okonomi* approach was common, it caused anxiety for customers and chefs alike: customers often could not tell what would taste good to them (and there was always the threat of the master's disapproving look), and chefs had the constant worry that the customer would order only inexpensive items, thus ruining the prized supply of expensive *toro* (flank or belly fat). Until recently, the telltale sign that a sushi course had reached its conclusion was a serving of *anago* (sea eel), followed by *tamagoyaki* (egg custard) and a roll, usually *kanpyō*.[44] *Wanmono* (soup), usually but not always miso soup, has also become a common option. The older chefs liked to say that one's coming of age as a sushi chef was marked by the ability either to make a decent *tamagoyaki* or to stew a good *kanpyō*. The ingredients for both dishes are inexpensive, but the preparation of each is time-consuming and requires extended training.[45] Knowledgeable customers used to believe that a good *tamagoyaki* was one reliable test of a chef's skill. Both *tamagoyaki* and *kanpyō* have begun to disappear, however, given the time and skill that each demands, and some restaurants now outsource their preparation and buy them ready-made. Longtime sushi aficionados, not to mention sushi chefs, can become indignant when they discover that one sushi venue or another doesn't offer these inexpensive, iconic, but labor-intensive items. "Unbelievable," one chef in his forties told me. "That's a sure sign we're in a sushi bubble." And this is one more area where customers' expectations cannot be ignored. Younger and more fashion-conscious diners often shun the less expensive fare associated with an *ojisan* (a word that literally means "uncle" but is a generic, largely demeaning term meaning "older man"). Once, after I ordered a *kanpyō* roll to end my meal, a young woman nearby whispered to her companion, "I wouldn't want to eat anything *binbōkusai*"—anything, that is, suggestive of poverty. One chef told me that he would like to serve *kanpyō* but has decided to forgo it because it's just not a luxury item.

Not surprisingly, people who have ventured beyond the friendly confines of a neighborhood sushi shop often return to their base. Indeed, a remarkable feature of *yoyaku konnanten* is the small number of customers who are in their fifties or older. Sometimes an intrepid soul, often with a comrade or two, seeks out a new and noteworthy place, but this adventurer tends to be a man with time on his hands and money to spare. The effort required to secure a reservation at some venues is not the only thing that keeps older people away. The primary deterrent is that the contemporary understanding of fine sushi leaves out much of what many aficionados have long taken for granted, including the freedom to order à la carte and the promise of *kanpyō* or *wanmono* at the end of the meal. A more cynical explanation might be that older customers no longer have access to expense accounts, for reasons that include their retirement and the public's disapproval of what used to be a system of profligate spending. But, whatever the reason, fine dining in the world of sushi, except at several legendary establishments, has been taken over by the post-Bubble generation, with its young chefs and its customers in their thirties and forties.

At any rate, when the feast, like all other good things, comes to its end, someone has to pay up. There is no itemized tab. The universal practice is for the chef to give the customer a small slip of paper inscribed with numbers, and for the customer to accept it without question. This lack of transparency has bewildered many diners and repelled many potential customers, past and current. The payment system is admittedly imperfect. In the 2010s, a television program surreptitiously filmed a chef charging a pair of attractive young women much less than he charged a pair of older, not very attractive men. On this topic, one comment from a seasoned chef was "What would *you* do?" Likewise, in the early 1990s a famous Ginza chef openly acknowledged that he charged businesspeople the equivalent of two hundred US dollars, young women the equivalent of eighty US dollars, and his regular, retired customers the equivalent of thirty US dollars.[46] When I shared this information with a very old chef, he laughed. "I wouldn't go that far," he said, "but, yes, when there are people I hope will never come back, I charge them more." To be clear, most of the chefs I talked with denied that they would ever engage in such blatantly biased behavior, consciously or not, regardless of whether it would encourage the return of attractive women or deter the presence of unwanted customers. Nevertheless, most of the chefs allowed that they would like to attract good customers and repel bad ones—and here we see yet another manifestation of the truism from a generation ago, that one can judge a sushi place by looking at its customers.[47] But the unfortunate lot of almost all sushi chefs, even the famous ones, is that they do not have the privilege of discriminating. They are obliged to accept all paying customers. Here, one can only throw up one's hands and paraphrase Tolstoy: Good customers are all alike; each bad customer is bad in his or her own way.

Some of the chefs I talked with have openly challenged the payment system and its lack of transparency. Even when there is an *omakase* course, an *oyakata* often provides different items, and in distinct portions. "If a younger customer comes in," one chef told me, "I may make sushi from the tougher part of *chūtoro*, which is cheaper."[48] It is also common practice to vary the sizes of the pieces of sushi according to the customer's gender or size or the chef's perception of how hungry the customer is. Because the raw ingredients of sushi are so expensive, some chefs argue, it shouldn't be at all surprising that prices differ across customers, sometimes substantially.[49] Also not surprising is the fact that mistakes do happen.

Despite the many transformations in the sushi dining experience, one constant is the widespread sense of alimentary satisfaction. "When I eat sushi, I feel glad to be alive" is a typical, if gushing, comment from an elderly man. Everything in the experience happens very quickly, much as in some people's experience of a sexual encounter—the pleasure of anticipation, the relatively truncated nature of the act's consummation, and the long afterglow. The experience of eating sushi stimulates all the senses with its marvels of color and shape, its contrasting and changing textures, its fragrances and tastes, the crescendo and diminuendo of biting and chewing, the swallowing and the aftertaste. It turns an ordinary diner into a philosopher. When I ask people about the experience of consuming sushi, they tend to wax eloquent: "It's like eating the season," or "I become one with nature." And what makes this ecstatic response possible is the extraordinary effort of sushi artisans.

THE MAKING OF SUSHI CHEFS

What is life like for a sushi artisan? As we have seen, there is constant concern about polarization between types of sushi establishments, and about the emergence of superstar chefs, but the daily routines of all sushi chefs are remarkably similar.

The *oyakata*—more often called *taishō* (military general) by customers—or his trusted second-in-command makes a daily shopping trip to a market (formerly to the Tsukiji Fish Market, which closed in October 2018, and now to the Toyosu Market) and, keeping in mind the season as well as costs, selects and purchases the best or most appropriate types of seafood. The course menu is decided in part by the vagaries of the weather as well as by fishermen's catches, but the *oyakata* decides what is best and what his customers will (or should) want. The task of selecting the best fish is a crucial one, and the chef has prepared for it by spending years and decades learning about all sorts of seafood. *Suzuki* (perch-like fish) are popular in Japan, especially several types of *aji* (carangidae, a subcategory of *suzuki*). To the untrained eye, however—surely the eye of almost every American and of many a Japanese person, too—all fish look alike, similar to the generic fish in a child's drawing. And just to confuse things, *buri* (Japanese amberjack), one of the most popular fish in the *suzuki* category, goes by no fewer than six names, which change according to the fish's size and its stage in the growth cycle. *Buri* is what might be called an upwardly mobile fish (*shusseuo*); that is, just as in the past a successful Japanese person (such as a kabuki actor) might change his name to match his newly established skills and status, a so-called upwardly mobile fish does not simply grow but becomes known by a different name as it reaches each new stage of growth. What is even more confusing is that seafood nomenclature often varies across Japanese regions; for example, an American sushi eater will know *buri* as *hamachi*, the name used in the Osaka region for a youthful manifestation of *buri*. To add another layer of perplexity, some people in the Tokyo area also use the name *hamachi*, in part because they have been influenced by the name's widespread use in the United States.

The *oyakata* is a walking encyclopedia of seafood. A reasonably trained sushi chef will know when it's a good time to eat *buri*, which fish looks best, and which parts will be good for sushi. A serious chef can discourse for hours on the different taste and texture that results when *buri* is caught in one particular area or another, or in one manner or another. The most glamorous (or most expensive) fish is *maguro* (tuna), and its varieties and their subtleties are enough to draw chefs, fishmongers, and aficionados into endless conversations and debates. Yet some things are beyond dispute; for example, net-caught *maguro* is said to be gamy and hence inferior to its line-caught counterparts. The term *maguro* can refer to any number of types of tuna, which may all look alike—brilliant red in color, with areas of gleaming white—but there are numerous subspecies, including the inexpensive albacore, caught in temperate or tropical waters, and the prized *hon maguro* (Pacific bluefin tuna). Serious sushi people almost always look for *hon maguro* that have reached a certain size (bragging rights are enhanced by the weight of the tuna, which can exceed half a ton) and that were caught in preferred areas. The consensus favorite is *maguro* caught with a fishing pole off Ōma (in northern Honshū) and not flash frozen. The New Year's auction fetches the highest price for Ōma *hon maguro*; in 2019, the highest bid was the equivalent of more than three million US dollars for a fish that weighed 613 pounds.[50] The fatty, expensive parts of *hon maguro* caught off Ōma are a matter of pride for a sushi chef, who apprises his customers of the fish's authenticity, which in turn justifies the astronomical cost of the treasured meat.

One way the best chefs retain their place in the informal hierarchy of the sushi world is by establishing and maintaining ties to the best wholesalers; indeed, a chef in his thirties blurted out to me, "I didn't apprentice at a truly top place, so I wasn't able to establish a connection with the top wholesalers." Therefore, an indispensable element of the chef's daily round of shopping for seafood and vegetables is his network (which can span several generations) of trusted fishmongers and other purveyors. After six daily rounds of shopping per week, for perhaps fifty weeks a year, a chef develops an intuitive sense of suitable fish and fishmongers, a surety that resides in the realm of tacit knowledge, backed though it is by the chef's formal education in ichthyology. One *oyakata* told me, only half in jest, that he knew he had attained a particular level of mastery when he began to hear fish calling, "Eat me." A specific variety of tacit knowledge is known as *mekiki*—that is, the ability to discern the quality and taste of a fish simply by looking at it (the term also denotes the person, whether chef or fishmonger, who has this ability). But even a chef who is a *mekiki* cannot always tell when *maguro*, for example, is gamy. Only a trusted fishmonger, who in turn obtains his products from trusted fishermen (and a few fisherwomen), can ensure the procurement of the best *maguro* and other items. That's why an exceptionally seasoned chef told me that it's less important for a chef to become a great *mekiki* himself than to establish relationships with trustworthy fishmongers. Several of the chefs and fishmongers I spoke with bemoaned the general decline in skilled *mekiki*. In fact, a frequent claim was that there are only three truly skilled *mekiki* for tuna, and so there is a powerful gravitational pull toward the few trusted wholesalers who employ skilled, widely acknowledged *mekiki*. Most chefs confine themselves to visual and haptic cues as they shop for fish, but some insist on the primacy of the sense of smell—what strikes almost everyone else as a fishy odor discloses a splendid complexity to the happy few.

In the sushi industry, the cost of raw ingredients is prohibitive. Food costs may account for no more than 20 percent of a fast food restaurant's total operating costs but may constitute 40 percent of total outlays for a sushi establishment.[51] Some sushi chefs even claim that the cost of raw ingredients exceeds 50 percent. As one veteran chef reported, "I think I was at about 60 percent, but now I try to keep it below 50 percent. It's just too hard to sustain this place at such low margins."

Obviously, the cost and the decisive impact of sushi's raw ingredients make their sourcing absolutely crucial, but raw ingredients are important in another way, too. In the 1980s, it was not uncommon for sushi chefs to express gratitude not only to senior chefs and other colleagues, to fishmongers, and to customers but also to the bounty that came from the sea, from the mountains, and from nature in general. Such gratitude and respect were sometimes even extended to individual fish that had been sacrificed. Some chefs used to say that, to atone for the killing, they strove to make use of everything from mouth to tail (this was also, in part, a reflection of the ordinary virtue of not wasting). When they described the process of preparation, they often employed the euphemism *shimeru* (tightening) instead of using words that conveyed the reality of slaughtering or butchering. At the market, wholesalers and their customers held ritual funerals for the fish that had been caught and killed. It would be misleading to suggest that the chefs felt guilty, like the renowned French chef Alain Passard, who decided to stop serving meat at his restaurant in Paris. But a crucial part of the sushi chef's artisanal outlook is an appreciation of the riches received from the sea. Even today, according to a master chef, "The sense of gratitude cannot be forgotten."

With shopping and selection out of the way, the *oyakata* and his colleagues turn to the lengthy, laborious task of *shikomi* (preparation). A casual observer may form the impression that making sushi means nothing more than slapping raw fish onto rice. Such an observer would naturally believe that the chef's eye for quality and his tacit knowledge of seafood are far more important than *shikomi*. But that would be a mistake. It's true that the most visible aspect of dining at a sushi restaurant is watching the chef in the act of shaping individual pieces of sushi, but that is neither the most difficult nor the most important component of sushi making. One octogenarian chef claims that *shikomi* is 90 percent of making sushi; in other words, perhaps 90 percent of the work—buying and preparing raw materials—is done by eleven o'clock in the morning. Another seasoned *oyakata* says that *shikomi* accounts for 70 percent of the work.[52] In any case, no sushi master would deny the critical importance of *shikomi*. A chef in his early forties told me that he opens his establishment for dinner only three nights a week because he has not yet mastered *shikomi*. "I have so much to learn," he said, "and it all takes so much time." When I asked him about the economic challenge of having his restaurant open on such a limited basis, he shrugged. "This is the only way," he said.

Shikomi is the crux of Edo-style sushi—something is done to every ingredient in order to make it tastier than when it was raw.[53] In fact, there is an adage that many *oyakata* repeat almost verbatim: "The idea of Edo-style sushi is to make seafood tasty." Sushi means far more than simply fresh, raw fish. Everything is treated, and at times the ingredients are aged for days, or they are marinated, fermented, braised, or burned. The classical techniques used in making Edo-style sushi take years and sometimes decades to master. Almost any effort to simplify the tedious, time-consuming process of preparation, or to bypass any of its steps, is harshly criticized and considered an instance of *teochi* (neglect). One renowned *oyakata* claims that *shikomi* is a process of subtraction—that is, preparation is all about eliminating the negative aspects of the raw material in order to enhance its essential deliciousness. Most would say that a great deal of addition is also involved, but all seasoned chefs probably agree that the fundamental task is to draw out the tasty and the flavorful from seafood.

It seems that each generation has had to experience its own struggle over the boundaries of acceptability regarding seafood. Indeed, the perennial question concerns what, exactly, constitutes legitimate Edomae sushi. In the past, the most common form of dismissal was to label something new *jadō* (heretical, heterodox, or evil); for example, a renowned Ginza sushi chef recalls having a longtime customer accuse him of heresy for serving sushi that used fresh shrimp and squid.[54] Traditionalists balked at serving *uni* (sea urchin), though now no one hesitates. But almost every sushi chef still refuses to serve salmon except as *sakuramasu* ("cherry trout") in season.[55] Otherwise, salmon is not in the Edomae repertoire. Nevertheless, the boundaries of acceptability have expanded considerably over the past several decades, though when a customer asked a young chef whether he might begin making chicken sushi, the chef shook his head with uncharacteristic vigor. Be all that as it may, what defines Edomae sushi in the age of globalized supply chains is no longer geography, as in the era when the source of all Edo-style seafood was Tokyo Bay. Instead, the defining characteristics of Edomae sushi are now preparation and style.

The task of preparation extends to *shari,* which is carefully selected and often stored for a spell—aged rice is widely believed to be superior for sushi. Sushi chefs also experiment with different varietals and often come up with their own personal blends. Prod any conscientious chef, and he will discourse endlessly on the proper varietal of rice and the best way to cook it. (With apologies to Claude Lévi-Strauss, sushi is not just about the raw but also and emphatically about the cooked.) Ono Jirō, for example, has said that *shari* accounts for 60 percent of what makes sushi stand out.[56] The same care extends to wasabi, *gari,* and other sushi elements. Tea, however, may be an exception to the regimen of careful preparation. Tea that is less expensive and less refined is believed to go best with vinegar-rich sushi, and so there's not so much stress on tea selection and preparation. In fact, the rustic tea common at sushi establishments is often made from inexpensive leaves.

Given Edo-style sushi's humble origins as street food for commoners, no central authority, guild, or association has ever defined the boundaries of this kind of sushi. Nevertheless, because of the long-standing primacy of apprenticeship as the royal road to sushi mastery, a great deal of obeisance is paid to the notion of tradition and to the accumulated wisdom of past practitioners. Genealogy, then, is a popular topic of conversation, and it is of paramount significance to sushi chefs and gourmets because aficionados believe that proper training by a great master is what makes a great sushi chef. In addition, if a chef should become aware of a customer's visit to another sushi establishment, the chef may talk about his relationship with the other chef and, if so, usually mentions whether he is senior or junior to him or was his apprentice, especially if the other chef is famous. Not surprisingly, there may be a basic resemblance among generations of apprentices to the same *oyakata*, even years after they have left his side. A chef may even seek to indicate such an affiliation by naming his establishment in a certain fashion, such as by including a Chinese character that also appears in the name of the restaurant where he apprenticed. For example, former apprentices of Sushi Shō can be identified by their inclusion of the Chinese character that can be read either as *shō* or *takumi* (meaning "skill" in either rendering). Autopoiesis marks the sushi artisan.

It would be misleading to stress only the diversity and variety of sushi styles among Edomae chefs. As noted earlier, the practice of making daily rounds at the fish market, or of spending long periods in preparation, is an invariable feature of the sushi-making life. But there is also a commitment to cleanliness—something shared by many Japanese—that verges on the fanatical. Watching a sushi chef work comes close to observing someone with an obsessive-compulsive disorder. After just about every motion, there is what looks like an almost instinctive wiping and cleansing of the preparation surface or the knife. Many sushi aficionados claim that they can appraise an unknown sushi spot just by smelling it. For example, a lingering odor of vinegar is a sure sign that the restaurant doesn't take cleaning seriously, and this in turn is taken as clear evidence that the establishment is inferior.

Some chefs claim not to buy expensive knives. In this, they echo what has been said of the Buddhist monk Kūkai (774–835), the master calligrapher who didn't obsess about the brush he used. But all chefs take extraordinary care of their knives and constantly sharpen them, a practice made necessary by heavy use. Except at a few pretentiously upscale spots, almost all chefs wear clean white garments and keep their hair extremely short. As one chef observed, it's easy to spot other chefs out in the world at large—you've seen them at the fish market, or they have the same very short haircut.

Another expression of Edo style has to do with the kinds of fish a chef prizes and presents. Seasonal variations notwithstanding, two types of fish have come to define Edo-style sushi: *maguro* and *kohada*.[57] Some *oyakata* insist on the superiority of the cheek or the loin, but pride of place goes to the flank or the belly fat—that is, to the *toro*—whose meat is in turn usually divided into three categories of increasing fat content: *toro* (meat with regular fat content), *chūtoro* (meat with medium fat content), and *ōtoro* (meat with superior fat content). Because *hon maguro* is expensive, it is something of a loss leader. A few chefs told me the same thing: if they made too many pieces of sushi using *maguro*, their restaurants would go belly-up. Adding to the travail is the considered opinion of every *oyakata* that *maguro* is easily spoiled or squandered by careless thawing, rough handling, or poor slicing. In a rare blunder, one chef slipped while he was carrying a precious chunk of *ōtoro* and chose to protect the fish rather than his head. When he regained his composure, he was relieved that nothing had happened to the *ōtoro* but was oblivious to his own physical discomfort—and no wonder, since his filet, weighing perhaps a little more than two pounds, had probably cost him well over the equivalent of one thousand US dollars. It is easy to damage the *suji* (sinew or fiber) of good tuna meat and thus destroy its delicate flavor. Of particular and critical importance, then, is masterly slicing, the product at once of many years of training and of a well-made, well-maintained knife. But an obvious question is why the chef should bother serving *maguro*. The usual answer involves *iji*, a term whose translation is found somewhere in the vicinity of "will," "pride," and "obstinacy." In other words, it is a matter of self-definition, and it is unthinkable not to serve *maguro*. To say, "I am an Edo-style sushi chef, and an Edo-style sushi chef makes *maguro* sushi" is to utter a tautology, of course, but the statement's irrefutability makes it all the more powerful. And here, customers' expectations cannot be neglected. As one knowing sushi customer put it, using a generalization that would apply to Italian restaurants in Japan, "A sushi meal without *maguro* is like Italian food without pasta."

Kohada, too, is a matter of pride—and, more symbolically, so is its infantile form, *shinko*, which is only a few inches long and becomes much smaller after *shikomi*, so that each piece of sushi may include up to five pieces of *shinko*. Not only has *shinko* become expensive—often as expensive, by weight, as *maguro*—but its preparation is extremely tedious. Prepping *shinko* requires a great deal of skill and patience, and the chef who lacks either attribute won't have much *shinko* left to serve. The financial and physical outlay is justified, though, because making *shinko* sushi is another mark of an Edo-style chef's mastery. That's why, every summer, many chefs proudly announce the arrival of *shinko*. As one *oyakata* in his thirties said, "It's hard to explain to outsiders, but *shinko* marks a change of season. My *oyakata* said that for him it was a chance to reaffirm his beginnings as a sushi chef, and it's sort of like renewing a vow of commitment." Some renowned chefs do find their colleagues' commitment to *shinko* strange, but it would be hard to conceive of a meal that did not include *kohada*, which is served almost year-round. For many a tradition-inclined chef, *kohada* is an essential component of Edomae sushi as well as a good test of a chef's skill. But some young sushi eaters find the appeal of *kohada* mysterious, by contrast with the meat-like *maguro*. Their reaction is an expression of the growing carnivorous propensity in Japan.

The extended preparation time needed for Edomae sushi and the experience that goes into proper fish selection and *shikomi* are in service of only a few customers. The scale of an Edomae sushi restaurant is necessarily small. One sushi chef endures considerable financial hardship by opening his restaurant for only one round of six customers at lunch and for another round of six at dinner; that is, he and his wife work long hours to serve only twelve customers each day. The chef told me nonchalantly, "It takes a lot of time for me to prepare, and it would be hard to serve more than six people." He runs an expensive establishment, certainly, but a large fortune is not on the horizon even for a restaurant that charges the equivalent of more than five hundred US dollars per customer and serves two rounds of customers each night (and even more customers, if we include lunch). After all, it is not uncommon to find a restaurant that has empty seats in spite of having one or two Michelin stars. When I asked the proprietor of what is perhaps Tokyo's greatest sushi restaurant why he served only one set of customers a night, he replied, "That's about as many as I can handle. I can make enough money and still satisfy myself about the quality of my work." One master, for seven months after his second-in-command became independent, filled only seven of his restaurant's eleven available seats, and during that time his operation was in the red. "That was the moment I was being asked if I was a businessman or an artisan," he said. And what prevailed in his case was not the spirit of the merchant, the *shōbainin*, but that of the *shokunin*.

The long hours devoted to selecting raw materials, then preparing them, culminate in the act of serving. Some sushi restaurants have tables and private rooms, but in most only a narrow counter separates the *oyakata* from the customers (perhaps there are also one or two advanced apprentices in the *tsukeba*, the place on the other side of the counter from the diners). The *tsukeba* is a space of privilege. Traditionally, apprentices spent years longing to step inside and make sushi. A generation ago, it would have been more accurate to say that the *tsukeba* is a sacred place. But secular disenchantment is a contemporary aspect of urban Japanese life, and sushi workers are no less affected than other people by the decline in both religiosity and the use of spiritual language.

The actual combining of the *neta* (material for sushi) and the rice is the performative core of the sushi experience. (Several of the chefs I spoke with used the term "theater" to accentuate their time in the spotlight.) *Neta*, a sushi neologism, is an anagram of *tane* (seed), and the sushi world is rich in such slang and secret language—*shari* for sushi rice, *agari* for tea, and so on. This type of argot has long separated the trained professionals from the outsiders.[58] But if much of sushi's secret lingo has been leaked to the larger public through manga, television programs, books, and websites, traditionalist chefs still express dislike of customers who use the language of the professionals. One chef in his fifties remarked, "*Agari* is for us to use. Customers should just ask for tea." Likewise, in the mid-1980s there were renowned food writers like Ikenami Shōtarō who warned their readers that customers using professional sushi jargon risked the scorn of the people behind the counter.[59] But younger chefs seem indifferent to protecting the sanctity of their professional language.

Although there are numerous traditional ways to make *nigirizushi* (Edo-style sushi), there is one basic rule: the rice should be firm enough to pick up with the fingers, but once in the mouth it should dissolve.[60] Most chefs use some variation of *kotegaeshi*, which is a reliable and relatively quick way to make sushi, usually involving six distinct steps. Yet it would be misleading to say that most chefs make sushi in the same way. The series of hand gestures may be formally alike from chef to chef, but each chef expresses his individuality. Some are nonchalant and almost Zen-like. Others display extreme concentration, visibly contorting their faces and bodies. Some chefs I spoke with laughingly recalled having practiced in front of a mirror. All of them had watched their masters and other sushi chefs over the years. They also seek to respond to the customers in front of them, whether by offering smaller pieces or providing faster service. There is general agreement that the finished product should look delectable, even beautiful, but the most important point is that the rice should be softly compacted. A common ideal is that the sushi rice should not just dissolve but crumble—or, as a famous French chef said, explode—in the mouth. Japanese sushi chefs have different ways of expressing this ideal (never in the language of explosion, however). Several older chefs talked about how compacting sushi rice is like fondling a woman's breast. A new father (and certainly a more politically correct chef) said it's like holding a baby's hand. Another remarked that it is a matter of compacting air. Because the finished sushi rice does crumble easily, there's some urgency that customers eat the sushi quickly, and traditionalists often recommend using the fingers instead of chopsticks. Before the dominance of the *omakase* menu, the norm was to give the customer two pieces of the same sushi. That practice is said to have arisen from the size of the sushi pieces that were made in the past: during the Edo period, a piece of sushi was as large as an *omusubi* (rice ball) and would have been impossible to eat in a single bite; it had to be cut in two. The contemporary norm is to serve a single small piece at a time. This practice exacerbates the urgency of the customer's eating quickly, but it also avoids the embarrassing dissolution of a formed piece of sushi in the dish of soy sauce. As mentioned earlier, most chefs now add condiments (usually *nikiri* and sometimes salt), a custom that has put an end to sushi aficionados' long, convoluted debates about the proper way to dip sushi in sauce. There is scarcely an aspect of sushi making and dining that has not been the subject of controversy, though this debate, like most others, ended not because it was finally resolved but because the dominant practice of preparation and presentation changed.

Interaction with customers is widely deemed important, but customers' experiences vary greatly. Some chefs are taciturn. Others are quite talkative. In any case, most sushi ingredients are expensive and don't last very long, and so it is crucial to get the amount of food and the number of customers right. This is probably the main reason why most upscale restaurants almost exclusively offer only one *omakase* course, though the usual rationale, which is not false, is that the *oyakata* knows best, both about what is good on a particular day and about the order in which the items should be consumed. Some sushi chefs offer beverage pairings, but most leave that decision to the customer. There is a typical first order— "Toriaezu, bīru" ("Let's start with a round of beer")—but several chefs remarked with a chuckle that it all depends on what others around a customer have ordered; a customer who sees someone drinking sake is more likely to order sake instead of beer. Because I always drink sake when I am eating sushi, the topic of conversation with the chef can turn to the right pairing—and the *oyakata* almost always agrees, when prompted, that sake is generally the best accompaniment to sushi. At this point, the conversation turns to discussion of which sake region, maker, and grade is best and of the temperature at which it should be served; the contemporary norm is to serve it cold. There is also widespread agreement that the most expensive (and also the fruitiest) types of sake, favored by affluent customers, don't go well with seafood. Again, however, exceptions abound; for example, an elderly sushi chef in Ginza prefers to serve red wine with his sushi.

That said, beer or wine rather than sake is now the most common choice, in keeping with the demographic trend toward younger customers. Champagne in particular is a moneymaker, as indicated by most chefs' practice of offering to refill a customer's glass (this is not done for beer or sake). Although many Japanese restaurants seek to make money by selling expensive liquor, it is still extremely unusual to find a sushi chef who does so. Likewise, the industry norm in high-end restaurants is to charge three or four times the retail price of liquor, but most sushi chefs charge perhaps double. When I explicitly asked chefs about this practice, most shrugged and said either that they were following a norm (what they had learned when they were apprenticing) or that it would be unfair to make excess profit from liquor. As one young *oyakata* said, with a hint of indignation, "This is a sushi restaurant, not a bar."

The *oyakata* strives to perform at his peak, day in and day out. As shown in chapter 4, the ubiquitous phrase *ichigo ichie* points to the singularity of any encounter. It is not uncommon to hear an experienced sushi chef say, "This may be the only time this particular customer will eat at my place, and I would like to give her the best experience I can muster." People do have their off days, and there are inferior chefs. But, even though it would be easy to deride such a statement as a bromide, it speaks to the artisanal pride that lies close to the heart of any seasoned sushi master. In addition, it is important to recall that sushi masters don't operate on the usual incentives found in Western restaurants, such as customers' tips, though they devoutly wish for the loyalty of their customers, regardless of whether repeat customers bring gifts.[61] The rhetoric and the actions of sushi *shokunin* hew close to the nature of their work and to the pride they take in it.

In short, being a sushi chef is a challenge. According to the five attributes listed as desiderata by Kyūbei, the legendary Ginza sushi restaurant, a sushi master must be an excellent chef, a competent sommelier, a proficient keeper of accounts, a good manager of staff and customers, and an entertainer.[62] Most sushi chefs work from early in the morning until late at night, six days a week, fifty weeks a year. Again, why do they bother? For earlier generations of sushi chefs, the work they did was not a matter of choice. Some simply assumed the mantle of a family business. Others were sent to apprentice by their impoverished parents, usually right after graduating from primary school. Ono Jirō, for instance, did not want to become a sushi chef—the world of sushi was thrust upon him.[63] But his two sons followed in his footsteps, more or less by choice. And, indeed, in the postaffluent period, people have had some latitude in their occupational choices. There is also anagnorisis, with people attempting to find their way in one occupation or another before coming to recognize sushi as their path. For example, the former master at Sushi Shō chose to become a sushi chef partly because he had read an inspiring manga.[64] Similarly, an apprentice in his twenties told me, "I saw a video of Mr. Ono [the chef at Sukiyabashi Jirō] and thought he was *kakkoii* [cool]." Another sushi chef graduated from a prestigious university and worked for a while as a software engineer but later decided to work at what he really wanted to do. "My uncle was a sushi chef," he told me, "and I admired him." Still another was told that the career of a sushi chef would allow him to work abroad in Australia or France and make good money. But young would-be sushi chefs, whatever their motivations, must still enter the world of apprenticeship, with its long hours and low pay.

SUSHI AND THE ARTISANAL ETHOS

Variations and transformations notwithstanding, a unifying trait in the world of Edo-style sushi is the primacy of the artisanal ethos—that is, respect for tradition and training, and valorization of work in and of itself rather than as a means to something else. (Chapter 6 has much more to say about the artisanal ethos in general.) Exceptions exist, but sushi chefs overwhelmingly identify as artisans.

But Horie Takafumi, the disgraced internet entrepreneur (mentioned in chapter 3) who reinvented himself as a lifestyle guru and gourmet, suggests that the arcane world of sushi craft is obsolete, and he points to a future in which machine-made sushi will supersede the sushi made by human chefs.[65] In fact, however, Horie's line of thinking had already become manifest by the 1990s, if not earlier, in the prototype known as *kaitenzushi,* which became especially popular in Japan during that decade.[66] Indeed, conveyor-belt sushi can offer both efficiency and profit. Any would-be capitalist entrepreneur should be able to envision a chain of large restaurants, and to scale up the lucrative business of sushi. Extremely expensive high-end establishments might continue to provide a sense of exclusivity, but the general modus operandi of the chain restaurant would be mass production. In a scaled-up enterprise of this sort, standardization and division of labor would govern the manifold production tasks, from the purchase of fish to the fish's preparation and its presentation to customers. By ensuring the presence of more and more customers, such a chain could not only secure a larger supply of fish (presumably at a discount) but also make greater use of frozen fish, which can be bought in season, and relatively inexpensively, in large quantities. The establishment could also employ such labor-saving technology as sushi-making robots. In terms of raw materials and labor, this approach would offer massive cost savings. In this scenario, with sushi making understood as a means to the ultimate end of moneymaking, and with production quality satisfactory and consumer demand robust, it would be logical to expand the operation by enlarging the restaurant or opening more branches. This arrangement would also make sushi widely available beyond the narrow circle of wealthy consumers and connoisseurs. If it's true that younger customers are now visiting a more expensive type of sushi venue in part because of their wish to stand out for their conspicuous consumption (especially by way of social media), it's also true that *kaitenzushi* establishments (along with popular culture and, again, social media) have made sushi accessible to a larger clientele. Thus the modernist mode of sushi production would be efficient, scientific, rational, profitable, and demotic.

In contrast, the artisanal ethos, or the artisanal mode of work, rests on ideas and ideals that are distinct from, if not diametrically opposed to, those of the modernist mode. There may be partners, apprentices, and assistants, but the scale of production is small. Division of labor exists, of course, and apprentices in particular perform the menial tasks (cleaning the fish, washing dishes, scrubbing the counter, mopping the floor, acting as the *oyakata*'s factotum); in the postwar period, it was common to hear sushi aficionados say that a novitiate could hold a knife only after a decade of apprenticeship. The conventional wisdom of a generation ago was that it took three years to be able to cook rice, and eight to be permitted to make sushi. The rationale for what was often a decade-long apprenticeship was that it takes a long time to understand and appreciate the nature of distinct fish and to learn the various aspects of the trade, not just cleaning and preparing the fish but also interacting with customers. One chef told me matter-of-factly, "To be a mature chef, it takes ten years, but I think it's a lot tougher for traditional Japanese food, which takes fifteen years."[67] Especially in the early postwar decades, apprenticeship entailed long hours, abysmal pay, and sometimes an abusive boss. Therefore, apprenticeship was usually depicted in the language of *shugyō* (spiritual training); it was, in other words, no fun.[68] Older chefs today still recount horrible abuse from their apprentice years—not just the long hours and the low pay but also the *oyakata* who hurled invective at every turn and used his *geta* (wooden clogs) to hit apprentices. Moreover, the training itself was nominal. A common saying was that the apprentice should learn by stealing the *oyakata*'s secrets—his skills, his recipes, even his social networks. Perhaps most important, the training was all about being patient and putting up with whatever came one's way. This was the virtue of *gaman* (endurance). A generation ago, *gaman* surely would have been one of the greatest virtues to be inculcated into an artisan in the making.

By the early twenty-first century, the postwar common sense about apprenticeship had ceased to be true. It's now thought that only a few years, often at different establishments, may impart enough experience for a young chef to open and successfully operate his own place. And, indeed, younger sushi chefs in particular dismiss the idea that they engage in anything like *shugyō*. Instead, they use secular terms like *torēningu* (which simply means "training"). Yet today's truncated period of apprenticeship has not completely eliminated belief in the widespread notion that it takes at least a decade to master the craft.[69] When I told a group of Japanese sushi workers that the owner of a major US-based sushi chain, a Burmese refugee, uses his fellow refugees as sushi chefs and boasts about quality control on the basis of a two-week training period, they were incredulous (or they were dismissive, as if I were making a bad joke).[70] Even chefs who are already acknowledged masters tend to insist that mastery remains elusive, though they may say this in part because of the sushi world's pervasive norm of modesty. At the same time, sushi artisans stress the unassuming nature of their job. As a remarkably gifted older chef in Nihonbashi told me, "It really doesn't take that long to master sushi making. It's the simplest of food—fast food."[71]

Today's sushi chefs may be willing to reduce the gap between what are now the integrated processes of conception and execution. They may also be willing to avoid excessive division of labor. But the artisanal ethos makes them wary of scaling up or branching out. When I asked sushi chefs why they didn't want to expand their restaurants or create franchises, they were uniform in their resistance, though they expressed it in different ways. Usually they offered not so much a reasoned response as a curt dismissal, such as "dame" ("no good"). They denied the very possibility of expansion in part because they saw it as inconceivable to clone themselves, to create their doubles. Precisely because conception and execution *are* integrated, and because knowledge becomes embodied in the chef after his long apprenticeship, it is difficult for a chef to allocate tasks to disparate people except in routine matters like cleaning fish and scrubbing the counter.[72]

But there is something else that many sushi chefs find problematic about the kind of expansion that could lead to mass-produced sushi. It is not that most of them believe that tradition is sacred, or that there is only one way to make sushi. A

Michelin-star sushi chef, revered by his peers and sushi aficionados alike, says he has nothing against *kaitenzushi,* but it's just not the way he does things. "I want people to eat my sushi as I make it," he says, because that's when sushi tastes best.[73] Another chef told me, "You could write a manual, but then sushi making would become mechanical. In that case, people might as well just go to a *kaitenzushi* place." His point, though he never would have put it this way, was that mastery and artisanship hold the possibility of offering something transcendent.

Sushi chefs in general aspire to prepare the best slices of the best parts of the best (seasonal) fish. As a result, some become dedicated to finding the best sources of fish. Isshi Haruo wrote of one such chef, "There was a passion in the master's sushi that struck and moved people. This passion was a manifestation of the master's extreme obsession about food. A proof of love."[74] It is easy to get carried away, characterizing craftsmanship as a spiritual quest and using quasi-religious language to describe it. But none of the many chefs I talked with in Japan gave off a spiritual or religious air, nor did they use the language of the sacred. Instead, they talked about virtues like *kodawari* (commitment) and *shūchaku* (obsession). For them, making sushi was not so much a calling as a sense of having embraced life, or a way of life. In any event, the master chefs I spoke with, chefs with decades of experience, were hesitant to explain the philosophy or mechanics of sushi making, apart from offering somewhat nebulous comments about a way of life or their *ikigai*; as they told me, they just did their work. Indeed, artisans are not theorists. If there were a philosophy of sushi making, it would probably be "I make the best sushi I can."

But sushi making is also about relating to and serving customers. As another superstar chef puts it, "A sushi artisan makes sushi so customers can eat it and go home happy."[75] He defines his job as the business of *sarashi no shōbai* (exposure), by which he means that human interaction is the key to sushi making.[76] In other words, sushi chefs are not making sushi for themselves. They need customers to complete the circuit that includes fishing boats and fishermen, fishmongers, and the chefs themselves. The nature of their business requires conversation with customers, but sushi chefs tend not to be great raconteurs or eloquent speakers. They use the restricted code of simple declarative sentences.

Craftsmanship is not just about business or making money. It is first and foremost about *craft* and about the will and the spirit that undergird it.[77] But if work carried out in accord with the artisanal ethos is an end in itself, this is not to say that sushi chefs don't want to make money, build a reputation, or achieve renown. They feel strongly, however, that they are working not so much to make money as to make a living by integrating work and life in the pursuit of a craft or calling. The sushi chef mentioned at the beginning of this chapter, the one who couldn't wait to get back to work after the New Year's break, is not as unusual as he may seem. For example, there is a famous sushi chef who retired from his Michelin-star restaurant in Tokyo and promptly opened a new restaurant in Honolulu. I asked him how he was enjoying his "retirement." He smiled and said he was finding it interesting and challenging to explore the local marine life and turn it into sushi. Later, I visited another Michelin-star sushi chef who had also retired and almost immediately opened a restaurant in Honolulu. I was surprised to see that he was serving fish exclusively from Japan and that his new menu was a rough simulacrum of the one in his Japanese establishment. When I expressed curiosity about these two diametrically opposed approaches, with the first chef serving almost all local or regional food, and the second replicating what he had done in Japan, the second chef simply said that he and the other chef had different *porishī* (a word that sounds like the English word "policy" but in Japanese denotes something between "philosophy" and "practice"). Sushi chefs take it for granted that people work in different ways and engage in distinct alimentary practices, shaped as the chefs they are by their masters, their training, and their long immersion in their craft. They don't necessarily agree on what's best or how best to do their job, but they all say that they work in part because working is their way of living.[78]

Needless to say, however, many sushi chefs do have larger aspirations—not for fame and fortune as such but for the opportunity to become independent and perhaps open a restaurant in a major urban area like Ginza (which, as mentioned earlier, became the mecca of Edo-style sushi after the Great Kantō Earthquake of 1923, if not before).[79] And make no mistake: the sushi world is marked by competition (with masters or apprentices, with peers, with oneself), no matter how much the rhetoric of the craft downplays the fact of competition.[80] An elderly man of my acquaintance, who claims to have eaten at sushi restaurants more than ten thousand times, told me that the older *oyakata* tend to be Edoites, with a predominant character trait of *makezugirai* (meaning that they hate to lose), though he added that few *Edokko* remain. And some of today's young sushi workers are less than diligent. But the relative hardship of artisanal work is such that a truly undedicated apprentice will fall by the wayside long before an opening appears for him to ascend the sushi hierarchy.

The artisanal ethos or artisanal temperament—what the Japanese call *shokunin katagi*—is far from dominant in contemporary Japan, but it remains remarkably robust. It is not marginal, but neither does it flourish only for a luxury market. Sometimes it is viewed as a distinctly Japanese trait, but it is far from unique to Japan. In the artisanal ethos, work is valued as an end in itself and as a way of life. In this, the artisanal ethos stands out from the dominant, modernist mode of working and from the modernist way of thinking about work. Some sushi chefs add flourishes of their own to this view of life by adding to it a layer of the old Edoite spirit. For example, Morooka Yukio, a towering figure of the sushi world, takes as his motto the received Edoite philosophy of life: "Iki de inase de aru" (which translates roughly as being *kakkoii*, or cool, not to mention chic, dashing, and spirited).[81] Yet even the most successful sushi chefs don't exactly enjoy fame and fortune. The usual working rhythm—six days a week, from early morning to late night—is rigorous even by the workaholic standards of Japan. This is not the life for a bon vivant, and certainly not for anyone who seeks a high income.

Well into the 1980s, it was still taken for granted that the road to becoming an *oyakata* was mapped out for those who did not aspire to tertiary education and to the coveted life of a corporate worker. By the 2010s, however, there were more than a few sushi chefs who were graduates of four-year universities. What gave the late entrants access to this less traveled road was the radical contraction of what had previously been a long, arduous apprenticeship. These chefs may have entered the sushi world because they detested the routinized life of a desk jockey answering to an annoying boss, but they all knew that the life of a sushi chef is challenging and not well paid. Several of this new breed told me that they appreciated not just the autonomy of their adopted line of work but also the meaningfulness of making or doing something concrete. As one chef in his forties said, "It's like my *oyakata* said—we should all aspire to do something that makes us feel it's good to be alive, to have been born." Certainly, most *oyakata* express something approaching love for sushi—a demanding mistress, but endlessly enchanting. And there is undoubtedly an element of impression management in sushi chefs' stated enchantment with their work. After all, as one chef asked rhetorically, "Who wants to shell out a pile of cash to eat at a place with a gloomy chef?" All the same, it seems quite clear that to be a sushi chef is to have, if not quite a calling, a meaningful and satisfying occupation.

CAVEATS AND CONCERNS

Change is ineluctable, tradition is not static, and Edomae sushi has undergone considerable transformation in its less-than-two-hundred-year-old existence. It's a story not just of technological and commercial innovation but of shifting life trajectories and aspirations. Long gone are the tales of wretchedly poor prepubescent youth apprenticing in almost serf-like conditions. In my hundreds of excursions to sushi restaurants, I have never heard an *oyakata* scream at his assistants (though I have heard them offer criticisms) or seen the violent deployment of his *geta*. Whatever we make of sushi chefs and their artisanal orientation, the widespread, even worldwide, consensus is that sushi itself is a superlative Japanese achievement. This is evidently the mind-set of those sushi aficionados, not all of them wealthy, who dine regularly at expensive sushi establishments. As the writer Arashiyama Mitsugorō says, "My purpose in life is to eat sushi."[82] Or take one of my neighbors, a middle manager in his fifties who spends much of his discretionary income eating at top sushi places. He asks, "Is there a better or more cost-effective way to be happy?" And this is not even to mention all the people who like to eat at their local sushi joints, drop into an inexpensive *kaitenzushi* outlet, or pick up the humble offerings available at convenience stores. Sushi, a triumph of the artisanal ethos, helps make Japanese society bearable and keeps it viable. Be all that as it may, however, there are some reservations to be entertained about the world of sushi.

Disruption of the Artisanal Ethos

In *kaitenzushi* spots, some employees are undertrained as chefs and function more as general-duty workers, not so different from workers at fast food chain restaurants. A rough generalization is that the artisanal ethos survives most strongly in the most expensive and oldest sushi establishments. But how long can the artisanal heart of the sushi world keep beating? As early as 1986, the legendary sushi chef Morooka Yukio was lamenting the corrosion of the artisanal ethos.[83] In 1990, there were about fifty thousand sushi establishments with fewer than four employees; by 2006, there were only about twenty-two thousand.[84]

And consider all the younger chefs who rely on entrepreneurs or corporations to bankroll their establishments. The newer chefs—especially the younger celebrities, unmoored from the traditions of their craft—can look more like businessmen than artisanal chefs. In the increasingly globalized sushi world, they seem equally at home in New York or Paris as in Tokyo. And as they proffer their rich visual spectacles, they shortchange traditional concerns. Who cares, really, about the inexpensive but laborious *kanpyō* roll when younger customers want the easy, expensive *torotaku* (fatty tuna and pickled radish) roll? At one much-publicized establishment, the chef offers thirty pieces—but, as an experienced eater noted, they are all "child-size."

Moreover, sushi restaurants operate within a world of commerce. In the past, fishermen and fishmongers worked in smaller, artisanal operations. Today they find themselves up against stiff competition from corporate interests. There are also reports that *yakuza* (elements of organized crime) are extensively involved in the seafood business.[85]

But there is reason for cautious optimism. Partly because of the global fanfare over sushi and the widespread awareness of sushi in Japan, steady numbers of young men, and some women, are now seeking careers in the challenging but rewarding world of sushi. Some enter culinary academies or universities to pursue their path, though apprenticeship remains the royal road, if only because it offers ready access to networks of excellent fishmongers and wealthy customers.

At the same time, some *kaitenzushi* chains are beginning to emulate establishments in the sector of fine sushi dining. This change is due in part to the newly refined palate of the Japanese consumer, or at least to the consumer's confidence in his ability to differentiate good sushi from bad, as well as to the consensus view that low prices alone are no guarantee of a restaurant's success. Indeed, Sushirō, perhaps the most successful *kaitenzushi* chain, stresses its artisanal production methods and claims that raw materials account for at least 50 percent of its operating costs.[86] It is no accident that in 2019 the winning bid for the New Year's *maguro* was a *kaitenzushi* chain. What the sushi world is witnessing, then, is not a race to the bottom but a trend toward quality-based competition.

Misogyny

It is unclear whether sushi artisans are more misogynistic than workers in the modern world of corporations and bureaucracies. Nevertheless, the world of Edomae sushi is male dominated, and casual misogyny does prevail. It is not that there are no female sushi chefs, but almost all the famous chefs are men, and so are those who are less famous. In many establishments, women serve tea and clean up, and in the rare instance when a woman does make sushi, criticisms from male customers are not uncommon. "The old lady clearly wasn't trained," I heard one man grumble. "Her sushi falls apart when you touch it." But that didn't stop him from wolfing down one piece after another. For older chefs, the absence of women is simply the norm, though many hasten to give other reasons why women do not or cannot become good chefs. A commonly articulated rationale is that because women's body temperature is higher, their *nigirizushi* won't be as good as the *nigirizushi* made by colder-blooded men (but many men dip their hands in cold or iced water to lower their own body temperature). Other chefs, seeming to contradict that rationale, say that women don't have *kiai* (fire in the belly) and that women lack the tenacity and fighting spirit to flourish in the sushi world. The truth, though, is that there is no reason why women cannot dedicate themselves to the craft of sushi making.

Economic Vulnerability and Insecurity

Outsiders to the sushi world, and some sushi chefs, say that the career track of chef is for dropouts from the Japanese meritocratic system. Until the late twentieth century, the schooling of most sushi artisans was minimal. Nevertheless, there is a certain respect in the sushi world for educated people, especially among chefs who came of age in the immediate postwar decades. For example, a famous chef in Ginza, notorious for his gruff demeanor, had barely been able to grunt a greeting to me until the day I happened to mention that I write books. With a quick flicker of recognition, he held forth on all the famous authors who had frequented his establishment, and he concluded by expressing regret over his lack of formal higher education. The sense of inferiority born of not being a university graduate has prompted some older, financially successful chefs to insist that their offspring pursue tertiary education. Indeed, as noted earlier, by the 2010s it was not entirely uncommon for a university graduate to work for a time at a prestigious corporate job and only then become a sushi chef. In any case, it's not clear why everyone needs to enroll in higher education, or why attendance at a highly ranked university should be the ultimate arbiter of one's chances in life. As a celebrated chef in his forties said, "What's great is that an ordinary guy like me can come from a humble background and still make it. I just worked really, really hard, and now I have a job I like, and more money than I ever thought I'd have."

Outside observers may also be struck by the precarious nature of the sushi chef's existence. His business, not to mention the lives of his family and employees, depends completely on his restaurant's profitability, and the burden rests almost entirely on his shoulders. If he should ever get sick, he would have to close down until he recovered. Perhaps it is not so remarkable, then, that sushi chefs seem not to get sick—their obsession with cleanliness, including constant hand-washing, undoubtedly does much to keep viruses and bacteria at bay, as does their life of constant exertion, along with their healthy diet. To my knowledge, no one has undertaken any studies of sushi chefs' health or of the health of chefs in other types of restaurants, but it's not unreasonable to suppose that a meaningful, reasonably fulfilling job might do wonders for a chef's physical and spiritual health.

There is also the question of retirement. Many sushi chefs remain vital and vigorous into their eighties and even their nineties, long after other people in their age cohort have retired from work in different fields. In addition, sushi chefs, like others working in small, family-operated Japanese firms, habitually save a portion of their earnings.[87] They realize that in old age they will not be able to rely on their children, as older generations of sushi chefs did, or on Japan's chronically anemic government-based pension scheme.

Environmental Stressors

The sushi world is not immune to the environmental crisis. What was once abundant has become rare. What was once large is now almost always small. These and other trends are worrisome.[88] Overfishing, for example, a problem now for decades, has caused the depletion and even the disappearance of some types of fish that were once common in the waters off Tokyo and around the Japanese archipelago generally.[89] In addition, the already-declining fish stock has been squeezed by escalating global demand. Moreover, warming and acidification of the ocean have placed some species not just in peril but under actual threat of extinction. Many fishing villages, too, are in decline, partly because fishing is laborious, dangerous, and poorly paid.[90] Some chefs worry that the future of Edomae sushi is threatened, too. Regrettably, though, few customers seem worried about the impending crisis.

6

The Artisanal Ethos in Japan

The Larger Context

In Tokyo, not more than a five-minute walk from the sushi restaurant described at the beginning of chapter 5, there was a tempura place I used to go to about as often and as long as I had gone to that sushi shop. Its U-shaped counter seated eleven people, and the standard lunch set cost the equivalent of about seven US dollars, including tax and tip. Like the sushi shop, the tempura place hadn't raised its prices in years. The chef had been deep frying fish and vegetables for more than a half century. He displayed masterly facility with his elongated chopsticks as he turned over the breaded shrimp or squid, then found the right moment to serve the tempura to his waiting, ravenous customers. He had two assistants—a younger man, who was apprenticing, and an elderly woman, who was in charge of cooking the rice and washing the dishes. During one of my visits, in the off-hours, I overheard the assistants talking about the ridiculous prices that nearby purveyors were demanding for processed and prepared food. The chef grunted. This was just the way things were, he said—there was nothing to be done. When I asked him about raising his prices, he shrugged almost imperceptibly and remained silent. Many chefs who work behind a counter can be taciturn, saving their voices for initial greetings and departing thanks, but it would be wrong to think they're not observant. This tempura chef didn't know my name, but he knew that I had been coming to his place over the years. Later on, when I asked him if he would ever retire, he grunted again and said he would keep on frying tempura until he dropped dead. Sad to say, he got sick and his restaurant closed in 2018.

Between and beyond my many visits to *B-kyū gurume* (class B gourmet) restaurants, I prowled the same neighborhood for used books and magazines, since this

143

area was a center for that kind of reading material. My favorite redoubt was a century-old bookstore that had been renovated and was now a clean, well-lighted three-story building. It had a well-curated collection of books and magazines in diverse fields, and a long table in front of the cashier's station that displayed new books (regulars called this table "the battleship," because of its shape). As a bibliophile with intermittent outbreaks of obsessive-compulsive disorder, I always select the best-preserved copy of a title when several are available. On one occasion, having completed a lengthy browsing session and chosen several books, I took them to the register, where the cashier scanned their bar codes and began slipping a paper cover over each volume, as is the Japanese custom, carried out to protect the books as well as the customer's privacy. But suddenly the cashier stopped and closely examined one of the purchased books. He pointed out a tiny flaw on the cover and said he would find me a copy in better condition. I was dumbfounded. I hadn't noticed anything wrong with the cover, and when the cashier showed me the flaw, it looked incredibly minuscule even by my extreme standards. But I agreed to the switch, and the cashier came back with a pristine copy of the book.

In the same area of Tokyo, I often stayed at a small hotel that perches atop a knoll. It has only thirty-five rooms. The hotel is famous for accommodating writers who have been canned—that is, forced by their editors to hole up and write until a looming deadline is met. It's a place of unmatched serenity and understated service. As Yukio Mishima himself wrote, "I never thought there could be such a quiet inn right in the middle of Tokyo. The facilities are extremely clean, and it's great that the service is a bit amateurish. I hope it won't become too famous or too fashionable."[1] The hotel actually is well known, but these days, with its Art Nouveau construction redolent of a bygone era, it's definitely not fashionable. It is, in a word, retro, and it exudes the atmosphere of the Shōwa period. Yet Mishima's testimonial continues to ring true. The staff almost always evinces an artisanal ethos of service.[2] For example, in one of the hotel's several restaurants, there is a waitress who, unaccountably, remembers my preferences, even though I have stayed at this hotel just once a year, at most. The cleaning staff, too, is scrupulous about preserving what almost every other hotel's housekeepers would surely toss away.

In chapter 5, I could have written not just about sushi chefs but also about chefs and cooks of other cuisines, or about ceramicists and glassblowers, or about kabuki actors and traditional musicians. They all belong to the world of the artisanal ethos. But the distinct world of sushi was as good a place as any for me to begin describing the powerful strand of the artisanal ethos in Japanese life. Let's look now at some other, broader manifestations of the artisanal ethos in contemporary Japan.

The three vignettes at the beginning of this chapter may mean different things to different readers. Some readers may wonder whether the restaurant I described, and the one described at the beginning of chapter 5, are just greasy spoons pushing shoddy sushi and sodden tempura. It's true that both shops have a shabby gentility about them, but both are almost immaculately clean. Their chefs and employees are invariably polite and cheerful, and they take pride in serving fresh, tasty fare at a reasonable price. Other readers may wonder whether I'm describing venues that are beyond the reach of ordinary people, like the restaurants serving fine sushi that are described later in chapter 5. But having a meal at the tempura joint is cheaper than eating at McDonald's, and the boutique hotel I mentioned is not particularly expensive—certainly it's less expensive to stay there than at a Hilton or a Hyatt. Still other readers may have formed the impression that contemporary Japanese people are obsessed with order and purity. And perhaps that is true, but the restaurant and hotel employees described in these vignettes are not particularly authoritarian, bureaucratic, or militaristic in their pursuit of cleanliness. My interactions with them have been nothing if not casual and easy. Far from being authoritarian or unfriendly, chefs and their assistants are attentive, whether that means replenishing a customer's *tentsuyu* (tempura sauce) before he requests the refill or anticipating the customer's next move, such as his preparations to pay and leave. But this kind of exceptional service is certainly not enforced by an overbearing boss or mandated by employee guidelines. The bookstore cashier, for example, did not have to fetch a fresh copy of a minimally damaged book. To be clear, then, I am not talking about expensive establishments, and I am not attempting to convey information about a supposed Japanese national character. Rather, I am describing the artisanal ethos, a distinct orientation to work and to what work demands. As chapter 5 explains, the artisanal ethos is not universal in Japan, nor is it unique to Japan. But it persists, even in the face of considerable stress.

The idea of the artisanal ethos may seem inscrutable, and certainly irrational from an economic standpoint. After all, why not enjoy a well-deserved rest instead of itching to get back to work, like the sushi chef at the beginning of chapter 5, who could barely tolerate his New Year's break? And why not raise prices when the market will surely bear the increase, especially since the downside of many a *B-kyū gurume* restaurant is a long line and a long wait?[3] Although many such restaurants acknowledge the need to make money and do not ignore competition based on prices, they are not in business to maximize the income of their chefs and employees. Instead, these spots generally charge what seems right and fair to them, a price they arrive at after calculating what it costs to sustain the establishment and its employees, with a sideways glance at competitors' rates. Their chefs stay in business, continuing to work hard and put in long hours alongside their employees, because that is what artisans do. For them, the artisanal ethos and the artisanal mode of work are a way of life.

THE ARTISANAL ETHOS AS RELIC

The words "artisan" and "craft" may call up a cobwebbed, mothballed world of antiquated practices, such as embroidery, that are usually associated with decrepit elderly people. To be sure, as I elaborate below, there are contemporary enthusiasms for artisanal chocolate or craft beer, but items that are handmade or home-made have hearty, healthy connotations and evoke a sentimental past. But most people today surround themselves with things made under conditions of standardized mechanical production, which achieves both efficiency and affordability.[4] Giant mechanized operations, whether the factory farms of the US Midwest or the industrial edifices of southeastern China, make everything from the clothes we wear to the foods we eat and even the buildings in which we work and relax and sleep. A consumer may not know where or how her shoes were made, but unless she has paid a hefty sum for luxurious handcrafted footwear, she will surmise that they were manufactured at a factory somewhere, probably in China.

The world of mechanical production is all around us. We are influenced by industrial aesthetics, we operate under mechanical time, we believe in science-based technology, and we measure the drudgery of our work against the gains we'll derive from our consumption. But the word "manufacture" has been wrenched from its etymological roots. Once upon a time, it denoted items produced by hand, and in shops. Now it summons up a world of machines and automation, of mechanical contraptions and digital programs that organize, produce, and market goods in the process that we summarize with the phrase "modern manufacturing." Innovation and progress seem to depend on combining division of labor (in the form of bureaucracy) with science-based technology. And now, nearly two centuries after the Industrial Revolution, there looms the specter of artificial intelligence and robots.

If most of the products we buy are made in large factories and sold in large retail outlets, we should not be surprised that so many of us also work in large organizations, whether offices, stores, or factories. Indeed, the factory is the generic institutional manifestation of the modernist mode of work, a mode distinct from the feudal and medieval modes, though its permutations are found in such different types of workplaces as a call center and a large hospital, each of which values efficiency and standardization, which means that it divides tasks, employs technology, and expands the scope and scale of its particular kind of production. Under this arrangement, management handles conception—often with the aid of formal training in executive tasks, as represented by the prestige credential known as the MBA—and execution falls to everyone else. If Frederick Wins-low Taylor's program of scientific management were not already half forgotten, it would be even more frequently derided. Nevertheless, his recommendations for breaking tasks down into small, preferably irreducible, component parts—into "laboremes," to coin a term—continue to be widely accepted and implemented. Moreover, whatever an enterprise's stated reasons may be for producing or provid-ing a particular good or service, the ultimate rationale in competitive, commercial society is to make money, and preferably to maximize profit. As a result, the mod-ernist ethos of production and service is characterized by division of labor, tech-nology and efficiency, scale and scope, and productivity and profit. We have come to think of the modernist mode—founded on the principle of instrumental ration-ality, which valorizes the end of moneymaking and, thus, the means of efficiency—as a natural, commonsense way to organize work and society.

In this context, then, the idea of artisanal work is a relic, a residual category, one that entails an honorable but outmoded way of making and doing things or, very often, a piece of work performed as a hobby, usually for a holiday. To be sure, the idea of artisanal work often connotes the artisan's diligence, skill, and authenticity. As such, it may command a premium. Very few of us can resist the authenticity, beauty, and authority of well-made things, which is why tourists, especially visitors to the Global South, routinely seek out local crafts as trophies of their travel—mementos of the past, and of the Other, that embody something real and exotic. There is also growing awareness—coeval with the advent of industrial manufacturing—that large-scale mechanical production may not be the best way to provide a range of goods and services. Boutique products and brands proclaim their worth in terms of rare or superior materials and skilled, even traditional, artisanal work. This is true not just for expensive items, such as haute couture and fine wines, but also for such everyday commodities as chocolate and coffee, beer and ice cream. The claim that an object or a comestible was handmade or roasted by hand, necessarily in small batches, is a sign of authenticity and quality as well as a rationale for a higher price. Nevertheless, even if small is beautiful, small is still small, and to be small is to be marginal and marginalized in the age of mass and mechanical production.

ARTISANAL VALUES AND ELEMENTS OF
THE ARTISANAL TEMPERAMENT

An ethos, as described in chapters 3 and 4, is a habit of thought, action, and char-acter, one that marks a particular orientation toward life and the world.[5] The arti-sanal ethos is what fuels the artisanal mode of production—a way of organizing work distinct from the dominant modernist mode in terms of organization, technology, and the market. And, as discussed elsewhere, what is most important is that work performed in accord with the artisanal ethos is not a means, or a matter of *instrumental* rationality, but rather and primarily an end, a matter of *substantive* rationality. Artisans fashion things for use and, in so doing, they acquire a sense of self-fulfillment, which in itself constitutes a meaningful and purposive endeavor.

The sushi chefs featured in chapter 5 are certainly not the only people who embody the artisanal ethos in contemporary Japan. The artisanal ethos is ubiquitous in the food industry, in connection both with traditional fare like sushi or tempura and with foreign cuisines. In the Tokyo neighborhood where I was staying in the late 2010s, for example, there were two Italian restaurants. Each one seated roughly ten people, and in each one a single Japanese chef served his customers. Both chefs employed helpers from time to time, but in principle each of them worked alone and did everything from purchasing vegetables to washing dishes. Both had lived and worked in Italy to learn the regional cuisines of that country.[6] Neither was a celebrity chef, but both of them worked day after day to make *pasta c'anciova* and osso buco, evoking the same scents and tastes as those produced by their colleagues in Catania or Milano, but making subtle adjustments to accommodate the prevailing Japanese preferences. If, after a satisfying meal at one of these restaurants or the other, I decided to take a walk through the concrete jungle of skyscrapers that dominated the neighborhood, I would see artisans working late into the night. In a shop that sold *tatami* (the mats used as flooring in Japanese-style houses), an elderly man might be weaving straw with intensity and care. In a shop selling custom uniforms (many Japanese students are required to wear them), I might see a middle-aged woman hunched over a sewing machine. There were also small shops that made and sold glass products and metal parts. And outside Tokyo and the other big cities, the Japanese archipelago is dotted with regional specialty crafts: traditional swords and knives and pottery as well as a wide range of everyday goods made by carpenters, cobblers, and other skilled artisans working in small, family-owned and -operated shops.

While I was in Japan, I sought to immerse myself in the pursuit of several crafts. It seemed to me that learning a craft might be a good way both to understand it and to communicate with the artisans who were its practitioners. In the end, all I managed was to become the George Plimpton of those crafts, though I did find a role for myself as a collator of artisans' words and actions, since artisans are neither theorists nor academics. As one ceramist quipped, "I just play with dirt." But if I were to look for some deep commonality or essence among the small enterprises I visited and among the artisans I talked with, I would necessarily commit a fallacy of misplaced concreteness. Some of the artisans were superstar chefs or so-called national treasures.[7] Others, if not teetering on the brink of bankruptcy, were unable to find successors for their lines of work or for their establishments. Still others, conforming to an old stereotype about *shokunin* (skilled artisans), seemed only to revel in their nightly rounds of drinking. And for every dedicated artisan I encountered, I found another who was less than disciplined and diligent. In short, as I explored the world of Japanese artisans, I found the usual distribution of talent, dedication, skills, material rewards, and satisfaction.

At the same time, certain themes came up again and again when these artisans discussed their work (and, much less frequently, themselves). The sushi chefs gave me more than an exceptional taste of the contemporary artisanal ethos in Japan. And what they said was repeated, with the expected permutations, across disparate genres of artisanship, not just in other areas of the culinary arts but in knife manufacturing, too, as well as in ceramic work, furniture construction, and the traditional Japanese arts of kabuki and woodworking, among many, many others. As pride and passion showed through these artisans' calm, matter-of-fact way of talking about their work and their lives, they produced a living discourse of the artisanal ethos in Japan today.

Dedication, Discipline, and Doing the Right Thing

In the perennial, irresolvable debate concerning the salience of talent versus the importance of effort, there is no question that the artisans I spoke with considered diligence paramount. It is not that there are no natural-born artisans—one superstar sushi chef told me he was awestruck by the delicate, superb nose and tongue of the celebrated French chef Joël Robuchon. But the consensus was that almost anyone improves after years of dedication to the craft. The virtue of *majime* (seriousness and straightforwardness) is considered somewhat outdated—it is redolent of elbow grease, as shown in chapter 4—but from time to time it was invoked as a crucial attribute of any successful craftsperson. In particular, the artisans I talked with thought it necessary to be *ganbaru* (persistent). Mastery, they said, might be a forever-receding goal, but daily repeated effort is what brings improvement.[8]

At times I heard the virtue of persistence discussed in somewhat more elevated language (*shūchakushin*), and there was talk of *kodawari* (caring). The same idea was also expressed, with slightly more ambivalence, as *ganko* (stubbornness) or more simply as the virtue of honesty. On one occasion, at a Michelin-star tempura restaurant, I expressed my surprise that there were only three guests. The chef cheerfully replied that he hadn't found enough good fish that week and had decided not to take any new reservations. At another establishment, the chef accidentally dropped a morsel of food onto an impeccably clean surface and then refused to serve it, despite the intended customer's entreaties. "This is what I have to do," the chef said. In other words, both chefs wanted to do the right thing, which was to serve their food in its best possible state. It's not that the chefs I spoke with thought there was only one right way to do things, but they did see many wrong ways to do things, and they held strong internal judgments about right and wrong.

In the world of the artisanal ethos, peccadilloes abound, such as *me wo otosu* (lapses of attention). As an amateur observer, I was startled to see a ceramicist deliberately smash one beautifully fired piece after another. He explained that he had been preoccupied by personal troubles when he was making those pieces and that the finished products clearly reflected his inattention—but the flaws were invisible to anyone but himself. *Teochi* (literally, "hand falling," meaning an omission, halfhearted work, or failure caused by not doing one's best) is another cardinal sin in the world of those committed to doing things right. For example, I saw a leather craftsman toss a series of superb bags onto a trash heap. When I asked him what was wrong with them, he pointed to areas of poor craftsmanship, but I was unable to see the flaws even after several careful inspections. When I suggested that he sell the bags at a discount, he scoffed at the very idea that an imperfect product might make its way from his shop out into the world. "I cannot do that," was his final answer.

The commitment to doing the right thing does come up against the realities of money, but that very commitment puts a damper on material temptations, since getting rich is not a prized goal in the world of the artisanal ethos. Indeed, the very effort to enrich oneself is seen as corroding the possibility of maintaining the commitment to rightness in the exercise of one's craft. The pursuit of money or profit is seen as corrosive because the whole point of the work is to do it right. Making money from a product, if making money is the primary goal, is understood as rendering the product inferior or *dame* (useless). A middle-aged potter said, "I suppose I could make more money, but what would be the point? I could have stayed on at the big corporation where I used to work, and kept my job security and my good pay, but the work was meaningless. Why make this work meaningless, too?" Of necessity, the artisans I talked with did sometimes make compromises, but only after grappling with their pride in their work and with their commitment to doing it the right way.

Embodied Habit and the Middle Voice

According to an apocryphal tale, the Buddha twisted a flower, and only one of his many disciples broke into a smile of recognition.[9] Thus Nengemishō (Flower sermon) conveys the paradigmatic instance of nonverbal or extraverbal communication employed in the transmission of embodied knowledge. Just as one candle is used to light another, person-to-person transmission enables communication of nonexplicit, nonformalized, nonalgorithmic, noninformational knowledge. Background knowledge that is acquired, then embodied, allows one to decipher the meaning of a twisted flower, or the unspoken, uncodified elements of a craft.

In the world of the artisanal ethos, the primacy of practice implies the priority of tradition. Books and videos are widely available to anyone who wants to learn a skill or technique, and so it may seem less important now than in the past to observe a master at work and emulate his skills. But even though learning is highly mimetic, emulation is not as simple as it may seem. Emulation requires not only a great deal of background knowledge and skill but also the ability to discern the unspoken and hidden elements of a craft. For example, there are many technically proficient players of the three-stringed Japanese instrument called the shamisen, and some even seem to play perfectly, but only those who "understand the silence," as one shamisen master told me, can become great players. In other words, as in the case of a sushi chef who must develop *mekiki,* learning entails a great deal of embodied, or tacit, knowledge—an awareness of things that are not easily formalized, formulated, or inscribed as clear steps to be followed. In the case of the shamisen, reverberation (the sound produced after a string is plucked) has central importance, and only those who have mastered this elusive element can truly become shamisen masters.

Artisanal work is full of baffling moves and decisions. Why did the sushi master make an incision in this particular fish, in this particular way? Where, exactly, is the invisible grain on this piece of wood in which the master woodworker is making a cut? What made the toymaker implant the hair on this doll's head in that particular way, so different from what he did yesterday with the hair on this other doll's head? It's one thing to discover the eponymous figure in *Where's Waldo?* It's quite another to find something if you don't know what it is you're looking for. Or, as the old cliché has it, if a joke has to be explained, it just isn't funny.

When I asked individual artisans whether transmitting a craft to later generations was worth the trouble of writing a book, the response was not always negative. But there was general doubt that the essential elements of the craft could be expressed in print or captured in photography. As a maker of traditional toys said, "It is worthwhile to write a book and leave something behind. The problem is that it's easy to misinterpret what's written down. But there's no mistaking what you've learned in your body." A notable paradox is that print, which seems fixed on the page, is precisely what becomes fluid and ambiguous, and thus open to misinterpretation. In fact, anyone who has attempted to do something as apparently simple as using printed instructions to tie a knot can attest to the near impossibility of moving from formal instruction to concrete practice. Similarly, anyone who has tried to assemble an IKEA product will have a tale to tell about how hard it was to follow the prescribed steps, no matter how explicitly they were outlined, and no matter how many supposedly helpful illustrations were included with the instructions.

Habituation, by which a complex of activities becomes second nature, is the royal road to embodied knowledge. It is both an ontological attribute and a matter for epistemology. Mastery emerges in the concrete act of making or doing. To reach the goal of mastery is at once to dissolve oneself in tradition and, in so doing, to embody it. Only from this standpoint can the artisan hope to flourish and express his or her singularity and individuality or to achieve what might be called innovation. The idea is not to hold explicit instructions in one's head but to be able to make or do something without benefit of conscious reflection. This is to say that movement becomes a matter of habit—of embodied knowledge or embodied action. What is required is complex, contingent, flexible knowledge that entails cognitive dispersal—like an octopus, one has not just a brain but also hands that think. Practice may not make perfect, but muscle memory does develop, and it works with or on the materials at hand. And here, habit—the habit of achieving excellence and striving for perfection—becomes a supreme achievement. It is important to stress, however, that the term "habit," in this context, does not denote reflexive behavior by which a skill, once acquired, can be mindlessly reproduced. Rather, habit in this context is mindful, or it is intelligent, but it does not depend on reflection. Habit understood in this sense is also purposive, or teleological, with no split between conception and execution. Anyone who has learned to play the piano knows that mastery of the instrument is not about banging on its keys from memory. Instead, one embodies the music and strives to reproduce it after hours of practice, hours during which the mind and the body have necessarily operated as a unit. Thorstein Veblen spoke of the instinct, or sense, of workmanship as combining intelligence and teleology.[10] We might say, echoing Aristotle, that what constitutes the artisanal disposition is a propensity for action and achievement, aimed at fulfilling one's potential and at constructing something of worth on the basis of years of habituation.

Given the reigning grammars of modern Western languages, we have come to believe in a fundamental duality between the active voice (the realm of intention and will) and the passive voice (the arena of enforcement and servitude). Therefore, another way to talk about embodied habit is to say that it resists this dualism, which is also common to most thinking in the social sciences. Discussions of artisanal work lead to the idea that artisans, in much of what they do, aim to use the *middle voice*, which is to say the voice of habitual action freed from formalism and explicit protocols.[11] For example, a chef who is making Edo-style sushi is not passively and mindlessly replicating learned movements. He does not explicitly conceive the notion of making sushi according to a learned algorithm. Instead, he does what he does by virtue of the ingrained habit of mastered movements that fall somewhere between the active and the passive voices, so to speak. Artisans—and, indeed, most other people, most of the time—inhabit the middle voice and dance to the music of embodied habit.

Diversity and Flexibility, Tradition and Innovation

An important implication of the middle voice is that an artisan's finished products or performances are not all uniform. The artisan may strive for perfection, but that's no guarantee that the goal will be achieved. Each piece wrought by an artisan is a distinct accomplishment, regardless of how much it resembles the artisan's other pieces. Instrumental reason involves some received beliefs, and one of them is faith in the application of scientific, theoretical knowledge to the quest for mechanical replication and, thus, for uniformity (in other words, it's a matter of engineering). But every new piece by an artisan is neither a product of that belief nor a random construction born of ill-considered, imperfectly followed steps and processes. In kabuki or Noh plays, as in classical music and other types of perform-ances, repeated practice is not meant to create a mechanically reproduced, seem-ingly perfect series of movements and statements. Paradoxically, the absence of uniformity is a necessary outcome of mastery.[12]

Lack of uniformity—diversity, that is—is considered to be far from inferior in the world of the artisanal ethos. From the modernist standpoint, lack of standardi-zation means failure. But from the perspective of the artisanal ethos, it is precisely because each piece or performance is different—a product of tacit, embodied knowledge, rendered concrete—that the piece or performance expresses the spirit of artisanship. At times, the Zen-like aesthetic of *wabi-sabi*, too, valorizes irregu-larities and imperfections. For example, as mentioned in chapter 4, the term *ichigo ichie*—which comes from the Japanese tea ceremony, another artisanal endeavor—has moved into the wider life of Japan. Based on the Zen Buddhist notion of ephem-erality, *ichigo ichie* evokes the miracle of an encounter that in all likelihood is unique. The vague awareness that *this* may be *it* lends a certain urgency to the potter's turn-ing and firing of her cup, or to the chef's creation of his signature dish. The notion of memento mori is of course not uniquely Japanese, but artisans in particular are fond of citing it to make sense of their work and their lives.

Artisans often talk about the weather—how the overcast sky is affecting the wood, how the rain has changed the nature of the clay, how cold dry air can alter foodstuffs—and every variation in the weather requires some kind of adjustment, however minor or even negligible. Nor is the audience uniform. A smaller cus-tomer may want a smaller portion, or an older customer's fading vision may mean she needs a bolder drawing. The idea, then, is not rigidity but flexibility, born of the contingent nature of life. And, curiously, flexibility works in other ways, too. Artisans are mindful of the myriad ways in which any product can be used, just as the living room in a traditional Japanese house may also be used as a dining room and a bedroom. A maker of traditional Japanese kimonos told me, "Japanese clothes are often cut in a simple way. They're not bespoke, like Western suits, with each part and segment measured for a perfect fit. Japanese clothes have a simple cut because they need to be flexible. There are different reasons for wearing them, and different ways to wear them."

For each particular craft, generations of artisans have devised and developed a range of tools, of implements that must be mastered in the course of learning the craft. Improvements and innovations are possible, as shown by the long chain of refinements and revisions that enhance any repertoire of the essential gadgets without which a craft cannot be practiced. Thus tools, which are received as elements of the production process, are also prosthetics of embodied knowledge. They become extensions of the hand and enable construction or performance. For example, a traditional Japanese carpenter talked with me about the *kanna*, an implement for smoothing a wooden surface by shaving or filing down excess wood fibers. "It's a strange thing," he said. "If I don't have the right posture, the right attitude, it just doesn't seem to do its job. It's only when it becomes part of my body—when I'm standing properly, and thinking straight—that the *kanna* does what it's supposed to do."

Many Japanese artisans talk about their tools in a way that might suggest a stark dichotomy between things Japanese (soft, flexible artisanal tools) and things Western (hard, rigid machine tools).[13] The use of machine tools depends on formal procedures that are applied to the task of producing uniform goods. Tools of this kind tend to transform raw materials in a standardized way, overpowering the resistance of raw materials and shaping them in homogeneous fashion. In contrast, artisanal tools are designed to work not just on but also with raw materials. When artisans use their tools, they strive to adjust to any resistance that the raw materials may offer. Thus a carpenter building *sukiya* or *minka* (what are taken to be traditional wooden Japanese houses) works not only with soft tools but also with soft materials. Flexibility is present from conception (as the carpenter considers and adjusts to the ground and the soil on which the house will stand) to execution (as he brings the soft timber into conformation with the architectural plan). This approach is very different from the one used in Western-style, hardness-dominated construction, which entails boring into the ground, pouring concrete, and erecting a rigid frame. But, according to the same carpenter who described his use of the *kanna*, softness and flexibility in construction may actually prove superior to precision-engineered toughness and rigidity. For example, earthquake damage can be minimized by soft wood and joints designed to sway with the rolling and thrusting of the ground. Industrial hardness, artisanal softness—the contrast discloses a diametrical opposition between two types of tools, by their nature and in their conception.

Any artisanal endeavor is grounded in tradition, which takes concrete form in what is often a long and challenging apprenticeship. Artisans, learning from others who have traveled the path before them, know that their craft has a long history. But even as they work to master the craft's received skills and techniques, they come to understand that as the world changes, the craft is also evolving. In other words, they recognize that the craft has developed over the years precisely because of their forebears' useful improvements—indeed, the spirit of improvement is the bridge between past and future. Therefore, notwithstanding their reverence for tradition, artisans don't talk about turning back the clock, even though their craft may have reached its peak decades or centuries ago. They accept their place in time and space, and they seek to repeat, continue, and improve upon past achievements. The language they use is sometimes that of re-creating a level of perfection that was achieved by a master or by a master's master, and so they are forever apprentices, forever polishing their skills. Somewhat like performers of classical music, they understand that practice and mastery do not necessarily rule out the possibility of improvement and innovation. The point is always to approximate perfection more closely, or perhaps to fail less, or fail better. In the words of the Noh master Zeami (1363–1443), "Life has an end. Noh should have no end."[14] An artisan's life is finite; artisanship—tradition—is infinite.

Emulation and Beyond

As discussed earlier, the heart of training is emulation. Just as aspiring painters may copy a work by an old master, artisans learn by observing and reproducing the movements of their own models and teachers. Because earlier generations of masters were not inclined to be overtly helpful, an adage arose to the effect that the aspirant must steal the master's skills (as seen in chapter 5, in connection with the apprentices of an *oyakata*). Today's elders tend to be kinder and gentler. Nevertheless, learning by doing, that is, by observing and imitating others, remains paramount on the road to mastery. Here, however, a fundamental distinction must be noted between striving to emulate a model (ultimately an autonomous activity, with the aspirant doing the work of conception and execution in unison) and being told what to do (a heteronomous affair); that is, emulation, far from rote learning, must be a mindful experience. Emulation is not the outcome or residue of repetition. Rather, it is a vehicle by which its practitioner reaches a higher plane of potential. Thus, even though artisanal work may seem to entail subjugation, one of its greatest points of pride and attraction is that it affords autonomy and independence.[15]

The artisanal ethos—which requires dedication and discipline, endless practice and emulation, habit and tradition—may appear to produce isomorphic disciples. Yet mastery by definition means transcending the necessity of emulation and striking out on one's own. Precisely because emulation is a process that is necessarily mindful, mastery is not mere acquisition of a skill set. It is the inhabiting of a new state. The rhetoric of imitation, of following a path or a tradition, is misleading in one sense—the goal is not to acquire a repertoire of techniques but rather to cultivate artistry and become an autonomous master oneself.[16] As mentioned earlier, one dissolves oneself in the pursuit of mastering a craft. In so doing, one synthesizes the past, sublimates it, and achieves a new state, sometimes called *shin'i* (true intention).[17] It is only then, as one tempura chef told me, that one's individuality can flourish.[18] This is the same point made by Zeami, the Noh master, who characterizes the mastery of craft as suppression of *jibun no hana* (the youthful, temporal and temporary flower) in favor of *makoto no hana* (the mature, true flower).[19] Or, to paraphrase Zeami, the aspiring artisan may thrive on youthful, natural talent, but its beauty is fleeting and he should not mistake it for his own; the singular fuel of mastery is practice, and practice is a matter of mimesis.[20] Aging brings decline, but through persistent practice one can generate the true, beautiful flower that the heart commands (*kokoro no mamanarubeshi*).[21] Mastery, in short, develops from practice and from remembering the repertoire of skills and techniques one has pursued from the beginning.[22]

An important implication here is that Zeami's state of mastery—the ability to respond to the heart's command—is not produced through rote memorization or automatic replication but rather through cultivation of a state in which artistry flows effortlessly, as second nature. Paradoxically, then, mastery requires the forgetting of accumulated skills, the suspension of consciousness, and an entry into mindlessness. A saying and practice among kabuki actors is that one learns the lines but forgets them when one steps onstage to perform; the point is to avoid awkward, self-conscious repetition of the lines, which must flow naturally.[23] Likewise, a common injunction in the traditional Japanese arts, whether in a tea ceremony or a judo match, is to remove the tension from the shoulders (*kata no chikara wo nuku*) or to relax; that is, one should not perform consciously, putting one's eager (or overeager) self above embodied mastery, the performance of which should unfold in a mindful but also mindless state. Relax, inhale, exhale deeply— one cannot will the materialization of mastery, just as one cannot will oneself to sleep. Again, embodied habit operates in the middle voice.

One manifestation of mastery is beauty of movement. Observing a seasoned artisan at work is akin to watching a superb dancer. Every action, seemingly spontaneous but also calculated, participates in a continuum, an uninterrupted flow that has an undisclosed but definite endpoint. A tempura maker standing over a vat of hot oil uses efficient, effective motions to swirl and scoop the pieces of fish and vegetables; no step seems wasted, every one is elegant. His expression of utter concentration, his erect posture, the minimal arm movements, the ever so slight swaying of his body—all come together to create yet another moment of pleasure for the customer.

Zeami's gnomic account may offer an excessively individualistic description of apprenticeship and mastery, but artisanal work is not necessarily a solo endeavor. In fact, in some types of artisanal work, the ideal of dedication justifies an extensive division of labor. For example, the division of labor is almost total in the world of traditional knife manufacturing. In a small shop, one person may take charge of the forging, another of the shaping, a third of the polishing; yet another may sharpen the blade, one more may produce the handle, and someone else may undertake the final assembly.[24] Each task is apparently simple, and certainly repetitive, but each of the artisans involved emphasizes how long it took to acquire mastery of his ostensibly routine task. Autonomy is a nice idea, but it's an impossible ideal. Even a chef who does everything by himself at his restaurant told me, "It's not as if I grow the rice or make the sake. It's very important to find people who share your ideals. It's always about working with others." Thus, though it seems a paradox, the artisan is always mindful of working with others, and yet there is a striking emphasis on individual cultivation. In this respect, consider the nature of a kabuki production. Each play is necessarily an ensemble effort, but almost everyone in the production spends large amounts of time preparing individually. Artisanal work carries the weight of tradition and involves a web of relations, but at one level it remains a singular journey of discipline and of dedication to achieving mastery over oneself and one's work.

Awareness of the Audience and Care of Raw Materials

As artisans pursue their craft and seek mastery, they remain conscious of the audience, for without the audience, the artisan's craft and livelihood would be unsustainable. For this reason, to ignore the importance of the audience is to violate the spirit of the artisanal ethos. There are no delusions of artisanal autonomy. Artisans forswear the beguiling temptation to regard themselves as *artistes*.[25] A craft is not practiced for its own sake but in service of other people.

Apart from the dialectic between artisan and audience, there is the dialectic between artisans and raw materials. Most obviously, artisans concern themselves with the excellence and appropriateness of the materials with which they work—the quality of the clay that the potter will shape and fire, the freshness and tastiness of the seafood that the sushi chef will prepare and serve. Thus raw materials, just like craft, become embodied. And the artisan, in order to appreciate his raw materials and take proper care of them, must understand them with the entirety of his embodied craft.

A curious aspect of concern for raw materials is that this attitude does not necessarily involve a search for those that are the best or the most refined. After all, artisans find themselves in a particular place and time, and even if they are not necessarily committed to using local materials, they do tend to use those that are at hand. For example, a potter mentioned to me that the clay he works with is actually very poor and of low quality, but he stays where he is: "I learned everything about pottery here. I grew up here. And people here have been making great things." The artisan makes a virtue of necessity. Needless to say, artisans would prefer to be working with the best raw materials, but they make do with what they have, at every level. "I don't think I'm a born umbrella maker," said an octogenarian master artisan. "I don't have the right sort of hands and fingers. But I've worked at it."

Working on raw materials is simultaneously an act of construction, destruction, and transmutation. A sushi chef told me, "Western cuisine often works as addition. You add sauce to meat. In sushi, it's often subtraction. You eliminate negative aspects in order to bring out positive features." In the process, raw fish becomes Edo-style sushi. The effort to bring out what's essential or what's best is at the heart of craft.

A consequence of the dialectic of care between artisan and materials is that many artisans sublate the subject-object distinction.[26] Chapter 5 tells of a sushi chef who said he could hear fish speaking to him and asking him to eat them. And this is far from unusual—many chefs mention listening to the inner voices of raw foods as they prepare and cook them.[27] Similarly, a woodworker told me that the wood called out to him: "I don't choose the woods I use in my work. They choose me." The ne plus ultra of this sort of magical thinking is the archer in Nakajima Atsushi's "Meijinden" (The life of a master), based on an anecdote in the *Liezi* in which a masterly archer, able to strike a bird without using his bow and arrow, ultimately forgets what these tools are.[28] A fantastic story, to be sure, but true mastery comes tantalizingly close, as when a superbly made teacup seems to merge with one's hands as one holds it.

The language of the heart or soul (*kokoro*) captures this dialectic and its sublation. Artisanal excellence entails inspiring, breathing life into, whatever the artisan touches. A typical expression of this idea is "It's important to put your heart into it." Infusing materials with care, putting one's soul into the endeavor—these attitudes speak to care of and concern for the craft's raw materials, and to its audience and its tradition.

As mentioned in chapter 5, wholesalers and their customers in the sushi world sometimes hold ritual funerals for the seafood from which they gain their livelihood, and it is not mere superstition that prompts such rites. Artisans are concerned about the preciousness and sustainability of their raw materials. Sushi chefs, for instance, often express gratitude toward fish and shellfish, vowing not to waste them. A master dyer of traditional Japanese clothes says, "I receive the lives of flowers. It's only natural that the flowers should bloom, but I'm sorry to be stealing from them. . . . I feel responsible for making the flowers bloom again on the clothes."[29] Thus the ethic of care is a critical component of the artisanal ethos. Or, to put the same idea more abstractly, artisans seek to uncover and restore the truth immanent in their raw materials.

Work as an End in Itself

When artisans say they are *shokunin*, not *shōbainin* (businesspeople), perhaps they're simply repeating a common justification for their lot in life. A cynic might allege sour grapes. In any case, artisans are almost uniformly committed to their craft. But to be dedicated to one's craft does not mean to lack a sense of humor or to have no other interests. And immersion in any activity—the experience of flow—is a ludic and profoundly satisfactory experience.[30] When I mentioned this idea to a middle-aged ceramicist, she added, "Yes—and it helps that we drink a lot." She is fond of making sake cups (hers are unusually large), and it would be hard to find many other people who enjoy their work or their after-work baccha-nal more than this woman enjoys hers as she toils away in the middle of nowhere.

I can say, having talked with hundreds of artisans in scores of crafts, that most seemed to enjoy their work and their lives. Like many other Japanese people, arti-sans would be embarrassed to speak overtly about "loving" their work. But if a single word could amalgamate the sentiments expressed by the words "care," "con-cern," "passion," and "commitment," that word might come close to capturing arti-sans' relationship to their work.

Status distinctions in Japanese society are not as stark as in the past, but there is still considerable social and economic inequality in contemporary Japan. And many artisans come from humble backgrounds and have had comparatively little formal education. In addition, they often find themselves serving precisely those people who have enjoyed a privileged upbringing, including extensive higher edu-cation. An older artisan may sometimes confess to having a chip on his shoulder because he did not graduate from college and feels undereducated. Even so, one would be hard put to pick up indications from most artisans that they resent their lot in life, envy their customers, or feel miserable and inferior. One master tailor, extremely proud that his son is a college graduate, was even more pleased that his son, too, chose to become a tailor. Again, artisanal work, though certainly a means of earning income, is also seen as an end in itself, and one of the most common attributes of artisans is their understated pride in their work.

The world of artisanal work may look grim—a long period of training followed by years of repetitive tasks performed over and over, with few holidays and even fewer vacations. But appearances can deceive. First, many artisans offer an instru-mental reason to maintain a positive mind-set. "If I found the work miserable," said one artisanal furniture maker, "the work would carry my misery." Likewise, the proprietor of a restaurant who does everything by himself, including cleaning the bathroom, remarked, "If I weren't enjoying it, the restaurant would be boring, and the food wouldn't taste as good," which would mean that his customers, and ultimately the proprietor himself, would suffer.[31] And, second, many artisans, using the common language of Japanese life philosophy, speak of their work as giving them *ikigai,* a reason to live. As Aristotle observed, human beings enjoy fulfilling their potential—becoming who they are—and exercising their power; human flourishing, especially when it involves the attainment of excellence in a chosen activity, goes hand in hand with human happiness.[32]

In the language of Romantic poetry, the cultivation of negative capability comes close to capturing some of the elements of artisanal work.[33] That is, what makes artisanal and aesthetic goals more important than goals that are pecuniary or philosophical is not the mindless execution of a received conception—that is, standard, mechanical production—but rather the ability to work with uncertainty and confusion. The novelist Dencombe in Henry James's masterly 1893 story "The Middle Years" captures some of the passion and mystery of artisanal work when he says, "We work in the dark—we do what we can—we give what we have. Our doubt is our passion and our passion is our task. The rest is the madness of art."[34] I've tried to draw a clear line between artisans and artists, but when I transliterated this passage from James for several Japanese artisans, the most common response was "This writer is an artisan."

A craft, though moored in tradition, is open to innovation. Its vocabulary is not one of efficiency but rather one of mastery based on practice and experience, of polishing skills rather than pushing the envelope, of work as an end in itself rather than as a means.[35] The goal is to master techniques, get the work right, and produce something worthwhile. The craft, and the artisan, thrive in the connection to raw materials and tools as well as in the connection to customers. It's true that the whole operation would collapse if there were no one to buy what artisans produce. But moneymaking is not the manifest goal, and the customer's satisfaction is a secondary reward. The primary psychic reward is work well done.

CRITICAL AND MODERNIST PERSPECTIVES ON ARTISANSHIP

The received stereotype of the *shokunin*, as described in chapter 5, depicted a figure who was far from praiseworthy. The artisan, said to be short-tempered and stubborn, was also alleged to indulge the common vices of drinking and gambling.[36] Moreover, people who were poorly schooled and who worked alone or in unstable family firms were neither admired nor valued in modern Japan, which prized formal educational credentials and prestigious jobs in the state bureaucracy or in large corporations. Kitaōji Rosanjin, something of an ur-gourmet in modern Japan, wrote of Imada Hisaji, founder of the famed Giza sushi restaurant Kyūbei, "If he had gone to university, he would now have been at least a department head or vice-minister, possibly even a minister."[37] But what's wrong with being a great sushi chef? This was class prejudice. In general, though, at least where sushi chefs are concerned, what was believed in the middle of the twentieth century is no longer held to be true.

To judge from Japanese historical and social-scientific writings, the *shokunin* of the Edo regime were occluded by the political economy of the Meiji regime, with its strong state and modern organizations. Social scientists in the West assumed that Japanese artisanal workers were transitional, doomed to disappear in the near future, and Japanese social scientists shared that assumption. In any case, the strength of Western domination in Japan can be gauged from the fact that aspiring artisans in pottery and other traditional arts usually enrolled in high school and university art classes that focused on and valorized Western art.[38]

Perhaps the only notable Japanese intellectuals to champion *shokunin* culture were Yanagi Muneyoshi, influenced by the English arts and crafts movement, and the journalist Hasegawa Nyozekan. Hasegawa, in his search for Japanese characteristics, argues that Japan is a "civilization of the hand" rather than an Athenian "civilization of the brain"; acknowledging that European societies had their own craft traditions, he specifies that Japanese *shokunin* focused on practical constructions and achievements, and that *shokunin* lived and worked more like English gentlemen than like English workers.[39] But Hasegawa, despite having grown up in an artisanal household, came to recognize the significance of *shokunin* culture only quite late in his career—toward the end of his long life, in the 1960s—and his recovery of the world of *shokunin*, hardly discussed in the large literature on his writings, is also excluded from his eight-volume collected works.[40]

The postwar period of rapid economic growth was certainly challenging for artisans. The valorization of educational credentials and salaried employment was enough to make artisans feel that they were behind the times. Many, overwhelmed by mechanical production or fast food, certainly thought their future was in peril. As an elderly maker of traditional Japanese footwear told me, "It was tough in the sixties and seventies because everyone wanted to be a *sararīman* [salaryman, or office worker]. No one wanted to apprentice in a traditional craft that had no future." And a somewhat younger *urushi* (lacquerware) master recalled envying his friends and neighbors as they went off to school in their uniforms: "I felt like I was being left behind. What was the point of lacquerware in the age of plastics? We were slow, they were fast. We were expensive, they were cheap. Who was going to buy what I made?" Moreover, for youngsters growing up in artisanal households, the prospect of sober, steady, usually low-paying artisanal work could not compete with the lure of bright lights and dark vices; few of these young people wanted to follow in their parents' unglamorous footsteps. Nevertheless, the 1980s, a time when few were entertaining doubts about Japan's affluence, marked the precise moment when the media reappraised Japan's traditional crafts, as evidenced by a spate of books and articles.[41] Ever since then, traditional handiwork and artisanship have enjoyed greater resonance and acceptance. But is the existence of Japanese artisans sufficient to warrant the assertion that artisanal work and the artisanal ethos constitute a vital sector in contemporary Japan? Objections to that assertion can be raised.

An economist might dismiss Japanese artisans as an extremely small group of workers producing handcrafted luxury products that account for a minuscule slice of the economy. A Marxist might agree with the economist while also pointing to artisans as the very definition of the petite bourgeoisie—a transitional, disappearing class. A progressive, though not in disagreement with the Marxist's characterization, might ask whether I am romanticizing sushi chefs and other artisans, and the progressive might go on to ask whether artisanal workers are exploiting their apprentices, or themselves. Here, a feminist might chime in, not just with criticism of the artisanal world's masculinist, even misogynistic culture but also with a report of never having laid eyes on a female sushi chef. And all four observers, though disagreeing about any number of other things, would join forces to interrogate the significance, viability, and desirability of the artisanal ethos.

Before we could address the remarks of the economist and the Marxist, we would need to know the size and nature of the Japanese artisanal sector. Unfortunately, because the artisanal sector is not a bureaucratic category in Japan, there are no government-collected data to reflect its specific contributions. But we can extrapolate from the data available for 2014, when there were more than three million small- and medium-size enterprises in Japan, with total sales equal to 95 percent of the sales of large enterprises.[42] Throughout the postwar period, non-Marxists and Marxists alike could not ignore the large contribution, often more than half the total, that small- and medium-size firms were making to the national economy. The most celebrated acknowledgment of this fact was the Japanese government's *Economic White Papers* for 1957 (the year after the government announced the end of the postwar period), which discussed the economy's "dual structure," that is, the simultaneous existence in Japan of an "advanced country" and a "backward country," the latter defined by such "premodern" elements as the preponderance of family-managed firms.[43] After this pioneering analysis by the government, the emerging consensus was that the so-called dual structure was a regressive and undesirable feature of Japan. Neoclassical and Marxist economists are diametrically opposed on most issues, but they are united in denigrating smaller firms as premodern or traditional and in assuming that such enterprises will be superseded by modern, large firms.[44] According to this line of thinking, artisans—the petite bourgeoisie—are destined to wither away. In the words of the 1960 benchmark work *Industrialism and Industrial Man,* "The technology and specialization of the industrial society are necessarily and distinctively associated with large-scale organizations."[45] Smaller firms and craft sectors did not fit into the grand narrative of Japan's rapid economic growth, fueled as it was by celebrated exports like radio and television sets, freight ships, and automobiles. Nor did smaller firms and craft sectors offer any of the vaunted benefits of the Japanese employment system. The idea of the dual economy did capture the evident persistence of smaller firms, but it also rendered them homogeneous and presumed their transitional character. In the heroic postwar epic of export-oriented industrialization, there was no place for stories about sushi chefs and knife makers, potters and anime artists.

The criticisms offered by the progressive and feminist observers do have validity. Artisanal work itself, precisely because of its autonomy, tends paradoxically toward long workdays and self-exploitation. An artisan may spend long hours at work because of financial need or competitive pressure from the market, but a long workday is at least as likely to result from the artisan's deep absorption in the work itself. In fact, the artisanal ethos accentuates the inherent significance of the labor process. I don't want to romanticize artisanal work, but because artisans have flourished in Japan's postsubsistence economy, they are far less burdened by the dictates of survival than premodern peasants were.[46]

But what about apprentices and assistants? The challenging nature of much artisanal work has led many a novice to flee the master as well as the craft. None of the artisans I talked with claimed that the work was easy. They all recognized that there are other, less arduous ways to make a living. But many artisans also insisted that they were providing an education for their apprentices, teaching them skills that they could not learn from books or in classrooms, and that they treated their apprentices like family members. The relationship between a master and an apprentice is analogous to a relationship in which a parent nurtures and guides a child until the child grows up. It's easy to cast a cynical eye on what looks like a paternalistic ideology and merely another way to justify exploitation. But the foundation of artisanal work is precisely that it is learned and reproduced through a long period of apprenticeship, after which the novice is mature enough to be capable of independence.

As for the gendered character of traditional artisanal work, that is undeniable, in Japan and elsewhere. Where fine cuisine is concerned, for example, between 1932 and 2019 only a dozen women chefs, primarily in France and Italy, were awarded three Michelin stars, and not one of them was a sushi chef; the only renowned female sushi chef is a manga character.[47] The persistence of male domination stems from the tradition-bound character of artisanal work itself, and the work's traditional character is precisely why it has been able to resist pressure toward mass production. Be that as it may, there is no point in denying past or current male domination and even misogyny in many lines of artisanal work. There are successful women artisans in Japan, and there is nothing inherent in artisanal work that requires men to dominate or women to be excluded.

If Japanese people sometimes claim that the artisanal ethos is distinctive, even unique, to Japan and to Japanese *shokunin,* it is also true that twenty-first-century Japanese artisans have seen exquisite examples of artisanal production from abroad, even if they have never traveled outside Japan themselves. A sushi chef told me that he had considered the Japanese superior in their handling and preparation of seafood until he encountered the superb techniques and raw materials at Le Bernardin, the French restaurant in New York.[48] Many other Japanese artisans have also told me about their deep appreciation of craft traditions from various parts of the world.

Moreover, when I was living in Paris, my apartment was a one-minute walk from a bakery that had won a coveted prize. Not only were this bakery's prices the lowest around, but the baker went so far as to halt the sale of any croissant or baguette he judged unworthy of his establishment. I also met an esteemed wine-maker south of Dijon who was no less punctilious.[49] As I observed her utter dedication to tending her vines and making the wines, it seemed that the last thing on her mind was reviews or sales. She was delighted that a visitor from the United States had heard of her wines and even tasted them, but she seemed content just to keep on working, without seeking further attention. "This is what I want to be doing," she told me. Winemaking, she said, was simply what she did, just as her father had done all his life. The owner of a neighboring wineshop told me that the winemaker routinely declassified prized grapes and sold the wines off at a lower price, in view of their purported lower level of quality. When I asked the wine-maker about this practice, she said, "It's the right thing to do."

Regrettably, the misleading narrative of progress has relegated artisanal work all over the world to a small and shrinking pigeonhole. At the same time, a robust tradition of artisanal work, and regions around which particular traditions of arti-sanship still thrive, can be found throughout Europe, and indeed everywhere. Italy, for instance, may not be the source of the best mass-produced automobiles, but few car buffs can resist the allure of a small, craft-based maker like Bugatti or Ferrari, and Italy's more traditional artisanal powerhouses, from clothes to wine, also do much to shore up the tottering Italian economy. Germany, in partial con-trast, boasts outstanding large-scale auto manufacturers, such as BMW, but is also notable for the prevalence and excellence of its regional craftwork industries, some of which can be dated to the Middle Ages.[50] Advocates of the artisanal ethos can even be found in the United States, where artisans themselves have largely disap-peared, not so much because of the obsolescence imposed by progress as because of a complex concatenation of factors, including the extraordinary power of monopolistic firms, remarkable innovations in technology, and a constant stream of unskilled migrant workers.[51] The United States—home not just of mass produc-tion but also of the greatest concentration of economists and social scientists—projected the naturalness and necessity of giant factories and large bureaucracies, and we have yet to shed the modernist myth of mechanization's inevitability. In general, though, we should be rethinking the place and significance of artisanal work. Its depreciation and derogation are due to a massive misrecognition of what it is to be modern in a world where, now more than ever, artisanal work is a crucial element of a more sustainable life.

Everyone has heard about superbly skilled Japanese makers of sushi and knives.[52] But the artisanal ethos, long a significant factor in areas outside traditional production, has influenced activities much more numerous than sushi making and knife manufacturing. In fact, the artisanal ethos and traditional artisanal work were central to the first stage of modern Japanese industrialization. In what was ostensibly preindustrial Japan—during the Tokugawa period, before the 1868 Meiji Restoration—there were numerous protoindustrial enterprises that often took the form of adjunct employment for farmers. These rural industries ranged from farming and fishery to food processing and ceramics, and they played an important role in the post–Meiji Restoration economic expansion of Japan. Thus Tokugawa-era technological and organizational developments not only generated viable products for export but also supplied the foundation of modern managerial skills.[53] And in modern, Western-imported Japanese industries like shipbuilding and machine production, artisans have played a crucial role in adopting or adapting Western machinery while bringing about important innovations.[54]

Artisans are also a vital presence in small- and medium-size Japanese firms.[55] For example, the artisanal ethos is at the heart of some modern, science-based high-tech enterprises, especially at smaller companies. Consider one of the most spectacular breakthroughs in technology—the invention of the blue light-emitting diode (LED). Beyond its scientific value (three scientists who had worked on the blue LED at Japan's Nichia Chemical won the 2014 Nobel Prize in physics for their invention), its practical significance is incontrovertible. The creation of the blue LED made possible the white laser, which in turn makes possible, among other things, smartphone screens and long-lasting white LED bulbs.[56] When the owner of Nichia, a company with only two hundred employees, devoted millions of dollars to this project, whose success or profit was far from certain, was that not the artisanal ethos in action? Or, to take another case, this one less celebrated, in 2002 Tanaka Kōichi's contribution to mass spectrometric analysis earned him the Nobel Prize in chemistry. Tanaka, reflecting on his achievement, mentioned not just the benefits of working at Shimadzu Corporation but also the influence of his carpenter-craftsman father.[57] A number of conclusions can be adduced from these two examples, but there is one that stands out. Contrary to a powerful strand of thinking about modern industrial societies, smaller and regional companies in Japan have been responsible for important breakthroughs, and in these cases it has been the "wrong" half of the so-called dual economy—the artisanal half—that turned out to be modern and innovative.

Artisanal work may also come to be incorporated into a much larger commercial outfit, one where artisans' autonomy is reduced to an illusion against the background of their structural subservience.[58] Manga artists, for example, embody the artisanal ethos in many ways. Most work for love of the genre, and they seek, like artisans, to produce manga as an end in itself. But even many highly successful manga artists are struggling financially, are overworked, and suffer commercial interference with their art, given their dependence on serials (usually weeklies, sometimes with circulation in the millions).[59] We should remember, of course, that Hayao Miyazaki, the great anime auteur, resisted mechanical and industrial production and insisted on sustaining the artisanal ethos.[60] Nevertheless, many independent manga artists or artisans today are being turned into content providers and performers of outsourced tasks, in no small measure because of the greater involvement of large financial and commercial enterprises and the consequent commodification of manga.[61]

That said, one striking instance of a successful Japanese export in the immediate post-Bubble years was *Pokémon* (*Pocket Monsters*), first devised in 1996 as a video game and later the fountainhead of what became a vast empire of anime and movies, stuffed animals and software. The creator of *Pokémon* is Satoshi Tajiri, a self-identified *otaku* (nerd or geek), who spent his childhood so completely fascinated by insects that his peers called him Dr. Bug. *Pokémon* developed from a six-year incubation period. Once emerged from its chrysalis, it almost immediately became a global sensation.[62] Is the creation of *Pokémon* an example of artisanal work? And is *Pokémon* in any way a product of the artisanal ethos? Both questions can be plausibly answered in the affirmative. First, like so many other Japanese artisans, Tajiri did not take the standard route of diligent study followed by a university degree and employment with a large organization. Instead, he pursued his obsession with video games—an obsession initially sparked by *Space Invaders*—and he launched a self-financed, solely authored video game magazine, *Gēmu furīku* (*Game Freak*) before going on to build relationships with other video game fanatics and create his own games. Second, and perhaps more important, by nurturing his private passions (insects and video games), Tajiri cultivated what was tantamount to the artisanal ethos. In the process, he endeavored to foster children's capacity for imagination and social communication and to offer them relief from the rat race of the Japanese examination system.[63]

Salaryman Agonistes

The artisanal ethos does not represent a utopian ideal. It should not be the only basis on which to work or the only way to operate an enterprise, especially in the twenty-first century. There should be room for mass production, if only to satisfy the demands of mass consumption. (To take only the example of industrial agriculture and mass-produced fast foods: for all their many faults, they may lower food insecurity.) The artisanal ethos can create spectacular products and offer a meaningful way to work and live. In some respects, it may even facilitate the task of running a mass transit system. Nevertheless, conceiving and carrying out the operation of thousands of trains on dozens of lines is the province of a large, complex organization. Therefore, instead of holding the artisanal mode of work up to one ideal or another, we should contrast it with the dominant way of working in contemporary Japan, the way of the office worker known as a salaryman. Here, we'll refer to him as the hegemonic archetype he is—as Salaryman.[64]

The Birth of Salaryman.   Salaryman, true to his name in the postwar period, generally *was* a man. Women at that time were office ladies, or OLs, filling an inevitably inferior, transitory role and often serving as "office wives."[65] Salaryman's work entailed a large organization, regular wages (or a salary), educational credentials, a uniform, a commute, and human relations that were both complex and hierarchical. Many Japanese people, including artisans and their children, were enchanted by the splendor of modernity that was Salaryman's life, if only because of its requisite uniform—a Western-style suit, a tie, and a briefcase for good measure.[66] As Ueki Hitoshi's 1961 hit song "Dontobushi," had it, Salaryman's life was "carefree."

Salaryman exemplified the modern and the urban. He commuted to his job— which, unlike traditional agricultural or artisanal work, involved a gender-based division of labor that was sharp and complete—and his wife maintained and watched over what was, in effect, Salaryman's haven from the cold, cruel (or at least competitive) world.[67] Thus both Salaryman and his wife were confined within and regimented by a gender-specific space during the day and sometimes into the night, and both of them pursued their gender-divided tasks in the name of the family. Their sharp spatial and temporal separation placed Salaryman and his wife in parallel universes, though the phenomenon that was Salaryman would not have been possible at all without his wife's household labor and emotional nurturance.[68] Salaryman and his colleagues, frequently portrayed as corporate warriors, were the shock troops of Japan's postwar economic growth. Even after almost everyone had finally acknowledged the full extent of Salaryman's misery, his lifestyle continued to embody not just the typical form but also the very goal of employment in Japanese life.

At bottom, Salaryman was a *kaishajin* (company man). His company—the larger, the better—selected new hires from among recent university graduates, trained them, set them on a life course of shifting duties and struggles with upward mobility, turned them into workaholics, and discharged them at the age of fifty-five or sixty with a modest pension. In turn, the company's employees found security and prestige in addition to the usual benefits of financial and psychological compensation. There was deep faith in the university-to-corporation pipeline, and widespread belief that educational credentials would be transformed into desirable employment.[69] Even though the postwar period valued freedom and democracy, the company's hierarchical organization was taken for granted, as was the expectation that its employees would execute the tasks conceived by their superiors. Indeed, the postwar corporation, not entirely unlike the prewar Japanese military, reified prestige-based hierarchy and placed the whole above the individual.

Salaryman's desire for a decent place to live often meant an excruciatingly time-consuming commute. Long working hours and six-day weeks were the norm for him, with overtime as well as transfers—and never mind that at the whim of a superior, all the time and effort he had put into endless meetings and meticulously prepared reports might come to nothing. Self-sacrifice and diligence, humility and loyalty—these were Salaryman's ultimate virtues. Maybe he would climb the corporate ladder—after all, somebody had to—or maybe he would bide his time until retirement. His life, a gauntlet of the slings and arrows he endured while identifying with the company, was in practice a legitimation of his superiors' power, however capricious and sadistic their exercise of it may have been.

But even if Salaryman failed to be promoted, his life was not without its joys and compensations. Is it any accident that the significance Salaryman attached to his work was something that consistently made his life bearable? Or that the same things Salaryman appreciated about his job—opportunities to be properly evaluated and appreciated for his ability and his attainments, to hone his skills, to learn and improve—are also prominent features of artisanal work?[70] And the company was his family away from home. It offered lifelong employment and was a community of destiny. Salaryman's company gave him not only a powerful form of identification but also a role, a meaningful place, and it served as a psychic bulwark against the anxieties and uncertainties of life. There was also the camaraderie of working, dining, and drinking with his colleagues.[71] As chapter 5 shows, sometimes Salaryman, under cover of work, was able to engage in various forms of entertainment, from the mindless solitude and solace of playing *pachinko* (Japanese pinball) to occasional forays into the water trade (as well as the services of the sex industry). And to soothe the anguish of his slow spiritual death by desk work, there was always the possibility of schadenfreude over the friends, acquaintances, and colleagues who worked at less prestigious companies or, worse, had dropped out by way of social extinction (unemployment) or its physical counterpart. Salaryman may have had moments of satisfaction about being able to support himself and his family. He may even have enjoyed his life at home (often called "family service"), in the sovereign realm of his wife. Even so, is it any wonder that Salaryman so often placed his work above his home life?

Salaryman in Popular Culture.   For the wartime and immediate postwar generations, the monotony and grind of Salaryman's life shone brilliantly against what they knew to be the alternative.[72] By the 1970s, however, the war had come to be remembered in sepia tones. Much of the population by then had been born after the end of the war, into general silence and amnesia (apart, that is, from the vague acknowledgment that the war had been tragic). It was taken for granted that Salaryman's work at the office was preferable to sweating on a farm or toiling with greasy machinery. At least his job was secure and his wages rose steadily. And so

Salaryman soldiered on, long after the memory of the meaningless war had faded, and well after Japan had developed a successful, wealthy economy. Salaryman had become just one more unique feature of Japanese life.[73]

What is remarkable in retrospect is that the brilliant mythology of Salaryman—a being at once modern, prestigious, and normative—persisted for so long after Japan had become prosperous. Arthur Miller's play *Death of a Salesman* was first staged in 1949, but it took until 2018 for a Japanese version to appear: *Aru sararīman no shi* (Death of a salaryman). Instead, the postwar period was filled with novels, movies, and manga that extolled the virtues of Salaryman's life or at least redeemed Salaryman as a figure of respect. In addition, a vibrant genre of literature celebrated the organization man, and Salaryman and his colleagues—who read voraciously, if only to endure their long commute by train—made up a large part of this genre's readership. Already by 1951, Genji Keita had begun publishing his popular picaresque novels about the organization man's life, focused now on Salaryman's business negotiations, now on his extramarital philandering.[74] After the 1960s, *jidai shōsetsu* (historical novels) depicted samurai in their struggles with lack of freedom and lack of autonomy, against the broad background of societal stability during the Tokugawa period.[75] But many readers of these long novels found in them ready analogies to corporate life. In fact, one self-identified organization man came up with a nickname for Yamaoka Sōhachi's twenty-six volume *Tokugawa Ieyasu*. He called it *sararīman dokuhon* (the salaryman reader).[76] Yamamoto Shūgorō, Shiba Ryōtarō, and Fujisawa Shūhei followed Yamaoka's lead and wrote extremely popular but critically derided chronicles of samurai (read: office workers). One recently retired organization man, discussing Fujisawa Shūhei's tales about the searing, soul-shattering trials of low-level samurai who must face the irrational, incomprehensible dictates of their superiors, said to me, "When I'm reading Fujisawa's stories, I can't stop crying." Salaryman also devoured books on the economy and business management, in surprising numbers, and he helped make Peter Drucker a rock star for middle-aged middle managers.[77] By the 1970s, however, pornographic stories and manga had begun to eclipse serialized novels and management tracts.[78]

Salaryman's Disintegration and Half-Life. The power and the glory of Salaryman's life were always more fantasy than reality. Salaryman might enjoy modest upward mobility at work, but after a lifetime of devotion to the company he would find that he had become *sodai gomi* (bulky trash)—pushed out of the corporation, alienated from and unwanted by his wife and children.[79] In the end, he would come to regard himself as someone who had started out as a promising, vibrant recruit but had turned into an ordinary employee coasting toward forced retirement, an unremarkable man in middle age.

As for his home life, there had always been tensions underlying the postwar ideal of the nuclear family, with its foundational units of Salaryman and a full-time

housewife who would uncomplainingly perform all the tasks of household production and reproduction, from cooking and cleaning to child-rearing. In works
of fiction from the 1960s, it was becoming possible to discern in Salaryman's wife
a simmering irritation that was about to boil over into frank hatred.[80] And by the
1970s, there were visible cracks in the veneer of Salaryman's ideal domestic
arrangement.[81] But the full secularization of the postwar myth—including its twin
pillars, Salaryman and his wife—coincided with the bursting of the Bubble. This
was when Salaryman, in particular, commenced the long descent from his privileged perch to his existence as an object of pity, even derision. Salaryman's long
commute, his hard work, his overtime, the stiff upper lip he maintained against the
arbitrary humiliations handed down by his superiors—all of this had once been
seen as heroic, but to younger Japanese people it now seemed depressing, if not
altogether dreadful. To them, the idea of passing one exam after another for the
sake of getting into a good university, all for the opportunity to become Salaryman, meant living life on a hamster wheel.[82]

What was more spectacular, the postwar employment regime itself appeared to
have gone into free fall. Salaryman's protective shell was breaking down, and so
was the security it had provided. In the late 1990s, the aftereffects of the Asian currency crisis intensified the previously unthinkable wave of bankruptcies and *risu-
tora* (restructuring, a euphemism for "layoffs") that had already been rattling corporations throughout Japan. And the turn of the new century brought no reprieve.
Structural reform, the leitmotiv of Prime Minister Koizumi, posed a head-on
challenge to the stability and security that had come with lifetime employment.
Flexible production and no-strings employment were the signature of the American vogue for privatizing public companies and deconstructing stable arrangements. Inequality worsened in Japan, as in much of the rest of the world, and
everyday talk now centered on winners and losers. No wonder, then, that the new
millennium brought a spate of Shōwa nostalgia that harked back to the Golden
Age of rapid economic growth and economic security. As Salaryman's life in all its
grandeur continued to implode, the gender binary became difficult to sustain, as
an ideal and in fact. It's no surprise, then, that Japanese women workers had begun
to throw off their OL uniforms by the first decade of the twenty-first century. They
no longer saw the workforce as a waystation to marriage. Now they were in it for
the long haul, and vanishingly few among them harbored dreams of a loveless,
sexless marriage to Salaryman. Salaryman does still exist, but in diminished form,
without much spark or shine. And almost no one today wants to be Salaryman.[83]

Artisanship in Light of Modernist Modes of Work

Having taken a close look at the dominant, modernist form of labor in Japan, the
mode of Salaryman, we can now ask how it compares to the artisanal form of
work, the mode of *shokunin*. In contrast to the received notion of work in modern

industrial societies, the work of almost all artisans is performed on a small scale and usually in a room at home, in a separate studio, or possibly in a small shop. In addition, artisans own their tools. They also decide what they will do as well as when and how they will do it, within the broad constraints of received practices and external demands. In Marx's vocabulary, then, artisans not only own the means of production but also control the labor process. They take enormous pride in their skill, and they express commitment to their craft. They are embedded in distinct structures or networks of production and exchange—sushi chefs, after all, do not go fishing for the seafood they will prepare and serve—but they exercise a great deal of autonomy, and this too is a point of no little pride. Paradoxically, however, artisans' autonomy often becomes routinization and self-exploitation, which is to say that artisans often work very long hours and do the same things, day after day. Freedom has its price. What makes these conditions bearable is the pride that artisans take in their work, in addition to their understanding that only tedium and repetition can bring mastery (and perhaps innovation) and their recognition that they've chosen their path.

The contrast with modernist modes of production should be clear. Workers in modernist settings don't own their tools or devise their working conditions and processes. Commuting to work is both normal and time-consuming. For the sake of maximum productivity and profits, skilled work is often carried out through division of labor and the application of technology. The phenomenon of deskilling, which exists in every factory and every office, raises the specter of automation (accentuated by ubiquitous discussion of robotics and artificial intelligence) and, therefore, the threat of workers' redundancy and irrelevance. Work is generally thought of as drudgery. Some workers may find satisfaction in their work, but most simply endure it and find pleasure after work, in leisure activities. Workers in these settings can seek better opportunities by looking for employment elsewhere (the language of careers and human capital turns human beings into commodities) or by organizing into unions. Almost always, however, the struggle is not so much about transforming the work itself as about agreeing on wages and work hours. Work in this situation is purely instrumental, a means of earning money to ensure one's livelihood and, very often, to support one's family.

In contrast, there are no capitalists or managers to shape an artisan's conception of the work to be done, nor do rulebooks or lists of techniques dictate the work's execution. As many artisans say, their knowledge is in their hands. It lives in muscle memory as embodied skills. Artisans generally receive their skills from their masters, and they go on to practice their skills, and sometimes improve on them, in such a way as to produce items of perceptible quality (though judgments will vary, of course, regarding the excellence of any individual producer or product). In short, conception and execution occur simultaneously, in the single moment of an artisan's exercising his or her received, embodied skills and techniques. The embodied knowledge of artisanal work is not explicit. It resists formalization. For example, when a chef was asked why he didn't formulate a rule for exactly how much salt to use in a particular dish, he said that this was not a mechanical issue but depended instead on complex contingencies like the weather, the texture of the ingredients, and so on, and that to formalize the issue would be to mechanize it, which in turn would be tantamount to making the work inhuman, something for robots to do.[84]

In contrast, the prevailing modernist mode of work valorizes extensive division of labor, routinization, and mechanization. As mentioned earlier, even though Taylor's recommendations for scientific management have been discredited, his ideas remain alive. Consequently, breaking up workers' tasks is thought to be efficient, and so the work of management is to deconstruct and rearrange those tasks while inserting as much machinery and automation as possible. Under this style of management, workers focus on executing their defined tasks, and their skills are devalued. The long chain of command, almost always organized hierarchically, makes for an impersonal work environment, which becomes a site of authority and discipline as workers are managed and controlled. The bitter pill of being told what to do is worsened by deskilling as well as by the devaluation of work, and the work in turn is often boring and meaningless. The ultimate realization of Taylor's line of thinking would be a fully automated factory or office.

Mass production has its defenders, and there is no reason to dismiss it. Standardized, rules-based, machine-based production can save labor as well as costs. Modern transportation, for instance, would not operate well without mass production. Nevertheless, despite the benefits of mass production, its virtues are too often exaggerated, as in the American cliché that a particular innovation is the greatest thing since sliced bread.[85]

Mass production is predicated on mass consumption. But, if it would be problematic to dismiss the widespread benefits of mass-produced commodities, the long litany of tirades against shoddy products should give anyone pause. For example, both John Ruskin and William Morris pointedly criticize the type of industrialization that not only destroys the countryside but also offers inferior products while eliminating the role of traditional artisans and craftspeople. If concern for quantity and cost supersedes concern for quality and aesthetics, a post-subsistence economy is not necessarily well served by mass consumption. Ruskin and Morris are right to worry about the deleterious impact of mass production on people's taste and quality of life.

Consumers, after all, are human beings who learn and evolve. If Jean Anthelme Brillat-Savarin is at least partly right in saying that we are what we eat, it follows (and few would disagree in principle) that what we eat should matter, and that we should care about what we eat. No one wants to gorge on pollutant-drenched, pesticide-laced produce, and who needs the concentrated dose of pain caused by food poisoning? But many people, rightly skeptical about the so-called expertise of self-styled experts, are tempted to say that everything tastes the same, and they happily receive the news that more drinkers in a blind tasting chose the less expensive beverage over the one that costs fifteen times more. Nevertheless, experience and expertise do exist, and there is no substitute for learning—perhaps from reading, but more likely from actual drinking—that craft-produced, pollution-free wine is superior to mass-produced, chemical-infused wine. In other words, consumer education can be significant even though it does not form part of any formal curriculum. In fact, one reason why artisanal chefs flourish in Japan is that many Japanese diners are not only discerning but also educated and informed about matters of cuisine. Thus chefs and diners alike are able to maintain and support the hope that quality can trump quantity, if only in part, and to reject a race to the bottom on the basis of competitive pricing.

Or consider plates. Older Japanese ceramicists and *urushi* craftsmen often talk about the disastrous period of the 1960s and 1970s, the high tide of Japan's rapid economic growth, when people began to jettison traditional housewares in favor of modern industrial products, such as plastic dishes and similar tableware. Lacquer plates, properly cared for, can look splendid even after a century of constant use. As I heard from one elderly *urushi* master, however, "People got rid of all their lacquer plates that had been in the family for generations. They just put them out on the street. The new plastic plates were American. They were shiny." And why stop at plastic? Why not paper plates, which at least eliminate the drudgery of dishwashing? One answer is that if industrial products can have a beauty of their own, most people resist the slide to full utilitarian ugliness. People appreciate beauty in small things. For example, a particular delicacy may look more pleasing, and therefore taste better, when it is arranged on a beautiful plate, and the plate's fragility inspires care and commitment, even if that level of attention amounts to an inconvenience. Taking care of a beautiful plate—living with it, aging with it—is a form of commitment and conviviality. Although the beauty of a small thing is minor and ephemeral, it can still play a small but positive role in one's life, and it can represent a meaningful relationship. Indeed, fragile handcrafted pottery inevitably chips and cracks, but there is an aesthetics of transforming imperfections into points of appreciation. As a last resort, a broken plate can be put back together through the technique of *kintsugi,* in which the shards are glued with lacquer and dusted with gold or other minerals, and the plate, thus reborn, becomes a renewed artisanal object of beauty.

To generalize, then, educated consumers constitute a critical foundation of the artisanal mode of work. Yanagi Muneyoshi, a founding figure in the modern Japanese revival of *kōgei* (arts and crafts), says that a thing has a "life before," as something created, but also a "life after," as something to be used.[86] In an anticipation of reception theory, Yanagi points to the irrefutable idea that an artisanal product comes to life when it is used. Instead of being stored as a work of art, whether for investment or pleasure, an artisanal product that is used is one that lives, enmeshed as it is in the present. Thus consumer education is a crucial but neglected component of the artisanal mode of work. As Ruskin puts it, "We need examples of people who . . . have resolved to seek—not greater wealth, but simpler pleasure; not higher fortune, but deeper felicity."[87] Or, as Morris instructs, every object should be "made by the people for the people as a joy for the maker and the user."[88]

7

The Book of Bathing

It is a commonsense observation that most Japanese people bathe before they retire for the night. They may not bathe every day, and some, especially young urbanites, may prefer to shower in the morning.[1] Yet few Japanese people would deny that bathing is normative in Japan, and many have much to say, often with eloquence, about the virtues of bathing. An office worker in his fifties told me, "During the day, there's nothing I look forward to more than going home, sinking into warm water, opening a cold beer, and relaxing." "It makes me feel Japanese," a restaurant server in her thirties said, and she added, with self-conscious exaggeration, "I'm lucky I was born Japanese and can drown all my troubles in the tub." But the ultimate bathing experience takes place at an *onsen* (a hot spring, mineral spring, or spa). Indeed, *onsen* are a top destination for domestic tourists. The overt purpose of *onsen* travel is to allow the visitor to plunge repeatedly into thermal mineral water, but there are latent pleasures, too, such as feasting. Bathing in general and *onsen* travel in particular are touched by the glow of tradition—many Japanese people like to talk about the inextricably intertwined nature of the Japanese self and its aquatic ensconcement. A fact convenient for this self-presentation is that almost all nineteenth-century Western visitors to Japan remarked on the ubiquity of bathing in the Japanese archipelago. As the itinerant Isabella L. Bird declared in the late nineteenth century, "The public bath-house is one of the features of Japan."[2] Likewise, the expatriate manga artist Yamazaki Mari recalls Japan as a place where "food is tasty and one can bask in wonderful *onsen*."[3] In short, bathing occupies a prominent place in the pantheon of Japaneseness, right alongside Mount Fuji, cherry blossoms, and sushi.

What is the significance of bathing? Just as with sushi, bathing comes with a bewildering variety of practices, and over time they have undergone considerable transformation. Bathing, on the basis of its association with religious rituals of purification and medicinal acts of detoxification, emerged during the Edo period as a daily ritual that provides extraordinary moments of repose. Bathing—the antidote to work, however remunerative or satisfying one's work may be—allows relaxation and restoration. It is a haven of not-doing in a world of busyness.

THE PHENOMENOLOGY OF BATHING

In contemporary affluent societies, people learn alphabets and numbers, even foreign languages and statistical methods, but they get by with minimal instruction about matters of everyday sustenance. In some cases, the lack of instruction is paradoxical, as when people pursuing training and qualification as academics are not taught pedagogy. In others, as in the case of sexual interaction, parents and teachers are not reliable sources of instruction—they mostly talk about what *not* to do. And so young people, in the absence of formal or traditional modes of instruction, turn to such readily available sources as video porn.[4] Nor are parents or professionals (with the possible exception of dental hygienists, who are zealous about demonstrating the proper way to floss and brush one's teeth) always attentive guides to and enforcers of personal hygiene. How, then, do we learn to shower?

Bathing rules and routines are widely known and understood in Japan because many people participate in one form of communal bathing or another.[5] Apart from all the unspoken rules and communal norms, in a *sentō* (public bathhouse) or *onsen* there is invariably a placard that delineates the dos and don'ts.[6] The *sentō* or *onsen* is housed in an imposing structure, often reminiscent of temple architecture, as befits a place of secular purification.[7] And the sanctum sanctorum is the bathtub, which one may enter only after a rigorous cleansing or ritual ablution. In fact, the first item of the posted guidelines usually states that rule, and the visitor who fails to obey can expect disapproving comments from the other guests. In any case, many Japanese bathers do engage in a preliminary round of vigorous washing, and it can be breathtaking to observe this cleansing routine in the setting of a Japanese venue for public bathing.[8] One sits on a low stool, repeatedly splashes water on oneself, and uses a soap-infused towel to lather and massage the entire body. In the past, the prevailing norm was to have another person wash one's back.[9] For the past several decades, however, especially among men (this is one instance of a difference in gender-based norms), the usual procedure has been to wash one's own back by pulling the towel back and forth against it. At times when one concludes this routine, one's body is so thoroughly reddened as to resemble a bright-red lobster after a plunge in boiling water. But then comes immersion in the tub, and the exhalation of cortisol-tinged air. Indeed, the soak is the highlight of the contemporary bathing process, the point at which one finally relaxes and seems to float to a higher plane.

Nostalgia for public bathhouses has brought a retro boom, but attendance is sharply down. Nevertheless, *sentō*-based bathing rituals are still carried out in private households. After the war, in part because members of a household shared the same tub of water, people continued the practice of washing the body before soaking in the bathtub, a practice that is both economical and ecological. But this practice is still observed even by people who live alone. Almost any Japanese person, even the most self-consciously hip *Yankī*, will acknowledge following the received mode of cleansing before soaking. (A determinedly nonconforming young man gave me a crooked smile as he explained, "It's not as if you can just do *anything*, or be different on every point. How can you not be clean before getting in the tub?") The point is not just to wash dirt off one's body and keep the water clean but also to leach out any pollutants that may have accumulated during the day. In Japanese bathing, purification, whether it's the washing away of physical dirt or the soaking that seems to release spiritual pollution, is about expunging external grime and restoring the self. It is no accident that bathing is one of the day's last activities.

Submersion times vary greatly. The human body cannot perspire adequately in water, and so a long soak raises the body temperature and threatens *yuatari* or *nobose* (extreme bodily fatigue caused by overheating). The contemporary norm seems to be submersion for ten to fifteen minutes, long enough for the body to retain internal heat after the bath.[10] The absence of central heating in many Japanese homes makes the process of warming the body functional in the winter, though people are no less likely to soak in the tub during other seasons. Time in warm water may seem like the last thing anyone would yearn for in the intense heat and humidity of a typical Japanese summer, but many people insist on the invigorating and refreshing effects of a soak, in part because it is a form of homeopathy and in part because of the cooling effect of perspiration. But the primary reason is often the ingrained habit of bathing, along with what almost amounts to dependence on its salutary effects. Some people say they read in the tub—books available for bathtime reading can be viewed on an e-reader equipped with a waterproof sheath. Others admit, somewhat sheepishly, that they take their smartphones with them. But it seems that most people don't do anything in particular in the tub apart from reflecting a bit and spacing out. In Japan, bathing and soaking in the tub are equated because many Japanese people bathe not just to get clean or warm up but also to relax and rejuvenate.

Then there is the after-bath routine. The received practice, once one is flushed and perspiring and radiating heat from within, is to hydrate oneself. Many middle-aged men (but people in other demographic groups, too) take distinct pleasure in the first swallow after cracking open a beer. The sweating glass, the seductive froth at its rim, the perfect gulp giving way to a satisfied smile—this ritual has been enacted in many a television commercial. For several decades, a brand of fruit-flavored milk that began production in 1958 was a mainstay of many public bath-houses, though almost no one admitted drinking it (and it basically escaped the attention of younger people). The enterprise that manufactured this so-called *furo-age no aji* ("taste after the bath") went out of business in 2019.[11] Be that as it may, in Japan the after-bath drink is almost as mandatory as the postcoital smoke in a classic Hollywood film.

The Japanese way of bathing, like sushi, crystallized during the Edo period, but the postwar period gave the Japanese their daily bath, which continues to function as something between a habit and a basic necessity. The postwar husband, upon returning home, would bark, "Meshi, furo, neru" ("Food, bath, and sleep"), but bathing was crucial for almost every other member of the household, too.[12]

THE JAPANESE VICE AS VIRTUE

Bathing is as old as civilization, and surely even older. *The Epic of Gilgamesh*, the oldest surviving work of fiction in the human repertoire, has Gilgamesh and Enki-du bathing together, and classic works from the Christian Bible to *Man'yōshū*, from Homer's epics to *Exodus*, feature bathing scenes. As the hilarious manga *Thermae Romae* revealed to many Japanese readers, the ancient Romans, too, were crazy about bathing.[13] The Roman public bath, which included lounges and librar-ies as well as restaurants and brothels, offered a complete package of pleasures (and vices), and Diocletian may have built the largest public bath in world history—it spanned fourteen acres and could accommodate more than three thousand peo-ple.[14] Bathing, then, is hardly unique to Japan, but confusion on this point stems in part from the myriad ways in which the word "bathing" is used. Although the word can denote physical as well as symbolic cleansing, its connotations also include the soaking in a tub that most Japanese people think of when they talk about bathing.

At any rate, it has become an article of faith for many Japanese people that they are bathing aficionados and virtuosos. This ethnocentric belief is strengthened by foreigners' impressions, as noted earlier. From the time of the sixteenth-century Portuguese missionary Luís Fróis (the first Western visitor to write a book about Japan), Western chroniclers almost always mentioned the frequency with which Japanese people bathed.[15] Another common observation has to do with the high temperature of Japanese bathwater.[16] Pierre Loti, in the late nineteenth century, was horrified to see that "in front of an isolated house, an old man and an old woman were cooking two small girls, probably in order to eat them." Upon closer inspection, he was relieved to discover that the children were only being bathed.[17] In Nagasaki, he found it "comique" that in the early evening ("five or six o'clock") "everyone [was] naked ... [and] in some sort of tub."[18] But what was comical to

Loti struck Commodore Matthew Perry (usually credited with "opening" Japan) as "foul corruption": "A scene at one of the public baths, where the sexes mingled indiscriminately, unconscious of their nudity, was not calculated to impress the Americans with a very favorable opinion of the morals of the inhabitants. . . . [T]he Japanese people of the inferior ranks are undoubtedly . . . a lewd people."[19] That is, in the minds of some Western observers, mixed-gender bathing was a cardinal Japanese vice. In addition, exported *ukiyo-e* prints—many of them *shunga* depicting nudity and sexuality, with the public bathhouse as a frequent locus—undoubtedly confirmed both the Japanese penchant for bathing and the supposed perversion that was the mixed-gender public space.[20] The Meiji leaders, by and large, agreed with this Western judgment. But by the early twentieth century, mixed-gender bathing had also become a point of pride and a source of Japanese identity for some, a perspective that continues to this day.[21]

Why would an otherwise perceptive Westerner mistake children being bathed for children being cooked, or find the practice of mixed-gender bathing so offensive? The simple answer is that from the Middle Ages to the nineteenth century, most Europeans suffered from a generalized form of dysmorphic disorder as well as from aquaphobia (for them, the so-called French bath was more than enough).[22] Although this is an overgeneralization, there is some truth to the rumor of the medieval Christian abomination of the body. Natural shame and unnatural hatred combined to form a potent brew. Many Europeans imbibed it and struggled to cover their sin-drenched nakedness. By the early modern era, Europeans had also begun to believe in the deleterious consequences of exposing the body to water.[23] At that time, the latest scientific thought proscribed prolonged immersion in water because water was supposedly inimical to humoral balance and, therefore, to good health. Needless to say, the reluctance to be naked and the resistance to being in water spelled hygienic disaster and olfactory nightmare. Even without these ideational proscriptions, however, clean water was in short supply, and heating it was costly, which made daily bathing a wild extravagance. Only after the nineteenth century did Europeans begin to bathe regularly and stop worrying about removing the scum from their skin.[24] The coeval technological transformations also made running water possible, along with sewerage and other infrastructural preconditions of the modern bathroom, which itself was largely a twentieth-century invention.[25] The widespread abhorrence of nudity, the reluctance to bathe, and the difficulties of bathing account for Western observers' curiosity about and horror of Japanese bathing, which sometimes meant men, women, and children bathing together.

The Edo-era *yuya*, or *sentō*, opened up the possibility of daily bathing for ordinary people. In 1591, Ise Yoichi established the first demotic bathhouse near Zenigamehashi (contemporary Ōtemachi), and it caught on rapidly. By 1614, according to writer Miura Jōshin, every town had a bathhouse.[26] What made the *yuya* accessible, apart from its ubiquity, was its low price.[27] It was also open during daylight hours.

A popular genre of Japanese entertainment involves time travel (presumably through a wormhole) with the protagonist, usually an ordinary twenty-first-century person, ending up in the war-torn Japan of the late sixteenth century. That time traveler would be rather startled by an Edo-era *sentō*. She would note some ready similarities, both in the interior design (the entrance where one pays, the changing area, the washing area, the tub) and in the clientele (a mass of individuals cleansing themselves). But other features would be alien to her. For instance, Edo-style bathhouses were dark and claustrophobic, and they served as *karaburo* (literally, "empty baths"), or steam baths.[28] In addition, the usual bathing setup was much closer to that of the Finnish sauna or the Slavic *banya*. Nor did Edo-era bathers quite soak in a twenty-first-century-style bathtub filled with warm water.[29] Instead, Edoites often sat in a tub of shallow water, reportedly muddy because there was no filtering mechanism. But bathhouses were popular enough to encourage incremental improvements, which eventually brought higher water levels and longer immersion times. By the early nineteenth century, certainly, the Edo bathhouse had come to closely approximate the postwar *sentō*.

As in ancient Rome, the purpose of bathing culture in the Edo period was not just hygiene. It also served as entertainment, since it offered tea, conversation, and other activities that "tempt men's hearts," as Miura puts it.[30] Accordingly, by the eighteenth century it had become common for a bathhouse to change, after four in the afternoon, from a place of cleansing to a place of entertainment.[31] A two-story system, with the ground floor for bathing and the floor above for (male) entertainment, also became popular.[32] There were also *yuna* (professional scrubbers), who initially served to wash men's bodies or comb their hair but later became bathhouse geisha, entertaining the bathers and engaging not just in social but other forms of intercourse.[33] In other words, the bathhouse came to be synonymous with the male vices of boozing, gambling, and whoring.[34]

Before the eighteenth century, bathhouses in Edo, as well as those in western Japan, were often stratified on the basis of price and did not invite cross-status interaction. In fact, high-status people avoided bathhouses altogether, precisely in order not to mingle with the masses.[35] But eventually the Edo bathhouse, apart from its manifest and latent functions—hygiene and entertainment, respectively—came to serve as a public space where people of different ranks could mingle.[36] In effect, the Edo bathhouse became the equivalent of the coffeehouse in Enlightenment Europe.[37] After-bath conversations, undoubtedly fueled by alcohol, could unfold in a protected arena of relatively open speech—there's nothing like nakedness to strip away the pretensions of rank and prestige.[38] Isabella L. Bird may have been reiterating an informant's take on the matter, but she was nevertheless right to declare, "The public bath-house is said to be the place in which public opinion is formed."[39]

Shikitei Sanba's "Ukiyoburo" (The world of the bath), published in the early eighteenth century, is popular entertainment, complete with scatological humor.[40] Between interpolated tales of flatulence and reports of gossip, Shikitei's comic story captures, as few other records have done, the everyday concerns and conversations of Edoites around the time when *nigirizushi* (Edo-style sushi) appeared. Indeed, in "Ukiyoburo," women's discussions about children's schooling or about what to put in a child's *bentō* (lunch box) might just as easily be overheard in Tokyo's neighborhood parks today.[41] Even more striking is the fact that Shikitei opens his story with an eloquent assertion of human equality in the nakedness of the bathhouse. He articulates the five virtues of bathing—warming the body, removing dirt, curing illness, relieving fatigue, and caring for others—while depicting a culture of clean bodies and dirty stories.[42] By 1808, when *yuya* were organized into *ton'ya* (guilds), the bathhouse had already become a defining public institution of ordinary life in Edo.[43]

It should not be assumed that Japanese bathers at an Edo-era *sentō* were prelapsarian innocents sauntering about naked and indifferent to the male (or female) gaze.[44] In an Edo *sentō*, by contrast with the norms in a *kon'yoku* (mixed-gender) *onsen*, a time traveler would not find open celebration of mixed-gender bathing.[45] In fact, the government sought to ban mixed-gender bathing, though most *sentō* blithely ignored the proscription, since they lacked the funds needed to make major renovations.[46] The early nineteenth century saw the advent of the bathhouse with a female-only area, a development that points to what until then had been the male-dominated character of Edo bathing culture, and to women's desire to be liberated from the male gaze as well as from men's unwanted behavior.[47]

Nineteenth-century Western observers often commented on mixed-gender bathing in Japan because, like gender-integrated public spaces, it was relatively rare in their home countries. In contemporary Japan, open-air bathing, whether in *onsen* or streams, necessarily involves no barrier between the sexes. In such a setting, families often bathe together, as happens in similar places almost everywhere else in the world. But public mixed-gender bathing is not an invitation to an orgy. Rather, it entails considerable decorum.[48] Indeed, in a *kon'yoku*, most Japanese bathers, especially those who have not grown up with public bathhouses, are somewhat diffident and invariably cover their private parts outside the water. Some facilities even prescribe swimsuits, to the consternation of traditionalists. To be sure, Peeping Toms and sexual provocateurs are common enough in Japan, and there is the occasional exhibitionist. In general, however, Japanese people in outdoor, mixed-gender *onsen* fall somewhere between shy and shameful on the scale of feelings about public nudity.[49]

THE MODERN BATHING EXPERIENCE

The Edo period formed the basis of contemporary Japanese bathing culture, but we should also consider the developments of the past century and a half. The proximate source of the modern Japanese bathing experience is the *kairyōburo* (new and improved bath) that opened in Tokyo in 1887. With its open, large, well-lighted interior and big tub, it shaped the contemporary *sentō*. Connotations of modernity and the West can be gleaned from the bathhouse's Western-style architecture. Massive reconstruction after the 1923 Great Kantō Earthquake gave rise to the last major flourish of the contemporary *sentō*—its imposing exterior, befitting a premodern castle or a temple. The new Meiji format allowed ample space for lathering as well as the opportunity to soak in warm water. The bathhouse, gender-segregated from the outset, made bathing a clean, family-friendly affair. Instead of *yuna*, who were sometimes also sex workers, *sansuke* provided straightforward scrubbing services.[50] To be sure, this type of facility was available only in urban areas, and it was neither open to nor attractive to everyone. Moreover, the technological and infrastructural improvements of the postwar period, and the accompanying enrichment of the Japanese population, were necessary before Japanese people could approach the contemporary ideal of universal daily bathing.[51] In the second half of the twentieth century, the widespread use of gas and electricity made possible not only a bathhouse with a larger capacity but also a much cleaner establishment.[52]

In the postwar period, most urban Japanese people went to public bathhouses. The client, carrying a small pail and a towel, would pay the price of admission (usually considered affordable, and a necessity in any case), enter the gender-appropriate area, and disrobe. The main bathing area was large, with a fresco on the wall that held the tub. *Sentō* art constituted a genre in itself, with artisans limning one popular image or another; Mount Fuji was most common. The client would then wash vigorously in the area reserved for cleansing, perhaps wash the back of a relative or even a stranger (who might return the favor), and then soak in the large tub. Given the presence of other bathers, many of them neighbors and acquaintances, the client was more likely to engage in casual banter or gossip than to talk about personal matters. After immersion in the tub, the client would emerge clean, refreshed, and warm. That was the moment for more conversation, perhaps, or a beverage, and maybe, very occasionally, a massage. This cleansing routine, including the centrally important soak in the tub, was crystallized in the postwar *sentō*, but the element of privacy was still missing.

By the mid-1960s, rapid economic growth had made the contemporary Japanese ideal of daily bathing a reality, one that preferably included a long soak in hot water. But it was just when public bathhouses became readily accessible and affordable that a gradual yet irreversible decline in the number of bathhouses began. From the peak, in 1968, when there were nearly 2,700 bathing establishments in Tokyo, their number dropped steadily until there were roughly 1,350 public bathhouses in 1999 and only about 700 by the mid-2010s.[53] More dramatic, however, was the decreasing frequency with which people in Tokyo went to public bathhouses—between 1975 and 1996, the average number of daily visits to individual bathhouses plunged from 440 to 160.[54] Now, instead of bathing in public, people were turning to their private bathrooms, and a private bathroom meant a private tub.[55] Ownership of a bathtub did not spell the end of visiting public bathhouses. For example, 26 percent of respondents to a 1993 survey reported having a bathtub at home but also going to public bathhouses because of their plentiful hot water, their spaciousness, and the pleasure they provided.[56] But the public bathhouses did not offer privacy, and the household bathroom, thanks to the declining cost and greater convenience of at-home bathing infrastructure and equipment, became a personal haven from the gazes and gossip of neighbors as well as from wearying social interaction itself.

As a reaction to the advent of the private bathroom, public bathhouses differentiated along two major lines. First, the contemporary *sentō*, no longer conceiving of itself as a place for daily bathing, strove to deliver an experience much closer to that provided by a visit to a hot spring. Decked out for special occasions, it became a veritable tourist attraction offering a variety of entertainments and levels of service. Second, in 1951, as a throwback to the Edo-era bathhouse, Tokyo Onsen pioneered the *Torukoburo* (Turkish bathhouse), which gained popularity over the course of the 1960s. At this type of bathhouse, the client can enjoy a sauna, a steam bath, and massage services, but it is best known for erotic massage as well as for its function as a brothel, a function enhanced by the closure, in 1958, of Japan's redline, or red-light, districts. Indeed, the *Torukoburo,* wildly popular throughout the country, is postwar Japan's indisputable king of *fūzoku* (sexual services). In 1984, under pressure from Turkish students in Japan, these establishments came to be known as *sōpurando* (soap lands). At any rate, what an Edo-era observer might have said about the ubiquity of public bathhouses in his own time, his contemporary reincarnation would be able to say about Tokyo's *sōpurando.*

ONSEN AND THE RATIONALE FOR BATHING

As mentioned earlier, the ultimate in Japanese bathing experiences is a visit to a hot spring. The closest English translation of *onsen,* "spa," does not begin to capture the profound connotations of rest and relaxation, nor does it do justice to oneiric evocations of pleasure and longing.[57] Japanese vacationers go to *onsen* not just for the thermal mineral waters but also for the opportunity to enjoy ancillary activities like walking, shopping, getting a massage and (extra) sleep, and especially eating and drinking. The mere mention of *onsen* stirs warm memories and wistful yearnings in many Japanese people.[58] Hot springs remain prime vacation destinations, and many *onsen* are reasonably close to major Japanese cities. A glance at the stacks of guides in bookstores confirms the prominent place of *onsen* in the fantasy lives of Japanese people.[59]

When it comes to *onsen*, the Japanese penchant for thinking Japanese culture extraordinary, even unique, is on full display. Because *onsen* are believed to be a defining characteristic of Japanese culture, the mere mention of the word unleashes a discourse whose truncated translation is "I'm glad I was born Japanese." Even Japanese monkeys are known to enjoy a dip, as Japanese lovers of *onsen* are often eager to point out. (When I visited Jigokudani, however, the local simians appeared less keen on taking the waters than on snatching food from tourists.) Literary types who want to affirm the long-standing Japanese obsession with *onsen* can mention *Man'yōshū*—the oldest poetry compilation, from the eighth century— and drop the names of Japanese literary figures who loved *onsen,* a list that can seem almost synonymous with the pantheon of great Japanese writers.[60] Moreover, a famous *onsen* proprietor will make sure that his guests have been filled in on the glorious history of his little corner of paradise, a history that will perforce include his enumeration of past eminent visitors.[61]

Until recently, *onsen* were the almost-exclusive preserve of the Japanese, a situation validating the belief that foreigners find it difficult to understand Japanese culture.[62] Recent years have seen a steady increase in the number of foreign tourists, especially from neighboring Asian countries, but most foreign visitors are ignorant of the well-established norms of *onsen* tourism, such as washing oneself thoroughly before entering the mineral spring. Therefore, the *onsen* setting becomes a good barometer of who the Japanese people are, and of how they are different from non-Japanese people. At times, then, a Japanese hot spring can become a literal hothouse of ethnocentrism, even xenophobia. I heard one *onsen* aficionado exclaim, "Japanese bathing culture is the greatest! If foreigners don't like it, they can stay out of Japan. *Onsen* are the spirit of the Japanese people."

Japan, like other fissured, earthquake-prone areas, is blessed with numerous mineral springs, and people have been soaking in the thermal waters of the Japanese archipelago for some thirty thousand years. From the earliest recorded times, a mixture of motives—the most important ones were religious and medical— legitimated the pleasure of bathing, though bathing has been common enough in other cultures.[63] Ki no Tsurayuki, in his tenth-century *Tosa nikki* (Tosa diary), recounts a walking journey of fifty-five days and expresses marked interest in mineral springs. Nevertheless, as in his near contemporaneous *Utsuho monogatari* (The story of Utsuho) and later writings, his emphasis is on interesting sights and people.[64] At one hot spring, he cleansed himself—that is, he experienced *gyōzui* (a quick bath in a shallow wooden tub)—but did not take a prolonged soak in a pool of thermal water. Be that as it may, travel and leisure were the province of nobles like Ki no

Tsurayuki, and they were joined from time to time by long-distance merchants and religious wanderers. In other words, *onsen*, apart from their accessibility to a few local inhabitants, were largely restricted to the nobles, the samurai, and the monks who constituted the elite strata of Japanese society. Because mineral springs everywhere tend to be found in remote mountainous areas, it was hard for most people to reach them before improvements in transportation, communication, and general economic conditions had occurred. In the case of Japan, those improvements took place at the outset of the Edo period. Even then, however, travel was hampered by factors that were bureaucratic (government-issued passes were necessary), infrastructural (the roads were poor), and economic (few people had the means for leisure travel).[65] Not surprisingly, then, until the twentieth century most *onsen* areas lacked well-developed networks of inns, restaurants, and shops. Even in a famous *onsen* area like Arima or Kusatsu, it wasn't until the nineteenth century that the number of inns began to exceed a score.[66] Kusatsu Onsen, renowned from time immemorial for its extremely acidic, sulphur-rich thermal water, remained closed during the long winter months until the Meiji period, and its inaccessibility discouraged mass tourism until the twentieth century.[67]

Travel to Japanese mineral springs is very popular today, but the origins of *onsen* lie shrouded in the mists of time. And with *onsen*, as with bathing in general, we should resist presentism, that is, the temptation to see the past in terms of the present. The fact is that in the past, mineral springs were viewed mostly with ambivalence. A particular *onsen* might offer spiritual or physical benefits, but it was just as likely to evoke the image and foul vapors of hell.[68] What could be more repellent, if not downright frightening, than the sight of bubbling water and the stench of sulphur? In any event, visitors to *onsen* until the eighteenth century or so usually remained clothed, and many *onsen* were set up as steam baths.[69]

Until the eighteenth century, *onsen* travel in Japan did not begin to approximate its modern version. Apart from the relative inaccessibility of *onsen* areas and the small scale of *onsen* travel, most *onsen* facilities were primitive affairs. *Onsen* travelers of the past, like their Edo-era counterparts in public bathhouses, often were not able to enjoy the contemporary mode of soaking. The difficulty of transporting mineral water meant that bathers had to go right to the source, and, given the extremely high temperature of many springs, bathers reposed in simple structures that were steam baths. These arrangements were far from what is suggested by idyllic images of luxuriating in a large open-air bath.

It was the long interval of peace and prosperity in the latter half of the Edo era that gave rise to the prototype of modern *onsen* tourism, which was now available even to ordinary people.[70] Some *onsen* towns doubled as market towns, and they experienced economic and cultural growth, especially in coastal areas with easy access to main avenues that initially had been developed in part to facilitate the transportation of *daimyō* (feudal lords) and later were used for interregional commerce. Atami, close to Edo, was an exemplary beneficiary and distinguished itself as a favorite vacation spot of many *daimyō*.[71] Wealthy and powerful patrons sought spiritual cleansing or bodily cures, but they also viewed *onsen* as places for rest and relaxation. Over time, there emerged inns featuring gourmand meals and geisha entertainment. Thus the Edo-era *onsen* came to function as an elaboration of the Edo-era public bathhouse, but for a more affluent clientele.[72]

The early nineteenth century brought group tours masquerading as religious excursions, and these made *onsen* tourism possible and popular for townspeople.[73] There was now better security on interregional roads. In addition, the government now readily approved one-night travel, and news of *onsen* was spreading via travel writings and *ukiyo-e* prints.[74] It was in the nineteenth century, then, that ordinary people began to enjoy a scaled-down version of *onsen* travel, which previously had been restricted to the affluent and the powerful.

The Meiji Restoration marked a turning point. The new leaders sought to emulate the West and to reject the past, if selectively. Among practices considered traditional and supposedly backward, *onsen* and *onsen* travel were on the chopping block, and so was mixed-gender bathing, a source of acute embarrassment to the modernizing leaders. Starting with the 1879 legislation against *kon'yoku*, the post–Meiji Restoration state proscribed mixed-gender bathing. Equally problematic was the seemingly nonscientific cast of *onsen* cures. The anticapitalist logic of *onsen* rest made it, too, suspect. Some people continued going to mineral baths, and some scientists defended them. But the modern Japanese state also held to Western notions of hygiene and focused on sanitation, in the form of battling contagious diseases, so as to promote industry and the military.[75] In this worldview, bathing was not of critical importance.

Japanese people in the early 1940s were compliant students of the West, even on the topic of *onsen*. Thus the early scholarly literature on *onsen* went beyond geological features and medical benefits to include suggestions for improving the experience of *onsen* travel in Japan by developing infrastructure like that found in the spa towns of Europe and elsewhere.[76] That is, not only were Japanese scientists in the early 1940s aware of the existence of mineral springs elsewhere in the world, but they also thought the Japanese should learn from them. Udagawa Yōan, a pioneering nineteenth-century Western-style chemist, wrote his treatise largely by translating portions of an English-language textbook, but he included observations on *kōsen* (mineral springs).[77] Most other nineteenth-century discussions of mineral springs, in common with Udagawa's treatise, revolved around the medical benefits of thermal water, including its chemical characteristics. The most famous of these was a seminal work by a German doctor, Erwin O. E. von Bälz.[78] Von Bälz, the putative father of modern medicine in Japan, found much to celebrate in the salutary effects of Kusatsu Onsen. Thus his work legitimated *onsen* in the minds of government bureaucrats and medical practitioners and led inevitably to discussion of the benefits of *onsen* for the modern military.[79] But von Bälz failed to realize his vision for a spa at Kusatsu, one that would be superior to the spa at Karlsbad.[80] Even so, he influenced generations of Japanese scientists and boosters of *onsen*, and his German-inflected idea of a spa for health and relaxation would go on to inspire a large, persistent following.[81]

Von Bälz notwithstanding, the idea of *onsen* had associations with the decadent, not with the onward and upward march of Japanese industry and empire, or even with the genteel spa resorts of Bath or Baden-Baden. It is no accident that *onsen* came to be associated with literary lions, many of whom had rejected the world of wealth and power, and that *onsen* became both their Alps and their Bohème. Nature worship, inspired by Romanticism, was very much a Western notion, and it was embraced not only by the likes of von Bälz but also by the new Japanese intellectuals. It should not be surprising, then, that much of early Meiji literature, such as Ozaki Kōyō's *Konjiki yasha* (Golden Demon; set at Atami) and Tokutomi Roka's *Hototogisu* (Cuckoo; set at Ikaho), arcane and traditional though these works seem today, used mineral springs as a modern setting for such novel phenomena as romantic love.

Yasunari Kawabata wrote incessantly about *onsen* life, usually depicting a male character suspiciously like himself, along with a local woman who is invariably younger and of lower status. One of the modern literary texts most widely assigned to Japanese pupils is Kawabata's 1924 short story "Izu no odoriko" ("The Dancing Girl of Izu"), in which the protagonist, to escape the toil of student life, ventures to Yugashima, an *onsen* town, where he meets a fourteen-year-old itinerant dancer, falls in love, and leaves refreshed, free of ennui and melancholy as well as of the girl, for good measure.[82] But even in the early twentieth century, travel to Yugashima entailed walking from Ōhito, the final stop on the rail line, to Shuzenji and then to Yugashima. The age of mass tourism was yet to come. In his masterpiece, *Yukiguni* (*Snow Country*), Kawabata, with a fine brush, paints the life of an *onsen* town and the affair of his protagonist, Shimamura, with a local geisha.[83] Shimamura's visit to this distant hot spring, putatively modeled on Yuzawa Onsen in Niigata Prefecture, has been made possible by a new train and a tunnel, completed in the early 1930s, that links Tokyo to Niigata. *Yukiguni*, with its speeding train that penetrates and passes through a dark tunnel to the white snow country, and with the index finger that holds Shimamura's tactile and olfactory memories of his erotic encounter, is at times high pornography masquerading as pure literature, like much other *onsen* fiction. The association of male *onsen* travelers with women would continue well into the postwar period. In the mid-1980s, for example, the elderly proprietress of an inn in rustic Tōhoku asked me after dinner whether she should "call a girl." When I demurred in embarrassment, she said, "That's what men come here to do." At the time, the hiring of female escorts had long been illegal, thanks to the postwar reforms, but escorts remained an integral element of the *onsen* experience for men, young or old.

Eloping couples were another common category of *onsen* visitor. In Kenji Mizoguchi's 1939 film, *Zangiku* (*The Story of the Last Chrysanthemum*), a famous kabuki actor, after initial failures, runs off with a woman, and they move from one *onsen* town to another, a feat made possible in part by their staging kabuki performances in the towns.[84] And in the novel *Shitsurakuen* (A lost paradise), by Watanabe Jun'ichi, an adulterous pair abandons the glittering life of Tokyo for a modest existence in shabby rustic towns, which of course include *onsen*.[85] In short, hot springs offer a background of nudity, including mixed-gender bathing, and therefore sexuality, and this is what has privileged *onsen* as the setting for many popular novels and films.

The rise of mass tourism occurred during the Shōwa period. In the 1910s and 1920s, the developmental state built a nationwide network of railways, and the trains stopped at many *onsen* towns.[86] As a result, a town like Kusatsu, until then inaccessible at nearly four thousand feet above sea level, could be transformed almost overnight into a destination easily reached from a number of major cities. The trains brought not just tourists but also construction workers as well as workers of other kinds, and the population of Kusatsu, 645 in the late nineteenth century, had increased four- or fivefold by the early twentieth century.[87] *Onsen* themselves expanded rapidly, too, in large part because of modern construction technology.[88] Today almost all *onsen* visitors enjoy hot-water bathing on the premises of the inns or hotels where they are staying, whether the facilities offer *uchiyu* (indoor bathing) or *rotenburo* (outdoor, open-air bathing).[89]

Also important to the growth of *onsen* tourism was the transformation of the group tour into a particular kind of *onsen* getaway. This type of sojourn might be arranged by a corporation or a military unit as a way for executives or commanders to build morale by rewarding their employees or subordinates. But patriarchal corporations and the patriarchal state also proved paternalistic in that they sought, by way of *ian* (comfort or relaxation) outings, to satisfy their charges' desire for leisure and entertainment. It was this approach that would lead to the innovation of furnishing Japanese and, later, American soldiers with *ianfu* (comfort women, which is to say sex workers, voluntary or not). Another change had to do with the typical duration of an *onsen* visit. During the Edo era the normal stay had been twenty-one days, but now an overnight trip, if not a day trip, became the norm.[90] With the democratization of the *onsen* experience, the benefits of *onsen* were implanted in the Japanese psyche. Except during the last years of World War II and the immediate postwar years, *onsen*'s popularity would continue.[91]

The trends of the prewar period only intensified during the era of rapid economic growth, and as group tours and mass tourism expanded in the 1950s and 1960s, the character of many *onsen* towns and facilities was transformed. Between 1953 and 1973, the total number of *onsen* tourists grew threefold. From the 1950s to the 1970s, *onsen* became strongly associated with the worldly pleasures of drinking, singing, and gambling.[92] In addition, lavish vulgarity turned many an *onsen* into a miniature Las Vegas. Some *onsen* brought in alligators and banana trees. Others added indoor golf courses or nightclubs. The ensuing construction boom brought massive hotels with modern amenities. Until the last third of the twentieth century, most inns at *onsen* locales had walls that were thin partitions, at best, and there were no private toilets, partly as a legacy of travel during the Edo era, when most guests slept in a single large room. Whatever the nature of the sleeping quarters, however, group tours had become bacchanals. The closest that non-Japanese people could come to observing the raucous nature of an *onsen* trip was the sad scene in Yasujirō Ozu's 1953 film, *Tokyo monogatari* (*Tokyo Story*), in which an elderly husband and wife, sent by their adult children to Atami, the famous *onsen* town near Tokyo, are kept awake all night by noisy revelers. Isabella L. Bird, writing about *onsen* facilities in the late nineteenth century, was already complaining about the noise.[93] But even at the high point of rapid economic growth, solitude or repose was far from the usual experience for most Japanese *onsen* tourists. In imagining the past, we must be mindful that the tranquil *onsen* visit is a presentist fantasy, as is the notion of soaking in a spacious tub at a public bathhouse.

The leisurely sojourn and relative tranquility were not the only things to disappear during the period of rapid economic growth. The enormous Western-style hotels, with their varied entertainments, blurred the focus on the hot spring itself as well as on the surrounding natural environment. Even the thermal water was increasingly filtered, chemically treated, and recycled, innovations that prevented bacterial and viral infections and offered economies of operation but also undermined a primary purpose of *onsen* tourism—receiving the mineral spring's benefits.[94]

It was precisely when Japan's rapid economic growth decelerated that the *onsen* experience solidified into the form that most Japanese people in the 2010s could recognize.[95] The nature of the experience had been transformed by the swift decline in group tours, with more and more visitors arriving in small groups or, often, as couples, and by these visitors' higher expectations for sanitation and service as well as for privacy and relaxation. Previously, guests had indulged in late-night bouts of drinking worthy of a fraternity party. Now they wanted to turn in early and get a good night's sleep. And instead of sharing a large tub with scores of strangers (of the same gender or not), they began to express their strong preference for a more private bathing experience.[96] By the 2010s, the more expensive inns were not only catering to single travelers (a practice virtually unheard of during much of the postwar period) but also offering a private bathing experience, which they could do either by renting out separate bathing rooms or by placing a tub in each of the inn's rooms. These arrangements were actually rather close to those enjoyed by the many celebrated writers who had spent time at hot springs and experienced them as a quiet setting for work, reflection, and rest—though scribbling away during the daylight hours certainly didn't rule out a private, alcohol-drenched session of sexual debauchery in the evening. In any case, the dominant trope came to be that of *onsen* as a getaway, as a suspension of the hurly-burly of everyday life in the city.[97]

The temptation here is to expound on the cosmic significance of bathing and, in the process, touch on urgent topics such as religion and spirituality, health and the environment, and the like. Instead, I will stress the disjunction between bathing and the contemporary political economy of Japanese life. Tokyo and other large metropolitan areas are all about efficiency and rationality, whereas bathing seems inefficient and irrational. A shower, after all, takes less time and uses up less water and energy. This is to say that bathing and *onsen* militate against the reality principle of work and efficiency. And in a world where, otherwise, one works at everything—getting and spending, eating dinner, forming a friendship—a hot spring in particular is a place to do nothing, to disregard kenophobia, or horror vacui.

Japanese people who are asked to reflect on the question of why they bathe usually offer justifications involving the virtue of cleanliness, the benefits of improved blood circulation, and so on. Furukawa Akira, a self-professed bathing addict, claims that compulsive bathing supports weight loss and is also refreshing, and he says that bathing at hot springs promotes conversation and social life.[98] Tatsuno Kazuo writes that bathing relieves fatigue, cleanses the soul, restores a sense of the wild, and enables immersion in nature.[99] For Yokoo Tadanori, bathing at mineral springs enhances "love for one's being" and "a sense of gratitude."[100] Hikita Satoshi says that bathing makes one "stress-free," eliminates "all confusion, gloom, and worry," and offers a moment of bliss, day after day.[101] According to Kurayasu Anzai, an unheralded bard of bathing who wrote in the nineteenth century, "A warm bath renders one selfless and disposed to flow with nature, heaven, and earth."[102] And a high school girl told me that if she didn't bathe every day, others might be able to detect her body odor. At any rate, Japanese people say many different things about bathing in general and *onsen* in particular. But—notwithstanding positive inducements to bathe and regardless of negative sanctions for not bathing—the habit of daily bathing is deeply embedded in the sense of pleasure, not as ecstasy but as immanence. Bathing, in other words, is a secular ritual of relaxation and redemption, an ordinary luxury of everyday life.

SERVICE AS CRAFT

Onsen lodgings run the whole gamut, but there are two broad types—hotels and *ryokan* (inns). The hotels tend to be larger and outwardly Western, with Western-style beds and rooms in which guests are not required to remove their shoes. For the most part, the hotels also belong to one chain or another. This does not mean that the hotels lack high-quality service, but in the interest of discussing the craft character of hospitality, I will focus here on the inns.

The *onsen* aesthetic has almost always been traditionalist. The representative architectural style of an *onsen* inn, *sukiya*, takes its inspiration from the sixteenth century and from the minimalistic aesthetic of tea culture. The typical room is characterized by a Zen austerity, is minimally furnished and sparsely decorated, has *tatami* (straw mats) covering the floor, and is separated from adjoining rooms by sliding doors covered in rice paper. The room tends to have three separate areas. The outer area faces a garden, which usually features a pond or a stream and offers pleasing, relaxing views and sounds.

Reservations, increasingly made online, are a must. Chauffeur service from the nearest train or bus station, once widespread, is now becoming less common except at very remote or traditional inns. Guests' separation from the outside world begins with their removing their shoes, which are promptly stowed away, often for the rest of the vacation. After the guests have been formally greeted, they are ushered into a waiting area where they are served Japanese sweets and tea. Once they have been escorted to their rooms, most guests immediately change into the *yukata* (bathrobe) that will be their attire for the whole stay. Most of the time, what comes next is a dip in one of the baths, followed either by a massage (increasingly a spa treatment) or by relaxation until dinner is served. Dining in one's room used to be very common but is now becoming rare, largely because of the shortage of staff members and the cost of employing them. Most guests will dip once more into the bath before going to sleep. They may bathe when they wake up (the morning bath is considered a great luxury); then breakfast is served, and guests usually bathe again after breakfast, until they check out.

The service, though pleasant and polite, may seem perfunctory to an unknowing guest, who will have direct experience of the service primarily at meals and will otherwise experience it indirectly, as when he or she notes the condition of the room and the baths. But from the standpoint of the staff, the workday is extremely long and requires constant dedication. Because the number of staff positions is necessarily limited, most staff members perform several different kinds of tasks. Not even the owner can just sit back and add up his take. He has to carry tea and coffee to the guests' rooms and may also be required to drive guests between the inn and the train station. "The day is certainly full," I heard from the proprietor of an inn at the bucolic, if radioactive, Misasa hot spring. He quickly added, "It's interesting to welcome guests from far away, and it's satisfying to see that they've had a relaxing, enjoyable time." A third-generation proprietor, he is extremely proud of the hot spring's magic, the historical nature of his inn, and all the famous people who have stayed there.

An inn's employees typically include *nakai*, servers who are almost always female in kimonos and who take charge of particular guests. Their day begins early, when they help with the breakfast preparations, and it ends late, since they clean up after dinner. For some of these servers, being a *nakai* is a short-term job that offers a mix of money and adventure. Rooms at the inn or at nearby dormitories are usually available free of charge to *nakai,* an arrangement that allows younger workers to enjoy a measure of independence away from home. For other servers, being a *nakai* can become a career, with promotions and raises as they move up the hierarchy. At one expensive inn, a *nakai* in her mid-twenties told me, "It was my ambition to work here because I'd heard about this place when I was working at a *ryokan* near my hometown. I had to uproot myself and move more than six hundred miles away from home, but this is an amazing place to work, with a lot of very interesting guests."

Maintaining the baths can be time- and labor-intensive. Almost every inn has at least two baths in order to sustain gender-segregated arrangements, and many have more than two. And because *onsen* aficionados insist on having the tubs filled with fresh hot water directly from the spring, rather than water that has been recycled or mixed with anything else, the tubs have to be drained every day so the bathing area remains clean. It's true that many *onsen* take various shortcuts, including the use of chlorine, which often defeats the whole purpose of soaking in natural mineral water. But public health officials have put great pressure on *onsen* managers ever since the notorious episode in 2002 when seven people died of legionellosis contracted at an *onsen* in Miyazaki Prefecture, and nearly three hundred more were infected with *Legionella.* Virtually no guest arrives with a chlorine meter or the inclination to police an inn's cleaning routine, and so the burden of safety rests squarely on the establishment. In other words, the inn's trustworthiness depends on the proprietor's and the staff's commitment to the artisanal ethos.

Ikigai

Reasons for Living

The polymath Hashimoto Osamu, born in 1947 and therefore a member of the postwar *dankai* generation, recalls his upbringing in Suginami Ward in west central Tokyo. His grandparents, from a modest background, lived in a house on a lot larger than 3,500 square feet. Today that would be a gargantuan estate. Half the lot was a vegetable garden, with potato flowers, strawberries, and corn. But this paradise vanished after Hashimoto and his parents moved in with his grandparents. First an expansion of the house eliminated the garden. Then Hashimoto's father cut down the chestnut and fig trees to build a garage. The neighborhood finally disappeared altogether in the 1960s, when construction companies bulldozed small shops and independent houses and replaced them with paved roads and high-rise apartment buildings. In retrospect, Hashimoto realizes, he was happy at his grandparents' house in the time before their neighborhood vanished, and he believes that the era of rapid economic growth actually lowered the quality of life.[1]

It would be easy to make light of Hashimoto's idyllic pastoral. After all, many people look back fondly on childhood. And aren't Hashimoto's fellow baby boomers swimming in collective nostalgia for the period of rapid economic growth? But this is precisely where Hashimoto differs—he is not celebrating economic growth but lamenting the destruction it wrought. The per capita GDP of Japan is clearly higher now than it was fifty years ago, but how can we be sure that the quality of life has also gone up? Are high-rise apartment buildings, with their overlapping and redundant security systems in what is perhaps one of the safest cities in the world, really an improvement over one- or two-story houses with yards and gardens? Air conditioning has brought relief from heat and humidity, and housing built from concrete and glass keeps pesky mosquitos and moths out (though pesticides and the built environment have reduced their numbers). But what about the environmental and energy burdens? Have paved roads made up in convenience for what they replaced—entire neighborhoods that were dismissed as vacant lots? Is it better to shop in a clean, well-lighted supermarket or in a neighborhood grocery store? Is it better to grow one's own vegetables and fruits, with all the dirt and worms that come with them? The logic of growth says, "One more, then another," and in contemporary Tokyo there's no end in sight to the graying of the built environment. The achievement of affluence—defined by GDP figures or by the proliferation of glass-and-concrete skyscrapers—may or may not mean a good or better life.

But all is not lost. The artisanal ethos survives, as do ordinary virtues. Many Japanese people enjoy rest and relaxation, even idleness, and not just by way of *onsen* travel. Meaning and purpose can be found and cultivated in leisure activity. The sustainable society is ludic. And what underlies it is the search for *ikigai*—for meaning, for reasons to live—reasons that in turn sustain the artisanal ethos and ordinary virtues.

RELIGION AND ITS DEMISE

For many human beings, the whole issue of reasons for living is moot. The self-evident character of the survival instinct—the will to live—requires no extended commentary, especially when food and security are of utmost concern. Yet the arrival of affluence, or at least of the potential for rest and reflection, and the lengthening of the life-span provoke incessant and irrepressible questions about the meaning of life, if not life in general, then surely life in this or that particular. Is my life worth living? Or, as the more usual formulation has it, is my life meaningful and significant? Basic curiosity about life's meaning (not as a semantic question) is grist for the philosophical mill everywhere, and it evokes a number of generic responses. The most common of these is religion.

The Meiji regime propounded State Shintō, with the emperor at the apex, as the wellspring of spiritual and secular authority and answers.[2] The emperor system was the state-sanctioned ideology that turned Japan—and, over time, the Japanese empire—into the family-state, with the emperor as the ultimate patriarch and his subjects as his children.[3] The emperor ruled from his appointed place in a singular lineage that had begun with the birth of Japan, as described in the oldest extant Japanese text, *Kojiki* (Records of Ancient Matters), compiled from oral tradition in 712. Thus the purpose of State Shintō and the emperor system was to eliminate, or control and contain, competing religious or spiritual authorities (including, among others, animism, Buddhism, and Christianity) as well as folk rituals and practices.[4] In other words, the Meiji regime established a national belief system that sacralized political rule and instituted ideological control (and during the prewar regime, the fanatical articulation of this system became a proto-totalitarian war effort). Now every Japanese person had, in theory, all the answers to life's basic questions about meaning and identity.

Needless to say, reality is much more complex and confusing. Not everyone had unquestioning faith in the emperor system or State Shintō. The deviants included Marxists and adherents of other faiths, and if many of them followed the dictates from above, especially during the final years of the Pacific War, they did so without much enthusiasm or apodictic certainty.[5] Be that as it may, there was one focal point in modern Japanese life before 1945: the sacrosanct character of the emperor and the divine mission of the modern Japanese nation. This is to say that the Meiji regime provided a belief system, however creaky, and a source of both social solidarity and personal identity.

After the end of World War II, the extensive apparatus of the emperor system, including State Shintō, was either disestablished or disrupted. Almost overnight, the imperial project lay in ruins, and the central religious institution was shattered (though, again, I would not deny that there were some true believers and stragglers). Postwar Japan was now a nation without a national religion, a country bereft of a dominant belief system or a centralized religious institution. By the 1960s, to the extent that State Shintō survived at all, it was primarily as an object of opprobrium, criticized with equal intensity by pro-American politicians and anti-American student radicals.[6] Except on New Year's Day and some other special occasions, most people seemed to ignore Shintōism, though some right-wingers did rally around it in an effort to generate a new nationalist movement.[7]

After the war, a certain nullity threatened to rule the spiritual life of Japan. The Communist Party proffered a secular religion, but the party never came close to seizing power and, in any event, it maintained a secular face. Democratic and leftist intellectuals appeared to have become the unacknowledged legislators of postwar Japan, but they too never came close to assuming the mantle of prophets and pastors on behalf of the Western ideology of progress, democracy, and science. Moreover, their enthusiasm was decidedly tepid by comparison with the power and glory of the prewar emperor system, which they scorned after the fact. If some had been willing to give their lives for their country before 1945, almost no one now seemed ready to die for the sake of democracy or science.

Thus postwar Japan, with nothing like a national religion, remained staunchly secular. The end of the Meiji regime seems to have pulverized not just the emperor system but all adherence to any kind of transcendental belief system. As Joseph Kitagawa, a leading student of Japanese religious history, observed in the 1960s, "One of the basic problems of Japan is the rootlessness of the Japanese people.... The tragedy of postwar Japan is that the people have lost [any] fundamental religious orientation."[8] Surveys conducted since the 1950s have revealed that perhaps only 33 percent of the population claims any type of religious affiliation, and much Japanese religiosity is tepid in any case, which means that Japan is one of the most secular societies in the world.[9] As Yamaori Tetsuo characterizes the postwar Japanese, they maintain a "nebulous atheism" as their central belief system.[10] Adding to the sense of Japan's being a predominantly atheist country is the fact that religion is a private matter for the Japanese.[11] Nevertheless, it would be problematic to call Japan a strictly secular, much less atheist, society. For one thing, there are visible populations of Shintōists, Buddhists, and Christians, along with various new religious groups.[12] For another, some argue that the real religion of Japan is the so-called Japanese Religion, that is, belief in Japaneseness.[13] Even so, it remains true that, apart from a small minority, Japanese people do not look to organized religion or formal belief systems to find meaning in life.[14]

ROMANTIC PASSION, TAMED AND TEPID

Especially in the modern West, the individual, emancipated from such ascriptive ties as the family, the community, and the faith into which he was born, seeks life's fulfillment in romantic love. Indeed, there are few private passions as turbulent or as celebrated.[15] In contemporary Japan, however, the abatement of ambition (see chapter 4) has its correlate in the sphere of intimate interpersonal relationships. That is, the tepid nihilism of everyday life seems to have dethroned romantic love in favor of ordinary feelings, however important interpersonal relationships continue to be. This disenchantment with grand passions has also diminished expectations with respect to intimate life.

It was not always this way. The people of Tokugawa Japan were no strangers to sexual and romantic longing. But, given the predominance of arranged marriages among the samurai and the landlords, and the proscription on interstatus unions, depictions of romantic love in popular culture tended to focus on the forbidden and the transgressive (for example, an extramarital liaison between a patron and a courtesan that ends in double suicide). Such depictions contained little psychology. Death was the almost inevitable outcome of passionate hearts beating against an inflexible social structure.[16]

After the Meiji Restoration, despite the era's puritanical mind-set, modern Japanese people avidly consumed Western cultural imports that idealized romantic love, from Romantic poetry to love songs.[17] By the postwar period, in the wake of the prewar regulation of private emotions, many young urbanites were inclined to express their feelings by way of that most common phrase heard in popular music, "I love you," using a Japanese rendition of the English-language utterance if not the Japanese equivalent (*aishiteru*) or its permutations. The phenomenal popularity of the radio drama *Kimi no na wa* (Your name), later made into a three-part film series, featured two lovers who, over and over, barely missed meeting each other.[18] Somewhere, somehow, there surely would be someone—a true love. Sports manga dominated in the 1960s and 1970s, but manga for girls and boys alike featured tales of great passion, often between star-crossed lovers. The characters in these stories knew whom they loved and hated, and, as un-Japanese as this may have seemed, they expressed their loves and hatreds, if only via confessional missives. *Ai to Makoto* (Ai and Makoto) recounts the romantic passion of Ai, a bourgeois lady in the making, and Makoto, a poor delinquent. Everything is straightforward—her name means "love," his means "sincerity." Makoto tells Ai, "I would die for you!" The sheer number of obstacles thrown in the lovers' path recalls the impediments of *Wuthering Heights*.[19] In a more philosophical and literary vein, Fukunaga Takehiko's 1956 novel, *Ai no kokoromi* (An attempt at love), captures the postwar idealization of romantic love: from existential loneliness, we strive to pass through and realize the divine mystery of romantic love, of love as burning passion and ultimate spiritual encounter.[20] Eurocentric though Fukunaga may have been, his exaltation of romantic love was not uncommon for a modern Japanese writer. Indeed, in the immediate postwar decades, Fukunaga's existentialist ruminations on romantic love were anything but unique. In 1963, *Ai to shi wo mitsumete* (Facing love and death) became a phenomenal best seller, and in 1964 it was made into an equally popular television program.[21] Based on some four hundred letters between its two authors, which were written and exchanged when they were both university students and while the female protagonist was hospitalized with a terminal illness, *Ai to shi wo mitsumete* ends with her death, but not before she loses half her face to a botched operation. Watching the television adaptation is one of my earliest memories; grisly though the experience was, *Ai to shi wo mitsumete* is a testament to the ideal of *jun'ai* (pure love), beyond disfigurement and the grave. Clearly, love is not for the faint of heart.[22]

By the 1980s, the dominant tenor of romantic relationships had become one of *yūjū fudan* (indecision). Popular manga like *Tonda kappuru* (The jumping couple) and *Mezon Ikkoku* (Maison Ikkoku) depicted male protagonists who were decidedly indecisive.[23] In both works, a young man cannot choose between two young women, and the arc of the narrative swings back and forth as he is unable to decide or commit himself. There is passionate intensity but also Hamlet-like deliberation: Whom should I be with? Whom do I love? These protagonists are a universe away from the violence-loving delinquent Makoto, capable of declaring his willingness to die for his love. In the most popular romance of 1990, *Tokyo rabusutōrī* (Tokyo love story), there is a girl who can express her love openly, but once again there is a boy who cannot make up his mind, much less express his feelings.[24]

The life of indecision took a gentler turn in the post-Bubble decades. No longer were there loud proclamations of love. Now there was only a whispered "Sukidesu" ("I like you"). Needless to say, this semantic drift may warrant translating the language of like (*suki*) as a declaration of love (*ai*). Regardless, the tepid expression of romantic passion came to mark the outer limit of what was permissible, or imaginable.

A casual foreign observer might take the Japanese for a people so taciturn that a narrow range of romantic expression should be expected. Yet Japanese culture is drenched with tears and emotion about falling in, falling out, and even staying in passionate, erotic love. You've got to hide your love away, but it's all over the place. Sōseki Natsume, that colossus of modern Japanese literature, frequently holds forth on love. For example, the elder brother in *Kōjin* (*The Wayfarer*), has this to say: "What's truly sacred is not the relationship between husband and wife, created by human beings, but romantic love, concocted by nature. . . . And so it's not wrong to say that someone who subscribes to morality is a temporary winner, but a permanent loser. And someone who follows nature is a temporary loser, but a permanent winner."[25] To take another example, in Natsume's *Sorekara* (*And Then*), a male character, Daisuke, declares his love to a married woman, Michiyo. At first Michiyo calls Daisuke's declaration "cruel," but in time she decides to pursue an extramarital relationship with him, even unto death: "If you say die, I'll die. . . . I don't care when I get killed."[26] The theme of *Liebestod* is not just for a Romeo and a Juliet who accidentally die in the throes of young love, or even for a Werther who shoots himself because of unrequited love—though I hasten to add that both Shakespeare's famous drama and Goethe's *Die Leiden des jungen Werthers* (*The Sorrows of Young Werther*) were staples for the modern Japanese reading public. Rather, the course of modern Japanese love has often run to murder-suicide or to *shinjū* (double suicide). Thwarted love ending in double suicide is of course far from unique to Japan—consider only the 1889 Mayerling incident or its near contemporary, Tchaikovsky's 1876 ballet *Swan Lake*. But *shinjū*, both in abstract rhetoric and in concrete action, has long been a major trope in the humid, sticky world of Japanese passion, with all its erotic vexations and outbursts. Western-style romantic love was yet another import, but it would be egregiously condescending to claim that premodern and modern Japanese people had not already been suffering almost all the sorrows and pangs, the exaltations and ecstasies, of romantic love.[27] If they were not entirely clear on the concept, they were not necessarily innocent of its substance.

By contrast, Japanese lovers in the twenty-first century seem sober and lacking in ardor. After 1997, the year that marked the publication of Watanabe Jun'ichi's best-selling novel *Shitsurakuen* (A lost paradise) and the release of the film based on the novel, it has been difficult to find any major manifestations of *Liebestod* in Japanese culture.[28] Even in 1997, Watanabe, then in his sixties, seemed to appeal almost exclusively to his contemporaries and elders. Younger audiences were perplexed by the success of the novel and the film and regarded both as entertainments for *ojisan* (middle-aged men). For most Japanese people of the post-Bubble era, the coupling of love and death is unimaginable. For them, passion has largely been tamed, and love has become like. As Louise Bogan puts it, "What the wise doubt, the fool believes— / Who is it, then, that love deceives?"[29] Perhaps the best-known work of romantic love in contemporary Japanese literature—Haruki Murakami's *Norway no mori* (*Norwegian Wood*), published in the same year as Watanabe's *Shitsurakuen*—announces itself as a "100 percent romantic-love novel."[30] The male protagonist, Watanabe (a common Japanese surname), is kind and gentle, ever solicitous. He seeks a relationship based on gender equality and is all but devoid of old-fashioned patriarchal attitudes and macho behavior. The novel is not without its carnal moments, but the climactic sex scene leaves Watanabe's love, Naoko, unmoved. In the ups and downs of his romance, Watanabe is taciturn, with almost no wild swings of emotion. To be willing to die for one's love is one thing, but the kinder, gentler version of love seems to smother, even come close to extinguishing, romance and passion. The popularity of *Norway no mori* is emblematic of contemporary Japanese norms regarding romantic love. Or take Okazaki Kyōko's *Ribāsuejji* (*River's Edge*), in which every romantic longing is thwarted and the only sustained relationship is between the young female protagonist and her gay male friend, a relationship transacted primarily through their looking at an abandoned human body on the banks of a river.[31] There is death, but there's no love. The post-Bubble Japanese, disenchanted with fairy tales, are reluctant to follow the palpitations of the heart or to set out over the terra incognita of an emotional whirlwind. Sobriety rules. It's as if everyone can see the final stages of love—disenchantment and disbelief—and know that there is no transcendence.

Perhaps the most popular love story in the late 2010s was *Nigeru wa haji daga yaku ni tatsu* (We Got Married as a Job). Like so many other popular movies and television shows, it was originally a manga.[32] Thirty-six-year-old Tsuzaki Hiramasa, an engineer and a self-identified professional single man, is still a virgin. He's a softer version of an *otaku* (a geek or nerd). He needs someone to cook and clean for him, and Moriyama Mikuri applies for the job. Over time, their employer-employee relationship becomes a contractual marriage, an extension of their cash-basis connection into a long-term employment agreement. Because the story follows the conventions of romantic comedy, the two eventually develop a romantic attachment to each other, and the story concludes with substantive fulfillment of what had been their formal, empty contractual matrimony. There were feelings and passion somewhere, but they blossomed from the cold logic of the pair's contract, as if the two had been parties to an arranged marriage.

At the same time, women writers were abandoning the heteronormative world of patriarchal romantic love. Matsuura Rieko explores lesbian relationships and experimental sexual acts in *Nachuraru ūman* (Natural woman), which seems downright conventional next to her subsequent *Oyayubi P no shugyō jidai* (The training period of the big-toe P), in which the female protagonist's big toe opens up new possibilities by metamorphosing into a penis.[33] And in Matsuura's *Kenshin* (Dog body), a woman becomes a dog. A dog was the love object in Tawada Yōko's earlier *Inumukoiri* (Dog marriage).[34] Mizumura Minae's *Honkaku shōsetsu* (True novel), loosely based on *Wuthering Heights,* upsets the conventions of modern romantic love stories by starting off with a physically unattractive heroine, and the course of true love runs nowhere.[35] Needless to say, not all Japanese women writers have given up on traditional boy-meets-girl love stories, but one explanation for why South Korean television dramas are so popular among Japanese women may be that Japanese writers increasingly find it a challenge to narrate the received arc of romantic love, which may entail a rough journey, though all's well that ends well.

As for realism, it reflected what people were actually doing. And in the postwar period, that meant getting married ("till death do us part") and having children (at least two). In Haruki Murakami's novel *Kokkyō no minami, taiyō no nishi (South of the Border, West of the Sun),* the protagonist-narrator recalls his unusual upbringing: "In the world I grew up in, a typical family had two or three children. . . . I was an only child. . . . What other people all had and took for granted I lacked."[36] The narrator then goes on about how he hated his deviant existence, and about all the pejorative connotations of being an only child (most obviously, he was assumed to be spoiled). Normality, especially in one's family situation, was a requirement of the postwar decades, when the family was a haven and a bulwark against the unpredictable, potentially cruel and heartless world. Yet even then the rampart was cracking, if it had not always already been cracked. Recall Yasujirō Ozu's 1953 film *Tokyo monogatari (Tokyo Story),* discussed in chapters 4 and 7. In the film, an elderly man and his wife visit their adult children and receive only a lukewarm welcome. Especially for viewers of a certain age, the film often evokes the asymmetrical character of love between parents and children, or it exemplifies the delusions of gerontocracy—elderly parents, far from reigning as paterfamilias and materfamilias, fade and then pass away. The ambitious *dankai* generation, which sought to replace patriarchy with modern family life, found that it was not only the extended family but also the nuclear family that was breaking down.[37] Although contemporary Japanese people may yearn for love and marriage, for cohabitation and children, there is no question that the institution of the family is under assault. And marriage? It is now subsumed under *konkatsu* (spouse hunting), just another of the many activities that Japanese people engage in.

The family remains the typical form of cohabitation, but it has fractured into distinct models of living together. Even in the postwar decades there was still a widespread sense of the premodern, extended family or household as the bedrock of Japanese life. But the truths of past generations are no more. And the modern nuclear family of the postwar decades is also in crisis. In this regard, Japan is no different from many other wealthy countries. There are now more single people and unmarried couples in Japan, and more homosexual and transgender couples live together. The postwar myth of the normative heterosexual nuclear family is all but dead, and the prevailing norm is social tolerance, at least in urban areas. Thus twenty-first-century Japan, in its acceptance of different sexual orientations and lifestyles, has returned to its Tokugawa roots. BL (boys' love) manga has served as something of an avant-garde for alternative love relationships and lifestyles. What is curious about the genre is that it is written almost exclusively by and for women (the exceptions to the female readership are such occasional deviants as a curious researcher). It would be easy to see a projection of desire in BL manga's plethora of dashing, emotionally sensitive characters, who seem never to populate the living or working environments of the readers. The manga *Kinō nani tabeta?* (What did you eat yesterday?) is exemplary. In this illustrated recipe book, two likable gay men—one a lawyer, the other a hairdresser—have ordinary, contented lives, with occasional problems and crises around which the issue of what to cook and eat is a central motif as well as a master solution.[38] It is not that there aren't BL stories with suggestions of wild sex or turbulent relationships. After all, BL's readers grew up with the likes of Ikeda Riyoko's epic-heroic *Berusaiyu no bara* (*Berubara,* or *The Rose of Versailles*).[39] It is nevertheless striking, even in stories that depict the LGBTQ community, how passion has been tamed and how life has been routinized. This is not the world of Charlotte Brontë's Mr. Rochester or Emily Brontë's Heathcliff.

Many Japanese people have told me that they live in order to work—not just the sushi master discussed in chapter 5 but even some businessmen—yet no one has mentioned the notion of living in order to love. To be sure, a few people have identified a connection with a pet as their most important relationship and reason for living. And mothers do say that they find solace and significance in childrearing. It is common enough for mothers, and some fathers, to say that the births of their children have been the best moments of their lives. But that form of love, *agapē,* is distinct from romantic love between two adults. In other words, love is important to Japanese people, and worth living for, but romantic passion appears not to be. It may be that inequality and asymmetry between women and men—including the vast infrastructure of the sex industry, which doubles as an emotion industry—have cut off the possibility of passionate relationships based on equality.

It would be easy to deplore the diminished Japanese passion for romantic love, but it is also possible that the Romantic legacy of valorizing passionate love has already visited havoc on many relationships. This is a world from which transcendent sources of meaning and value have disappeared or are disappearing, whether we mean old-time religion or tightly knit communities. In the circumstances, expecting romantic love to stand as a pillar of ordinary, intimate life is tantamount to inviting a dragon to live in the bedroom. Reality is rife with small indignities as well as massive deviations from the impossible ideal of romantic love, and companionable, compatible intimate relationships involve many compromises. Some people forgo sexual relations altogether, whereas others find the absence of sex unbearable. Consider the popularity of the novel and manga *Otto no chinpo ga hairanai* (*My Husband Won't Fit*).[40] The protagonist suffers from what is regarded as a devastating flaw in her marriage, not to mention from the couple's inevitable failure to conceive a child, but eventually she comes to accept her imperfect, unrealized marriage as right for the two of them. The perfect romantic relationship is an abstraction, and beguiling though the ideal of romantic love has been for many people, romantic love is surely not a panacea for people who seek meaningful relationships or love in their lives. Again, it would be inaccurate to say that most Japanese people don't seek romance, passion, and relationships, but romantic love is not seen as the solution to existential anguish or existential questions.

OTAKU

If most contemporary Japanese people are ambivalent or wary about religion or romantic love—or, for that matter, in the nation or the family—what is left for building a meaningful life? Surely one answer is work. On that score, artisans provide a model for the well-lived life. But many people don't find a personally satisfactory occupation, to say nothing of all the jobs from which almost no one could derive any meaning. And other people don't like any kind of work at all. What hope is there for these people? A clue lies in a much-derided Japanese character type— the *otaku*, the nerd or geek encountered in earlier chapters.

The *otaku* belongs to the generations after the *dankai* generation. The term *otaku*, coined in 1983, is usually credited to Nakamori Akio, a manga critic. It denotes a young man or young men (the original *otaku* were almost always male) of a certain appearance—an unkempt mop of hair, casual clothing—considered to be not quite delinquent but somewhat strange. *Otaku* have poor social skills and an obsession with one or another aspect of pop culture, particularly manga and anime (though the actual range of human interests that an individual *otaku* pursues may be wider).[41] *Otaku*, whose efflorescence is coeval with post-Bubble Japan, are closely associated with the rise of consumer society and the proliferation of youth subcultures. The received stereotype of the *otaku* is the relentlessly negative image of young adults (again, usually male) who are incapable of dealing with the world. "They're no good," a woman in her forties told me. "They're socially unacceptable."[42] And the father of two *otaku* sons thundered, "They have no spirit, no will. They're parasites!" What prompts much of the discussion about the *otaku*, apart from their obsession with manga and anime, is their antisocial character. They are said to avoid the complexities and complications of real-life relationships, including sexual or romantic relationships, and to seek regulated and controlled encounters, whether online or in person with professionals. The *otaku* are also easy targets for people seeking to discover the causes of Japanese ills, including the struggling economy (indolent youth are said to be taking the place of the nation's corporate workers) and Japan's declining fertility rates.[43] In any case, few have much that is positive to say about this character type. As one man in his thirties told me, "I'm an *otaku* myself, and even I don't like the *otaku*."

Akihabara

The area in central Tokyo known as Akihabara, once a mecca of electronics shops, has been transformed into the capital and spiritual home of *otaku* culture. (It should be noted, however, that Akihabara increasingly attracts men older than the typical *otaku*, as well as some girls and women, not to mention foreign tourists.) Two notable cultural offerings are available there. The first (and dominant) of the two is what the *otaku* call "two-dimensional" products—primarily manga, anime, and video games. In this domain, the most prized type of female is a young and beautiful girl-woman described as *dōgan kyonyū* (having a baby face and big breasts). By contrast with three-dimensional (that is, real) girls and women, these two-dimensional representations preoccupy the imaginative and affective lives of many *otaku* boys and men, who are marked by *Rorikon* (a Lolita complex). The second offering is the *meido kissa* (maid cafés), featuring young women clad in French maid's uniforms who greet and serve their customers (again, almost all men) as lords and masters and may also play card games, board games, and video games with them. The hapless *otaku* shells out the equivalent of about five US dollars to enter the café, another five for each game he plays, and five more to take a photo with a maid. (The café's food and drinks, usually of substandard quality, are priced at approximately the going rate.) There is almost never any physical contact between the maids and their *otaku* customers. It is as if the *otaku* are at play in a Barbie DreamHouse version of the hostess bars that their fathers and grandfathers frequented.[44]

The all-female Japanese idol group known as AKB48 (AKB is the acronym for Akihabara) and its satellite groups, girl bands that represent the apotheosis of fan participation, provide insights into *otaku* culture. The annual AKB48 election, a nationally televised affair, was routinely one of the most watched programs of the year during the 2010s; it captured more attention and generated more excitement than the national legislative elections. AKB48's membership is determined by music fans, who vote with their wallets by purchasing the CDs in order to vote—one CD, one vote. The performer with the most votes becomes AKB48's lead singer, and the top twenty or so singers get to perform regularly in public. An uninformed foreigner might believe that this election rewards beauty or talent, but it almost always comes down to which performer best approximates the ideal of the girl next door. It is widely agreed by fans and nonfans alike that a beautiful (or tall or bright) young woman intimidates the *otaku*, who form the core of CD buyers (voters), which is why beautiful, tall, or bright contestants often fail to make it in the world of AKB48. Indeed, the mean height of AKB48's members is lower than the national mean.

Recall the language of *suki* (like) as opposed to the language of love. In this context, the chief aesthetic virtue is not to be beautiful but to be *kawaii* (cute). The exemplary *kawaii* figure, Hello Kitty, does not have a mouth or teeth, and the AKB48 stars are similarly nonthreatening. Here, communication and expression can flourish—*kawaii* culture, for the *otaku,* means never having to risk revealing anything personal, and never being menaced by the real world.[45] The *otaku* knows he is in control because he is the one who has chosen and created the stars.

It is true, of course, that in the postwar period there were many movie stars and singers who also became idols. Fans saw their films, bought their albums, and may have bought their posters, too. But these stars and singers were *idols,* sacred objects of passionate veneration. Consider only the fact that in English the title of Hiraoka Masaaki's book about the 1970s teen singing sensation Yamaguchi Momoe would be *Momoe Is Bodhisattva.*[46] What Hiraoka sees in Yamaguchi's hollow eyes is the look of the proletariat. In this respect, Yamaguchi embodied the spirit of *supokon manga* (sports manga; see chapter 4), that is, the struggle for upward mobility in postwar Japan. And the postwar idols' fans did worship them, believing them incapable of entertaining a polluted thought or committing an irreverent act—an image clearly at odds with that of idols like the members of AKB48, who represent the utter secularization of pop culture idols. How could it be otherwise, when the top vote-getter in the 2016 AKB48 election had been a contestant in a televised farting contest held in a school library? Many of AKB48's older fans do retain a spiritual orientation toward the group, but for the *otaku* these stars are not sacred figures.[47] Indeed, the *otaku* shows little overt passion. The figures who were icons for his parents are for the *otaku* mere dolls, material and disposable. The *otaku,* as a denizen of the world of the lukewarm bath (see "Ambition and Its Diminution," in chapter 4), makes the necessary (and considerable) effort to indulge his private interests, but he is not about to sacrifice himself like a kamikaze pilot, nor is he disposed to enact a lover's suicide.

Beyond the Stereotype

The stereotype of the *otaku* obfuscates more than it illuminates. Some self-described *otaku*—not unlike Tsuzaki Hiramasa, the fictional engineer in his thirties who is the protagonist of *Nigeru wa haji daga yaku ni tatsu*—hold prestigious jobs by day, and by night they gallivant about town, dine at expensive restaurants, visit *kyabakura* (cabaret clubs, that is, nightclubs), and generally behave more or less the way successful businessmen of their fathers' generation behaved with Ginza hostesses. As another challenge to the stereotype, the best-selling 2004 novel *Densha otoko* (Train man) features an *otaku* protagonist who is courageous enough to stop a sexual harasser and thus becomes a romantic hero of sorts.[48] Furthermore, the idea of Cool Japan and the vitality of Japanese subcultural products abroad (manga, anime, and video games, most obviously) suggest that *otaku-*

based industries are thriving export economies that also partake of the artisanal ethos.[49] In addition, more than a generation after the birth or invention of the *otaku*, it remains far from clear just who the *otaku* is. At times it is difficult to differentiate an *otaku* from a *Yankī*—this label has supplanted the archaic *furyō* (delinquent)—or, for that matter, to differentiate an *otaku* from any other young man (or woman). Therefore, some critics suggest that the *otaku* doesn't exist except as a by-product of discrimination.[50] As in Jean-Paul Sartre's conception of anti-Semitism, it is anti-*otaku* discrimination that produces the *otaku*.

The contemporary Japanese, however covert their public displays of affection may be, are not quite at the point of saying, "Not to be born comes first by every reckoning."[51] Nor are they still at the point of never having fallen in love, and this is no less true of the *otaku*. It would be easy to mistake ostensible quietude for a soulless existence, but the beating human heart maintains its interest in and devotion to one aspect of the world or another, perhaps in the arts, perhaps in the natural environment. An amateur psychoanalyst, tempted to see the *otaku*'s behavior as a projection of thwarted human relationships onto transitional or permanent objects, would be mistaken to overlook the vibrant inner world of interests beneath the contemporary Japanese *otaku*'s apparent indifference. The *otaku* seek, in their idiosyncratic ways, to make life worth living, to find *ikigai* beyond the received verities of family, community, company, or nation. No bitter taste of the real has killed their appetite for a slice of life, however mediated, among other reportedly problematic and antisocial youth.

The individual *otaku*, then, no exemplar of post-Bubble burnout, almost always has an enthusiasm or two. He (sometimes she) readily joins fan clubs and collects everything related to a favorite genre or object. Contrary to the stereotype, the *otaku* may actually be less interested in consumption and collection than in experience and matters of the spirit. Indeed, the *otaku* is defined by that very pursuit.[52] A moment's conversation with an *otaku* almost always reveals an engagement and an erudition akin to those of a research academic. I know a historian who began subscribing in high school to the prestigious *Journal of Modern History*, and after four decades he has been unable to let go of his all-consuming interest in early modern European history. Generally rumpled, and indifferent to most luxuries, he is the very picture of the absent-minded professor; the *otaku* in contemporary Japan is precisely this type of character. The received stereotype of the *otaku*—that he is unkempt, dresses indifferently, has trouble communicating, and displays little affect—also holds for a sizable swath of research academics. The only difference is that a university-based historian is an eccentric but laudable professional, whereas a lifelong passionate enthusiast of anime about Gundam (sci-fi robots) doesn't project the same status to most businessmen and bureaucrats.[53]

Needless to say, the research academic's mode of expression and dissemination is different from that of the *otaku*, but not qualitatively so. The research academic writes up and publishes his findings and his theses. The *otaku* writes his blog and perhaps even publishes a book. Both attend conventions to discuss matters of mutual interest with their colleagues. Here, though, one difference is that most academics at conventions and symposia eventually fall into discussing extra-academic matters (gossip about others, about who got what job, and so on), but *otaku* tend to talk shop most of the time, with the occasional digression into other common interests, such as *B-kyū gurume* (class B gourmet) restaurants.

Otaku also make their marks in different ways. For example, a manga *otaku* I met at Japan's supreme research library, the National Diet Library, had been conducting a bibliographic analysis of a manga series. His project would have put the great philologists of the past to shame. He had examined variations across distinct issues, or compared the serial version to its book variants, and his work had been so painstaking that he was in a position to publish an *editio cum notis variorum*. It might be argued that Dryden, say, is more important than *Kyojin no hoshi*, but the latter surely has more active readers. As another example, my seatmate on a flight in 2015 was an airline *otaku* who talked for hours about every aspect of contemporary commercial flying. In the previous decade, he had flown more than three million miles. He knew all the ins and outs of several airlines' frequent-flyer clubs, the details of airlines' seating arrangements, the levels of service that applied to different classes of air travel on distinct routes, and so on. As yet another example, a railroad *otaku*, my fellow passenger on a train trip, exhibited encyclopedic knowledge about types of trains and compartments as well as about various routes and their historical variations. There are history *otaku* and other types of academic *otaku*. I even encountered an *otaku* of social theory (one of my own specialties) whose knowledge of Max Weber was astounding. I could easily have dismissed this autodidact—he had not earned a graduate degree. But he did earn my respect with his seriousness and his dedication to the study of Weber (how many Weber scholars own the *Gesamtausgabe*?). And, as suggested earlier, there are Gundam *otaku*, such as Suzuki Toshimi, a barber who constructed ten large-scale models of Gundam robots outside his shop. "Sure," he says, "it's a hobby. But instead of just living my life, I wanted to give people something to be excited about."[54] Another Gundam *otaku*—this one in his forties, with hundreds of plastic models in his apartment—has amassed his own encyclopedia of model types and variations. "This is my life's work," he told me, in English.

THE LEISURE SOCIETY

The genius of the contemporary economy lies in its transformation of leisure and idleness into consumption and activity.[55] After work, we keep on working, this time in our role as consumers. We even provide free advertising by way of the corporate logos on our clothing and in the presumably personal views we transmit over social media.

People in Japan, too, like people elsewhere, are enjoined to go out and spend money, or to spend money at home by clicking links on the smartphones that have entered the inner sanctum of personal privacy, the last redoubt of idleness. Indeed, picking up a smartphone is often the first action upon waking and the last before going to sleep. Instead of cultivating their gardens or soaking in a warm bath, Japanese people are glued to the small screen where the central drama is fame and fortune, getting and spending. And if the temptation to soak in a warm bath should break through the continuous injunction to busyness, the smartphone is equipped with a waterproof cover.

If it were possible to summarize, in a simple way, the life of a contemporary Japanese corporate employee, the summary would come down to a series of *katsu* (activities): studying to get into a college or a university, *shūkatsu* (looking for employment), *konkatsu* (looking for a spouse), and, finally, *shūkatsu* (dying). To the extent that leisure enters the picture at all, it is usually devoted to conspicuous consumption, which itself is a struggle to achieve social recognition, often by establishing invidious comparisons between oneself and others. Thus, as we saw in chapter 5, some people spend more time and energy taking photos of sushi than enjoying the sushi chef's delectable concoctions. Leisure in Japan is certainly not devoted to sleep. On average, Japanese people don't sleep much at all.[56] Moreover, Japanese workers of all kinds—almost all Japanese adults, for that matter—are expected to be other-directed, and the demands on their time can become onerous.

In the past, people managed to find moments of fun. As noted in chapter 5, executives and other businessmen often frequented nightclubs and *kyabakura,* as well as the less expensive *sunakku* (literally, "snacks"; the term derives from these establishments' specialty of serving light meals and drinks).[57] There, they kept up a stream of banter and flirted, all the while drinking to excess. Not surprisingly, some people describe these establishments as having been fueling stations for businessmen. And there were games, played in the batting cages or on the driving ranges that cropped up in most postwar Japanese neighborhoods. There was also *pachinko* (Japanese pinball), with all its permutations, a game that probably consumed more of the average office worker's leisure time than any other activity. What all these pursuits had in common was that they satisfied the desire for either physical pleasure or mindless amusement. Needless to say, people's free time was not devoted entirely to pursuits like these. People also read books, went to movies, and played music. Still, as a self-described anime *otaku* in her thirties told me, "I have no idea what my father did in his free time. Sleep? My mother was always doing stuff around the house—cleaning, cooking—though I'm not really sure, since she never talked about it. Anyway, older Japanese people didn't know how to have fun. They just worked all the time."

That may or may not have been true. Perhaps office workers in the past were actually less busy than they wanted to appear. Today, though, thanks to the dissemination of *otaku* culture, it's not just the young and the restless who are engrossed in a life-consuming hobby. More and more office workers now lead double lives as nocturnal, ostensibly antisocial *otaku*. The habits of the *otaku* have spread widely, and Japanese people are increasingly embracing their inner geek.[58] In fact, the extent of *fascinatio nugacitatis*—enchantment with triviality—is nothing short of impressive in Japan. In the face of the daily grind of meaningless work, people are finding meaning and purpose in leisure activity. Hobbies and similar obsessions are ubiquitous.

This plethora of hobbies pursued with diligence—a consequence of affluence and the advent of the leisure society—had already become a notable feature of Japanese life by the 1970s, but the explosion of leisure activity coincided with the emergence of the *otaku*.[59] The passionate engagement of the *otaku* represents the modest happiness discussed in chapter 4, a happiness that relies more on fulfillment and experience than on material possessions. Paradoxically, then, the allegedly antisocial, parasitical *otaku* have shown their elders possibilities for a life beyond the workplace.[60]

The post-Bubble years were particularly important in the dissemination of serious leisure activities, and in some office workers' transformation into *otaku*. One middle-aged corporate employee began taking piano lessons after reading a manga about a young woman's struggle to become a great pianist. "I must have listened to classical music when I was in school," he said, "but after reading a scene where the protagonist plays a Beethoven sonata, I went out and bought a CD. It was mesmerizing. I discovered a new world." Another relates a similar story: "I happened to see an illustration by Itō Jakuchū. It was nothing like what I'd thought Edo-era art was like. I read some books, went to galleries and museums, and became an Edo art *otaku*." Others simply took what they were already doing to a new level, one that looked fanatical to outsiders but meant, in practice, the sublime level of the *otaku*. For example, a retired executive said, "I always enjoyed drinking, and I began to enjoy drinking alone. At an *izakaya* [a tavern or pub-like restaurant], you don't really drink alone anyway [but I began solo drinking]. I read books about drinking alone and searched for interesting *izakaya* all around Japan."

Leisure activity, like life itself, is all about flow. The feeling of aimlessness—the sense of being buffeted by random, incomprehensible forces—can be overcome in part through the pursuit of something in which it is possible to become passionately engaged. As long as that engagement lasts, it can offer meaning and a sense of purpose. Yet there is a long-standing, often troubling (and troublesome) practice of condemning leisure activity. For example, a volatile mixture of resentment and envy was once brought to bear on housewives because they pursued hobbies while apparently enjoying the economic support of their hardworking husbands (some women were even said to devote their free time to extramarital affairs). That misogynistic discourse has faded with women's reentry into the labor market, but it contained a grain of truth in the sense that Japanese women in general, and housewives in particular, have been less careerist than men, and therefore more inclined to pursue one hobby or another. Some of women's hobbies have been traditionally female pursuits with a touch of cachet and sophistication, such as tea ceremony or flower arrangement. Others have been faddish, such as hula dancing in the postwar decades or, at the turn of the twenty-first century, listening to K-pop music and binge-watching South Korean television dramas. As an example of the latter obsession, I was seated next to a middle-aged Japanese woman on a flight from Tokyo to Seoul. Immediately after takeoff, she opened a portable DVD player and proceeded to watch a popular South Korean drama. When she noticed that I had a Korean-language newspaper, she began to speak to me in excellent Korean. I asked her how she had learned the language, and she said she had been immersing herself in popular South Korean TV dramas and wanted to understand what the characters were saying. She added that she had traveled to South Korea more than twenty times in the previous five years or so, and that she enjoyed nothing more than being able to talk with an ordinary South Korean about a drama they had both watched (her knowledge of those dramas was breathtaking, by the way). I met another middle-aged Japanese woman who was extremely enthusiastic and well informed about K-pop. Her deep knowledge and dazzling analyses of the genre were the equal of what might be expected from an academic expert. Both women were effectively *otaku,* and women like the two of them are everywhere now in Japan.

Aristotle, in contrast to almost all other philosophers, takes leisure activity seriously, not only as a means of recovering from fatigue and of preparing for another round of work, but also as something to be pursued for the sake of fulfilling one's personal potential. Indeed, for Aristotle, leisure activity is "the fundamental principle"; thus leisure activity is not mere play or relaxation but has a purposive element in that it must incorporate such skills and learning as can be used to turn free time in the direction of "pleasure, happiness, and the good life."[61] (It is not for nothing that Greek *skole* and Latin *scola,* the etymological roots of English "school," denote "leisure.") Frivolous though an activity may be, there are meanings and purposes to be gained from its pursuit. And, if not everyone can find fulfillment in work by becoming a consummate artisan, there is also no reason to believe that a good society will be one in which everyone endeavors to find and pursue a professional career. This would be a society of diligence, probably an ascetic society. But another avenue is open to almost everyone in an affluent society, an avenue made all the richer because it is enjoyable, fulfilling, and uplifting, with no hangover and no emptiness at the end. As William Morris, echoing Aristotle, puts it, "What other blessings are there in life save . . . fearless rest and hopeful work? [T]o have space and freedom to gain such rest and such work is the end of politics; to learn how best to gain it is the end of education; to learn its inmost meaning is the end of religion."[62] I am not sure that we should expect everyone to hew to the two goals of work and leisure. There should be a place for believers as well as for lovers and others who take meaning and sustenance from different sources. In a postaffluent society, a society in which most people have abandoned the comforts of the traditional faiths and social collectivities, or have been through the whirlwind of egoistic hedonism or romantic passion, leisure activity seems the likeliest and most reliable goal.

Leisure activity is a necessary component of the good life, and of a good society. All work and no play makes Jack a dull boy, or so we believe (though we're skeptical of those who play all the time). Yet there is a sense in which leisure activity has features in common with artisanal work. Both provide meaning and purpose in life, and both involve projects that enhance personal potential and self-worth.

IKIGAI

What is thought to be the meaning or worth of an individual life has varied enormously across cultures and throughout history. To take one example, the reigning Western historiography stresses the salience of the Christian God, often omniscient and omnipotent, in order to endow an ephemeral, seemingly pointless life with significance and immortality. To take another, Japan's wartime imperial-military ideology affirmed that the ultimate fulfillment of life's purpose was self-sacrifice for the sake of the emperor.[63] In the immediate postwar decades, recovery and growth were posited as ultimate values, given the debacle of the war. The contraction of ambition and the curtailment of passion spelled the end of transcendence, including the ideology of rapid economic growth and materialism. Nevertheless, as Epicurus (who was far from the embodiment of what we call Epicurean) might have said, life must offer modest pleasures. But if infinite desire is a self-defeating proposition, aphanisis—the extinction of desire—offers no nirvana, for we would be anxious precisely because we had no desire. This would be the life of acedia about which the medieval scholastics were so exercised. More important, it would be hard to extinguish the quest for meaning and purpose—the will to be, the desire to carry on. Ordinary virtues are not without their rewards, of course, but people still seek deeper reasons for living. For anyone who has even a moment for repose and reflection, the hermeneutical urge is almost irrepressible. Abulia and sloth, emptiness and nothingness—these are dark holes from within which we struggle to instantiate the will to live.

Existential and spiritual questions become all the more urgent once people have escaped the world of dire necessity (that is, when they have acquired adequate means of satisfying basic needs for food and shelter) and moved beyond the universe of received answers (that is, when there are no longer any hegemonic belief systems, such as religion and its secular permutations). In the twenty-first century, grand narratives about God or emperor, nation or revolution, sound hollow to most Japanese people. Despite deep-seated suspicions that contemporary Japanese people remain collectivist and holistic in their orientation, they are usually acutely aware of their individuality as well as of their potential, or actual, loneliness.

We are thrust into the world, where our time is necessarily limited. Alcohol and drugs offer one practical, moderately effective answer to existential anxiety, as does immersion in one total institution or another, whether a "black" corporation (one of the superexploitative companies in contemporary Japan) or a cult, of which there is a wide selection. For most Japanese people, however, there is no immediately available transcendental recourse, no possibility of escape into a received traditional mind-set, and no relief (barring serious cognitive deficits) from existential questions about their personal place and significance in the world. The overwhelmingly worldly orientation of contemporary Japanese life makes the consolations of Christianity or Buddhism incredible and implausible. Without the promise of an afterlife, how do Japanese people find consolation for nothingness, for the apparently meaningless universe and the inevitability of death and extinction? The received answers are unsatisfactory, and the crumbling of the postwar regime can be seen in the inefficacy of the standard postwar bromides about what makes life worthwhile.[64] The unexamined life, *pace* philosophers, is worth living, but the ubiquity of the idea of *ikigai* makes reflection on one's life (How should I live? What should I live for?) a common theme of thought and conversation in everyday Japanese life.[65]

Kamiya Mieko, a psychiatrist, has written searchingly about *ikigai*. "For people to continue to live vivaciously," she says, "there's nothing more important than *ikigai*. Therefore, there's nothing more cruel than to take away people's *ikigai*, and there's no greater love than to give people *ikigai*." For Kamiya, *ikigai* is intimately intertwined with *hariai* (something worthwhile). "People find it intolerable to live alone, in a vacuum," she says. In order to live well, people need validation—the sense that they exist and matter, that they have efficacy in and responses from the world. Kamiya goes on to say that the sense of having a life worth living entails an orientation toward the future and a sense of purpose—devotion to a cause, a pursuit. *Ikigai*, she writes, is not a matter of the usefulness one has developed and accumulated over time, nor of the sheer length of time one has lived. Rather, *ikigai* is all about mattering, about meaningful living, and it leads to a series of questions: What is the purpose of my life? What is my purpose in life? Is my life worth living? Is life worth living?[66] The answers are necessarily very idiosyncratic, and they differ from one individual to another. *Ikigai* is a general concept, but its individual articulation is particular—it is mine.

Ikigai overlaps with happiness, but there are important differences. Happiness, as studied by positive psychology and preached by the popular Japanese religious group Happy Science, tends to be conflated with pleasure, with what makes one feel good. The notion of happiness is subjective: to say that one is happy is to offer a descriptive statement, but the description includes no temporal dimension or values-oriented content. The idea of *ikigai*, by contrast, does include a temporal dimension, which links the past (through the faculty of memory) and the future (through the faculty of imagination and the shaping provided by a sense of purpose). In addition, *ikigai*'s purposive teleology closely conforms to the sense of self and entails a values orientation.[67] Happiness, in short, is desire fulfilled. *Ikigai* spiritualizes desire and locates it within one's life span and life project.

For Kamiya, *ikigai* exists beyond biological needs and is not synonymous with sociological security. It cannot be cultivated in desperate times—during famine or war, for example—because the life force itself and the need to survive will preclude opportunities for sustained reflection on life's purposes. Nor can *ikigai* be planned and implemented, because determinism, or outside forces, will squelch the sense of possibility required for *ikigai*. Without individual freedom, striving is meaningless; that is, without a sense of efficacy, of the power to produce effects in the world, there can be no sense of life that has been lived. The undermining and weakening of *ikigai* stem from the darkness of death, biological or sociological. Kamiya does not claim that people are completely free. The individual's agency is limited. But the individual must believe in his personal agency before he can have reasons for living. As in Stoicism, there are areas of life that one can change and areas that one cannot change. The challenge, once basic needs have been met, is to strive to accomplish what one can but accept that there are things one cannot do, such as avoid mortality.

A classic reference point for thinking about *ikigai* is Akira Kurosawa's 1952 film *Ikiru* (*To Live*). The movie opens with a voice-over narration describing an office worker: "Busy, always so very busy. But in fact this man does absolutely nothing at all. Other than protecting his own spot." But this consummate bureaucrat has received a death sentence—a diagnosis of terminal cancer. Moved as he is to drain what is left of his life down to the dregs, he looks for consolation in alcohol and sex. But a young hostess asks him if there is anything he would like to make or to do, and his moment of epiphany comes concretely, in the form of his desire to build a park. In so doing, he finds his life's purpose—his meaning. Hirokazu Kore-eda's 1998 movie, *Wandafuru raifu* (*After Life*), offers a slightly different perspective. In the film's version of purgatory, each person must come up with a memory of a defining moment, of something the person is most proud of or finds most striking, and around this memory a film will be made about his or her life. When I asked people in Japan to perform this exercise, it was interesting that nobody mentioned a memory of work. Central though work is, most corporate employees cited memories from childhood. One proudly recalled running a race at school and finishing first. Another remembered his first, unrequited romance. Several women talked with wonder about giving birth for the first time. In general, it seems, life's significance lies in what one pursues with purpose, whether that means winning a playground race or becoming a mother. The discourse of *ikigai* occasions reflection and, necessarily, regret. One thinks of redoing or resetting one's life (the childhood wasted on frivolity, the occupation not pursued, the love that was not to be).[68] Reflecting backward, living forward—*ikigai* makes a richer inner life possible, though perhaps it will be accompanied at times by pain and regret.

Among artisans and others for whom work is fulfilling in and of itself, the problem of *ikigai* is not a clear and present danger. Yet *ikigai* is a serious challenge for office workers who face mandatory retirement at the age of sixty or sixty-five.[69] As a septuagenarian retiree remarked, "If you have nothing going on in your life when you retire, it's too late for you. Some of my colleagues died. Others became incapacitated. We need *ikigai*." Many office workers—forced to overachieve or overwork, or having chosen to do so—have led lives devoted to their organizational roles and have built many major relationships around their work lives. For them, retirement comes as a rude shock. In other words, in an extended act of what Jean-Paul Sartre called *mauvaise foi* (bad faith), they have spent years turning a blind eye and a deaf ear to the existential question of *ikigai*.

There are retirees who crash and implode. No one keeps statistics on those who die from a sense of obsolescence—from lack of *ikigai*—but it is not hard to get older people to name people they knew who died when they lost their place at work, and therefore in life. Some retirees suffer from loss of meaning, a loss intensified by having nowhere to go and nothing to do. Boredom and apathy are common outcomes for these retirees—idleness begets incapacity. Others, having lost their daily commute, decide to colonize the family home; they hijack the family's life and place undue stress on their wives to serve them during the day, or they make demands for more efficient household management.[70] In Yōji Yamada's 2016 film, *Kazoku wa tsuraiyo* (*What a Wonderful Family!*), one of many twenty-first-century representations of the postretirement blues, the protagonist, an office worker who has been put out to pasture, finds all his hopes for his golden years dashed when his wife of fifty years demands a divorce. The film ends well for this protagonist, but the same cannot be said for many white-collar retirees, whose wives and grown children call them (and treat them like) *sodai gomi* (bulky trash), unattractive and with no apparent purpose in life. Some of these men even go on to live in a place overwhelmed by trash, as in *Junrei* (Pilgrimage), a novel by Hashimoto Osamu, in which an elderly man turns his house into a virtual garbage dump reminiscent of the house and grounds in the film *Grey Gardens* (1975).[71]

The logic of the bureaucratic organization, however small that organization may be, is that the individual plays a role and is therefore replaceable. No one, no matter how charismatic or brilliant, is indispensable to any bureaucratic organization of any size. As a result, no matter how easily one has been able to find meaning and purpose in life while employed by the organization, it becomes very difficult to do so when one's employment comes to an end. One may have enjoyed high status in the organization, but retirement imposes a rough equality. One's organizational title and rank are stripped away, and one must now move through the social world as an old person. Especially when one has enjoyed organizational success, coming to terms with the reality of its loss is like experiencing all the bitterness of the samurai's life, but without the customary sartorial markers and social sustenance.

Hagakure is regarded as the bible of samuraihood. The prewar military generals were said to read it every day. Like most other classics, it has been reduced to a few selective quotations, which are tantamount to misquotations, such as that "the foundation of *bushido*," or the way of the samurai, "is death."[72] The author of *Hagakure*, Yamamoto Tsunetomo, propounds absolute loyalty for the samurai—obedience unto death—but his life philosophy is larger than this occupational injunction. In his autobiographical reflections, he does not regret that he left his job after his lord's death, and he suggests guidelines for living.[73] "A human being's life is very short," he says, having himself retired early. "Therefore, one should spend time doing things one likes. . . . It is stupid to spend life in pain, not doing things one likes."[74]

Not everyone wants to be like Yamamoto and write a treatise on *ikigai*. But when it comes to finding reasons for living after retirement, a leaf can be borrowed from the book of the *otaku*, and a surprising number of retirees are seriously interested in studying.[75] There are retirees who are involved in numerous other pursuits as well. For instance, a woman in her seventies found her life's work after retirement when she volunteered to help impoverished refugees and immigrants learn the Japanese language and explore Japanese culture. "I've found nothing more rewarding than trying to teach them," she told me. "I feel really useful, and I think I'm really helping them." Others look to more self-centered pursuits, such as mastering a sport (golf, for example) or a board game like Go. These retirees have no interest in acquiring professional-level skills in these sports or games, but there are many tournaments and other venues where the competition is challenging yet friendly.

What has been striking about the post-Bubble decades in Japan is the strong tendency of Japanese people in general to embrace the ordinary and to find *ikigai* in everyday life. As for retirees, one plausible way for them to live is to embrace their decline and resist the dictate of busyness that dominates so many lives. Thus Higuchi Yūichi encourages those who are sixty-five and older—those who have retired—to have "the courage to do nothing."[76] What Higuchi is proposing is not the achievement of a Zen state of nothingness but rather self-emancipation from the externally imposed imperative to *do* something. Time is precious, but it is one's own to burn or waste freely—and honorably.

SHINIGAI

Then there is death. If philosophy is preparation for death, then either contemporary philosophy has lost its way, or many have been wrong about the task of philosophy. The striking achievement of the twentieth century, at least in the affluent parts of the world, is that death is no longer an everyday affair. One can go a long time without seeing anyone dying or dead. Life expectancy has nosed up into the ninth decade, and there's a common saying in Japan that people should expect to live for one hundred years. No wonder the Grim Reaper and the Japanese equivalent, Shinigami, have such a low profile. At the same time, the news about Japan's aging society is not all good. Many people in their last years are burdened with pain and other kinds of suffering, and their desire for a peaceful death, perhaps at home, surrounded by loved ones—their *shinigai* (reasons for dying), we might say—often remains unfulfilled.[77] It is a strange form of biopolitics that seeks quantitative lengthening of life—*vita* without vitality—but does not ponder the quality of life. As in economic growth, so too in life—more is not necessarily better. A person benefits at least as much from reflection on *ars moriendi* as on *ars vivendi*.

Kobori Kōichirō, a retired surgeon, observes that in modern Western medicine as he practiced it, death was seen as defeat, pure and simple, and aging was to be resisted.[78] According to this line of thinking, the longer the life, the better; patients are enjoined to fight aging and struggle against death. After Kobori's formal retirement from surgery, he became involved with a regional hospital and made home visits to dying people. He witnessed hundreds of cases in which the patient, the patient's family members and friends, and the medical staff, all in denial about the finality of death, made unfortunate choices that exacerbated pain and suffering.[79] Kobori now argues for a paradigm shift in palliative care, with more investment in end-of-life care infrastructure, a shifting of the site of death from the clinic back to the patient's home, and greater involvement of the patient's family members. Kobori's fervent hope is that more doctors will spend time individually with dying people in their last days.[80] And perhaps family members and friends, too, will find that their involvement in hospice work serves as a reminder of their own mortality, illuminating the lives of the dying but also shedding light on the preciousness that life still has for the living. The pursuit of *shinigai* is another sort of *ikigai*.

Just as different regimes have honored different ways of death—consider, for instance, the celebration of the kamikaze pilots under the prewar regime—Japanese people over time have held various views about life, death, and the afterlife.[81] And despite the dissemination of progressive ideology, there is still widespread awareness of life's simultaneous preciousness and finitude, a concept that is often expressed as *mono no aware* (the pathos of things), one that incorporates both the assumption of impermanence and an appreciation of the haecceity—the "thisness" or "thusness"—of things, the ephemeral beauty of existence.[82] Premodern samurai and, later, the modern Japanese military appropriated this concept for purposes of their own, but it serves as a contemporary reminder of mortality, an ordinary realization of ontological finitude. It serves, in other words, as a final chapter in the consideration of *ikigai,* or *shinigai.*

Ikigai and *shinigai,* like love and life, can be discussed only in the abstract but in fact are experienced and expressed only in the concrete. The inevitable chasm makes it difficult to say anything meaningful about *ikigai* or *shinigai.* Let me conclude, then, by noting the sheer distance between, on one hand, the people of the Edo era, who, though plagued by disease and surrounded by death, seem to have been insouciant about mortality and, on the other hand, their contemporary descendants who live with exaggerated fear for their safety and their lives even as they enjoy unprecedented security and longevity.[83] Kōda Rohan's Edo-era novella *Gojūnotō* (The five-storied pagoda) offers a vivid sketch of the inaccessible Edo *shokunin* spirit. The protagonist—Jūbei, a carpenter—is nicknamed Nossori (meaning, roughly, "slow and quiet"). He has achieved nothing of significance but wants to build a pagoda, or tower. He says repeatedly that it would be fine for him to die if only he were first able to undertake his life's work.[84] It is not that Jūbei hungers for fame or fortune, or that he seeks to realize his desire out of vanity. Rather, the tower will be a proof of life, and its realization will be a moment of both transcendence and immanence, a synthesis that sublimates his being. Kōda makes it clear that the novella is not about dense networks of human relations and expectations—it is not, in other words, about *giri ninjō* (ethical obligations and humane feelings)—nor does it represent the modern quest for the true self. In fact, Jūbei's struggle to build the tower, a job entrusted to him by a Buddhist priest, has almost nothing to do with self-satisfaction or self-development. It is simply embedded in his life as a carpenter, a *shokunin.* In the teeth of a ferociously destructive storm, Jūbei becomes despondent, but only because he believes that the priest has lost confidence in his artisanship. This artisan is willing to go down with his tower— the artisanal ethos is free of egocentric desire, untouched by the hubris of human autonomy. The tower and the story are all that remain.[85] Very few people today could resuscitate Jūbei's *shokunin* spirit within themselves (and it is unclear how desirable that would be). That spirit is alien to modern temperaments. But it points to a way of living life: if one should lose what makes life worthwhile, it would not matter if one died; knowledge of what makes life worthwhile is what is worth recognizing and preserving.

In the novel *Junrei,* mentioned earlier, Hashimoto traces the life of his protagonist, a straight arrow who has lived through the period of Japan's rapid economic growth but now, in retirement, lives in a house overflowing with discarded objects not unlike his own life, objects whose value he tries to redeem. Only when his younger brother comes to help him does the protagonist allow all the accumulated detritus to be hauled away. His brother urges him to go on a pilgrimage to Shikoku so as to discover the meaning of living, and is relieved to see his older brother smiling with delight while eating tempura. "My brother has finally chosen to live," the younger brother says to himself, but he is surprised when his older brother dies in his sleep that very night.[86] In the end he decides that his brother, upon realizing that he had undertaken a pilgrimage with no purpose, finally accepted his life and his death and let himself be pulled into the void. A life without a reason for living is hollow, like the mindless accumulation of things and pleasures. And so it goes in the quest for *ikigai*.

POSTFACE

It is tempting to believe, with the long-forgotten Friedrich Gundolf, that "Methode ist Erlebnisart" ("method is experience"), and therefore to narrate the genesis and genealogy of this book.[1] But to do so would be tantamount to producing another volume, maybe a book longer than this one. It is true that my protracted if intermittent residence in Japan made me skeptical toward one or another of the grand narratives about Japan. Perhaps my having dwelled among academics—fond as they are of generalizations, such as that the Japanese are hierarchical or holistic, collectivist or compulsive—made me resist the proverbial *unum noris omnes* (know one, know all), blanket generalizations that occlude more than they illuminate. That said, I have tried to provide something like a general view, rendered after a series of immersions in distinct life paths, craft worlds, and trivial pursuits. Readers may be surprised by how often I ate sushi or visited *onsen*, but someone had to take up the challenge in the name of science. Suffice it to say that sushi was good to think with, that *onsen* were great to think in, and that eating sushi or enjoying *onsen* is not a bad first step in the search for a sustainable future.

Nevertheless, the ordinary virtue of honesty compels me to a confession. I am not at all sure that the slices of life compatible with the age of limits will thrive in Japan (or anywhere else, for that matter). It would require a committed suspension of disbelief to remain ignorant of the fact that so many intriguing categories of *shokunin* are disappearing.[2] For one thing, while writing this book, I learned that several people with whom I talked at length had died, and there is no one to carry on the work that they did. Artisanal work can be challenging, whereas the lure of easy, casual work feels irresistible. And instrumental rationality, a powerful conceptual tool, favors measures of satisfaction or happiness that make the artisanal ethos look irrational, or at best quaint. For another, neighborhoods of Japanese houses and family merchants have given way (as they've been doing now for a half century) to high-rise apartment buildings and supermarkets.[3] The ordinary virtues discussed in chapter 4 seem to be disappearing, too, and many Japanese people are now drunk on free-wheeling American-style liberties. For example, though the dreaded older men in small restaurants are surprisingly polite and quiet (not just once or twice did they apologize for disturbing my peace, or offer me sake in compensation for their rowdiness or as a friendly gesture), some of their younger counterparts clearly feel entitled to be as loud as they want to be, and to laugh just as much as they please, to hell with everyone else. In addition, there are still strong impulses within Japan to catch up with the West. And the Meiji regime, in its permutation as the postwar regime, rolls on. Worse, some people in Japan are even power-fully drawn to the prewar mayhem of violence and discipline.

In any case, the value of writing in the social sciences remains ambiguous. Such writing can aspire to the exalted status of an exact science, pursuing but falling short of a progress that can only prove illusory, given the hubris of the endeavor. Yet how much light does this kind of writing truly shed on concrete lives and social contexts? This book might have been more readable and easier to understand if I had conceived of it as a novel and put concrete (or concrete-seeming) individuals in motion, then observed them as they passed through time in all their historical and geographical particularity. This is what novelists often try to do, though this method, too, doesn't always make for a compelling read.[4] But one works with what one can, hoping for the best. For me, there is only the trying.

CHAPTER 1. FROM JAPAN AS "NUMBER ONE"
TO THE LOST DECADES

1. Ezra F. Vogel, *Japan as Number One* (Cambridge, MA: Harvard University Press, 1979).

2. See Ezra F. Vogel, *Japan as Number One: Revisited* (Singapore: Institute of Southeast Asian Studies, 1986), 1.

3. In 1989, the value of all the land in Japan was four times the value of all the land in the United States—a country twenty-six times larger. As another measure, in 1989, with respect to total capitalization, seven of the ten largest corporations in the world, and twenty-one of the world's thirty largest corporations, were Japanese; by 2019, no Japanese company ranked in the top thirty. See Yoshino Hiroki, *Heisei no tsūshinbo* (Tokyo: Bungei Shunjū, 2019), 12–14.

4. An emblematic novel of the era follows a young fashion model who appears to perceive and evaluate everything in terms of brand names and their status-enhancing effects; see Tanaka Yasuo, *Nantonaku, kuristaru* (Tokyo: Kawade Shobō Shinsha, 1981), a work notable for, among other things, its extravagantly large number of footnotes, at once erudite and vacuous.

5. Takemura Ken'ichi, *Gōruden naintīzu* (Tokyo: Shinmori Shobō, 1989), 50, 112, 150–53.

6. For an erudite Martian, the recovery of Japan and Germany would have been axiomatic, given the penchant in human history for the cyclical as well as for karmic transferences. The first recorded Western defeat, the destruction of Troy, led not only to *The Iliad* and *The Aeneid*—the supreme works of classical Western literature—but also, at least according to early national myths, to the founding of Rome, France, and England.

7. As late as the 1980s, the typical American response to consumption of raw fish was one of polite incredulity or impolite disgust. Likewise, in a 1966 discussion, Jean-Paul Sartre

remarked that the strangest thing about Japan for a foreign tourist was the eating of raw fish; see Katō Shūichi, *Katō Shūichi taiwashū*, vol. 2 (Kyoto: Kamogawa Shuppan, 2000), 189.

8. Philip K. Dick, *The Man in the High Castle* (New York: G. P. Putnam's Sons, 1962). In fact, fourteen Okinawan emigrants to rural Brazil returned to Tokyo in 1973 and were convinced that Japan had won the war. One of them, responding to a reporter's challenge, pointed to the survival not only of the emperor but also of the Yasukuni Shrine, which honors war heroes, and asked how it was that a defeated country could be so prosperous; see Fujisaki Yasuo, *Heika wa ikite orareta!* (Tokyo: Shinjinbutsu Ōraisha, 1974), 4.

9. This novel about the US-Japanese economic conflict is Michael Crichton, *Rising Sun* (New York: Knopf, 1992).

10. For the views on Japan expressed by this Manhattan property developer and future US president, see Glenn Plaskin, "The 1990 *Playboy* Interview with Donald Trump," *Playboy*, 1 March 1990, https://www.playboy.com/read/playboy-interview-donald-trump-1990.

11. George Friedman and Meredith LeBard, *The Coming War with Japan* (New York: St. Martin's Press, 1991).

12. "Japan's Lost Decade," *The Economist*, 28 September 2002, 21.

13. Kishida Shū and Yamamoto Shichihei, *Nihonjin to "Nihonbyō" ni tsuite* (Tokyo: Bungei Shunjū, 1995); Sugiura Tetsurō, *Byōmei "Nihonbyō"* (Tokyo: Kōsaidō Shuppan, 2002); Kaneko Masaru and Kodata Tatsuhiko, *Nihonbyō* (Tokyo: Iwanami Shoten, 2016).

14. The reference here is not to the 1980 pop hit by the Vapors but to Japan's image as the basket case among OECD countries (Organisation for Economic Co-operation and Development); see the cover of *The Economist*, 30 July 2011, which portrayed Barack Obama and Angela Merkel in traditional Japanese clothing.

15. Takahashi Genichirō and Saitō Minako, "Taidan Heisei no shōsetsu wo furikaeru," *Subaru*, May 2019, 134–56, 136.

16. Azuma Hiroki, *Genron o* (Tokyo: Genron, 2017), 19.

17. The terms *sengo* (the postwar period) and *Shōwa* are often used synonymously (even though *sengo*, more accurately, means the second half, or post–World War II portion, of Hirohito's reign), and both terms are also used in connection with the period of Japan's rapid economic growth. The *sengo* notion has been remarkably robust, in spite of efforts to do away with it soon after the end of World War II. Thus, as early as 1956, Nakano Yoshio declared in an influential monthly, "It is no longer the 'postwar' period"; see Nakano, "Mohaya 'sengo' de wa nai," *Bungei shunjū*, February 1956. Most accounts stress the prologue of Keizai Kikakuchō's *Keizai hakusho* (1956), archived at Cabinet Office, http://www5.cao.go.jp/keizai3/keizaiwp/wp-je56/wp-je56-010101.html. The genealogy of these words and phrases is replete with antecedents and predecessors. By the early 1950s, for example, the end of postwar literature had already been announced by Shiina Rinzō, in "Sengo bungaku no sōkessan," *Kindai bungaku*, January 1953.

18. Scott O'Bryan, *The Growth Idea* (Honolulu: University of Hawai'i Press, 2009), 172–73.

19. See the early account by Shinobu Seizaburō, *Sengo Nihon seijishi*, 4 vols. (Tokyo: Keisō Shobō, 1965–1967).

20. John Lie, *The Dream of East Asia* (Ann Arbor, MI: Association for Asian Studies, 2018), 66–67.

21. Ishiwara Kanji, "Heiwa no senshinkoku," *Yomiuri Hōchi Shinbun*, 28 August 1945.

22. On the origin of the "peaceful nation" idea, see Wada Haruki, *"Heiwa kokka" no tanjō* (Tokyo: Iwanami Shoten, 2015), chaps. 1–3. It would be misleading, however, to assert that martial orientation disappeared abruptly from everyday life. Well into the 1970s, war games were popular among children, and pachinko (Japanese pinball) parlors played military marches. Manga and anime often featured battle scenes, frequently ending with the protagonist engaged in an act of kamikaze (for example, Tetsuwan Atomu self-destructing by diving into the sun to alter its course and thus save humanity—a laudable goal, needless to say).

23. For the figure, see Handō Kazutoshi, *Shōwashi*, vol. 2 (Tokyo: Heibonsha, 2006), 34–35.

24. Shirai Satoshi, *Eizoku haisenron* (Tokyo: Ōta Shuppan, 2013), esp. 47–50.

25. The most flagrant description of Japanese subservience to the United States can be found in Numa Shōzō, *Kachikujin Yapū* (Tokyo: Toshi Shuppan, 1970); see also the five-volume edition (Tokyo: Gentōsha, 1999). In this sadomasochistic, scatological, matriarchal fantasy that depicts a world two thousand years hence, the Yapū are descendants of Japanese and serve as (sex) slaves of white people, whose feces feed both the Yapū and black slaves. The work is also notable for its rampant parody of academic writings and classical Japanese literature. The rare literary transgression of the other taboo—denigration of the emperor—is Fukazawa Shichirō, "Fūryū mutan," *Chūō Kōron* (December 1960), in which the emperor is decapitated.

26. Perhaps the most decisive decree was that the bureaucrats pass the ultimate test of government efficacy—the trains must run on time. A best-selling mystery published in the late 1950s hinged on the notion that platform 15 of Tokyo Station could be seen from platform 13 for only four minutes per day because of the myriad trains arriving and departing from the hub station; see Matsumoto Seichō, *Ten to sen* (Tokyo: Kōbunsha, 1958). Thus, by 1958, a plot premise that would have seemed implausible to almost anyone anywhere—the timely coming and going of all of a large city's trains—was already taken for granted in Japan.

27. The most famous such celebration was Shiroyama Saburō, *Kanryōtachi no natsu* (Tokyo: Shinchōsha, 1975).

28. Lie, *The Dream of East Asia*, 19–21.

29. On consumption and rapid economic growth in postwar Japan, see Penelope Francks, *The Japanese Consumer* (Cambridge: Cambridge University Press, 2009), chap. 6.

30. See Murakami Ryū, *Ushinawareta 10nen wo tou* (Tokyo: NHK Shuppan, 2000).

31. See, inter alia, Richard Katz, *Japan* (Armonk, NY: M. E. Sharpe, 1998); William W. Grimes, *Unmaking the Japanese Miracle* (Ithaca, NY: Cornell University Press, 2001); and Gary R. Saxonhouse and Robert Stern, eds., *Japan's Lost Decade* (Malden, MA: Blackwell, 2004).

32. Murakami Haruki, *Andāguraundo* (Tokyo: Kōdansha, 1997).

33. Ikezawa Natsuki, *Ikezawa Natsuki, bungaku zenshū wo amu* (Tokyo: Kawade Shobō Shinsha, 2017), 8. See also Takemura Ken'ichi, *Korede iinoka "saigai taikoku"* (Tokyo: Taiyō Kikaku Shuppan, 1998).

34. Paul Krugman, "Japan's Economy: Crippled by Caution," *New York Times*, 11 September 2015, https://www.nytimes.com/2015/09/11/opinion/paul-krugman-japans-economy-crippled-by-caution.html; Joseph E. Stiglitz, "Japan Is a Model, Not a Cautionary

Tale," *New York Times*, 9 June 2013, https://opinionator.blogs.nytimes.com/2013/06/09
/japan-is-a-model-not-a-cautionary-tale/.

35. Steven K. Vogel, *Japan Remodeled* (Ithaca, NY: Cornell University Press, 2006),
218–20.

36. Joseph A. Schumpeter, *Capitalism, Socialism, and Democracy*, 3rd ed. (New York:
Harper Perennial, 2008; 1st ed., 1942), chap. 7.

37. Alan S. Milward, *The Reconstruction of Western Europe, 1945–1951* (Berkeley: University of California Press, 1984), esp. 462–64. See also Andrea Mayer and Martha Wilhelm,
Das Wirtschaftswunder: Die Bundesrepublik 1948 bis 1960 (Berlin: Elsengold Verlag, 2018);
and Rolf Petri, *Storia economica d'Italia* (Bologna: Il Mulino, 2002).

38. Hannah Arendt argues that a metropolitan polity often engages in policy experiments in its colony, freed as it is from the ordinary constraints of countervailing political
forces or moral misgivings; see Arendt, *The Origins of Totalitarianism* (New York: Harcourt,
Brace, 1951), part 2.

39. Land reform remains a neglected but important precondition for industrialization.
One of the preconditions of industrialization in northeastern Asia is the destruction of the
premodern landed oligarchy; in the Philippines and much of southeastern Asia, the survival of that oligarchy acts as a powerful bulwark against self-sustaining industrialization
and growth. See John Lie, *Han Unbound* (Stanford, CA: Stanford University Press, 1998),
chap. 2.

40. For an early rumbling of the coming trade tension, see R. W. Napier and P. A. Petri,
The U.S.–Japan Trade Conflict (Washington, DC: US Department of State, 1979).

41. Niikura Takahito, *"Nōritsu" no kyōdōtai* (Tokyo: Iwanami Shoten, 2017), chap. 4.

42. No one even employed the term "economic growth" until 1954; see Takata Yasuma,
ed., *Keizai seichō no kenkyū*, 3 vols. (Tokyo: Yūhikaku, 1954–57).

43. Hyōdō Tsutomu, *Rōdō no sengoshi*, vol. 1 (Tokyo: Tokyo Daigaku Shuppankai, 1997),
23–29.

44. Ishimure Michiko, *Kugai jōdo* (1969–74; complete ed., Tokyo: Fujiwara Shoten, 2016).

45. The other three major pollution-related illnesses that arose in the 1960s are Niigata
Minamata disease (again, like Minamata disease, caused by mercury poisoning), Itai Itai disease (caused by cadmium poisoning), and Yokkaichi asthma (generally attributed to smog containing sulfur dioxide). For a compact account, see Masano Atsuko, *Yondai kōgaibyō* (Tokyo:
Chūō Kōronshinsha, 2013).

46. On *kōgaigaku* (pollution studies), see Tsuru Shigeto, ed., *Gendai shihonshugi to
kōgai* (Tokyo: Iwanami Shoten, 1968); and Ui Jun, *Kōgai genron* (Tokyo: Aki Shobō, 1971).

47. Later, the term also entered the English lexicon; see Katsuo Nishiyama and Jeffrey V.
Johnson, "Karoshi—Death from Overwork," *International Journal of Health Services* 27:4
(1997): 625–41.

48. President Charles de Gaulle's disparaging remark about the visiting Japanese prime
minister, Hayato Ikeda, is cited in Ha-Joon Chang, *Bad Samaritans* (New York: Bloomsbury,
2009), 21.

49. Joan Robinson, *Economic Philosophy* (1962; reprinted, Harmondsworth, UK: Penguin, 1964), 46.

50. The importance of social movements should not be overlooked; see Kiyoteru Tsutsui,
Rights Make Might (New York: Oxford University Press, 2018).

51. Nor, in the after-hours realm, should we forget the expansion of *mizushōbai* (the so-called water trade, or the nocturnal entertainment industry).

52. Satō Masaru, *Kanryō kaikyūron* (Tokyo: Ningen Shuppan, 2015), 226-37.

53. Although the phenomenon is widely acknowledged, there are very few extended treatments of this topic. See, however, Inose Naoki, *Nipponkoku no kenkyū* (Tokyo: Bungei Shunjū, 1999), esp. 42-44, 93-96.

54. Inoguchi Takashi, *"Zokugiin" no kenkyū* (Tokyo: Nihon Keizai Shinbunsha, 1987).

55. Inose, *Nipponkoku no kenkyū,* part 3.

56. The airbags were a component of automobiles manufactured by Honda. In the mid-1980s, a Honda engineer told me that the goal of his group was to build "no faults forever" (NFF) cars.

57. Tsutsumi Kazuma, *Kyodai shōchō amakudari fuhai hakusho* (Tokyo: Kōdansha, 2000); and Shiohara Toshihiko, *Naze kanryō wa fuhai surunoka* (Tokyo: Ushio Shuppansha, 2007).

58. Ishihara Shintarō, *Kurutta kajitsu* (Tokyo: Shinchōsha, 1956). In the same year as its publication, the novel was made into a movie directed by Nakahira Kō and starring the author's younger brother, Ishihara Yūjirō.

59. Kojima Nobuo, *Hōyō kazoku* (Tokyo: Kōdansha, 1965).

60. Etō Jun is exemplary in this respect. His exposure to American life awoke in him not only renewed appreciation of Japan but also a comparatively negative reevaluation of the United States that he had so admired. He would go on to question Japan's postwar Constitution as an *oshitsuke* (American-enforced) instrument; see Etō Jun, *1946nen kenpō* (Tokyo: Bungei Shunjū, 1980). The most remarkable thing is that this argument, however debatable, was only explicitly articulated more than three decades after the fact.

61. Koyano Atsushi, *Hanbei to iu yamai* (Tokyo: Asuka Shinsha, 2016).

62. For an overview and criticism of this idea, see Tanimoto Mayumi, *Sekai de baka ni sareru Nihonjin* (Tokyo: Wani Bukkusu, 2018).

63. The Democratic Party, which replaced the Liberal Democratic Party from 2009 to 2012, was widely deemed incompetent, above all for having bungled the aftermath of the calamitous earthquake and tsunami of 2011. Never mind that 3/11 had in part been a consequence of cozy collusion among Liberal Democratic Party politicians, bureaucratic elites, and executives of the Tokyo Electric Power Company. The Democratic Party was in the wrong place at the wrong time, and even though correlation does not imply causation (a truth all the more salient because the mistake of linking the two is so common), Japanese voters in 2012 switched back, faute de mieux, to the tried-and-true Liberal Democratic Party, which was promising not just competence but also prosperity. The Liberal Democratic Party's appeal was credible partly because almost everyone seemed to agree that Japan was in trouble, though that trouble had been caused in no small measure by the forty-year reign of the Liberal Democratic Party.

64. For example, the hallowed Ōkurashō (this name was a direct import from the Tang dynasty) became the pedestrian-sounding Zaimushō. It was as if the United Kingdom had renamed its chancellor of the exchequer and chosen to call it the treasurer. The ministry's new name is analogous to that of the equivalent governmental department in the United States—and in this detail it is possible to note a deep continuity in Japan's habit of emulating superior powers.

65. Crucial in this regard is the Americanization of higher education in Japan. In the postwar period, the elite bureaucrats, especially at what had been the prestigious imperial universities, were inevitably influenced by Marxists and institutionalists in their under-standing of political economy. Even in the mid-1980s, an economics major at the University of Tokyo could still choose between the modern (neoclassical) and Marxist tracks. At that time, a major Japanese bookstore in Jinbō-chō still had a shelf of German-language books from the Reclam publishing house, and no English-language books at all. After the 1990s, neoliberal thinking—more market, less state—steadily increased its influence. By then, more members of the Japanese elite had studied in the United States than in Europe, and more information was arriving from the United States than from the Old World.

66. I recall discussing university reforms with several high-ranking Japanese education bureaucrats in 2005. Whenever my suggestions included concrete figures, such as when I mentioned the endowment of Harvard University or the stipend for PhD students at Berke-ley (already very low), their response was invariably to drop one or two digits from the proposed amount. *Hōjinka* (privatization), to them, seemed to mean less public funding and more bureaucratic control. And rule changes, instituted for the sake of introducing more competition, almost always brought about more red tape. See Yamaguchi Hiroyuki, *"Daigaku kaikaku" to iu yamai* (Tokyo: Akashi Shoten, 2017).

67. But see Koike Kazuo, *Kōhinshitu Nihon no kigen* (Tokyo: Nihon Keizai Shinbunsha, 2012), 35. Koike argues that Japan is marked by a commitment to quality and to the partici-pation of mid-level employees.

68. See, respectively, Global Entrepreneurship and Development Institute, "2018 Global Entrepreneurship Index rankings," https://thegedi.org/global-entrepreneurship-and-development-index; SoraNews24, "Survey Finds Only 6% of Japanese Workers Motivated; 7th Lowest in the World," *Japan Today*, 8 February 2020, https://japantoday.com/category/features/lifestyle/survey-finds-only-6-of-japanese-workers-motivated-7th-lowest-in-the-world; World Economic Forum, "The Global Gender Gap 2018," https://www.weforum.org/reports/the-global-gender-gap-report-2018; Transparency International, "Corruption Per-ceptions Index," 2018, https://www.transparency.org/cpi2018; Reporters Without Borders, "Japan," https://rsf.org/en/japan; Wikipedia, "List of Countries by Spending on Education (% of GDP)," https://en.wikipedia.org/wiki/List_of_countries_by_spending_on_education_(%25_of_GDP); Yale Center for Environmental Law and Policy, Yale University, and Center for International Earth Science Information Network, Columbia University, in collaboration with the World Economic Forum, "2018 Environmental Performance Index: Global Metrics for the Environment; Ranking Country Performance on High-Priority Environmental Issues," https://epi.yale.edu/downloads/epi2018policymakerssummaryv01.pdf; Wikipedia, "Good Country Index," ttps://en.wikipedia.org/wiki/Good_Country_Index; and Wikipedia, "World Happiness Report," https://en.wikipedia.org/wiki/World_Happiness_Report. Need-less to say, there are many other indices and rankings.

69. David Pilling, *Bending to Adversity: Japan and the Art of Survival* (New York: Pen-guin, 2014), xxiv.

70. The film is based on a long-running manga series by Saigan Ryōhei, *Yūyake no shi*, 65 vols. (Tokyo: Shōgakkan, 1974–2016). Contemporary works that peddle nostalgia tend to skip over the pain and darkness of the past, and the late-1950s Tokyo depicted in the movie

does indeed whitewash the overcrowding, pollution, and other negative aspects of that period's urban life. In the 2007 sequel, a climactic dusk is shown from Nihonbashi, which was shortly to be covered by a freeway.

71. The term *senchūha*, by contrast with *senzenha* (denoting the prewar generation) and *sengoha* (denoting the postwar generation), usually refers to those who were in their youth during the Pacific War. The term *dankai* (unified fragment) comes from a novel by Sakaiya Taichi, *Dankai no sedai*, in *Sakaiya Taichi chosakushū*, vol. 1 (1976; reprinted, Tokyo: Tokyo Shoseki, 2016), 313–539. The linked stories that compose the novel depict college-educated white-collar workers born between 1947 and 1949 (the first high tide of the postwar baby boom in Japan) and are set in what was, at the time of publication, the near future of the 1980s and 1990s. Sakaiya was prescient in envisioning a future of slowing growth, environmental constraints, and an aging society.

72. Yoshiyuki Junnosuke, "Honoo no naka" (1956), in *Yoshiyuki Junnosuke zenshū*, vol. 5 (Tokyo: Shinchōsha, 1998), 153–234 (quotation on 233–34).

73. Compare Tateishi Yasunori, *Sensō taiken to keieisha* (Tokyo: Iwanami Shoten, 2018), 86–88.

74. Miura Masashi, *Seishun no shūen* (Tokyo: Kōdansha, 2001), 11–12.

75. Sekikawa Natsuo, *Shōwa ga akarukatta koro* (Tokyo: Bungei Shunjū, 2002).

76. Toru Suzuki, *Low Fertility and Population Aging in Japan and Eastern Asia* (Tokyo: Springer, 2013), 50–53, 77.

77. Erdman B. Palmore, *The Honorable Elders* (Durham, NC: Duke University Press, 1975). Palmore, an American gerontologist born in Japan, has attributed the trait of honoring the elders to a particular Japanese form of social organization—*tate shakai* (vertical or hierarchical society)—and to the Confucian legacy of filial piety.

78. Ariyoshi Sawako, *Kōkotsu no hito* (Tokyo: Shinchōsha, 1972). In 1973, Ariyoshi's novel was made into a much discussed movie directed by Toyota Shirō, and the novel has been adapted as a television series three times (in 1990, 1999, and 2006).

79. Tachibanaki Toshiaki, *Rōrō kakusa* (Tokyo: Seidosha, 2016), 15–19.

80. Fukazawa Shichirō, *Narayamabushi kō* (Tokyo: Chūō Kōronsha, 1957).

81. The term *furītā* is a neologism derived from English "free" and German "arbeiter"; *nīto* is derived from the British technocratic acronym NEET (not in employment, education, or training).

82. The term was introduced by the sociologist Yamada Masahiro, *Parasaito singuru no jidai* (Tokyo: Chikuma Shobō, 1999).

83. Hayamizu Toshihiko, *Tanin wo mikudasu wakamonotachi* (Tokyo: Kōdansha, 2006), 16, 54–55, 78–80, 207–8.

84. Asai Hirozumi and Morimoto Kazuko, *Nīto to iwareru hitobito* (Tokyo: Takarajima-sha, 2005), 15.

85. Genda Yūji, *Hataraku kajō* (Tokyo: NHK Shuppan, 2005), 59–62, 167–72.

86. To be sure, inequality is being reproduced, but it is not being exacerbated; see Ishida Hiroshi, "Kakusa no rensa, chikuseki to wakamono," in Ishida Hiroshi, ed., *Kyōiku to kyaria* (Tokyo: Keisō Shobō, 2017), 35–36.

87. See, respectively, Genda Yūji and Maganuma Mie, *Nīto—furītā demonaku shitsugyōsha demonaku* (Tokyo: Gentōsha, 2004); and Mary C. Brinton, *Lost in Transition* (Cambridge: Cambridge University Press, 2011), 178–87.

CHAPTER 2. GROWTH RECONSIDERED

1. For Japanese military deaths, see John W. Dower, *War without Mercy* (New York: Pantheon, 1986), 297–99. Another researcher estimates that there were almost six million victims of Japanese aggression; see Rudolph J. Rummel, *Statistics of Democide* (1997; reprinted, Münster: LIT, 1998), 32. Still another puts the figure at more than twenty-seven million; see Werner Gruhl, *Imperial Japan's World War II, 1931–45* (New Brunswick, NJ: Transaction, 2007), table 2.2.

2. It is not that no battles or even wars (including internal rebellions and wars against the Ainu) were fought between the Battle of Sekigahara (1600) and the Boshin War (1868), but without question the post-Meiji decades brought one bloody war after another.

3. See, respectively, Funase Shunsuke, *Washoku no teiryoku* (Tokyo: Kadensha, 2014); and J. A. Levine, "Lethal Sitting," *Physiology* 29 (2014), 300–301. According to one comparative survey, on average the Japanese sit for seven hours a day, the longest duration in the world; see *AERA*, 8 April 2019, 11.

4. In one study, the typical 1975 Japanese diet, with its emphasis on legumes, seafood, and fermented foodstuffs, proved superior on most metrics to the later 1990 or 2005 diet; see *Asahi Shinbun*, 8 October 2018, 29.

5. Iino Ryōichi, *Sushi tempura soba unagi* (Tokyo: Chikuma Shobō, 2016), 3.

6. Miyamoto Tsuneichi, *Wasurerareta Nihonjin* (Tokyo: Miraisha, 1960); Watanabe Kyōji, *Yukishiyo no omokage* (Fukuoka: Ashi Shobō, 1998).

7. Inoue Katsuo, *Bakumatsu, ishin* (Tokyo: Iwanami Shoten, 2006), 235–40.

8. Watanabe, *Yukishiyo no omokage*, chaps. 2, 3, 7.

9. Mark Blaug, *Economic Theory in Retrospect,* 5th ed. (Cambridge: Cambridge University Press, 1997; orig. 1st ed., 1962), 59.

10. Adam Smith, *An Inquiry into the Nature and Causes of the Wealth of Nations* (1776), ed. Andrew Skinner (Oxford: Clarendon Press, 1976), iv, 9.51.

11. To be sure, this blanket generalization leaves out the plethora of dismal economists, especially in the nineteenth century, who worried endlessly about another form of growth—population—and feared economic stagnation or even decline. Thomas Robert Malthus, we should remember, was a critic of slavery and imperialism, and it is precisely these concerns that informed his demographic worries. See Alison Bashford and Joyce E. Chaplin, *The New Worlds of Thomas Robert Malthus* (Princeton, NJ: Princeton University Press, 2016), chaps. 9–10.

12. As Paul Baran, in *The Political Economy of Growth* (New York: Monthly Review Press, 1957), 1, wrote, "Economic growth was the central theme of classical economics."

13. For an overview, see Dani Rodrik, *Economics Rules* (Oxford: Oxford University Press, 2015), chap. 6.

14. Philippe Aghion and Peter Howitt, *The Economics of Growth* (Cambridge, MA: MIT Press, 2009), 1.

15. Benjamin M. Friedman, *The Moral Consequences of Economic Growth* (New York: Knopf, 2005), 11–12, 14.

16. As mentioned later in this chapter, there are exceptions, and in growing numbers, usually because environmental constraints have been recognized. These divergent perceptions are often afterthoughts, however, and they usually come out of nowhere at the end of

a book or article. Typical in this regard is E. A. Wrigley, *The Path to Sustained Growth* (Cambridge: Cambridge University Press, 2016), which sustains a long, largely triumphant narrative and then concludes as follows: "In the absence of [coordinated action to reverse environmental pollution] . . . the industrial revolution may come to be regarded not as a beneficial event which liberated mankind from the shackles which limited growth possibilities in all organic economies but as the precursor of an overwhelming tragedy—assuming that there are still survivors to tell the tale" (205).

17. Jacobellis v. Ohio, 378 U.S. 184, 197 (1964). Justice Potter Stewart's 1964 opinion exposes the subjective—or, more accurately, intersubjective—foundation of legal reasoning.

18. The basic idea of the GDP metric, of course, is that it sums up all of a nation's commercial activities (minus net income earned abroad) over the course of a fiscal year. For an early but comprehensive history, see Paul Studenski, *The Income of Nations, with Corrections and Emendations*, 2 vols., revised ed. (New York: New York University Press, 1961; 1st ed., 1958). See also Philipp Lepenies, *Die Macht der einen Zahl* (Berlin: Suhrkamp, 2013).

19. Gross domestic product has been characterized as the US Department of Commerce's "achievement of the [twentieth] century"; see Bureau of Economic Analysis, "GDP: One of the Great Inventions of the 20th Century," *Survey of Current Business* 80:1 (2000), 6–9, https://apps.bea.gov/scb/account_articles/general/0100od/maintext.htm. That said, GDP is also remarkable for its belated emergence, usually traced to a government report by the Nobel laureate Simon Kuznets: *National Income, 1929–1932* (Cambridge, MA: National Bureau of Economic Research, 1934), http://www.nber.org/chapters/c2258.pdf. The curious reader will note, however, that Kuznets did not actually use the concept of GDP in his 1934 report; rather, the idea of gross national product appears later on, in Simon Kuznets, *National Income and Capital Formation, 1919–1935* (New York: National Bureau of Economic Research, 1937), 1. More important, Kuznets was surely not the inventor of the idea of national income, or of the practice of national income accounting; instead, it was William Petty's political arithmetic, in the seventeenth century, that sought to measure national wealth, though not national income. Petty's project was not a disinterested study but rather an exercise in "a science of social engineering," the purpose of which was "to improve [society] by direct and in some cases violent means"; see Ted McCormick, *William Petty and the Ambitions of Political Arithmetic* (New York: Oxford University Press, 2009), 206. Petty's effort to aggregate data notwithstanding, it was only with the massive expansion of governmental bureaucracy in the twentieth century (along with the coeval development of statistics and computers) that we became awash in vital statistics and economic data, not only nationally but also internationally. Statistics as an autonomous academic pursuit has a belated origin, and it assumed a rough family resemblance to its current form around the turn of the twentieth century; see Stephen M. Stigler, *The History of Statistics* (Cambridge, MA: Harvard University Press, 1986), part 3. In this regard, the massive contemporaneous expansion of the modern state laid the groundwork for government-based statistical collections and analyses. At any rate, since Kuznets did not employ the term "GDP" in his report of 1934, the received attribution to him of GDP's paternity is problematic, but the progress of GDP itself is replete with refinements and controversies. As Kuznets himself stressed, GDP is a metric of convenience (as all metrics are) and should not be mistaken for an indicator of collective well-being or human welfare. After all, the accounting exercise counts income rather than capital or wealth, and flow rather than stock. In fact, Kuznets warned

against employing "national income [as] the sole social desideratum in theory or the dominant motive in fact in a nation's economy"; see Simon Kuznets, *National Income: A Summary of Findings* (New York: National Bureau of Economic Research, 1946), 127. Along this line of reasoning, Kuznets sought to exclude from national income accounting such antisocial activities as racketeering and prostitution as well as some government spending, such as military expenditures; see Kuznets, *National Income and Capital Formation, 1919–1935*, 5–7.

20. One of Prime Minister Shinzō Abe's plans to stimulate economic growth was called womenomics. In basic terms, this was a plan to turn Japanese housewives into wage earners by bringing them into the workforce. Such a policy would have been welcome as a way to empower Japanese women, and yet it is hardly clear how the resulting GDP growth in and of itself would necessarily have enhanced the collective welfare.

21. For a pioneering analysis of the dysfunctions of automobiles, see Uno Hirofumi, *Jidōsha no shakaiteki hiyō* (Tokyo: Iwanami Shoten, 1974).

22. Lorenzo Fioramonti, *Gross Domestic Problem* (London: Zed, 2013), chap. 3.

23. As early as 1973, William D. Nordhaus and James Tobin wrote, "A long decade ago, economic growth was the reigning fashion of political economy"; see Nordhaus and Tobin, "Is Growth Obsolete?" in Milton Moss, ed., *The Measurement of Economic and Social Performance* (New York: National Bureau of Economic Research, 1973), 509. To be sure, they concluded their essay by posing and answering the question "Is growth obsolete? We think not" (532).

24. On the situation in the United States, see Carol Graham, *Happiness for All?* (Princeton, NJ: Princeton University Press, 2017); on the situation in Japan, see David Chiavacci and Carola Mommerich, eds., *Social Inequality in Post-growth Japan* (London: Routledge, 2017).

25. Richard A. Easterlin, "Will Raising the Incomes of All Increase the Happiness of All?" *Journal of Economic Behavior and Organization* 27 (1997): 35–47.

26. Easterlin, "Will Raising the Incomes of All Increase the Happiness of All?" 38–41.

27. A restaurant with prices below the equivalent of about ten US dollars is known as a *B-kyū gurume* (class B gourmet) restaurant.

28. Shiriagari Kotobuki, "Chikyū bōeike no hitobito," *Asahi Shinbun*, 15 April 2019, 10.

29. Jeremy Davies, *The Birth of the Anthropocene* (Oakland: University of California Press, 2016).

30. In this vein, the most widely publicized work of the past half century is Donella H. Meadows, Dennis L. Meadows, Jorgen Randers, and William W. Behrens III, *The Limits to Growth* (New York: Universe Books, 1972).

31. Rachel Carson, *Silent Spring* (1962; reprinted, Washington, DC: Library of America, 2018). To be sure, Carson's focus was on the impact of DDT on human health, and in many ways her volume was preceded by Murray Bookchin, *Our Synthetic Environment* (New York: Knopf, 1962), which also provides a better point of departure (Bookchin's work was originally published under the pseudonym Lewis Herber).

32. See Kenneth Strong, *Ox against the Storm* (Tenterden, UK: Paul Norbury, 1977).

33. Daniel J. Fiorino, *A Good Life on a Finite Earth* (New York: Oxford University Press, 2018), 19.

34. A pioneering analysis of risk inequality is set forth in Ulrich Beck, *Risikogesellschaft* (Frankfurt am Main: Suhrkamp, 1986).

35. Mary Midgley, *Science as Salvation* (London: Routledge, 1992); David F. Noble, *The Religion of Technology* (New York: Knopf, 1997).

36. According to a commentary on Revelation 6:1–8, the four seals of destruction are conquest, war and bloodshed, famine (which follows war), and pestilence and death; see Michael Coogan, ed., *The New Oxford Annotated Bible*, 5th ed. (Oxford: Oxford University Press, 2018), 2212. Given World War I and the Spanish flu, 1918 was a horrible year for excess mortality; see, respectively, Antoine Prost, "War Losses," in *International Encyclopedia of the First World War*, updated 8 October 2014, https://encyclopedia.1914-1918-online.net/article /war_losses; and Christopher J. L. Murray et al., "Estimation of Potential Global Pandemic Influenza Mortality on the Basis of Vital Registry Data from the 1918–20 Pandemic: A Quantitative Analysis," *Lancet* 368 (2006), 2211–18.

37. Consider the refusal by China, at one time the world's recycling center, to suffer the consequences of recycling materials from the wealthy countries of the world; see Livia Albeck-Ripka, "Your Recycling Gets Recycled, Right? Maybe, or Maybe Not," *New York Times*, 29 May 2018, https://www.nytimes.com/2018/05/29/climate/recycling-landfills-plastic-papers.html.

38. The arms race between antibiotics and bacteria is surely interminable—but, disturbingly, pathogens seem to be winning in the early twenty-first century; see William Hall, Anthony McDonnell, and Jim O'Neill, *Superbugs* (Cambridge, MA: Harvard University Press, 2018). There is no doubt that human health has been greatly improved by cleaning, and by a clean water supply in particular, as well as by the maintenance of sanitary conditions in general, but medical progress still confronts the resistance of microbes and microparasites, along with the environmental destruction that produces a human-unfriendly planet; see, respectively, William H. McNeill, *Plagues and Peoples* (Garden City, NY: Anchor Press, 1976), 290–91; and David Quammen, *Spillover* (New York: W. W. Norton, 2012), 515–18. Contributing to our woes is the general decline in public health institutions; see Laurie Garrett, *Betrayal of Trust* (New York: Hyperion, 2000).

39. On the uneven focus of scientific and technological research, see Richard R. Nelson, *The Moon and the Ghetto* (New York: W. W. Norton, 1977).

40. Robert J. Gordon, *The Rise and Fall of American Growth* (Princeton, NJ: Princeton University Press, 2016).

41. Tyler Cowen, *The Great Stagnation* (New York: Dutton, 2011), chap. 3.

42. The most influential exposition of the idea of the falling rate of profit is found in David Ricardo, *On the Principles of Political Economy and Taxation* (1817), ed. Piero Sraffa, vol. 1 of Maurice Herbert Dobb, ed., *The Works and Correspondence of David Ricardo*, 11 vols. (Cambridge: Cambridge University Press, 1951), 125–26.

43. Dirk Philipsen, *The Little Big Number* (Princeton, NJ: Princeton University Press, 2015), 224–26.

44. Boosters of nuclear energy have been unable to find suitable and safe storage solutions for nuclear waste; on this point, see William M. Alley and Rosemarie Alley, *Too Hot to Touch* (Cambridge: Cambridge University Press, 2013). And, more important, meltdowns and near meltdowns, as at Chernobyl and Fukushima, have had devastating impacts; see, respectively, Serhii Plokhy, *Chernobyl* (Cambridge, MA: Harvard University Press, 2018); and Richard Lloyd Parry, *Ghosts of the Tsunami* (New York: Farrar Straus & Giroux, 2017).

45. Richard Baldwin, *The Great Convergence* (Cambridge, MA: Harvard University Press, 2016).

46. On the Christian source of progress as the basis for Western historiography, see Karl Löwith, *Sämtliche Schriften*, ed. Klaus Stichweh, Marc B. de Launay, Bernd Lutz, and Henning Ritter, vol. 2: *Weltgeschichte und Heilgeschehen* (1953) (Stuttgart: J. B. Metzler, 1983).

47. Marshall Sahlins, "The Original Affluent Society," in *Stone Age Economics* (Hawthorne, UK: Aldine de Gruyter, 1974).

48. James C. Scott, *Against the Grain* (New Haven, CT: Yale University Press, 2017).

49. Susan B. Hanley, *Everyday Things in Premodern Japan* (Berkeley: University of California Press, 1997), 78–94.

50. Hanley, *Everyday Things in Premodern Japan*, 48–50, 68–73.

51. John Maynard Keynes, "Economic Possibilities for Our Grandchildren," in *Essays in Persuasion* (New York: W. W. Norton, 1963). See also Roy Harrod, *Topical Comment* (London: Macmillan, 1961), chap. 2.

52. George Eliot, *Middlemarch* (1871–72; reprinted, Edingurgh: William Blackwood & Sons, n.d.), https://www.gutenberg.org/files/145/145-h/145-h.htm.

53. On the duality and contradictory character of practical reason, see Henry Sidgwick, *The Methods of Ethics* (1874; reprinted, Bristol: Thoemmes Press, 1996), 461. "Egoistic Hedonism," Sidgwick wrote, "has clearly a prior claim [over] Universal Good." The problem is parallel to the temporary tension or contradiction of individual utility maximization. There are no rational reasons for negating short-term interests in favor of long-term interests.

54. Thomas Hobbes, *Leviathan* (1651), ed. Edwin Curley (Indianapolis: Hackett, 1994), 76.

55. Fred Hirsch, *The Social Limits to Growth* (Cambridge, MA: Harvard University Press, 1977). Hirsch's concept of positional goods is antedated by Harrod's synonymous notion of oligarchic goods; see Roy Harrod, "The Possibility of Economic Satiety," in *Problems of US Economic Development* (Washington, DC: Committee for Economic Development, 1958).

56. In 1989, 25 percent of Japanese youth went to college, but by 2018 that proportion had increased to more than 53 percent; see *Asahi Shinbun*, 30 April 2019.

57. Nicholas Xenos, *Scarcity and Modernity* (London: Routledge, 1989), 2–5.

58. Tim Kasser, *The High Price of Materialism* (Cambridge, MA: MIT Press, 2002).

59. Tibor Scitovsky, *The Joyless Economy*, rev. ed. (New York: Oxford University Press, 1992; 1st ed., 1976).

60. Avner Offer, *The Challenge of Affluence* (Oxford: Oxford University Press, 2006), 1.

61. John Richard Hicks, *Value and Capital* (Oxford: Oxford University Press, 1946), 172.

62. The idea of the commercialization effect is proposed in Hirsch, *The Social Limits to Growth*.

63. Avi Dan, "What Do You Call a 17-Year-Old Ad Campaign? Priceless," *Forbes*, 25 August 2014, https://www.forbes.com/sites/avidan/2014/08/25/what-do-you-call-a-17-year-old-ad-campaign-priceless/#75b570127142.

64. As Benedict de Spinoza put it in *Ethics* (1677), trans. Edwin Curley (London: Penguin, 2005): "A man who is guided by reason is more free in a state, where he lives according to a common decision, than in solitude, where he only obeys himself" (154).

65. Jeffrey D. Sachs, *The Age of Sustainable Growth* (New York: Columbia University Press, 2015), 3. Nowhere in this heavy tome does Sachs come close to discussing why growth is desirable.

66. In the realm of economics, the idea of the stationary state has a long conceptual history; see Joseph A. Schumpeter, *History of Economic Analysis*, ed. Elizabeth Boody Schumpeter (New York: Oxford University Press, 1954), 560–72, 963–71.

67. John Stuart Mill, *The Principles of Political Economy with Some of Their Applications to Social Philosophy* (1844), ed. William James Ashley, 7th ed. (London: Longmans, Green, 1909), 531.

68. Mill, *The Principles of Political Economy*, 533.

69. Mill, *The Principles of Political Economy*, 531.

70. John Stuart Mill, "On Liberty" (1859), in *Collected Works*, vol. 18 (Toronto: University of Toronto Press, 1977), 262–63.

71. See the dystopian story by Kurt Vonnegut, "Harrison Bergeron" (1961), in *Welcome to the Monkey House* (New York: Delacorte Press, 1968).

72. We should recall that the socialists and revolutionaries of the early twentieth century, in Germany and elsewhere, ruthlessly criticized Bolshevism for its suppression of democracy and dissent and for its championing of dictatorship; see Karl Kautsky, *Die Diktatur des Proletariats* (Vienna: Wiener Volksbuchhandlung, 1919), esp. chap. 10.

73. The greatest literary achievement in this vein remains Aleksandr Solzhenitsyn, *The Gulag Archipelago* (1973), trans. Thomas P. Whitney and H. Willetts, 3 vols. (New York: Harper & Row, 1974–78).

74. Needless to say, women in general did not fare as well as men in general.

75. Wallace Stevens, "The Noble Rider and the Sound of Words," in *The Necessary Angel* (New York: Knopf, 1951), 29.

CHAPTER 3. THE REGIME AS A CONCEPT

1. Thorstein Veblen, *The Theory of the Leisure Class* (London: Macmillan, 1899), 88–91ff.

2. Shiomi Sen'ichirō, *Kinjirareta Edo no fūzoku* (Tokyo: Gendai Shokan, 2009).

3. Eiko Ikegami, *The Taming of the Samurai* (Cambridge, MA: Harvard University Press, 1995).

4. Clifford Geertz, *The Interpretation of Culture* (New York: Basic Books, 1973), chap. 1.

5. Dazai Shundai, *Keizairoku* (1729), 145–46, archived at National Diet Library Digital Collections, http://dl.ndl.go.jp/info:ndljp/pid/799312/167. The slogan's provenance takes us to the ancient Chinese classics, but the most influential expression can be found in Yokoi Shōnan, *Kokuze sanron*, trans. Hanatachi Saburō (Tokyo: Kōdansha, 1986); the original edition, published in the mid-nineteenth century, is difficult to locate.

6. For a comparative analysis of Edo-era proto-industrialization, see Saitō Osamu, *Purotokōgyōka no jidai* (Tokyo: Nihon Hyōronsha, 1985), esp. part 2.

7. Takahashi Yoshio, *Nihon jinshu kairyō ron* (Tokyo: Ishikawa Hanjirō, 1884). Lest the reader be tempted to dismiss Takahashi as a crank, note that no less an authority than Fukuzawa Yukichi wrote the preface to this work.

8. Maruyama Masao and Katō Shūichi, *Hon'yaku to Nihon no kindai* (Tokyo: Iwanami Shoten, 1998), esp. 43–49.

9. Mizumura Minae, *Nihongo ga horobirutoki* (Tokyo: Chikuma Shobō, 2008), 261–65.

10. Kaneko Mitsuharu, *Zetsubō no seishinshi* (Tokyo: Kōdansha, 1999), 37–40. Kaneko calls the post–Meiji Restoration period the "era of facial hair."

11. Douglas Sladen, *Queer Things about Japan* (London: Anthony Treherne, 1904), vii.

12. Emil Lederer and Emily Lederer-Seidler, *Japan in Transition* (New York: Yale University Press, 1938), 260.

13. Nakae Chōmin, "Ichinen yūhan," in *Nakae Chōmin zenshū* (1901), vol. 10 (Tokyo: Iwanami Shoten, 1983), 155, 156.

14. See, respectively, M. L. West, *The East Face of Helicon* (Oxford: Clarendon Press, 1998); and Dag Nikolaus Hasse, *Success and Suppression* (Cambridge, MA: Harvard University Press, 2016).

15. See Sei Shōnagon, *The Pillow Book,* trans. Meredith McKinney (New York: Penguin Classics, 2007); and Murasaki Shikibu, *The Tale of Genji,* trans. Royall Tyler (New York: Penguin Classics, 2002).

16. The most extreme manifestations, to be sure, occurred during the Pacific War; see Hayakawa Tadanori, "*Nihon sugoi" no disutopia* (Tokyo: Seikyūsha, 2016).

17. Watanabe, *Yukishiyo no omokage,* chap. 7.

18. Yasumaru Yoshio, *Nihon no kindaika to minshū shisō* (Tokyo: Aoki Shoten, 1974).

19. Natsume Sōseki, *Sanshirō,* in *Teihon Sōseki zenshū,* vol. 5 (Tokyo: Iwanami Shoten, 2017), 292. The work was first serialized in 1908 and was published as a whole in 1909.

20. See Abe's 1 January 2015 statement at Prime Minister's Office of Japan, https://www.kantei.go.jp/jp/97_abe/statement/2015/0101nentou.html.

21. Stockholm International Peace Research Institute (SIPRI), "Military Expenditure (Current USD)—Japan," in *Yearbook: Armaments, Disarmament, and International Security* (Stockholm: SIPRI, 2018), cited by World Bank at https://data.worldbank.org/indicator/MS.MIL .XPND.CD?locations=jp.

22. See Meiji 150, https://www.kantei.go.jp/jp/singi/meiji150/portal/index.html.

23. This slogan from 1942, said to be the creation of an eleven-year-old girl, though it was actually her father's composition, was one of many expressions that valorized warfare in Japan's manic militarist phase. See Tanabe Seiko, *Hoshigarimasen katsumadewa* (Tokyo: Shinchōsha, 1981).

24. The term "Grundyism" comes from the hapless character in Thomas Morton, *Speed the Plough* (1798; reprinted, London: T. N. Longman, 1800).

25. Tateishi, *Sensō taiken to keieisha.*

26. The postwar regime did not achieve hegemony until the early 1960s, though 1958 seems especially significant since it was the year when large clusters of *danchi* (apartment buildings) made their first appearance, along with rockabilly music and instant ramen.

27. Katō Shūichi, Nakamura Shin'ichirō, and Fukunaga Takehiko, *1946—bungakuteki kōsatsu* (Tokyo: Shinzenbisha, 1947), 23.

28. This line of thinking has been especially acute in the social sciences. The study of Japan has become the study of the unique, when in fact the study of Japan is redolent of insights into other places. Consider, for instance, the concept of *kūki* (atmosphere). During the first Shinzō Abe administration, in 2007, it became common to talk about *kūki yomenai* (KY, or inability to read the atmosphere). The obsession with KY was all about being hyper-

conscious of one's surroundings, especially of what others wanted and expected. In this sense, atmosphere—that is, the mood or spirit of the social situation—is a universal attribute of social life, as important as a norm; see Yamamoto Shichihei, *Kūki no kenkyū* (Tokyo: Bungei Shunjū, 1977), esp. 22–23. In Durkheimian fashion, *kūki* is said to reign as a social fact, the imposition of an unstated norm or reality that cannot be challenged or changed, at least not easily. It is something almost tangible: think only about stepping into a room where others have been discussing something very serious, and it is easy to grasp at least the emotional import of the situation; see Kathleen Stewart, "Atmospheric Attunements," *Environment and Planning D: Society and Space* 29 (2011), 445–53. In spite of the considerable salience of *kūki* in all social life, there is a tendency to believe that it is a phenomenon distinct, and perhaps unique, to Japan. For Yamamoto Shichihei, the primary theorist of *kūki*—which he calls the basis of *Nihonkyō* (Japanese religion)—*kūki* is not salient in the United States, in contrast to Japan; see Yamamoto, *Kūki no kenkyū*, 56–59.

29. Majima Ayu, *"Hadairo" no yūutsu* (Tokyo: Chūō Kōronshinsha, 2014).

30. Daisetz Teitaro Suzuki, *Zen and Japanese Culture*, revised ed. (Princeton, NJ: Princeton University Press, 1959; 1st ed., 1938), 230. Kuwabara Takeo, "Dai2 geijutsu," *Sekai* (November 1946).

31. Almost 80 percent of the respondents to a 2006 survey said that Japan should aim to achieve economic growth; see Nihon Keizai Shinbunsha, *Saredo seichō* (Tokyo: Nihon Keizai Shinbunsha, 2008), 28.

32. It is true that the central fish market in Tokyo had been moved before, but the point here is the keenness of the authorities to close down "the greatest fish market on Earth"; see "One of Japan's Great Institutions Makes Way for a Car Park," *The Economist*, 13 October 2018, 41.

33. *Asahi Shinbun*, 30 April 2019, 4.

34. The phrase, originally copied from a television advertisement, became a "key symbol" of the time; see Fukagawa Hideo, *Kyatchifurēzu no sengoshi* (Tokyo: Iwanami Shoten, 1991), 121–24.

35. Naikakufu, *Kokuminsei ni kansuru yoron chōsa* (Tokyo: Naikakufu, 2011).

36. For a quick view of the transition, see *Tokyo Shinbun*, 30 April 2019, 28.

37. The name Genroku, like the names Shōwa and Heisei, corresponds to the reign of the emperor; in the Edo period, however, it was common enough to change the name if the emperor's affairs were not going well.

38. Shizuki Tadao's 1801 translation of Engelbert Kaempfer's work on Japan, based on Kaempfer's travels from 1683 to 1693, rendered *Abschlusspolitik* as *sakoku*; both Shizuki and Kaempfer wrote about Tokugawa-era foreign policy positively, but later histories depicted it as one of the many negative aspects of Tokugawa rule. See Ida Kiyoko, *Edo chishikijin no sekai ninshiki* (Tokyo: Suiseisha, 2008), chaps. 5–6.

39. On changes in the treatment of *sakoku* found in high school history textbooks, see Takahashi Hideki, Mitani Yoshiyuki, and Murase Shin'ichi, *Kokomade kawatta Nihonshi kyōkasho* (Tokyo: Yoshikawa Kōbunkan, 2016), 114–15.

40. Fujita Masakatsu, *Nihon tetsugakushi* (Kyoto: Shōwadō, 2018), 356–58.

41. Shimazaki Tōson, *Yoakemae*, 4 vols. (1900; reprinted, Tokyo: Iwanami Shoten, 2010). In an intellectualist reading, the epic depicts the failure of *kokugaku* (national studies, or the philology of Japan) and its worldview.

42. Nakano Mitsutoshi, in *Edo bunka saikō* (Tokyo: Kasama Shoin, 2012), 30–31, argues that contemporary Japanese people who are able to read Edo literature from 150 years ago amount to 0.004 percent of the population.

43. Kuki Shūzō, "Iki no kōzō," in *Kuki Shūzō zenshū*, vol. 1 (1930; reprinted, Tokyo: Iwanami Shoten, 1981).

44. The Japanese original is *majimeninaruka hito no otoroe*. The anonymous phrase was included in Keiki Itsu, ed., *Mutamagawa*, vol. 1 (1750; reprinted, Tokyo: Iwanami Shoten, 1984), 152.

45. On the Meiji virtues of diligence and study, see Maeda Ai, "Kindai dokusha no seiritsu," in *Maeda Ai chosakushū*, vol. 2 (1973; reprinted, Tokyo: Chikuma Shobō, 1989), 97.

46. Yasumaru, *Nihon no kindaika to minshū shisō*.

47. Nagai Yoshio, *Edo no funyogaku* (Tokyo: Sakuhinsha, 2016), 9–13.

48. Nakano Mitsuya would stress the eighteenth century; surely the long span from the Genroku period to the end of Tokugawa rule marks a period of remarkable cultural achievement; Nakano, *18seiki no Edo bungei* (Tokyo: Iwanami Shoten, 1999).

49. Ishinomori Shōtarō, *Manga Nihon rekishi*, vol. 38 (Tokyo: Chūō Kōronsha, 1992).

50. Sugiura Hinako, *Ichinichi Edojin* (1991; reprinted, Tokyo: Shinchōsha, 2005), 20–21.

51. Azuma Hiroki, *Dōbutsuka suru posutomodan* (Tokyo: Kōdansha, 2001), 14–38.

52. Fujiwara Masahiko, *Kokka no hinkaku* (Tokyo: Shinchōsha, 2005).

53. Fujiwara, *Kokka no hinkaku*, 179–81, 191.

54. Hirata Oriza, *Kudarizaka wo sorosoroto kudaru* (Tokyo: Kōdansha, 2016), 12.

55. Hirata, *Kudarizaka wo sorosoroto kudaru*, 37–39.

CHAPTER 4. ORDINARY VIRTUES

1. The fons et origo is Kondō Marie, *Jinsei ga tokimeku katazuke no mahō* (Tokyo: San Māku Shuppan, 2011), which sold more than a million copies in Japan and was translated into more than thirty languages. The English translation—Marie Kondo, *The Life-Changing Magic of Tidying Up* (New York: Ten Speed Press, 2014)—propelled Kondo onto *Time* magazine's list of the one hundred "most influential people"; see Jamie Lee Curtis, "Marie Kondo," *Time*, 16 April 2015, http://time.com/collection-post/3822899/marie-kondo-2015-time-100/.

2. The Japanese term associated with what the translation describes as sparking joy is *tokimeki*, which means palpitation or excitement, as when one's heart skips a (usually metaphorical) beat upon a thrilling experience or encounter. Skipping one too many beats would lead to the Swedish *döstädning*—decluttering, as if one had died; see Margareta Magnusson, *The Gentle Art of Swedish Death Cleaning* (2017; reprinted, New York: Scribner, 2018). If Plato is right to suggest in *Phaedo* (61c–69e) that philosophy is preparation for death, then wouldn't it to be proper for us to declutter in preparation for death?

3. William Morris, "The Beauty of Life" (1880), in *Collected Works*, vol. 22 (London: Longmans Green, 1914), 76.

4. On England as the first consumer society, see Joan Thirsk, *Economic Policy and Projects* (Oxford: Clarendon Press, 1978). On the belongings of homeless people, see Elliot Liebow, *Tell Them Who I Am* (New York: Free Press, 1993), 32–37.

5. Michael Landy, *Break Down* (London: Ridinghouse 2002), and the video of the project, "Documentary: Breaking Down (2001)," *Vimeo*, https://vimeo.com/144144220.

6. Jennifer Roberts, "Barbara Kruger," in Deborah Wye, ed., *Artists and Prints* (New York: Museum of Modern Art, 2004), 244, https://www.moma.org/collection/works /64897.

7. Alastair Sooke, "The Man Who Destroyed All His Belongings," BBC Culture, 14 July 2016, http://www.bbc.com/culture/story/20160713-michael-landy-the-man-who-destroyed-all-his-belongings.

8. Toyama Shigeru, *Nihonjin no kinben, chochikukan* (Tokyo: Tōyō Keizai Shinpōsha, 1987).

9. Nakano Kōji, *Seihin no shisō* (Tokyo: Sōshisha, 1992).

10. Nakano, *Seihin no shisō*, 33.

11. Nakano, *Seihin no shisō*, 32, 34.

12. Tachibana Akemi, *Dokurakugin* (1878), in Mizushima Naofumi and Hashimoto Masanobu, eds., *Tachibana Akemi Zenkashū* (Tokyo: Iwanami Shoten, 1999). The title slyly evokes onanism, as in Harry Mathews, *Singular Pleasures* (New York: Grenfell Press, 1988).

13. Nakano, *Seihin no shisō*, 192–93. The film was based on the novel by Tsuboi Sakae, *Nijūshi no hitomi* (Tokyo: Kōbunsha, 1952). Nakano is slightly off—the teacher may be pure (though she is suspected of being a "Red" and is cynical about war aims and consequences), she may be beautiful, but she is not particularly poor. After all, she wears Western clothes and possesses what was then the luxury good of a bicycle. One could be forgiven for regarding the film as largely an indictment of war and only secondarily an indictment of poverty, as exemplified by the deaths of male students in battle and the economic hardship of some of the female students.

14. Nakano, *Seihin no shisō*, 194–99.

15. In making this suggestion, however, Nakano neglects the indigenous tradition of vulgar materialism. The countervailing philosophy of thrift and modest living can be found in Tokugawa-era merchants and townspeople, as exemplified by the merchant-philosopher Ishida Baigan; see Takenaka Yasukazu, *Sekimon shingaku no keizai shisō* (1962), expanded ed. (Kyoto: Mineruva Shobō, 1972), esp. part 2, chap. 2.

16. Tsutsui Yasutaka, "Nōkyō tsuki e iku," in *Nōkyō tsuki e iku* (Tokyo: Kadokawa Shoten, 1973).

17. Ikenami Shōtarō, *Otoko no sahō*, rev. ed. (Tokyo: Shinchōsha, 1984; 1st ed., 1981), n.p.

18. Sasaki Fumio, *Bokutachini, mō mono wa hitsuyō nai* (Tokyo: Wani Bukkusu, 2015).

19. Minimarisuto Shibu, *Tebura de ikiru* (Tokyo: Sankuchuari Shuppan, 2018).

20. Bashō himself traveled with servants who carried many things; for a revisionist account, see Arashiyama Kōzaburō, *Akutō Bashō* (Tokyo: Shinchōsha, 2006).

21. Honda Naoyuki and Yosumi Daisuke, *Mobairu bohemian* (Tokyo: Raitsusha, 2017).

22. Yosumi Daisuke, *Jinsei yaranakute ii risuto* (Tokyo: Kōdansha, 2018).

23. The anime—based on a novel by Sakemi Ken'ichi, *Kokyū shōsetsu* (Tokyo: Shinchōsha, 1989) and directed by Toriumi Hisayuki—depicts the rise and fall of an imperial palace. The protagonist, Ginga, the only daughter of a potter, is the source of vibrancy and decency in a corrupt court. It would not be a stretch to see this work as an allegory of Bubble-period Japan.

24. Katō Kyōko, *Aete eranda semai ie* (Tokyo: Wani Bukkusu, 2016).

25. Katō, *Aete eranda semai ie*, 154.

26. The ethos of *mottainai* (the term, derived from the Buddhist vocabulary for "inconvenient," means, among other things, regret over wastefulness) underlies Nakano's philosophy of poverty as well as the philosophy of the minimalists, and it remains a potent reflex in the everyday life of the Japanese. It would be easy enough to identify counterexamples, such as excessive use of packing materials, as if the nakedness of things must be covered up; many items in Japan are, like matryoshka dolls, wrapped in layer upon layer. Nevertheless, *mottainai* remains a strong norm in Japanese life. For an older survey on this topic, see NHK Hōsō Yoronchōsajo, *Nihonjin no shoku seikatsu* (Tokyo: Nihon Hōsō Shuppan Kyōkai, 1983), 130. Many virtues akin to *mottainai* can be traced to the later Edo period, when such norms as thrift, *kenjō* (humility), diligence, and honesty were the rule; see Yasumaru Yoshio, *Yasumaru Yoshio shū*, vol. 1 (Tokyo: Iwanai Shoten, 2013), chap. 1.

27. Doi Yoshiharu, *Isshiru issai de yoi to iu teian* (Tokyo: Gurafikkusha, 2016), 10.

28. Doi, *Isshiru issai de yoi to iu teian*, esp. 186–87.

29. Koizumi Kazuko, *Shōwa no kurashikata* (Tokyo: Kawade Shobō Shinsha, 2016), 5.

30. A common approach would be to stress the notion of *wabi-sabi*, especially the notion of impermanence and the aesthetic of imperfection, and its roots in Zen Buddhism. *Wabi* is all about unfashionable poverty, however, and *sabi* is about unpretentious rusticity. For the most influential account of Zen Buddhism and its impact on Japanese culture, see Suzuki, *Zen and Japanese Culture*. According to Suzuki, "Zen has entered internally into every phase of the cultural life of the [Japanese] people," and he speculates that this has something to do with "the racial psychology of the Japanese people" (21). A more reasonable perspective is offered by Okakura Kakuzō, who champions Muromachi-era ink drawings but traces their aesthetic to China and India; see Okakura, *The Ideal of the East* (New York: E. P. Dutton, 1920), 165–70. Contemporary Japanese culture is complex, with myriad influences.

31. Norms are both infectious and robust. Recall only Solomon E. Asch's experiments on conformity; see Asch, "Opinions and Social Pressure," *Scientific American* 193:5 (1955): 31–35. Rugged individualists, confident of their autonomy, nevertheless cower before the social force of collective judgment, however wrong it may be, and conform to its dictates.

32. G. W. F. Hegel, *Elements of the Philosophy of Right* (1821), ed. Allen W. Wood, trans. H. B. Nisbet (Cambridge: Cambridge University Press, 1991), 244–48.

33. Hegel, *Elements of the Philosophy of Right*, 197.

34. Simone Weil, *L'Enracinement*, 2nd ed. (Paris: Gallimard, 1962; 1st ed., 1949), 16, 30.

35. Samuel Smiles, *Self-Help, with Illustrations of Character and Conduct* (London: John Murray, 1859). See also Fukuzawa Yukichi, *Gakumon no susume* (1872–76), in *Fukuzawa Yukichi zenshū*, vol. 3 (Tokyo: Iwanami Shoten, 1959).

36. Clark stayed only eight months in Japan, but his commencement speech at the college went viral. According to Clark's biographer, there are several different accounts of what he said. Given Clark's commitment to spreading Christianity, one of the more credible versions seems to be "Boys, be ambitious for Christ!" See John M. Maki, *William Smith Clark* (Sapporo: Hokkaido University Press, 1996), 195–96 (as is usually the case, the passage of time has achieved the collective editorial work of producing a better copy). Clark was ambitious but feckless; as Maki observes, "Ironically, his students possessed what he did not:

the commitment and perseverance that led to the successful attainment of their ambitions" (288).

37. In the early decades of the Meiji period, the word *benkyō*, which earlier had meant "industriousness," came to mean "studying" (the instrument of upward mobility) and is the current word for "study"; see Takeuchi Yō, *Risshin shusse shugi* (Tokyo: Nihon Hōsō Shuppan Kyōkai, 1997), 33–41.

38. Although emulation of the West was dominant, it would be reductive to omit certain continuities with the Tokugawa period, or to ignore the resurrection of Edo-era ideas and practices; see Gregory M. Pflugfelder, *Cartographies of Desire* (Berkeley: University of California Press, 1999), 146–58.

39. The Meiji Restoration entailed a rejection of the Heian-era traditions associated with Kyoto court life; see Kawajiri Akio, *Heiankyō sento* (Tokyo: Iwanami Shoten, 2011), i–vii.

40. On the encouragement of meat eating to enlarge the Japanese body, see Hongō Kazuko, Ōtake Naoko, and Hotta Junji, *Nikushoku to sōshoku no Nihonshi* (Tokyo: Chūō Āto Shuppansha, 2011). On the discouragement of same-sex intercourse, see Gary Leupp, *Male Colors* (Berkeley: University of California Press, 1995), 202–4.

41. Nakamura Shin'ichirō, *Kono hyakunen no shōsetsu* (Tokyo: Shinchōsha, 1974), 7.

42. Shibuya Tomomi, *Risshin shusse to kahanshin* (Kyoto: Rakuhoku Shuppan, 2013), 199–204.

43. On the ideology of *ryōsai kenbo*, see Fukaya Masashi, *Ryōsai kenbo shugi no kyōiku*, expanded ed. (Nagoya: Reimei Shobō, 1990; 1st ed., 1966).

44. Kajiwara Ikki and Kawasaki Noboru, *Kyojin no hoshi*, 19 vols. (Tokyo: Kōdansha, 1966–1971); two substantial series of sequels have also appeared.

45. These lines are from the first (1936) version of the film *Jinsei gekijō*, directed by Uchida Tomu, and featuring the eponymous theme song, composed by the redoubtable Koga Masao and sung by Kusuonki Shigeo, with lyrics by Satō Sōnosuke. The film, which has been remade several times, is based on a long novel by Ozaki Shirō, *Jinsei gekijō*, 3 vols. (Tokyo: Takemura Shobō, 1935–38).

46. "Kirawaretakunaitte sugoito omou," *logmiBiz* 18 February 2018, https://logmi .jp/267211.

47. Takamori Asao and Chiba Tetsuya, *Ashita no Jō*, 20 vols. (Tokyo: Kōdansha, 1968–73).

48. On the limitations of egalitarian ideals during wartime mobilization, see Sasaki Kei, "Sōryokusen no suikō to Nihon shakai no hen'yō," in Ōtsu Tōru et al., eds., *Iwanami kōza Nihon rekishi*, vol. 18 (Tokyo: Iwanami Shoten, 2015), 98–99.

49. It is no accident that Kita Ikki was widely viewed as the ideological father of the Incident of 2/26, for which he was executed. Kita's principal books—*Kokutairon oyobi junsei shakaishugi* (1906) and *Nihon kaizō kōan taikō* (1919)—advocate imperialism and nationalism (including xenophobia) but also a form of socialism from above. See Kita Ikki, *Chosakushū*, 3 vols. (Tokyo: Misuzu Shobō, 1959–72), vols. 1 and 2.

50. The most elaborate articulation of this perspective is Murakami Yasusuke, Kumon Shunpei, and Satō Seizaburō, *Bunmei to shite no ie shakai* (Tokyo: Chūō Kōronsha, 1979).

51. Tachibanaki Toshiaki, *Kakusa shakai* (Tokyo: Iwanami Shoten, 2006).

52. Mita Norifusa, *Doragon sakura*, 21 vols. (Tokyo: Kōdansha, 2003–7). Other tales of unusual success abound, and they make for comforting bedtime stories.

53. Suda Yoshiki and Ida Hiroto, *Tōdai wo detakeredo,* 3 vols. (Tokyo: Take Shobō, 2006–10).

54. Tachibana Takashi, *Tennō to Tōdai: Dai Nihon teikoku no sei to shi,* 2 vols. (Tokyo: Bungei Shunjū, 2005).

55. To be sure, there is a persistent practice of using scripts other than katakana to label irrevocably foreign things as a way of stressing their assimilation into Japanese culture. But nativist Japanese people who have had good, standardized compulsory schooling would be hard put to deny that the adopted Chinese characters known as kanji, without which written Japanese would be all but illegible, are alien imports. Part of being comfortable, then, is xenophilia.

56. Kawaguchi Mān Emi, *Sundemita Doitsu* (Tokyo: Kōdansha, 2013). Kawaguchi gives eight points to Japan and two to Germany, finding Japan a much better place to live. She also finds that Japan is on an equal footing with the richest country in the world, Switzerland, and that the two countries are alike; see Kawaguchi Mān Emi, *Sekai-ichi yutaka na Suisu to sokkuri na kuni Nippon* (Tokyo: Kōdansha, 2016). These and other curious exercises in ethnocentric comparison make for bad pop sociology. To begin with, very few citizens of affluent countries prefer other countries or find it more convenient to live abroad. Moreover, such comparisons say nothing—in terms of educational attainment, gender, ethnicity, and so on—about the individuals who make them. Nevertheless, such comparative exercises do point to the widespread Japanese consensus that Japan is a good and convenient country in which to live.

57. The saying "The customer is a god" is from Minami Haruo's 1961 song.

58. In one study, Japanese customers who had suffered a bad experience were found to be the most unforgiving customers in the world; see Ryan General, "Why Japan's Customer Service Is the Best in the World," *NextShark,* 23 June 2017, https://nextshark.com/japans-customer-service-best-world/.

59. Futabatei Shimei's *Ukigumo* (The drifting clouds), appearing in three sections between 1887 and 1889 and published together in 1890, is widely regarded as the first modern (that is, Western) novel in Japan. It features a protagonist who is something of a *hikikomori.*

60. Azuma Hiroki, *Gēmuteki riarizumu no tanjō* (Tokyo: Kōdansha, 2007), 96–97. See also the criticism (its primary thrust being that Azuma is too old and behind the times) by Uno Tsunehiro, *Zero-nendai no sōzōryoku* (Tokyo: Hayakawa Shobō, 2008), 28–31.

61. An example is the best seller, by Kent Gilbert, *Jūkyō ni shihai sareta Chūgokujin to Kankokujin no higeki* (Tokyo: Kōdansha, 2017).

62. The official name is Zainichi Tokken wo Yurusanai Shimin no Kai (The Citizens' Association to Disallow Special Privileges for Zainichi), founded in 2007 by Sakurai Makoto. See Sakurai Makoto, *Zaitokukai towa "Zainichi tokken wo yurusanai shimin no kai" no ryakushō desu* (Tokyo: Seirindō, 2013). The basic idea behind Zaitokukai is that Zainichi have "special privileges" above and beyond what ordinary Japanese citizens enjoy in Japan; for example, there is the false claim that Zainichi don't pay taxes or utility bills. See Noma Yasumichi, *"Zainichi tokken" no kyokō* (Tokyo: Kawade Shobō Shinsha, 2013).

63. For a review of Zaitokukai's racist rants and neo-Nazi affinities, see Yasuda Kōichi, *Heito supīchi* (Tokyo: Bungei Shunjū, 2015), 12–17, 28–31.

64. On the Korean peninsular origin of rice cultivation and Buddhism, see, respectively, Ishikawa Hideshi, *Nōkō shakai no seiritsu* (Tokyo: Iwanami Shoten, 2010), 60–62; and

Yoshimura Takehiko, *Yamato ōken* (Tokyo: Iwanami Shoten, 2010), 12–17. On Zainichi, see John Lie, *Zainichi (Koreans in Japan)* (Berkeley: University of California Press, 2008).

65. Probably the best-selling novel of the 2010s was Hyakuta Naoki, *Eien no zero* (Tokyo: Ōta Shuppa, 2006).

66. The classic statement remains Maruyama Masao, *Gendai seiji no shisō to kōdō*, 2 vols. (Tokyo: Miraisha, 1956–57).

67. For a sustained critique, see Takeno Yōtarō, *"Shūdanshugi" to iu sakkaku* (Tokyo: Shin'yōsha, 2008).

68. See Asch, "Opinions and Social Pressure," and Stanley Milgram, "Behavioral Study of Obedience," *Journal of Abnormal and Social Psychology* 67 (1963), 371–78.

69. Eshima Ken'ichi, *Nihon dōtoku kyōiku no rekishi* (Kyoto: Mineruva Shobō, 2016), 182.

70. Ten seasons of *The Walking Dead* TV series had aired before production work on the eleventh season was interrupted by the COVID-19 pandemic. The comics series is Robert Kirkman and Tony Moore, *The Walking Dead*, 193 issues (Orange, CA: Image Comics, 2003–19).

71. Okamoto Takeshi, *Zonbigaku* (Kyoto: Jinbun Shoin, 2017), 213–33.

72. I have been measuring the noise levels in libraries around the world. The library I use most often in Tokyo, the Metropolitan Central Library, usually registers a decibel level in the mid-twenties. And books in that library are almost never marked up; after paging through thousands of volumes, I have yet to find any handwritten commentary. Where noise levels and careful handling of books are concerned, my current place of employment offers a painful contrast.

73. On the virtue of humility, see Max Scheler, "Zur Rehabilitierung der Tugend" (1913), *Gesammelte Werke*, vol. 3 (Berlin: Francke, 1972), 13–32.

74. On contemporary Japanese people's propensity for pursuing individual interests, and on the decline in Japanese people's close relationships with relatives and neighbors, see NHK Hōsō Bunka Kenkyūjo, *Gendai Nihon no ishikikōzō*, 8th ed. (Tokyo: NHK Shuppan, 2015), 162–68, 197–201.

75. Quoted in Anthony Abraham Jack, *The Privileged Poor* (Cambridge, MA: Harvard University Press, 2019), 148.

76. Jack, *The Privileged Poor*, 176.

77. Endō Isao, *Shinkansen osōji no tenshitachi* (Tokyo: Asa Shuppan, 2012), 46–51.

78. See also Endō, *Shinkansen osōji no tenshitachi*, 187–88.

79. Niitsu Haruko, *Sekaiichi seiketsu na kūkō no seifuin* (Tokyo: Asahi Shinbun Shuppansha, 2015), 16, 23.

80. Niitsu, *Sekaiichi seiketsu na kūkō no seifuin*, 57, 60.

81. Watanabe Yūsuke, "Sōji to shigoto wa onaji," *PHP*, 6 April 2017, https://shuchi.php .co.jp/article/907?p=1. See also Matsushita Kōnosuke, *Ketsudan no keiei* (Tokyo: PHP Kenkyūjo, 1979), 184–86, 189.

82. Quoted in Ōmori Shin, *Sōji shihonshugi* (Tokyo: NikkeiBPsha, 2015), 101.

83. Hirata Osamu, *Korekara no gakkō sōji* (Tokyo: Ikkei Shobō, 2018), 37.

84. On All Nippon Airways' ranking, see https://www.worldairlineawards.com/worlds-best-airline-cabin-cleanliness-2018/.

85. Handwashing, along with soap and clean water, may represent the greatest public health triumph in the history of humanity; see the Centers for Disease Control and

Prevention's instructions for handwashing at https://www.cdc.gov/features/handwashing /index.html. Ignaz Semmelweis is usually credited with having pointed out the medical benefits of handwashing in the mid-nineteenth century, but sushi artisans and others surely had adopted the practice before then. On Ignaz Semmelweis, see Theodore G. Obenchain, *Genius Belabored* (Tuscaloosa: University of Alabama Press, 2016).

86. Hirata, *Korekara no gakkō sōji*, 39.

87. Sugihara Satomi, *Sōji de kokoro migakerunoka* (Tokyo: Chikuma Shobō, 2019), chap. 1.

88. Endō Motoo, *Nihon shokuninshi no kenkyū*, vol. 1 (Tokyo: Yūzankaku, 1985), 245; Endō Motoo, *Nihon shokuninshi sōsetsuhen* (Tokyo: Yūzankaku, 1967), 37-43.

89. Tanaka Yoshio, *Dentō kōgei shokunin no sekai* (Tokyo: Yūzankaku, 2003), 3-5. But a merchant turned philosopher has spoken more systematically, famously denying any distinctions of rank or worth among occupations, and claiming that they are "all one thing under heaven," with "no two roads in heaven"; see Ishida Baigan, "Tohi mondō" (1739), in *Baigan zenshū*, rev. ed., vol. 1 (Osaka: Seibundō, 1972), 90.

CHAPTER 5. THE BOOK OF SUSHI

1. By the term "sushi" I mean the Edo-style sushi that emerged in the early nineteenth century, featuring *nigirizushi*. Sushi's history is coeval with rice cultivation—both arrived from southeastern Asia in the form of fermented fish with rice, called *narezushi* today; see Ishige Naomichi and Kenesu Radoru, *Gyoshō to narezushi no kenkyū* (Tokyo: Iwanami Shoten, 1990).

2. Sushi aficionados will note that I am simplifying here. There are different types of sushi—*nigiri, maki* (rolled in laver), *oshi* (made in a mold), *chirashi* (fish over rice, usually in a lacquered bowl, and undifferentiated into individual pieces, as in *nigirizushi*)—and there are occasional nonseafood items, most commonly vegetables and eggs.

3. There are several ways to denote the term "sushi" in Chinese characters, but a common way conjoins the "fish" radical with the one for "delicious." Probably the two other most common ways of rendering the term "sushi" in Chinese characters are either to combine the characters for "fish" and "make" or to use two distinct characters, one meaning either "longevity" or "congratulatory" and the other referring to rank or to someone who brings people together. These and other ways of using Chinese characters to denote the term "sushi" are just so many attempts to infuse meaning into a word that emerged gradually and spread in the same manner. To be sure, a plausible origin story would stress the first syllable, which refers to vinegar or sourness.

4. Yoshino Masuo, *Sushi, sushi, sushi* (Tokyo: Asahiya Shuppan, 1990), 56-61.

5. Nomura Yūjirō, "Tempura tsū" (1930), in Minami Hiroshi, ed., *Kindai shomin seikatsu*, vol. 6 (Tokyo: San'ichi Shobō, 1987), 118.

6. Nagai Kafū, *Reishō* (1915), in *Kafū zenshū*, vol. 7 (Tokyo: Iwanami Shoten, 1992), 3-191, 59.

7. Nagase Ganosuke, *Sushi tsū* (1930; reprinted, Tokyo: Doyōsha, 2017), 10-11.

8. Nagase, *Sushi tsū*, 10, 12.

9. In an unscientific survey, sushi emerged (ahead of curry and ramen) as the food that is most liked by Japanese people; see "Nihonjin ga ichiban sukina tabemono ga kettei!!"

excite news, 6 June 2018, https://www.excite.co.jp/news/article/Nicheee_2179082/. Most surveys, in fact, place sushi as the favorite food of the Japanese people; see "Nihonjin & gaijin ga sukina tabemono ranking," *ailovei*, 6 June 2015, https://ailovei.com/?p=25018.

10. Kitamura Nobuyo, "Kiyūshōran" (1830) in Kitamura Takaniwa, ed., *Nihon zuihitsu taisei henshūbu*, 4 vols. (Tokyo: Yoshikawa Kōbunkan, 1979), 3:80.

11. Nagase, *Sushi tsū*, 26-28.

12. Nagase, *Sushi tsū*, 19.

13. Bungei Shunjū Shuppankyoku, *Best of Tokyo iimise umaimise* (Tokyo: Bungei Shunjūsha, 2010), 192.

14. Kitagawa Morisada, *Kinsei fūzokushi (morisadamankō)*, ed. Usami Hideki, vol. 1 (1837-67; reprinted, Tokyo: Iwanami Shoten, 1996), 294.

15. *Edo meibutsu shuhan tebikigusa* (place of publication and name of publisher unknown, 1848), n.p.

16. Aoki Naomi, *Bakumatsu tanshin funin kakyū bushi no shokunikki* (Tokyo: Nihon Hōsō Kyōkai, 2005), 125, 128. On the relatively low price of Edomae sushi, see Ono Takeo, *Edo bukka jiten* (Tokyo: Tenbōsha, 2009), 352-53.

17. Shiga Naoya, "Kozō no kamisama" (1920), in *Shiga Naoya zenshū* (Tokyo: Iwanami Shoten, 1999), 265-79. The story, to be sure, is less about sushi than about envy, pathos, and unwanted and unwarranted charity and its consequences.

18. Nagase, *Sushi tsū*, 69-71.

19. Murai Gensai, *Kuidōraku*, 2 vols. (1904-5; reprinted, Tokyo: Iwanami Shoten, 2005). The two most extended discussions that concern sushi are about how fish heads can be procured cheaply at a sushi shop and about *ayu* (sweet fish) sushi, which is not served in Edo-style sushi.

20. Kumakura Isao, *Nihon ryōri bunkashi* (Kyoto: Jinbun Shoin, 2002).

21. Tokyo Nichinichi Shinbunsha Shakaibu, ed., *Mikaku gokuraku* (Tokyo: Kōbunsha, 1927), 47; in this pioneering work of the Tokyo restaurant guide genre, Shintomi Sushi is mentioned more than any other restaurant (67, 105, 107).

22. Yasui Tekiji, ed., *Dai Tokyo umaimono tabearuki* (Tokyo: Marunouchi Shuppasha, 1935).

23. Okamoto Kanoko, "Sushi" (1939), Aozora Bunko, https://www.aozora.gr.jp/cards /000076/files/1016_19596.html.

24. See Kojima Masajirō, *Kuishinbō* (1960; reprinted, Tokyo: Kawade Shobō Shinsha, 2011); and Shishi Bunroku, *Shokumi saijiki* (Tokyo: Bungei Shunjū, 1968). Neither of these books by well-known foodies mentions Edomae sushi.

25. Tanemura Suehiro, "Tokyo sushi konjakubanashi," in Nomura Mari, ed., *Sakka no betsubara* (Tokyo: Kōbunsha, 2007), 16-18.

26. Sugiyama Sōkichi, *Sushi no omoide* (Tenri: Yōtokusha, 1968), 186-87.

27. Itō Yōichi, *Kauntā kara Nihon ga mieru* (Tokyo: Shinchōsha, 2006).

28. Miyao Shigeo, *Sushi monogatari* (Tokyo: Inoue Shobō, 1960), 192-96.

29. The figure is taken from "Todōfubetsu tōkei to rankingu de miru kenminsei," Prefectural Statistics and Rankings, updated 17 November 2020, https://todo-ran.com/t /kiji/13428.

30. A study from the late 1970s revealed that only 44 percent of sushi establishments in the Setagaya Ward of Tokyo were privately owned; see Tokyo Shōkō Kaigisho Setagayashibu

Setagaya-ku Kuminbu Keizaika, *Shōwa 53-nendo Setayaka-ku Sushisō no Keiei Jittai Chōsa Hōkokusho* (Tokyo: Tokyo Shōkō Kaigisho Setagayashibu Setagaya-ku Kuminbu Keizaika, 1979), 3.

31. One writer has argued that sushi chefs test their customers and that their service is in fact a form of struggle with or against customers; see Yamauchi Yutaka, *"Tōsō" to shite no sābisu* (Tokyo: Chūō Keizaisha, 2015), esp. 1, 28, 52–53. When I summarized this argument to several sushi chefs, they uniformly found a grain of truth in it, but a rather small grain.

32. Sano Yōko, "Sushi," in Arashiyama Mitsusaburō, ed., *Watashi no shokujiman, ajijiman*, vol. 1: *Sushi* (Tokyo: Riburio Shuppan, 2006), 18.

33. Yamauchi, *"Tōsō" to shite no sābisu*, 28.

34. For a similar incident, see the memoir by Morooka Yukio, *Kanda Tsuruhachi* (Tokyo: Sōshisha, 2000), 48–52.

35. Ono Jirō, the famed sushi chef of Sukiyabashi Jirō, also frequently says that customers should eat whatever they want, in any order they want (see Satomi Shinzō, *Sukiyabashi Jirō shun wo nigiru* [Tokyo: Bungei Shunjū, 1997], 254), but he also says things that would undermine that stated principle (260–62).

36. As early as the 1990s, Kawaji Akira, in *Edomae nigiri kodawari nikki* (Tokyo: Asahi Shuppan, 1993), was reporting that the sushi chefs of a decade or two earlier had been routinely unfriendly, had not accepted reservations, and did not serve cold sake (32, 62–63).

37. Isshi Haruo, *Tabisuru Edomae sushi* (Tokyo: Bungei Shunjū, 2018), 190–91.

38. Sushi Shō Sawa, a forebear of Sushi Shō, had opened in 1989.

39. The three levels denote plants that are hardy and thrive even in the cold months. Their hierarchical order has nothing to do with their perceived value.

40. On the importance of critics and guidebooks for twentieth-century French restaurants, see Isabelle Terence, *Le monde de la grande restauration en France* (Paris: Harmattan, 1996), chap. 2.

41. To be sure, many such outings are "paid" dates (*papakatsu*), which is to say, as is usually the case, that an older man is out with a younger woman, employed by a nightclub or cabaret club or working as a freelancer, who offers him the "girlhood experience."

42. Ono Jirō, Kanemoto Kenjirō, and Sōtome Tetsuya, *Kyoshō no waza to kokoro* (Tokyo: Chūkei Shuppan, 2009), 15–17.

43. Many early guides to sushi restaurants provided guidelines for customers' behavior; see Kawaji, *Edomae nigiri kodawari nikki*, appendix.

44. One rationale for serving *anago* at the end of a sushi course is that it's usually sweetened and functions as a quasi-dessert. *Tamagoyaki*, too, is flavored (traditionally with Shiba shrimp) and sweetened.

45. *Tamagoyaki*, now almost always proffered last, was sometimes eaten first in the past; see Nagase, *Sushi tsū*, 83–84.

46. Kawaji, *Edomae nigiri kodawari nikki*, 118.

47. This truism is most frequently attributed to the scribbler-gourmand Ikenami Shōtarō; see Baba Keiichi, *Ikenami Shōtarō ga kayotta "mise"* (Tokyo: Isoppusha, 2009), 14–15.

48. The term *chūtoro* denotes a section of a fish's flank or belly fat that has a medium level of marbling.

49. See also Sagawa Yoshie, *Sushiya no kamisan uchiakebanashi* (Tokyo: Kōdansha, 1995), 85–86.

50. See "333.6 Million Yen for Tuna in 1999: The Highest Ever in Toyosu's First Auction," *Asahi Shinbun*, 5 January 2019, https://www.asahi.com/articles/ASM152F5QM15UTIL001 .html.

51. Most *oyakata* are reluctant to talk about financial matters, but the most commonly cited figure is 40 percent; in contrast, the ratio for sit-down restaurants in the United States is about 30 percent. See Priceonomics, "How Much Do the Ingredients Cost in Your Favorite Foods?," *Forbes*, 7 April 2017, https://www.forbes.com/sites/priceonomics/2017/04/07/how-much-do-the-ingredients-cost-in-your-favorite-foods/#788a3d9311ed. Interestingly, *kaitenzushi* places often spend more (40 to 50 percent or greater) because they face stiff competition as providers of inexpensive sushi; see Yonekawa Nobuo, *Kaitenzushi no keieigaku* (Tokyo: Tōyō Keizai Shinpōsha, 2011), vii.

52. Shimizu Kikuo, *Edomae sushi dentō to waza to shinzui* (Tokyo: Kōdansha, 2011), 101. The typical estimate is about 70 percent.

53. Long ago in the Tokugawa period, the term "Edo style" implied seafood from Edo or Tokyo Bay. By the twentieth century, with rapidly improving transportation and refrigeration technology, seafood from all over Japan had begun to appear in Tokyo's sushi restaurants.

54. Sugiyama, *Sushi no omoide*, 225–28.

55. Salmon is common, however, in *kaitenzushi* and North American sushi. In fact, salmon is not only the most frequently ordered fare but also (if nonscientific surveys can be trusted) the most popular. In the past, salmon was not served, because of its absence from the Tokyo area and because of the parasites in fresh salmon. Edo-style sushi chefs still resist the use of salmon, partly from tradition but also from their desire to differentiate themselves from chefs at *kaitenzushi* venues.

56. Ono, Kanemoto, and Sōtome, *Kyoshō no waza to kokoro*, 11.

57. *Kohada* (*Konosirus punctatus*) is sometimes known as spotted sardine or dotted-gizzard shad.

58. For a glossary of sushi argot from a generation ago (though many of the terms are still alive and well), see Ikuta Yoshikatsu and Tomioka Kazunari, *Tsukiji uogashi kotoba no hanashi* (Tokyo: Daishūkan Shoten, 2009).

59. Ikenami Shōtarō, "Sushiya to tsukiau hō," in Arashiyama Mitsusaburō, ed., *Watashi no shokujiman, ajijiman*, vol. 1: *Sushi* (Tokyo: Riburio Shuppan, 2006), 126.

60. Nagase, *Sushi tsū*, 59.

61. On the role of tipping, see W. F. Whyte, *Human Relations in the Restaurant Industry* (New York: McGraw-Hill, 1948), 98–99.

62. Imada Yōsuke, *Sushi no subete* (Tokyo: Shibata Shoten, 2017), 7.

63. On Ono Jirō's not having wanted to pursue a life as a sushi chef, see Usami Shin, *Sukiyabashi Jirō sushi wo kataru* (Tokyo: Bungei Shunjū, 2009), 195–96.

64. Ōbayashi Yūichirō and Tagawa Yasuyuki, *Tekka no makihei*, 8 vols. (Tokyo: Hōbunsha, 1978–81).

65. Horie Takafumi, *Horie Takafumi vs. sushi shokunin* (Tokyo: Pia, 2018).

66. Most historians date *kaitenzushi* to its appearance at Genroku Sushi, in 1958, but its signature innovation—the conveyor belt, which replaces the counter, and which parades a selection of sushi and other items before the customer—made its debut in 1974; see Yonekawa, *Kaitenzushi no keieigaku*, vii.

67. The same figures are reported in Sagawa, *Sushiya no kamisan uchiakebanashi*, 10.

68. The older language is *hōkō*, which has a feudal ring and sounds very old-fashioned, though *shugyō* sounds too serious and spiritual to younger sushi apprentices and chefs.

69. The idea of spending ten thousand hours, or roughly ten years, to master a skill is an idea that was popularized by Malcolm Gladwell, in *Outliers: The Story of Success* (New York: Little, Brown, 2008), chap. 2.

70. Hissho, a Burmese-owned sushi chain with more than a thousand locations in the United States, requires a two-week training course; see Miriam Jordan, "Ever Heard of Burmese Sushi Counters? You've Probably Been to One," *New York Times*, 29 October 2017. The Japanese sushi workers were skeptical about sushi chefs who were not of Japanese ethnicity, but they were even more skeptical about such a short training period.

71. Cf. Arashiyama Mitsusaburō, *Edomae sushi pin no pin no mise wo iku* (Tokyo: Shinkōsha, 2002), 42.

72. There is a time-honored way of reproducing a sushi establishment: sharing the *noren* (the cloth that hangs at the entrance to a sushi restaurant). The *noren* is usually inscribed with the restaurant's name but sometimes instead with something perfectly generic (such as the characters that spell out the word "sushi"). When an apprentice has mastered his craft and wishes to become independent (that is, open a new establishment), the end of his apprenticeship and the beginning of his independence will be marked by his (usually metaphorical) sharing of the older establishment's *noren*. Sharing the *noren* speaks to a sense of traditional continuity (though of course the generic logic of an apprentice becoming a master is universal wherever the idea of a craft or a guild operates). At least in the postwar period, the passing down of skills, knowledge, reputation, and goodwill has been the usual way by which a sushi establishment has expanded. But this time-honored mode of expansion is becoming much less common, as suggested by the proliferation of star sushi chefs opening their own restaurants in their thirties. Nowadays a promising young chef raises money, finds a sponsor, or may even be hired by a parent company.

73. Usami, *Sukiyabashi Jirō sushi wo kataru*, 188.

74. Isshi Haruo, *Ushinawareteyuku sushi wo motomete* (Tokyo: Shinchōsha, 2006), 18.

75. Nakazawa Keiji, *Sushiya no ningengaku* (Tokyo: Bungei Shunjū, 2007), 13.

76. Nakazawa, *Sushiya no ningengaku*, 73.

77. One master chef has observed that without *iji* (obstinacy or will) and *konjō* (guts or spirit), there's not much point in becoming a sushi chef; see Kosuge Keiko, *Aji no shokunin kodawari jiten* (Tokyo: Tokyodō Shuppa, 1994), 69.

78. In my experience, sushi chefs who are pressed to state their motivation for working at their craft tend to give a number of anodyne reasons: "I like the work"; "I enjoy making sushi"; "It's a very good life"; and so on. Others are more practical: "It's a good job. I make good money." In what is probably the most common response, though, the chef notes and affirms his place in a chain of social relations that gives him a sense of place and purpose: "Not a day goes by when I don't learn something. It makes me appreciate my elders and their hard work, and it makes me want to forge ahead." A sense of meaning may also come from customers' appreciation: "There's nothing more rewarding than watching a customer eat heartily and smile at the end of the meal." Some chefs worry about making ends meet. Others, especially senior chefs, are concerned about retirement and old age. As a group, however, sushi chefs seem to be of remarkably good cheer.

79. Yamada Gorō, *Ginza no sushi* (Tokyo: Bungei Shunjū, 2013), 37–39.

80. In the first major manga series to depict a chef, both a competitive and an artisanal ethic were stressed; see Gyū Jirō and Biggu Jō, *Hōchōnin Ajihei*, 23 vols. (Tokyo: Shūeisha, 1973–77). In the past, sushi chefs commonly tended to be dismissive of their rivals, and they had few kind words for celebrity chefs, but this is another generalization that holds less true for younger chefs.

81. Morooka, *Kanda Tsuruhachi*, 198.

82. Arashiyama, *Edomae sushi pin no pin no mise wo iku*, 105.

83. Morooka Yukio, *Kanda Tsuruhachi sushibanashi* (Tokyo: Sōshisha, 1986), 12–16.

84. Sōmushō Jimusho, *Kigyō tōkei chōsa* (Tokyo: Sōmushō Jimusho, 2006).

85. Suzuki Tomohiko, *Yakuza to sakana* (Tokyo: Shōgakkan, 2018).

86. On the cost of Sushirō's raw materials, see "Kaitenzushi, genkaritsu ga takai 'otokui-neta' saishin ranking," Moneypost; on the chain's artisanal production method, see "This Is Susilo," http://www.akindo-sushiro.co.jp/korezo. As for quality, as with McDonald's fries, surprisingly good.

87. In the past, the *oyakata* usually withheld a portion of the apprentice's income in order to defray the cost of his later opening his own store. This practice was known as *tenbiki chokin seido*. According to one source, the master subtracted and saved the equivalent of about five hundred US dollars from a monthly pay of what would have been the equivalent of approximately eight hundred US dollars; see Sagawa, *Sushiya no kamisan uchiakebanashi*, 15.

88. See Ikuta Yoshikatsu, *Annani ōkikatta hokke ga naze konnani chiisakunattanoka* (Tokyo: Kadokawa Gakugei Shuppan, 2015).

89. See, for example, Komatsu Masayuki, *Nihon no shokutaku kara uo ga kieru hi* (Tokyo: Nihon Keizai Shinbunsha, 2010), chap. 1.

90. Hamada Takeshi, *Nihon gyogyō no shinjitsu* (Tokyo: Chikuma Shobō, 2014), 234–46. Another environmental stressor is Japan's increased consumption of meat—curious, in a country that during the Edo period banned cruelty to and certainly consumption of animals, and ironic, too, in a sense, now that fish is considered a safer and healthier source of protein; see Komatsu Masayuki, *Nihon no umi kara sakana ga kieru hi* (Tokyo: Magajinrando, 2014), 32–33. The bans on meat and cruelty to animals were derided by modernizing Japanese intellectuals, but those bans now seem remarkably progressive when it comes to animal ethics and the human diet. On the proto–animal rights decrees of Tokugawa Tsuneyoshi, the fifth shogun, see Itakura Kiyonobu, *Shōrui awaremi no rei* (Tokyo: Kasetsusha, 1992). On the transformation of the Japanese diet, see Gotō Yoshiko, *Edo no shoku ni manabu* (Kyoto: Rinkawa Shoten, 2015); while Japanese people in the Edo period consumed about 6 percent of total protein from animal sources, the figure for contemporary Japanese people is 52 percent and growing (104–5).

CHAPTER 6. THE ARTISANAL ETHOS IN JAPAN

1. The quotation is from the Yamanoue Hotel's promotional pamphlet. Apparently Mishima, without having been asked, gave this glowing testimonial to the organization's founding president, Yoshida Toshio. See Tokiwa Shinpei, *Yamanoue hoteru monogatari* (Tokyo: Hakusuisha, 2002), 6.

2. Tokiwa, *Yamanoue hoteru monogatari,* 160–61.

3. No matter how popular a *B-kyū gurume* restaurant becomes, its standard practice is not to raise prices. Instead, customers line up, sometimes for hours. In effect, the customers offer their time and their dedication instead of their money, and chefs in turn reward their customers' dedication rather than their customers' wealth.

4. Joshua B. Freeman, *Behemoth* (New York: W. W. Norton, 2018), epilogue.

5. Compare Aristotle, *Nicomachean Ethics* (c. 340 BCE), ed. and trans. Roger Crisp, rev. ed. (Cambridge: Cambridge University Press, 2014), 23–24. The fact that an ethos operates at the level of the individual or the group is primarily what distinguishes it from a regime (see chapter 3 of this book), which operates at the level of the organization or the nation. Here, it is crucial to note that I am using the word "habit" in a sense quite different from the conventional notion of crystallized passivity, of acting or thinking almost reflexively, without reflection. It would perhaps have been helpful to discuss this idea in terms of the Aristotelian concept of *hexis* (disposition)—in terms, that is, of a state or a way of being that generates thought and action—especially because *hexis* is a concept that implies a distinct ethical, or value, orientation. All the same, I stick with pragmatist practice and talk about the habit of thought (and action and character) that constitutes an ethos. It was Aquinas who developed the Aristotelian concept of *hexis,* though Pierre Bourdieu's version reigns in contemporary thought.

6. There was a boom in Italian food (*Itameshi*) in the 1990s, and it led many aspiring chefs to train in Italy; see Ikawa Naoko, *Itaria ni itte kokku ni naru* (Tokyo: Shibata Shoten, 2003), 3.

7. Such a superstar is usually called a *ningen kokuhō* (human national treasure), though the official term is *jūyō mukei bunkazai* (important intangible cultural property).

8. Artisans can be a disputatious lot, however, and their almost inevitable disagreements should not be glossed over. For every point that was authoritatively stated and widely accepted, at least one other strongly contradicted it. For example, a master of *urushi* (lacquerware) told me, "It really doesn't matter how much you practice a craft if you don't have talent." He added, "It's more important for you to like what you're doing. You get better at what you're doing because you like what you're doing." An artisan could be born, he allowed, or he could become one almost overnight. But even for an artisan like that, mastery would remain "far away, and probably impossible to reach."

9. The Buddha—like other gurus, such as Socrates and Jesus—did not write his teachings down, nor did he permit his disciples to do so. It would be hard to reconstruct exactly what the Buddha said and did, since for four centuries his disciples obeyed his proscription against literary transmission, though it's only fair to add that the idea of exact reconstruction by way of writing is oxymoronic.

10. Thorstein Veblen, *The Instinct of Workmanship* (1914; reprinted, New York: W. W. Norton, 1964), 27–32, 235.

11. On the middle voice, see Émile Benveniste, *Problèmes de linguistique générale,* vol. 1 (Paris: Gallimard, 1976), 164–66.

12. In yet another paradox, artisans' explicit adherence to tradition contributes to the persistence of diversity. Convergences may result from an individual artisan's improvements, or they may be prompted by customers' changing tastes, but artisans follow different if not quite parallel paths because each artisan or group of artisans works from a particular

tradition, a tradition that the individual artisan or the group seeks to continue (and possibly advance). In other words, artisans mimic and emulate, but they don't bring about convergence and homogeneity.

13. Muramatsu Teijirō, *Dōgu to teshigoto* (Tokyo: Iwanami Shoten, 2014), 2–6.

14. Zeami, "Kakyō" (early fourteenth century), in *Zeami geijutsuron shū*, ed. Tanaka Hiroshi (Tokyo: Shinchōsha, 1976), 159.

15. Bandō Satoshi, *Shokunin to shimin shakai* (Osaka: Rōdō Chōsa Kenkyūjo, 1979), 113.

16. Otto Friedrich Bollnow, *Vom Geist des Übens* (Freiburg: Herder, 1978).

17. The term *shin'i* comes from classical Chinese aesthetics; Andō Masanobu, *Docchitsukazu no monotsukuri* (Tokyo: Kawade Shobō Shinsha, 2018), 52–54.

18. In the words of a poet writing in a completely different context, and from a different culture, "It is craft, after all, that carries an individual's ideas to the far edge of familiar territory"; see Mary Oliver, *A Poetry Handbook* (New York: Houghton Mifflin, 1994), 2.

19. Zeami, "Fūshikaden" (early fourteenth century), in *Zeami geijutsuron shū*, 11–98.

20. Zeami, "Fūshikaden," 76–77.

21. Zeami, "Fūshikaden," 57.

22. Zeami, "Fūshikaden," 18, 53, 84, 91.

23. See Hachimonjiya Jishō, *Kokin yakusha taizen* (1750), http://dl.ndl.go.jp/info:ndljp /pid/2533801.

24. Tim Hayward, *Knife* (London: Quadrille, 2016), 117–24.

25. It is important to distinguish between the modernist concept of art and the craft-based concept of artisanship. In the modern West (and it's no different in the contemporary Japanese art world), the ultimate task of the artist is to push the proverbial envelope—to achieve innovation and invention. An artist may emulate her predecessors, but there is never any question about where she finds her greatest rewards in terms of fame, money, or even self-satisfaction. The art world is deeply enmeshed in the world of money and power, but *l'art pour l'art*—art for art's sake, or artistic autonomy—remains a benchmark assumption. This mind-set is far from that of the artisan. For an artisan, innovation may come about from the effort to master and improve on traditional techniques. (There is something Platonic about many artisans' ideal of where they are heading; that is, their goal is perfection, which doesn't quite seem to belong in the real world.) But the goal is mastery, not innovation. In the world of the artisanal ethos, there's no point in seeking innovation for the sake of innovation; innovation emerges only from mastery. What is just as significant, moreover, the complex web of relations that sustains artisanal work is explicitly acknowledged as part of this mode of work. One art critic and philosopher has articulated the distinction between art and craft as follows: "Art is more beautiful the closer it comes to its ideal; craft is more beautiful the more it interacts with reality"; see Yanagi Muneyoshi, "Kōgei no michi" (1934), in *Yanagi Muneyoshi zenshū*, vol. 8 (Tokyo: Chikuma Shobō, 1980), 78. Here, Yanagi can be contrasted with Immanuel Kant, who influentially argues that beauty, which stems from the power of judgment, evokes pleasure, has universal validity, is purposive without purpose, and is necessary. To summarize this contrast briefly, Kant suggests that, in principle, the human faculty of judgment should arrive at a universal and necessary conclusion about the beauty of an object, which gives pleasure but is without explicit purpose; by contrast, Yanagi suggests that in craft, the beauty of the object is tied up with its explicit purpose. A teacup, for instance, is not just an object of admiration but

realizes itself in its use. Its purpose *is* to be used. Thus the notion of absolute art or universal beauty is foreign to the world of craft.

26. Interaction with a craft's raw materials can elicit synesthesia. A woodworker, for example, conflates the optic and the haptic, saying that his sense of touch allows him to see pieces of wood.

27. Koyama Hirohisa, *Aji no kaze* (Tokyo: Shibata Shoten, 1992), 195.

28. Nakajima Atsushi, "Meijinden" (1942), *Nakajima Atsushi zenshū*, vol. 1 (Tokyo: Chikuma Shobō, 2001).

29. Shirase Masako, *Nihon no takumi* (Tokyo: Shinchōsha, 1981), 24.

30. Mihalyi Cziksentmihalyi, *Flow* (New York: Harper Collins, 1991).

31. Kukkubizu, ed., *Ichiryū no honshitsu* (Tokyo: Daiwa Shobō, 2017), 260.

32. Aristotle, *Nicomachean Ethics*, 10–12.

33. Keats, writing to his brother in 1817, described negative capability as the capacity to be "in uncertainties, mysteries, doubts, without any irritable reaching after fact and reason"; see John Keats, *The Complete Poetical Works and Letters of John Keats*, ed. Horace Elisha Scudder (Boston: Houghton Mifflin, 1899), 277.

34. Henry James, "The Middle Years" (1893), in *Compete Stories, 1892–1898* (New York: Library of America, 1996), 354.

35. George Sturt, in his classic work *The Wheelwright's Shop* (Cambridge: Cambridge University Press, 1923), 197–203, notes the added benefits of laughter and camaraderie, which he compares favorably to the mandates of efficiency and prices under the regime of scientific management.

36. Yamada, *Ginza no sushi*, 17, 59.

37. Kitaōji Rosanjin, "Nigirizushi no meijin," *Doppo*, 1952, n.p. *Doppo* was a periodical.

38. Andō, *Docchitsukazu no monotsukuri*, 36; earlier, Andō discusses the salience, among traditional potters, of an inferiority complex vis-à-vis the West (7).

39. Hasegawa Nyozekan, *Nihon samazama* (Tokyo: Daihōrinkaku, 1962), 33–34, 37, 229–30.

40. Hasegawa Nyozekan, *Hasegawa Nyozekan shū*, 8 vols. (Tokyo: Iwanami Shoten, 1989–90).

41. See Nakae Katsumi, *Edo no shokunin* (Tokyo: Tairyūsha, 1986); and Nakamura Yūkō, *Gendai no takumi* (Tokyo: Kadokawa Shoten, 1986).

42. National Association of Trade Promotion for Small and Medium Enterprises, *2017 White Paper on Small Enterprises in Japan: Conveying the Buds of Growth to the Next Generation* (Tokyo: Ministry of Trade, Economy, and Industry, 2017), figs. 1-1-5 and 1-2-1, http://www.chusho.meti.go.jp/pamflet/hakusyo/H29/PDF/2017shohaku_eng.pdf.

43. *Keizai hakusho* (Tokyo: Keizai Kikakuchō, 1957), http://www5.cao.go.jp/keizai3/keizaiwp/wp-je57/wp-je57-010402.html.

44. Representative in this respect is the 1892 Erfurt Program; see Karl Kautsky, *Das Erfurter Programm in seinem grundsätzlichen Teil erläutert* (1892), archived at Marxists' Internet Archive, https://www.marxists.org/deutsch/archiv/kautsky/1892/erfurter/1-untergang.htm. Kautsky, its chief author, titles the first chapter "Der Untergang des Kleinbetriebs" (The decline of small producers).

45. Clark Kerr, John T. Dunlop, Frederick H. Harbison, and Charles A. Myers, *Industrialism and Industrial Man* (Cambridge, MA: Harvard University Press, 1960), 39.

46. As A. V. Chayanov observed of peasant labor, self-exploitation can arise from the fact that for a peasant working alone, more work means greater yields; see Chayanov, *The Theory of the Peasant Economy*, ed. Daniel Thorner, Basile Kerblay, and R. E. F. Smith (1966; reprinted, Madison: University of Wisconsin Press, 1986), 85. In contrast, a peasant working for someone else tends not to work as hard, because the extra effort is unlikely to offer any additional benefit.

47. This fact is yet another example of how so-called women's work, once valorized and professionalized, becomes a stronghold of male domination.

48. Eric Ripert, chef at Le Bernardin, did not appear out of the blue. As early as 1924, the French government established an award to honor artisans, "Un des meilleurs ouvriers de France" (One of France's best workers); the Japanese equivalent was not established until 1950. See Meilleurs Ouvriers de France, *Annuaire des Meilleurs Ouvriers de France*, http://meilleursouvriersdefrance.pro/.

49. Laure Gasparotto, *Les vins de Laure* (Paris: Grasset, 2009), 52–57.

50. Josef Kulischer, *Allgemeine Wirtschaftsgeschichte des Mittelalters und der Neuzeit*, vol. 1 (Munich: R. Oldenbourg, 1928), part 2, chap. 2.

51. W. J. Rohrabaugh, *The Craft Apprentice* (New York: Oxford University Press, 1986), 202–9.

52. See the documentary film *Jiro Dreams of Sushi*, directed by David Gelb (2011). See also *Kill Bill: Volume 1* (2003) and *Kill Bill: Volume 2* (2004), directed by Quentin Tarantino; both were inspired by the Japanese film *Shūra yukihime*, directed by Fujita Toshiya (1973), and both manifest fascination with Japanese swords and sword making.

53. Thomas C. Smith, *Native Sources of Japanese Industrialization, 1750–1920* (Berkeley: University of California Press, 1988), 45–46, 97–98.

54. Odaka Kōnosuke, *Shokunin no sekai, kōjō no sekai*, rev. ed. (Tokyo: NTT Shuppan, 2000), esp. chaps. 4–5.

55. It is precisely their size that gives many smaller manufacturers the flexibility to meet the shifting demands of the marketplace and the changing dictates of the larger corporations that they supply. On the significance of flexible production, see David Friedman, *The Misunderstood Miracle* (Ithaca, NY: Cornell University Press, 1988), 211–17.

56. One of the three Nobel laureates, a Japanese-born American named Shuji Nakamura, sued Nichia and eventually won the equivalent of about nine million US dollars in compensation for what he claimed had been an insufficient bonus for his indispensable contributions to the blue LED's invention; see Nakamura Shūji, *Ikari no bureikusurū* (Tokyo: Hōmusha, 2001). It seems unlikely, however, that Nakamura's colleagues did not contribute small innovations that led to the ultimate breakthrough.

57. Tanaka Kōichi, *Shōgai saikō no shippai* (Tokyo: Asahi Shinbunsha, 2003), chap. 1.

58. For one articulation of this possibility, see Michael Herzfeld, *The Body Impolitic* (Chicago: University of Chicago Press, 2004), 204–10.

59. One highly successful and extremely prolific manga artist, Satō Shūhō, works with five assistants twelve hours a day, six days a week, and sometimes puts off sleep for several days; see Satō Shūhō, *Manga binbō* (Tokyo: PHP Kenkyūjo, 2012), 74–75. More disturbingly, according to Satō, the entire manga industry would "instantaneously collapse" (73) if the authorities were to enforce the prevailing laws regarding minimum wage and maximum work hours. Satō estimates the annual mean income of manga artists who have published a

book (a population of a little more than five thousand) at roughly the equivalent of twenty-eight thousand US dollars, with apprentices earning on average less than they would from part-time work at a convenience store (76–77).

60. Uratani Toshirō, *"Mononokehime" wa kōshite umareta* (Tokyo: Tokuma Shoten, 1998), 152–58.

61. Nakano Haruyuki, *Manga sangyōron* (Tokyo: Chikuma Shobō, 2008), 4–5, 96–100.

62. Originally, Tajiri had intended to assemble a collection of 150 pocket monsters to complete his video game. Thanks to the game's worldwide popularity, however, by 2018 the total number of pocket monsters had grown to more than eight hundred. On Tajiri himself, see Miyamasa Tarō and Tajiri Satoshi, *Tajiri Satoshi* (Tokyo: Ōta Shuppan, 2004).

63. Anne Allison, *Millennial Monsters: Japanese Toys and the Global Imagination* (Berkeley: University of California Press, 2006), 197–203.

64. Although Salaryman is a Japanese character type, one that dominated the postwar period, it would be a mistake to exaggerate this figure's particular and peculiar Japanese provenance. Wherever bureaucracy thrives, there emerges Salaryman. Imperial and Weimar Germany may hold the dubious distinction of having produced, in *die Angestellten* (salaried employees), the prototype of the Japanese office worker; see Emil Lederer, *Die Privatangestellten in der modernen Wirtschaftsentwicklung* (Tübingen: J. C. B. Mohr, 1912), and Siegried Kracauer, "Die Angestellten: Aus dem neuesten Deutschland" (1930), in *Werke*, vol. 1 (Frankfurt am Main: Suhrkamp, 2006), 211–320. This should not be surprising, given the precocious development of large-scale organizations in a late-developing country that, not coincidentally, also produced pioneering sociological analyses. The post–World War II United States never produced a singular term or character type to match Japan's postwar Salaryman, but a family resemblance is seen in such kindred spirits as the US white-collar worker and organization man. Sloan Wilson, in *The Man in the Gray Flannel Suit* (New York: Simon & Schuster, 1955), captures the empty conformity of organizational life, including the protagonist's suburban home with its full-time homemaker.

65. The emergence of office workers is coeval with the modernization of Japan, and the pervasive character of bureaucratic work is a postwar phenomenon, the flip side of the rapid decline in farmwork. It may appear that the primary function of office ladies in postwar Japanese companies was to pour tea, but in fact they did yeoman's work (pardon the masculinist language) and suffered sexual harassment as well as other imposed rituals of inferiority. In the postwar period, female office workers were often expected to resign after marriage or childbirth, sometimes as a matter of company rules, until the 1985 institution of nominal gender equality in employment. This truncated term of employment, along with women's inferior starting position, rendered all women inferior to almost all men in many postwar companies. According to Mary C. Brinton, in *Women and the Economic Miracle* (Berkeley: University of California Press, 1993), the Japanese economy demonstrates the compatibility between high levels of female participation in the labor force and highly sex-segregated roles, though this generalization is more apt with respect to the modernist mode of work.

66. As good a place as any to look for the privileged life of the office worker of the 1950s is Yamaguchi Hitomi, *Eburimanshi no yūga na seikatsu* (Tokyo: Bungei Shunjūshinsha, 1962).

67. The phenomenon of the housewife (*shufu*) is part and parcel of Japanese modernization; see Muta Kazue, *Senryaku to shite no kazoku* (Tokyo: Shin'yōsha, 1996). For the same

reasons underlying the propagation of the office worker—the decline of the primary sector and the rise of the tertiary sector in the postwar period—the massive "housewifing" of Japan was a postwar product.

68. Amy Borovoy, *The Too-Good Wife* (Berkeley: University of California Press, 2005), esp. chaps. 2–3.

69. According to Sengoku Tamotsu, in *Hikaku sararīmanron* (Tokyo: Tōyō Keizai Shinpōsha, 1977), 259–61, the Harvard sociologist Talcott Parsons resisted the idea that an examination should shape one's life chances, as seemed to be the case in Japan; thus Sengoku points to the particular and peculiar character of the Japanese school-to-work transition.

70. Kikai Shinkō Kyōkai Keizai Kenkyūjo, *Howaitokarā no nenrei to hataraku ishiki ni kansuru chōsa kenkyū* (Tokyo: Kikai Shinkō Kyōkai Keizai Kenkyūjo, 1979), 56.

71. The solidarity of the small group is crucial to the workings of a large-scale organization, whether the organization in question is the prewar military or the postwar corporation. The near universal act of complaining—letting off steam—engages the valve that releases built-up pressure from particular situations and contexts. Thus the Japanese office worker turned restaurants, bars, and nightclubs into places of respite and relaxation. The dark side of this custom was that the sexism of the workplace was carried into the water trade (that is, also into the sex industry, which became ubiquitous in postwar Japan), in which women comforted the corporate warriors, psychically or somatically.

72. The absurdity of military life, a major motif of postwar Japanese literature, led to such masterpieces as Noma Hideo, *Shinkū chitai* (Tokyo: Kawade Shobō, 1952); and Ōnishi Kyojin, *Shinsei kigeki*, 5 vols. (Tokyo: Kōbunsha, 1978–80). And the last six years or so of the Pacific War, which brought food insecurity and ideological indoctrination, militarist authoritarianism and the elimination of all fun and humor, should not be underestimated as the backdrop of the office worker's existence. To his elders—the generation that not only suffered material deprivation but also had to face the prospect of charging into American fire or being coerced into individual or collective suicide—the office worker's life seemed vastly superior.

73. In this way, the prevalence of office workers—organizational men and women—in all other industrial societies was ignored; for an example of the claim that the West was completely devoid of any concept of the office worker, see Nihon Keizai Shinbunsha, ed., *Dokyumento sararīman* (Tokyo: Nihon Keizai Shinbunsha, 1981), 219.

74. See Genji Keita, *Hōpu-san* (Tokyo: Bungei Shunjūshinsha, 1951); and Genji Keita, *Santō jūyaku* (Tokyo: Mainichi Shinbusha, 1951).

75. Sekikawa Natsuo, *Ojisan wa naze jidai shōsetsu ga sukika* (Tokyo: Iwanami Shoten, 2006), 10–11.

76. The eponymous protagonist of the novel—which spoke to the newfound enthusiasm for peace, stability, and prosperity—unifies Japan after the bloody civil wars; the novel became a best seller in both South Korea and China and is a perennial contender for the title of longest novel in the world. See Yamaoka Sōhachi, *Tokugawa Ieyasu*, 26 vols. (Tokyo: Kōdansha, 1953–67). As for the Japanese office worker's US counterparts, they too had to endure intraorganizational struggles, irascible and irrational superiors, mindless and meaningless work, long commutes (with traffic jams), and, at home, unhappy wives and unruly children, all the while under orders to revel in the blessings of peace and affluence; Salaryman by any other name emitted the same bittersweet scent. The Americans didn't

read many samurai novels, with the exception of James Clavell, *Shogun* (New York: Dela-corte Press, 1975), whose Japanese protagonist, Yoshi Toranaga, was modeled on Tokugawa Ieyasu himself, and which reportedly sold fifteen million copies. At more than a thousand pages, this doorstop of a book may have been for its impatient American readers the same kind of marathon that Yamaoka's volume was for its Japanese audience.

77. To get a sense of Peter Drucker's fame and influence, consider the unlikely best-selling novel by Iwasaki Natsumi, *Moshi kōkō yakyū no joshi manejā ga Drucker no 'manējimento' wo yondara* (Tokyo: Daiyamondosha, 2009), in which a high school girl becomes the manager of her school's baseball team and—after reading Peter Drucker, *Management* (New York: Harper Business, 1993)—leads the team to a national championship.

78. Perhaps the most celebrated incarnation of the contemporary Japanese office worker is Shima Kōsaku, a manga protagonist who first appeared in 1983 and is still going strong. A self-identified baby boomer, Shima personifies the postwar fantasy of the organization man. As a middle manager, he leads the life of a Lothario but also becomes intimately involved in many challenging projects and negotiations. Shima bucks his company's traditional way of doing things, and he resists the firm's clique-based internal politics—that is, Shima is a principled individualist. Against all odds, he manages to ascend the corporate hierarchy, and he marries the younger, beautiful (though illegitimate) daughter of the company's charismatic founder. Shima lives a charmed life that would make any cardboard hero wince with embarrassment.

79. In the words of 1997's most popular poem about the Japanese office worker, "In our house / Pokémon for children / Papa unwanted"; see *Asahi Shinbun,* 23 May 2019.

80. Kōno Taeko, "Kani" (1963), in *Kōno Taeko zenshū,* vol. 1 (Tokyo: Shinchōsha, 1994), 171–93; Ōba Minako, "Sanpiki no kani" (1968), in *Ōba Minako zenshū,* vol. 1 (Tokyo: Nihon Keizai Shinbunsha, 2009), 9–250.

81. Suzanne Hall Vogel, with Steven K. Vogel, *The Japanese Family in Transition* (Lan-ham, MD: Rowman & Littlefield, 2013), chaps. 1, 5. The formal, Western-inspired women's movement was exerting its influence, too, and this included the importation and implanta-tion of ideas about gender equality. As one result, by the twenty-first century the ideal of *ikemen* (handsome men) was being supplanted by that of *ikumen* (men who participate in child-rearing). Everything was being questioned now, from heteronormativity to economic advancement and upward social mobility, and a variety of nontraditional families and households began to come into being. Marriage rates were down as well, and divorce rates were up. Nevertheless, more people sought refuge in the family even as it was collapsing. In 1958, for example, only 12 percent of people who were asked to name the most important thing in life mentioned the family, but that figure had increased to 44 percent by 2013; see Tōkei Sūri Kenkyūjo, "Nihonjin no kokuminsei chōsa," Institute of Statistical Mathematics, https://www.ism.ac.jp/kokuminsei/page2/page15/index.html.

82. You work hard, you suffer, you die—such is the life of Salaryman. No wonder, then, that the end of the Bubble decade saw the emergence of *shinjinrui* (new human beings) and *furītā* (the underemployed young people described in earlier chapters), who at first were described as free from the drudgery of commuting and from the boredom of full-time employment. *Furītā,* Salaryman's antithetical children, are engorged by and inured to the affluence of Japan's postwar economic growth.

83. In 2019, when Japanese adults were asked to name the occupations they would pursue if they could be reborn, they most often said they would choose to be researchers or professors, doctors, novelists, and *shokunin*; see *Asahi Shinbun*, 26 January 2019. A common feature of almost all their responses is that they point to challenging or interesting jobs that afford a degree of autonomy. Very few of the respondents appeared to be primarily interested in money or fame; their stated motivations were to be able to pursue a particular interest or to help other people. Three months later, children in the first grade were asked to name their own preferred occupations, and most of them, like the adults, did not report that they aspired to become office workers, though many did mention work that involved being a *shokunin*. Among the girls, the most desired occupation was pâtissier; see *Tokyo Shinbun*, 4 April 2019.

84. According to Peter Gaskell, in *Artisans and Machinery* (London: J. W. Parker, 1836), "It is . . . the great aim of machinery to make skill or strength on the part of the workman valueless, and to reduce him to a mere waiter of, and [to being] waited upon [by], *automata*" (357).

85. Even in the realm of food production, however, it would be churlish to ignore the role that mass-produced industrial food has played in alleviating hunger. If one has grown up eating sliced bread (Wonder Bread, no less, a standardized product widely available at very low cost) or the noncheese cheese known as Velveeta, one may be grateful for having had access to cheap calories. Then again, one may be disturbed by the existence of such unnatural, unnourishing foods. The consensus seems to be that craft-based food production is superior, especially since it has incorporated scientific and technological advances without jettisoning the embodied tradition of the skills and knowledge that enter into agricultural production, whether the ultimate product is wine or milk, cheese or charcuterie.

86. Yanagi Muneyoshi, "Sakubutsu no kōhansei" (1932), in *Cha to bi* (Tokyo: Kōdansha, 2000), 76–93.

87. John Ruskin, "Unto This Last" (1860), in E. T. Cook and Alexander Wedderburn, eds., *The Complete Works of John Ruskin*, vol. 17 (London: George Allen, 1903), 112.

88. William Morris, "The Beauty of Life" (1880), in *The Collected Works of William Morris*, vol. 22 (London: Longmans Green, 1914), 58.

CHAPTER 7. THE BOOK OF BATHING

1. The notion of the morning shower—or, more accurately, "morning shampoo"—emerged in the 1980s; see Ishikawa Yasuhiro, *Ofuro no tatsujin* (Tokyo: Sōshisha, 2011), 4.

2. Isabella L. Bird, *Unbeaten Tracks in Japan* (1881; reprinted, London: John Murray, 1911), 417.

3. Yamazaki Mari, *Bōen Nippon kenbunroku* (Tokyo: Gentōsha, 2012), 223.

4. See Wendy Maltz and Larry Maltz, *The Porn Trap* (New York: Harper, 2008), chap. 4.

5. It should be noted, however, that many young Americans also bathe (that is, shower) communally, as in locker rooms.

6. For some examples of bathhouse rules, see Kasahara Itsuo, *E de miru Nippon sentō bunka* (Tokyo: Ribun Shuppan, 2016), 104.

7. For visual examples, see Machida Shinobu, *Sentō isan* (Tokyo: Ebisu Kosho, 2008); and NHK "Bi no tsubo" Seisakuhan, *Sentō* (Tokyo: Nihon Hōsō Kyōkai Shuppan, 2009). For

regional variations, see, especially, Machida Shinobu, *Sentō* (Kyoto: Mineruva Shobō, 2016), chap. 2.

8. In my comparative investigation of bathhouses in the United States, the United Kingdom, France, Germany, New Zealand, Taiwan, China, and several other countries, Japanese bathers stood out for their practice of thorough cleansing. Until recently, urban South Koreans probably surpassed the Japanese in scrubbing scum off the body. The norm, usually enforced by a professional scrubber, was to rub the body with a towel until the skin reddened. Yet the recent turn to the shower instead of the bath, especially among young people, has reduced the practice of vigorous cleansing in South Korea. For a glimpse into the norm of vigorous washing in Japan, see Aori Michiyo, *Onnayu ni ukande mireba* (Tokyo: Shinjuku Shobō, 2009), 17–19, 46–48.

9. Paid help, almost invariably called *sansuke,* was available in the heyday of *sentō* (that is, in the immediate postwar decades, and earlier).

10. This figure derives from my informal survey. Reliable survey figures are for the entire time spent bathing, and they are not disaggregated. According to a 2008 government survey, the average time for men was twenty-eight minutes, and for women it was thirty-five minutes; see "Basic Survey on Social Life," *e-Stat,* 2016, https://www.e-stat.go.jp/stat-search/files?page=1&layout=datalist&toukei=00200533&tstat=000001095335&cycle=0&tclass1=000001095377&tclass2=000001095393&tclass3=000001095394&stat_infid=000031617880&second2=1. Another survey, less extensive but more recent, suggests that the mode falls roughly in the range of twenty to thirty minutes; see "Ichijikanijō ga niwarijaku," *Mainabi,* 25 February 2015, https://gakumado.mynavi.jp/freshers/articles/13766. There is broad consensus, based on informal surveys as well as on casual conversations, that bathing time has declined in the past decade; see "Nihon zaijū gaikokujin no nyūyoku ni kansuru jittai," *PR Times,* 25 September 2017, https://prtimes.jp/main/html/rd/p/000000643.000009276.html.

11. *Tokyo Shinbun,* 5 March 2019.

12. Maeda Kyōko, *Ofuro no tanoshimi* (Tokyo: Asuka Shinsha, 1999), 1.

13. Yamazaki Mari, *Thermae Romae,* 6 vols. (Tokyo: Enterbrain, 2008–13).

14. For an accessible overview, see Dominique Laty, *Histoire des bains* (Paris: Presses Universitaires de France, 1996).

15. Luis Frois, S. J., *The First European Description of Japan, 1585,* ed. and trans. Richard K. Danford, Robin D. Gill, and Daniel T. Reff (London: Routledge, 2014), 50, 73, 214. A typical comment is from Charles MacFarlane, in *Japan* (Hartford: Silar Andrus, 1856): "All classes of [the Japanese] make a very frequent use of the bath" (290).

16. One survey from 2011 puts the average water temperature at 41 degrees Celsius (105.8 degrees Fahrenheit); see "How to Take a Bath: Ranking by Prefecture," *Senior Guide,* 13 November 2018, https://seniorguide.jp/article/1152717.html. Mixed-gender bathing notwithstanding, the high water temperature is probably the feature of Japanese bathing practices that is most commonly mentioned by more coolheaded observers. See Vladimír Křížek, *Kulturgeschichte des Heilbades* (Leipzig: Edition Leipzig, 1990); and Alev Lytle, *Taking the Waters* (New York: Abbeville Press, 1992); in Japanese, see Nishikawa Yoshitaka, *Onsen genshi* (Kyoto: Jinbuin Shoin, 1943), 79–84.

17. Pierre Loti, *Japoneries d'automne* (Paris: Calmann Lévy, 1889), 113.

18. Pierre Loti, *Madame Chrysanthème* (Paris: Calmann Lévy, 1888), 235.

19. Commodore M. C. Perry, *The Expedition of an American Squadron to the China Seas and Japan*, ed. Francis L. Hawks, 3 vols. (Washington, DC: A. O. P. Nicholson, 1856), 1:404.

20. For examples of pictorial depictions of bathing during the Tokugawa period, see, Hanasaki Kazuo and Machida Shinobu, *"Nyūyoku" hadaka no fūzokushi* (Tokyo: Kōdansha, 1993); and Kogure Kindayū, *Nishikie ni miru Nihon no onsen* (Tokyo: Kokusho Kankōkan, 2003).

21. Nakagiri Kakutarō, preface to Mizuno Hōsō, *Furo no bishō* (Tokyo: Hirano Shobō, 1934), 1.

22. Peter Brown, *The Body and Society* (New York: Columbia University Press, 1988).

23. Katherine Ashenburg, *The Dirt on Clean: An Unsanitized History* (New York: North Point Press, 2008), chap. 4.

24. Julia Csergo, *Liberté, égalité, propreté* (Paris: Albin Michel, 1988), part 4, chap. 1.

25. The renowned Ritz Hotel in Paris made news in 1906 by adding a bathroom to every guest room. Even in the late twentieth century, however, it was common enough for an Englishman to boast about his infrequent bathing. An Oxonian quip from a generation ago was "I take a bath once a year, whether I need it or not." Similarly, the Japanese author of an influential eighteenth-century guide to healthy living advised bathing once every ten days, and then only in a very small amount of lukewarm water in a deep tub; see Kaibara Ekken, "Yōjōkun" (1712), in, Ishikawa Ken, ed., *Yōjōkun, wazokudōjikun* (Tokyo: Iwanami Shoten, 1961), 9–191, 111–12. Kaibara offers many other sensible pieces of advice, such as not to eat or drink too much, but three centuries later his advice is ignored by Japanese people, especially during an *onsen* vacation.

26. Miura Jōshin, *Keichō kenmonshū* (1614), ed. Nakamaru Kazunori (Tokyo: Shinjinbutsuōraisha, 1969), 161. Given that this volume contains observations about a much later period, the effective publication date must have been much later. Some of the information in *Keichō kenmonshū* is repeated almost verbatim in Miura Jōshin, "Sozoro monogatari" (1641), in *Kinsei fūzoku kenmonshū*, vol. 1 (Tokyo: Kokusho Kankōkai, 1912), esp. 12–13.

27. Santō Kyōden, "Kenguirikomi sentō shinwa" (1802), in Santō Kyōden Henshūiinkai, ed., *Santō Kyōden zenshū*, vol. 4 (Tokyo: Perikansha, 2004), 512–13. Santō's tale is a work of comic fiction, but his descriptions don't stray far from *yuya* life in the early nineteenth century. See also the later illustration in Hasegawa Keiki, *Edo Tokyo jikken garoku* (1848–72; reprinted, Tokyo: Iwanami Shoten, 2014), 204–5.

28. See the description in Miura, "Sozoro monogatari," esp. 13.

29. Hanasaki Kazuo, *Edo nyūyoku hyakushi*, expanded ed. (Tokyo: Miki Shobō, 2004; 1st ed., 1978), 43–112.

30. Miura, *Keichō kenmonshū*, 161.

31. Hanasaki, *Edo nyūyoku hyakushi*, 24–25.

32. See the description in Sanshōtei Karaku, *Edo jiman* (Tokyo: Yamaguchiya Tōbei, 1823), n.p.

33. See Nakano Eizō, *Nyūyoku, sentō no rekishi* (1970; reprinted, Tokyo: Yūzankaku, 1984), 86–105. Miura, in "Sozoro monogatari," 13, observes that eight or nine out of ten men could not tear themselves away from the *kōshoku*, a word that can be a euphemism for *yūjo* (sex workers).

34. Watanabe Shin'ichirō, *Onnatachi no yuami* (Tokyo: Shinchōsha, 1996), 12. Or, in the words of a renowned scholar of bathing, the Edo bathhouse was a place of *ianjo* (comfort);

see Fujinami Gōichi, *Tōzai mokuyokushi*, expanded ed. (Kyoto: Jinbun Shoin, 1944; 1st ed., 1931), 182–87.

35. After the invention of the *suefuro* (water bath) in the early eighteenth century, it became possible and affordable, at least in principle, to have a small bathtub in a private residence. But even affluent people tended not to own a bathtub; a wood fire was needed to heat the water, and there was general fear of fire. (If the flower of Edo was fireworks, its flower of evil was fire.) Moreover, the cost of land and kindling was prohibitive.

36. Nevertheless, the samurai class was officially proscribed from frequenting the plebeian *sentō*; the Tokugawa *bakufu* (military government) issued an ordinance against bathing by samurai in 1600, after a fight broke out. See Aoki Michio, *Fukayomi ukiyoburo* (Tokyo: Shōgakkan, 2003), 33–35; and Tozawa Yukio, *Edo chōnin no seikatsu kūkan* (Tokyo: Hanuka Shobō, 2013), 112–15.

37. As Habermas argues, the coffeehouse provided space for the open discussion that formed public opinion, and, as such, it constituted a powerful underpinning of the public sphere; see Jürgen Habermas, *Strukturwandel der Öffentlichkeit* (Neuwied: Luchterhand, 1962), chap. 2.

38. For Konno Nobuo, the origin of Japanese uniqueness is the Edo public bathhouse, in its promotion of equality among naked people; Konno, *Edo no furo* (Tokyo: Shinchōsha, 1989), 4.

39. Bird, *Unbeaten Tracks in Japan*, 205.

40. Shikitei Sanba, "Ukiyoburo" (1809–13), in Jinbō Kazuya, ed., *Shin Nihon kotenbugaku taikei*, vol. 86 (Tokyo: Iwanami Shoten, 1989), 4.

41. It would be a mistake, however, to assume that Edoites in the early eighteenth century were just like contemporary Japanese people in their bathing habits, or that Westerners' reports from that era can be accepted uncritically. Moreover, twenty-first-century Tokyoites would find their ancestors of two centuries ago uncouth because of their loud talking, their comparatively infrequent bathing, and their way of washing their clothes; see Santō, "Kenguirikomi sentō shinwa," 516–17.

42. Shikitei, "Ukiyoburo," 5.

43. Both in the West and in Japan, the invention of the bathroom was a twentieth-century achievement. Only the gaze back from the present—a time when bathing is a fixed element in the firmament of Japaneseness—leads to the assumption that bathing in the past was the same as bathing today. It is true, however, that the rudimentary features of contemporary Japanese bathing practices took definite form during the Tokugawa period. The fact that a handbook on public bathhouses was published during that period suggests both the prevalence and the importance of bathhouses at that time; see Kōkaitei Tōrin, *Sentō tebikigusa* (1851; place of publication and name of publisher unknown). Nevertheless, by 1814, when Edo had become more affluent, and when considerable improvements had been made to Edo's bathhouses, there were still only 600 *sentō* for Edo's 1,700 towns; see Ogawa Akimichi, "Chirizukadan" (1814), in Iwamoto Sashichi, ed., *Enseki jisshu*, vol. 1 (Tokyo: Kokusho Kankōkai, 1907), 272. This fact also suggests that until the twentieth century the vast majority of Japanese people did not bathe as frequently as Western observers and contemporary Japanese thought was the case, and they certainly did not bathe on a daily basis. Even in 1973 in Tokyo, when *sentō* were still a major presence in everyday life, there were 2,588 bathhouses, with an average of 530 clients per day, which meant nearly 1.4 million

people served on a daily basis, but this was in a city of what was then a population of more than 11 million; see Tokyo-to Seikatsu Bunkakyoku, *Tokyo-to kōshū yokujō kiso shiryō* (Tokyo: Tokyo-to Seikatsu Bunkakyoku, 1997), 3. Moreover, around the turn of the twenty-first century, one survey found that more than 75 percent of Japanese cities, towns, and villages were without a single public bath; see Shiraichi Tara, *Kyōdōburo* (Tokyo: Iwata Shoin, 2008), 20.

44. In any case, it would have been difficult for people to gaze at one another, because the bathing area was dark. Also, until the later Edo period, bathers wore underwear. As late as 1851, for example, men wore *fundoshi* (loincloths); see Kōkaitei, *Sentō tebikigusa*.

45. On the prevalence of mixed-gender bathing at hot springs, see Sekido Atsuko, *Kusatsu onsen no shakaishi* (Tokyo: Seikyūsha, 2018), 36–37.

46. The government's aim was not specifically to separate women and girls from men and boys but rather to regulate public morality and restrict the presence of the women who served as professional scrubbers and, often, as sex workers (a 1637 rule limited their number to three per bathhouse); see Nakano, *Nyūyoku, sentō no rekishi*, 89. It should be noted as well that male scrubbers also cleaned women.

47. Kōkaitei, *Sentō tebikigusa*. A constant nuisance for female bathers was the Peeping Tom, whose behavior is another indication of gender segregation and the absence of public nudity; see Watanabe, *Onnatachi no yuami*, 56–58.

48. Nudity was not as acute a source of shame in premodern Japan as in the Christian West, but it's also true that public nudity has not been celebrated, either in Japan's past or in the present. As one contemporary advocate of mixed-gender bathing says, "Precisely because this is a space in which men and women are naked together, it's important to be aware of manners and common sense"; see Yamazaki Mayumi, *Dakara kon'yoku wa yamerarenai* (Tokyo: Shinchōsha, 2008), 8.

49. At the time of this writing, according to Oguro Keita, in *Zekkei kon'yoku hikyō onsen* (Tokyo: Mediea sofuto, 2018), the number of *kon'yoku onsen* in Japan has fallen by 50 percent. Oguro cites two major reasons for the decline—the prevalence of bathers with bad manners, and intergenerational differences among *onsen* owners (126). In Germany, by contrast, a powerful culture of public nudity (*Nacktkultur*, or *Freikörperkultur*), initially inspired by a movement to reform the constrictions of civilized life (*Lebensreform*), has flourished since the late nineteenth century. By the early twentieth century, bathing in Germany had largely become the *Luftbad* (air bath), which also survives in the early twenty-first century but without its original ideological moorings or the earlier aversion to bathing in water. The unabashed display of the body in Berlin bathhouses, as compared with the normative concealment of the genitals in *kon'yoku onsen*, invites speculation on how mixed-gender bathing might have developed in contemporary Japan if the Westernizing Japanese leaders had heard more about the matter from the organicist Germans than from puritans like Commodore Perry. See Heinrich Puder, *Nackt-Kultur*, 3 vols. (Berlin: Heinrich Puder, 1906); and Michael Hau, *The Cult of Health and Beauty in Germany* (Chicago: University of Chicago Press, 2003), 10–13, 18–19.

50. Ishida Ryūzō, *Meiji hiwa* (Tokyo: Naigai Shuppansha, 1939), 191–204, esp. 202. There were three ranks of *sansuke—sotomawari, nakabataraki,* and *kamamae,* in order of ascending seniority—but, according to Ishida (196), the subtleties seem to have been lost on most bathers.

51. On the transformation in bathing technology and infrastructure, see Enatsu Hiroshi, *Ofuro kōgengaku* (Tokyo: TOTO Shuppan, 1997), chaps. 2–3.

52. Neotekunorojī, ed., *Hatsumei ni miru Nihon no seikatsu bunkashi sumai sirīzu*, vol. 2: *Furo* (Tokyo: Neotekunorojī, 2014), 5.

53. Statistics on public bathhouses are available from the Tokyo Metropolitan Government; see shouhiseikatsu.metro.tokyo.jp.

54. Tokyo-to Seikatsu Bunkakyoku, *Tokyo-to kōshū yokujō kiso shiryō*, 3.

55. Already by 1968 there was a private bathroom in 42 percent of Tokyo households, and by 1994 the proportion had reached 90 percent; refer again to the Tokyo Metropolitan Government figures: Tokyo-to Kōshūyokujō Kyōgitaisakukai,"Tonai no kōshūyokujō sū," https://www.metro.tokyo.lg.jp/tosei/hodohappyo/press/2020/08/24/documents/04_01.pdf. By 2020, it was de rigueur.

56. Tokyo-to Seikatsu Bunkakyoku, *Tokyo-to kōshū yokujō riyōsha ishiki chōsa kekka* (Tokyo: Tokyo-to Seikatsu Bunkakyoku, 1993), 7, 9.

57. The word *onsen* is said to have first appeared in the sixteenth century, though some claim a longer genealogy. In any case, *onsen* was anything but the prevailing name until three centuries later. Instead, the simple word *yu* (warm water) was the most common designation. In Meiji-era documents written by government officials or scientists, *kōsen* (mineral springs) was used, but *onsen* had become a popular term by the nineteenth century. See Nishikawa, *Onsen genshi*, 1–54.

58. According to Noguchi Etsuo, in *Nintei "onsen isan" Nihon no meiyu 100* (Tokyo: KK Besutoserāsu, 2007), *onsen* travel is "a delectable tour of the beautiful seasons of Japan" where hot water "melts away all stress and profane thoughts" and offers "a moment of *shifuku* [bliss]" (3).

59. Ishii Hiroko, in *Kandō no onsenyado 100* (Tokyo: Bungei Shunjūsha, 2018), offers a look at the seemingly limitless number of *onsen* guides. The most authoritative of the guides, by the self-styled Professor Onsen, observes that the Japanese "are rare in the world for having *onsen* as an everyday phenomenon"; see Matsuda Tadanori, *Onsen techō*, revised and expanded ed. (Tokyo: Tokyo Shoseki, 2017; 1st ed., 2012), 110. But the sum total of guidebooks easily represents a mere fraction of the available *onsen* magazines, which are often oversize publications featuring glossy photos; see, for example, the 2018 special issue of *Casa Brutus*. There are also at least two annual journals for *onsen* geeks: *Onsen hihyō*, which began publication in 2013, and *Onsen tatsujinkai*, which began in 2007.

60. At least these Japanese writers loved *onsen* enough to inspire a theory of *onsen* literature. See, for example, Kawamura Minato, *Onsen bungakuron* (Tokyo: Shinchōsha, 2007).

61. For example, in one old inn at Arima Onsen a room was devoted to memorabilia of Tanizaki Jun'ichirō. It included not only his publications but also his manuscripts and photos. The proprietor had even tried to align the inn's aesthetics with those advocated by Tanizaki in "In'ei raisan," an essay that encourages appreciation of the darkness that existed before the advent of electric lighting; see Junichiro Tanizaki, *In Praise of Shadows* (1939), trans. Gregory Starr (Yokosuka: Sora Books, 2017).

62. Suzuki Kazuo, *Edo no onsen zanmai* (Tokyo: Iwata Shoin, 2010), 24–25.

63. Křížek, *Kulturgeschichte des Heilbades. Onsen* offered a premodern version of medical tourism. The biomedical benefits of thermal water had already been presumed, but Gotō

Konzan and his students—scholars during the early Edo period—explicitly prescribed an *onsen* sojourn as a cure for many ailments. In 1738, Kagawa Shūtoku, Gotō's student, wrote the first text on thermal water as a cure. The water, he said, "improves the spirit, warms the body, removes the old blood, and improves blood circulation," among other physical and spiritual benefits; see Kagawa Shūtoku, *Ippondō yakusen*, vol. 4 (1738; place of publication and name of publisher unknown), n.p.

64. Likewise, some later pioneers of *onsen* literature wrote chronicles that are all about the wonders of travel—extraordinary sights and strange encounters that evoke a common plot of Noh plays. One might expect Ōhira Motoori's *Arima nikki* (Arima diary) to be all about Arima Onsen, but this eighteenth-century work is actually a tale of pilgrimage with descriptions of interesting people and events encountered on the road; see Ōhira Motoori, "Arima nikki" (1781), in Itasaka Yōko, ed., *Edo onsen kikō* (Tokyo: Heibonsha, 1987). These writings by Ōhira and others point to the growth of *onsen* tourism, but only with the writings of Sugae Masumi, who traveled across the Japanese archipelago from the late eighteenth century to the early nineteenth, do we encounter explicit attention to the characteristics of thermal water. Sugae's writings were not published, however, and so they did not have an immediate impact; see Ishikawa Rio, *Onsen no Nihonshi* (Tokyo: Chūō Kōronshinsha, 2018), 160–62.

65. Travel passes, issued for the purpose of visiting *onsen*, were usually granted on the basis of *tōji* (medical reasons). A list of physical and spiritual problems that might be ameliorated by *onsen* (and this was at a time when transportation and security had already improved markedly) can be found in Yasumi Roan, "Ryokō yōjinshū," in Imai Kingo, ed., *Dōchūki shūsei*, vol. 21 (Tokyo: Ōzorasha, 1996), 25–32.

66. Matsuda, *Onsen techō*, 125. In premodern Japan, needless to say, there were no reinforced-concrete structures, only wooden buildings, though these might contain up to a hundred rooms.

67. At the source, the pH of the waters at Kusatsu is 2.1, roughly equivalent to the acidity of lemon juice. Kusatsu's fame can be gauged by the existence of a large body of literature from the Tokugawa period, helpfully collected in Taihei Shujin, ed., *Kusatsu Onsen hanjōshi* (Tokyo: Taihei Shooku, 2012). See also Hagiwara Susumu, *Chūsei no Kusatsu* (1976; place of publication and name of publisher unknown), n.p.

68. Many *onsen* have *jigoku* (hell) as part of their toponyms.

69. Despite contemporary assumptions about the prevalence of mixed-gender bathing in the past, many premodern visitors to *onsen* appear to have been fairly modest, and they usually occupied gender-differentiated areas. See Ishikawa, *Onsen no Nihonshi*, 30–31, 45–48, 97, 109–10.

70. During the eighteenth century, before the era of peace and prosperity, interregional travel almost anywhere in the world was fraught with hazards both natural and social; see Watanabe Kyōji, *Edo to iu genkei* (Fukuoka: Gen Shobō, 2004), chap. 8.

71. Matsuda Tadanori, *Edo no onsengaku* (Tokyo: Shinchōsha, 2007), 31–32, 63–65.

72. One indication of the leisurely nature of premodern *onsen* travel is the usual length of stay. During the Tokugawa period, the ideal length of an *onsen* vacation was said to be twenty-one days. Kaibara Ekken's *Yōseikun*, an influential medical guide during the Edo period, recommended a cycle of seven days for the bathing cure, but three cycles of seven days were considered the average length of stay; see Matsuda, *Edo no onsengaku*, 169–71.

Older, Buddhist influences may have played a part here; see Kogure, *Nishikie ni miru Nihon no onsen*, 44.

73. Matsuda, *Edo no onsengaku*, 6–68.

74. Ishikawa, *Onsen no Nihonshi*, 151–54. The oldest *onsen* guide had been published as early as 1733, but more demotic guides were now available, especially those that ranked *onsen* in a way that was similar to the ranking of sumo wrestlers; see Matsuda, *Edo no onsengaku*, 3–38, 43–49 (the oldest extant chart is from 1817; the top two *onsen* were Kusatsu, in the east, and Arima, in the west). A collection of travel writings by Yasumi, "Ryokō yōjinshū" (1810), was perhaps the first sustained user-friendly guide.

75. See Ono Yoshirō, *"Seiketsu" no kindai* (Tokyo: Kōdansha, 1997), chaps. 3–4.

76. See, especially, Nishikawa, *Onsen genshi*, 36–39. Another scholar, impressed not only by Germany's scientific prowess but also by its *onsen* culture, begins his compendious treatise with a quotation from the hot spring–loving Goethe; see Fujinami Gōichi, *Onsen chishiki* (Tokyo: Maruzen, 1943), esp. 71–79.

77. For the chapter on mineral springs, see Udagawa Yōan, *Seimikaisō*, vol. 7 (1847; place of publication and name of publisher unknown), outer part, chap. 3.

78. Erwin O. E. von Bälz, *Nihon kōsenron*, trans. Chūōeiseikai (Tokyo: Chūōeiseikai, 1880). See also Naimushō Eiseikyoku, *Nihon kōsenshi*, 3 vols. (Tokyo: Naimushō Eiseikyoku, 1886). These books had a lasting impact on how mineral springs are classified and discussed.

79. Matsuda (*Onsen techō*, 156) remarks that von Bälz's "medical influence was overwhelming." The German doctor was familiar with the medicinal benefits of the spas in his homeland. But had an American doctor, from a culture without spas, been the "father" of modern Japanese medicine, mineral springs might have been understood more as settings for rest and relaxation than as a source of benefits to health.

80. To be sure, von Bälz is celebrated in Kusatsu, where there is a prominent bust of the German doctor. Moreover, any history of Kusatsu will mention him; see, for example, Ichikawa Zenzaburō, *Bälz to Kusatsu Onsen* (Kusatsu: Kusatsu Bälz Kyōkai, 1980). Von Bälz also had a very high opinion of Kusatsu's natural endowment; see Erwin O. E. von Bälz, *Das Leben eines deutsche Arztes im erwachenden Japan* (Stuttgart: J. Engelhorns, 1930), 336–43. Nevertheless, the residents of Kusatsu resisted his plan for a modern spa. Xenophobia probably played a part, as did fear of competition, but Kusatsu is also a traditionalist and hermetic place. Paradoxically, given the long-standing reputation of Kusatsu as one of the greatest *onsen* towns—and thus as, faute de mieux, a cosmopolitan spot—Kusatsu's residents and the proprietors of its inns are even today politically and socially conservative.

81. See Nishikawa Yoshikata, *Onsen to kenkō* (Tokyo: Nanzandō Shoten, 1932), 237–38.

82. Yasunari Kawabata, *The Dancing Girl of Izu and Other Stories*, trans. J. Martin Holman (Berkeley, CA: Counterpoint Press, 1998).

83. *Yukiguni* had a long and convoluted period of composition. Initially, in 1935, it was published as a discrete short story in a literary journal. Subsequent parts of what would later become the novel appeared in a number of other journals. The first edition of the novel proper was published in 1937, though the version that most people now read is based on the final edition of 1948. Both that edition and the earlier one were published by Sōgensha. See also Yasunari Kawabata, *Snow Country*, trans. Edward G. Seidensticker (New York: Vintage, 1996).

84. Kabuki actors, though they may be financially comfortable, are not known for being wealthy, and so the characters' ability to live this itinerant life speaks to the affordability of *onsen*. See also Yoshida Shūichi, *Kokuhō*, 2 vols. (Tokyo: Asahi Shinbun Shuppansha, 2018), which reproduces Mizoguchi's plot of a famous kabuki actor in exile in *onsen* towns.

85. Watanabe Jun'ichi, *Shitsurakuen*, 2 vols. (Tokyo: Kōdansha, 1997).

86. Sekido, *Kusatsu onsen no shakaishi*, 64–68.

87. Sekido, *Kusatsu onsen no shakaishi*, 55–56.

88. In 1879, machine-based boring expanded the source of thermal water in Beppu, and by the 1920s almost all major *onsen* areas were using this technology; see Ishikawa, *Onsen no Nihonshi*, 192–94.

89. *Uchiyu*, though it began in the early twentieth century, remained uncommon until the postwar period. Until then, most visitors had to leave their inns and go outdoors to naturally occurring springs (*sotoyu*), a limitation that made bathing in the cold months a challenge. See Sekido, *Kusatsu onsen no shakaishi*, 39–42.

90. Ishikawa, *Onsen no Nihonshi*, 224–25.

91. Toward the end of the war, many *onsen* facilities were used to house soldiers and citizens who were fleeing urban bombing raids; see Ishikawa Rio, *Onsen no heiwa to sensō* (Tokyo: Sairyūsha, 2015), chap. 6.

92. Kanno Takahiro, "Onsen imēji no hen'yō," in Nihon Onsenbunka Kenkyūkai, ed., *Onsen no bunkashi*, vol. 1 (Tokyo: Iwata Shoin, 2007), 324–26.

93. Bird, *Unbeaten Tracks in Japan*, 419.

94. See Iizuka Reiji, *Onsen shikkaku* (Tokyo: Tokuma Shoten, 2013), 44–49. This problem continued into the 2010s, though there was widespread appreciation of the significance of bathing in "original" springwater; see Komori Takemori and Iinuma Kakuju, *Kyūkyoku no gensenyado 73* (Tokyo: Shōdensha, 2016), 20–26.

95. Kimu Yoomi, an *onsen* sommelier, writes that visiting scores of hot springs, many of them quite difficult to reach, gave her *iyashi* (comfort) in the midst of work and relationship problems, and that *onsen* travel became her *ikigai*, her reason for living; see Kim Yoomi (Kimu Yumi), *Watashi no shiawase onsen jikan* (Tokyo: Media Sofuto, 2017), 5.

96. The late 1980s saw a boom in *hitō* (secret *onsen*) as a response to younger Japanese people who wanted a quiet, secluded getaway for healing and restoration; see Yatsuiwa Madoka, *Onsen to Nihonjin* (Tokyo: Seikyūsha, 1993), 165. On the decline of mixed-gender bathing, see Yasuda Yoshiaki, *Onsenron* (Tokyo: Ōtsuki Shoten, 2009), 52–56.

97. According to government statistics for 2016, there were 3,155 *onsen* towns in Japan, and *onsen* facilities received about 132 million overnight guests; see Kankyōshō, *Onsenchi ni kansuru sankōshiryō*, Env.gov, https://www.env.go.jp/press/files/jp/106545.pdf. Needless to say, the figure for overnight guests includes foreigners and repeat visitors, but it excludes *onsen* travelers on day trips, and so it suggests a thriving commerce in bathing vacations and the popularity of *onsen*.

98. Furukawa Akira, *Onsengaku nyūmon* (Osaka: Kwansei Gakuin Daigaku Shuppan, 2014), 7–8, 162–63.

99. Tatsuno Kazuo, *Bon'yari no jikan* (Tokyo: Iwanami Shoten, 2010).

100. Yokoo Tadanori, *Onsenshugi* (Tokyo: Shinchōsha, 2008), 220.

101. Hikita Satoshi, *Sentō no jikan* (Tokyo: Asahi Shuppansha, 2001), 230.

102. Kuratani Anzai, *Tajima Kinosaki tōji shinansha* (1820; place of publication and name of publisher unknown), n.p.

CHAPTER 8. *IKIGAI*

1. Hashimoto Osamu, *Tatoe sekai ga owattemo* (Tokyo: Shūeisha, 2017), 235, 243.

2. Helen Hardacre, *Shintō* (Cambridge, MA: Harvard University Asia Center, 2016).

3. The classic argument remains Ishida Takeshi, *Meiji seiji shisōshi kenkyū* (Tokyo: Miraisha, 1954).

4. Murakami Shigeyoshi, *Gendai shūkyō to seiji* (Tokyo: Tokyo Daigaku Shuppankai, 1978).

5. There are reasons to be skeptical about how many true believers there were in Japan even at the height of the prewar regime. As a proxy measure of true believers, the highest figure presented for the number of Japanese people who committed suicide at the end of the war is just over five hundred (they were primarily high military officials), and there are almost no reports of mass civilian suicide; see Oka Kiyoshi, "Jobun," in Nukata Hiroshi, ed., *Seiki no jiketsu* (Tokyo: Fuyō Shobō, 1968), 8. This is in striking contrast to Nazi Germany, where at least seven thousand people under the Third Reich committed suicide in Berlin alone, and there were also numerous reports of mass suicide; see Christian Goeschel, *Suicide in Nazi Germany* (Oxford: Oxford University Press, 2015), 159–66. Even more striking is the fact that so many German civilians committed suicide, presumably from despair as they saw the Nazi dream crumbling and going down to defeat. Some even enjoined their children to kill themselves; see Florian Huber, *Kind, versprich mir, dass du dich erschießt* (Berlin: Berlin Verlag, 2015). Whatever else one may say about Nazi Germany, it had its share of true believers.

6. Murakami Shigeyoshi, *Kokka Shintō* (Tokyo: Iwanami Shoten, 1970), i–ii. As for the previously divine Emperor Hirohito, in the 1960s he ranked only fourteenth among people whom the Japanese most respected, far behind Abraham Lincoln (in first place) and Florence Nightingale; see Mita Munesuke, *Gendai Nihon no seishin kōzō* (Tokyo: Kōbundō, 1965), 69.

7. See John Lie, *Multiethnic Japan* (Cambridge, MA: Harvard University Press, 2001), 130–36. According to a survey published by Japan's NHK Broadcasting Culture Research Institute, the imperial household remains popular, but it is safe to say that the dominant attitude toward State Shintō is benign indifference, to judge by data from the majority (60 to 70 percent) of the respondents; see NHK Hōsō Bunka Kenkyūjo, *Gendai Nihonjin no ishiki kōzō*, 7th ed. (Tokyo: NHK Hōsō Bunka Kenkyūjo, 2010), 119–23.

8. Joseph M. Kitagawa, *Religion in Japanese History* (New York: Columbia University Press, 1966), 331–32.

9. See Nishihara Shigeki, "Shūkyō," in Tōkei Sūri Kenkyūjo and Kokuminsei Chōsa Iinkai, eds., *Dai4 Nihonjin no kokuminsei* (Tokyo: Idemitsu Shoten, 1982); and Tōkei Sūri Kenkyūjo, *Dentōteki kachikan to mijikana seikatsu ishiki ni kansuru ishikichōsa hōkokusho* (Tokyo: Tōkei Sūri Kenkyūjo, 2011), 33–35. Only 16 percent of Japanese respondents to a survey conducted in the 1980s reported that they were willing to sacrifice their personal interests for the sake of a collective national goal, whereas more than 70 percent of respondents in the United States and South Korea expressed willingness to make that sacrifice; see Nishi-

hara Shigeki, *Yoron chōsa ni okeru dōjidaishi* (Tokyo: Burēn Shuppan, 1987), 98. More than 78 percent of respondents to a 2003 survey claimed not to participate in civic life of any kind, and fewer than 9 percent acknowledged being members of an organized religious group; see Ishii Kenji, *Dētabukku gendai Nihonjin no shūkyō*, rev. ed. (Tokyo: Shin'yōsha, 2007), 57–61. In the same year, 77 percent of respondents to another poll claimed to have no interest in religion; see Ichiro Tanioka, Noriko Iwai, Michio Nitta, and Hiroki Sato, *Japanese General Social Survey (JGSS) 2003* (Ann Arbor: Inter-university Consortium for Political and Social Research, University of Michigan, 2003), https://doi.org/10.3886/ICPSR04242.v1 (tellingly, later surveys in this series did not include questions on religion and religiosity). And, according to a 2017 Gallup poll, 29 percent of Japanese people are confirmed atheists, another 31 percent say they are not religious, and only 13 percent claim to be religious; see Worldwide Independent Network of Market Research and Gallup International, "Religion Prevails in the World," Internet Archive Wayback Machine, https://web.archive.org/web/20171114113506/http://www.wingia.com/web/files/news/370/file/370.pdf.

10. Yamaori Tetsuo, *Kindai Nihonjin no shūkyō ishiki* (Tokyo: Iwanami Shoten, 1996), 2.

11. The nineteenth-century Edoites, though worldly and relatively irreligious, were deeply superstitious. Their descendants have dropped such superstitions as not living on the fourth floor of a building (the Japanese word for "four" is a homonym of the word for "death") and seeking expert opinions on fêng shui (geomancy), though this is not to deny the curious persistence of interest in ways to divine personality traits and future romantic possibilities by way of astrology or blood types. But if the old superstitions have gone by the board, there is nevertheless widespread fear in Japan—of the unknown, of terrorists, and of religion in general with its connections to brainwashing and acts of terror.

12. Kōfuku no Kagaku (Happy Science) is as representative of these new religious groups as any. Initiated in 1986, it claims to be a religion of love, peace, and happiness that synthesizes the teachings of Jesus and Muhammad, Buddha and Confucius. Its founder, Ōkawa Ryūhō, has established a political party, in seeming rivalry with the Buddhist sect Sōka Gakkai (itself founded by Ikeda Daisaku) and its powerful political party, Kōmeitō. In his latest tract, the founder of Kōfuku no Kagaku has moved on to identifying the laws of bronze and discussing Socrates and Sakamoto Ryōma; see Ōkawa Ryūhō, *Seidō no hō* (Tokyo: Kōfuku no Kagaku Shuppan, 2018).

13. Yamamoto Shichihei and Komuro Naoki, *Nihonkyō no shakaigaku* (Tokyo: Kōdansha, 1981). But if contemporary Japanese people's belief in Japaneseness entails respect for the notion of the community and for the salience of the larger society, the Japanese nevertheless remain stubborn individualists. In 1971, for example, 32 percent were reported to privilege the individual over the country, and by 2011 that proportion had risen to 56 percent; see Naikakufu Daijin Kanbō Seifu Kōhōshitsu, *Shakai ishiki ni kansuru yoron chōsa* (Tokyo: Naikakufu Daijin Kanbō Seifu Kōhōshitsu, 2017), 21, 29. By contrast with the prewar generations, the overwhelming majority of Japanese people born after 1945 place greater value on the individual pursuit of personal likes and preferences than on the family, the community, or the nation; see NHK Hōsō Bunka Kenkyūjo, *Gendai Nihonjin no ishikikōzō*, 8th ed. (Tokyo: NHK Shuppan, 2015), 162–68; and Tōkei Sūri Kenkyūjo and Kokuminsei Chōsa Iinkai, *Dai5 Nihonjin no kokuminsei* (Tokyo: Idemitsu Shoten, 2003), 66–84. It is very difficult to shake most Japanese people's fundamental faith in the ontological uniqueness and distinctiveness of the individual.

14. What is more significant is the continuing legacy of folk spirituality, not only with respect to seasonal rituals but also regarding concern for *hotoke* (the dead, or a menagerie of living and deceased spirits). The Edo-era practice of splashing water or placing mounds of salt in front of a house remains remarkably persistent (though not in urban areas, given the dominance of high-rise apartment buildings). The archaeological accretion of Japanese religious history survives as an eclectic and syncretic modality of spirituality, which includes something like a religion of nothingness that still resonates deeply, as in the frequently invoked idea of *ichigo ichie,* or the ephemerality of life. Indeed, it has been suggested that the relative absence of religious affiliation in contemporary Japan is in fact an identification with the religion of nothingness; see Yamaori Tetsuo, *Shinzuru shūkyō, kanzuru shūkyō* (Tokyo: Chūō Kōronshinsha, 2008), 27–28.

15. In more mundane terms, and in the words of a quotation misattributed to Sigmund Freud, "Love and work are the cornerstone of our humanness"; see BrainyQuote, https://www.brainyquote.com/quotes/sigmund_freud_165464. On the misattribution as such, see Alan C. Elms, "Apocryphal Freud," *Annual of Psychoanalysis* 29 (2001), 83–104. Cf. Gillian Rose, *Love's Work* (New York: Schocken, 1995).

16. See, for example, the plays of Chikamatsu Monzaemon, in which what we would call romantic passion comes up against the intransigent realities of rigid social norms; a representative work would be *Sonezaki shinjū* (1703).

17. Yanabu Akira, *Hon'yakugo seiritsu jijō* (Tokyo: Iwanami Shoten, 1982), 89–97. See also the suggestive essay by Itō Sei, "Kindai Nihon ni okeru 'ai' no kyogi" (1962), in *Kindai Nihonjin no hassō no shokeishiki* (Tokyo: Iwanami Shoten, 1981): "We imported 'love.' But we didn't import prayer or repentance, the dowry or a sufficient income on the husband's part" (153). According to Itō, love became fallacious in Japan without a Western background of Christianity and economics; in the West, he argues, there is a tendency to achieve inner peace through stable social relations, whereas in the East, by contrast, there is a tendency to hesitate to form egalitarian relationships (140).

18. The 1953–54 film version, which aired on NHK from 1952 to 1954, was directed by Ōba Hideo and is loosely related to the 2016 anime directed by Shinkai Makoto.

19. Kajiwara Ikki and Nagayasu Takumi, *Ai to Makoto,* 16 vols. (Tokyo: Kōdansha, 1973–76).

20. Fukunaga Takehiko, *Ai no kokoromi* (Tokyo: Kawade Shobō, 1956).

21. Ōshima Michiko and Kōno Makoto, *Ai to shi wo mitsumete* (Tokyo: Daiwa Shobō, 1963). See also Sonia Ryang, *Love in Modern Japan* (Abingdon, UK: Routledge, 2006), 75–90.

22. It is possible to argue that for the wartime generation, before the end of World War II, the significance of death far outweighed the significance of love, and that after the war, economic recovery and material pursuits also outweighed love. In this respect, the sociologist Mita Munesuke's study of popular song lyrics considers more than twenty themes, including anger and joy, but not love (though Mita does consider *bojō,* which denotes affection or longing and possibly love, but only in the sense of agape); see Mita Munesuke, *Kindai Nihon no shinjō no rekishi* (Tokyo: Kōdansha, 1967).

23. Yanagisawa Kimio, *Tonda kappuru,* 15 vols. (Tokyo: Kōdansha, 1978–81); Takahashi Rumiko, *Mezon Ikkoku,* 15 vols. (Tokyo: Shōgakkan, 1980–87).

24. Saimon Fumi, *Tokyo rabusutōrī*, 4 vols. (Tokyo: Shōgakkan, 1990). To be sure, one of the two love interests in Yanagisawa Kimio's *Tonda kappuru* is also decisive and expressive.

25. Natsume Sōseki, *Kōjin* (1913). aozora.gr.jp/cards/000148/files/775_14942.html.

26. Sōseki Natsume, *And Then* (1909), trans. Norma Moore Field (Tokyo: Tuttle, 2011), 202.

27. These amorous symptoms are brilliantly anatomized by Roland Barthes, *Fragments d'un discours amoureux* (Paris: Éditions du Seuil, 1977).

28. Watanabe, *Shitsurakuen*.

29. Louise Bogan, "Juan's Song," in *The Blue Estuaries* (New York: Farrar, Straus & Giroux, 1968), 10.

30. The phrase is in the banner added to the cover of the book's Japanese edition. See Murakami Haruki, *Noruwei no mori*, 2 vols. (Tokyo: Kōdansha, 1997). See also Haruki Murakami, *Norwegian Wood*, trans. Jay Rubin (New York: Vintage International, 2010). In *Murakami Haruki Shinbun*, Murakami suggests that his preferred phrase would have been "This is 100 percent Murakami Haruki's realist novel"; see "It's a 100% Love Story," *Haruki Murakami Newspaper*, http://murakami-haruki-times.com/100percentlovestory/. Be that as it may, most readers regarded the novel as a love story, as is blatantly clear from the 2010 film version directed by Tran Anh Hung.

31. Okazaki Kyōko, *Ribāsuejji* (1994; reprinted, Tokyo: Takarajimasha, 2015).

32. Umino Tsunami, *Nigeru wa haji da ga yaku ni tatsu*, 9 vols. (Tokyo: Kōdansha, 2013–17). The original manga had a Hungarian subtitle, *Szégyen a futás, de hasznos.*

33. Matsuura Rieko, *Nachuraru ūman* (Tokyo: Kawade Shobō Shinsha, 1991); Matsuura Rieko, *Oyayubi P no shugyō jidai* (Tokyo: Kawade Shobō Shinsha 1993).

34. Matsuura Rieko, *Kenshin* (Tokyo: Asahi Shinbunsha, 2007); Tawada Yōko, *Inumukoiri* (Tokyo: Kōdansha, 1993). The word *mukoiri* (rather cumbersome to translate into English) denotes adoption by one's wife's family upon marriage.

35. Mizumura Minae, *Honkaku shōsetsu*, 2 vols. (Tokyo: Shinchōsha, 2002).

36. Haruki Murakami, *South of the Border, West of the Sun*, trans. Philip Gabriel (New York: Vintage, 2000), 4.

37. Divorce, once an affront to the sacrosanct family, became common, and if it still carried a whiff of embarrassment, it was seen as a garden-variety error, a venial sin. At the same time, there has been a precipitous decline in the total Japanese fertility rate (that is, the mean number of births per woman over her lifetime). Until 1974 the total fertility rate was higher than 2.0, but in the twenty-first century it has fluctuated between 1.26 and 1.45; see World Bank, "Fertility Rate, Total (Births per Woman)—Japan," 1960–2019, https://data .worldbank.org/indicator/SP.DYN.TFRT.IN?locations=JP. Whatever the causes of Japan's declining fertility—the usual suspects include the difficulty of childrearing in a two-career household and the considerable expense of having children, especially when it comes to their education—there is no doubt that the typical twenty-first-century Japanese family is not the same as in the immediate postwar decades. And not only are there fewer children, but there are fewer marriages, and the unions are of shorter duration. In fact, nearly 66 percent of respondents to a 2013 survey said that there is no need for marriage; see NHK Hōsō Bunka Kenkyūjo, *Gendai Nihonjin no ishikikōzō* (2015), 2.

38. Yoshinaga Fumi, *Kinō nani tabeta?*, 17 vols. (Tokyo: Kōdansha, 2007–20).

39. See Ikeda Riyoko, *Berusaiyu no bara*, 13 vols. (Tokyo: Shūeisha, 1972–73). The series depicts a turbulent love affair during the French Revolution (the very definition of turbulence and tumult). This work is significant in that it established gender-based manga written by and for women, though some trace the genre to Tezuka Osamu's *Ribon no kishi* (available in English as *Princess Knight*). From at least the era of Yamagishi Ryōko's *Hiidurutokoro no tenshi* (1980–84), the primary romantic relationship had been between two men. By the twenty-first century, this genre, often called *yayoi,* had come to be known as BL (boys' love) manga.

40. The novel is Kodama, *Otto no chinpo ga hairanai* (Tokyo: Fusōsha, 2017), and the manga version is Kodama and Gotō Yukiko, *Otto no chinpo ga hairanai*, 5 vols. (Tokyo: Kōdansha, 2018–20).

41. Ōtsuka Eiji, *Otaku no seishinshi*, rev. ed. (Tokyo: Seikaisha, 2016; 1st ed., 2004), 44; Azuma, *Dōbutsukasuru posutomodan.*

42. In 1988 and 1989, a number of girls were kidnapped and murdered by a young man whose room was overflowing with manga and anime, and this sensational crime helped cement the perfidious image of the *otaku;* see Ōtsuka, *Otaku no seishinshi,* chap. 6 (see also chap. 24 for the impact of the Aum Shinrikyō cult).

43. The *otaku* do not quite belong to the ranks of *furītā* and *nīto,* the under- and unemployed young people who are demonized as only slightly more functional than the *hikikomori* (Japan's urban agoraphobics, young adults suffering from acute social withdrawal and fear of leaving the house); see Honda Yuki, Naitō Asao, and Gotō Kazutomo, *Nīotte iuna!* (Tokyo: Kōbunsha, 2006), 38–41, 220–22 (the discourse of *nīto* stresses not only deviance from the previous generation's norms of work and ambition but also criminality). Willingly or not, however, the *otaku* do not lead the regimented life of the office worker, and so they deviate socially and psychologically from the dominant lifestyle of the postwar regime. In the mid-2010s there was considerable discussion about young men who, unlike their aggressive, "carnivorous" elders, had become meek "vegetarians" (more symbolic than actual culinary orientations); this discourse formed part of a story about declining masculinity, a putative cause of Japan's declining marriage and fertility rates.

44. The scale of sex work is staggering: an estimated 350,000 women work in the sex industry (*fūzoku*), with an array of services ranging from *deriheru* (health delivery, entailing the delivery of sex-related services) to the long-standing *sōpurando* (soaplands, that is, bathhouses with sexual services); see Nakamura Atsuhiko, *Nihon no fūzokujō* (Tokyo: Shinchōsha, 2014), 38–69. In addition, perhaps 10,000 women every year enter the vast industry of pornographic video, usually called AV (for "adult video"); see Mori Yoshiyuki, *Adaruto bideo ura no sekai* (Tokyo: Takarajimasha, 2012), 5.

45. See Miyadai Shinji, Ishihara Hideki, and Ōtsuka Akiko, *Sabukaruchā shinwa kaitai* (Tokyo: PARCO, 1993), 40–49.

46. Hiraoka Masaaki, *Momoe wa Bosatsu de aru,* complete ed., ed. Yomota Inuhiko (Tokyo: Kōdansha, 2015; 1st ed., 1979).

47. Hamano Satoshi, *Maeda Atsuko wa Kirisuto wo koeta* (Tokyo: Chikuma Shobō, 2012).

48. Nakano Hitori, *Densha otoko* (Tokyo: Shinchōsha, 2004).

49. On the political economy of Japanese subculture, see Nissim Kadosh Otmazgin, *Regionalizing Culture* (Honolulu: University of Hawai'i Press, 2013).

50. Ōizumi Mitsunari, *Otaku to wa nanika?* (Tokyo: Sōshisha, 2017), 240–47.

51. Sophocles, *Oedipus at Colonus* (c. 401 BCE), in Hugh Lloyd-Jones, ed. and trans., *Loeb Classical Library*, vol. 21: *Antigone, The Women of Trachis, Philoctetes, Oedipus at Colonus* (Cambridge, MA: Harvard University Press, 1994), 547.

52. Puzzled outsiders' reactions to the ubiquitous *otaku* slang term *moe*, which expresses strong attraction and enthusiasm, are symptomatic of the general misrecognition regarding the *otaku*'s passionate inner life. For example, the father of a single *otaku* woman in her thirties asked, "Why can't she say, 'I love you' or 'I like that'? Instead, it's 'moe.' What is that? Is it *moyamoya* [uneasy] or *moeru* [burning]? I don't understand." There is in fact a curious convergence between the meaning of *moe* and Motoori's classic definition of *mono no aware* (usually rendered in English as "the pathos of things") as "to feel deeply in the soul" about something. Thus the consummate eighteenth-century thinker anticipates the soul of *otaku* folk; see Motoori Nobunaga, "Isonokamisasamegoto" (1763), *Ashiwake obune, isonokamisasamegoto* (Tokyo: Iwanami Shoten, 2003), 177.

53. The object of study should not determine that study's worth (though I hasten to add that this illusory correlation does fuel much research in the social sciences). The pursuit of a dream, of purposefulness, is not something to be judged by its content. Just as one man's trash is another man's treasure, something that is of consuming interest to one person may leave many others cold. A passionate interest may fade over time and even disappear, but a new interest may appear. The point is not the transcendental importance or long duration of the interest. Rather, it is having something to be interested in.

54. *Tokyo Shinbun*, 11 May 2019.

55. The locus classicus of this argument remains Theodor W. Adorno and Max Horkheimer, *Dialektik der Aufklärung* (1944; reprinted, Frankfurt am Main: Fischer, 1988).

56. The average amount of sleep in Japan in 2015 was seven hours and forty-three minutes—a full hour less than the 1960 average. The 2015 US average was eight hours and thirty-six minutes. See Japan Institute of Sleep Science, "Sleep Situation of Modern People," https://www.nishikawasangyo.co.jp/company/laboratory/topics/01/.

57. There are more than one hundred thousand *sunakku* in Japan, which means that *sunakku* are more common than the ubiquitous *izakaya* (taverns or pub-like restaurants) and only slightly less common than real-estate offices. A *sunakku* is primarily for eating, drinking, and conversation. The *sunakku* exists outside the so-called water trade of sexually tinged clubs and bars, and so its servers, almost all women, must sit across from rather than next to their customers, who are almost all men. The figures regarding *sunakku* are from Taniguchi Kōichi, "Sunakku kenkyū kotohajime," in Taniguchi Kōichi, ed., *Nihon no yoru no kōkyoken* (Tokyo: Hakusuisha, 2017), 16.

58. Katō Hitoshi, *Teinengo* (Tokyo: Iwanami Shoten, 2007), 26–28.

59. On this point, the pioneering analysis is Miyadai, Ishihara, and Ōtsuka, *Sabukaruchā shinwa no kaitai*. The Tokyo neighborhood described in chapter 6 of this book has two shops dedicated to old jazz LPs, and the bookstore in that neighborhood has a full shelf of new books on jazz. Moreover, an almost maniacal devotion to waning musical genres (waning in the United States, anyway) can be observed in everything from the demotic (such as

blues) to the Olympian (such as Western classical music). The passionate pursuit of jazz or classical is surely *otaku* by another name.

60. Compare Furuichi Noritoshi, *Zetsubō no kuni no kōfuku na wakamonotachi* (Tokyo: Kōdansha, 2011), chap. 6; and Futagaki Nōki, *Nīto ga hiraku kōfuku shakai Nippon* (Tokyo: Akashi Shoten, 2012), chap. 2.

61. Aristotle, *Politics* (c. 350 BCE), in *The Complete Works of Aristotle*, Vol.2, ed. Jonathan Barnes (Princeton, NJ: Princeton University Press, 1986), 1337b. See also Josef Pieper, *Musse und Kult* (Munich: Kösel, 1947), chap. 2.

62. William Morris, "The Lesser Arts of Life" (1882), in *The Collected Works of William Morris*, vol. 22, 269.

63. The members of the *tokkōtai* (kamikaze pilots, as they're known to outsiders) and their ilk were not poorly educated. On the contrary, many of them were overeducated and excessively idealistic. It is bracing to read their diaries and letters, which convey the pilots' moral sincerity through references to a veritable Who's Who of modern Western philosophy, from Marx to Heidegger. To be sure, we should not overlook the curated and justificatory character of these accounts, often composed after the war by the pilots' survivors; see Hidaka Kōtarō, *Fujichaku* (Tokyo: Shinjinbutsuōraisha, 2006).

64. Gordon Mathews, *What Makes Life Worth Living?* (Berkeley: University of California Press, 1996), 232–38.

65. Mathews, *What Makes Life Worth Living?* 12–16.

66. Kamiya Mieko, *Ikigai ni tsuite* (1966; reprinted, Tokyo: Misuzu Shobō, 2004), 7, 11, 31.

67. Kamiya, *Ikigai ni tsuite*, 28–29.

68. When respondents to one survey were asked what they would do if they could live their lives over again, they most commonly replied that they would study more, or better; see *Asahi Shinbun*, 18 May 2019.

69. As late as 1981, Japan had more companies with a mandated retirement age of fifty-five or younger than companies with a retirement age of sixty or older. By the turn of the millennium, however, less than 1 percent of Japanese companies had a formal retirement age of fifty-five or younger. See Kōsei Rōdōshō (Ministry of Health, Labour and Welfare), *Koyō kanri chōsa* (Tokyo: Kōsei Rōdōshō, 2014).

70. Katō Jin, *Teinengo* (Tokyo: Iwanami Shoten, 1998). According to one writer, many diseases exist—*fugenbyō* (literally, "father-created illnesses")—that are caused by retired husbands who put stress on their wives; see Ishikura Fuminobu, *Fugenbyō* (Osaka: Osaka Daigaku Shuppankai, 2011).

71. See Hashimoto Osamu, *Junrei* (Tokyo: Shin'yōsha, 2009). (The 1975 film *Grey Gardens* was directed by Albert and David Maysles.)

72. Yamamoto Tsunetomo, *Hagakure* (1716), ed. Kanno Kakumyō, Kurihara Gō, Kizawa Kei, and Sugahara Reiko, vol. 1 (Tokyo: Kōdansha, 2017), 35.

73. Yamamoto, *Hagakure*, 466–68.

74. Yamamoto, *Hagakure*, 392.

75. For example, Tokyo's Asahi Culture Center, where many retirees enroll alongside younger people, offers more than a thousand courses and is much more comprehensive than many colleges and universities. The curriculum features classes geared to absolute beginners in various subjects, but past offerings have also included advanced physics,

recherché topics in classical Japanese literature, and a course in which students read Proust in the original French. One retiree, a Buddhist art and architecture *otaku*, has dedicated considerable time and energy to visiting Buddhist temples and looking at pieces of art that are usually not shown to the public. Having amassed a body of knowledge equal to that of a professional expert in the field, this man points to other *otaku* whose expertise far exceeds even his own.

76. Higuchi Yūichi, *65sai nanimo shinai yūki* (Tokyo: Gentōsha, 2018).

77. Sherwin B. Nuland, *How We Die* (New York: Knopf, 1994), chap. 1. As recently as 1951, almost 90 percent of Japanese people died at home, but today that proportion is only about 10 percent; see Kobori Ōichirō, *Shi wo ikita hitobito* (Tokyo: Misuzu Shobō, 2018), 1.

78. Kobori, *Shi wo ikita hitobito*, 5, 89–91.

79. My mother, for example, after her diagnosis of stage 4 cancer, wanted to spend her remaining time with family members and friends, and to visit hot springs. But my father and my siblings believed both in the miracle of modern medicine and in the notion that a dying loved one should be encouraged to scratch out every possible extra moment of life, and so they insisted on experimental interventions that caused my mother excruciating pain, great personal indignity, and, soon enough, loss of cognitive function.

80. Kobori, *Shi wo ikita hitobito*, 198.

81. See Shimazono Susumu, *Nihonjin no shiseikan wo yomu* (Tokyo: Asahi Shinbun Shuppan, 2012).

82. The consensus is to credit Motoori Norinaga's reading of *Genji monogatari* (*The Tale of Genji*); see Watsuji Tetsurō, *Nihon no seishinshi* (Tokyo: Iwanami Shoten, 1926).

83. On ordinary Edo-era people's attitudes toward death, see Watanabe, *Edo to iu genkei*, 81–87.

84. Kōda Rohan, *Gojūnotō* (1887; reprinted, Tokyo: Iwanami Shoten, 1927), 24–26, 36–37.

85. Kōda, *Gojūnotō*, 112–16.

86. Hashimoto, *Junrei*, 231.

POSTFACE

1. Friedrich Gundolf, *Shakespeare und der deutsche Geist* (Berlin: Georg Bondi, 1914), viii.

2. Kawahata Yū, *Machikado no Shōwa isan* (Tokyo: Saizusha, 2018).

3. Nakagawa Hiroko, *Tokyo kakusa* (Tokyo: Chikuma Shobō, 2018).

4. Okuizumi Hikaru, *Tokyo jijoden* (Tokyo: Shūeisha, 2014); Hashimoto Osamu, *Kusa-yanagi no tsurugi* (Tokyo: Shinchōsha, 2018).

Founded in 1893,
UNIVERSITY OF CALIFORNIA PRESS
publishes bold, progressive books and journals
on topics in the arts, humanities, social sciences,
and natural sciences—with a focus on social
justice issues—that inspire thought and action
among readers worldwide.

The UC PRESS FOUNDATION
raises funds to uphold the press's vital role
as an independent, nonprofit publisher, and
receives philanthropic support from a wide
range of individuals and institutions—and from
committed readers like you. To learn more, visit
ucpress.edu/supportus.